AppleWorks 6
THE MISSING MANUAL

*The book that
should have been
in the box*

AppleWorks 6
THE MISSING MANUAL

Jim Elferdink & David Reynolds

POGUE PRESS™
O'REILLY®

Beijing • Cambridge • Farnham • Köln • Paris • Sebastopol • Taipei • Tokyo

AppleWorks 6: The Missing Manual

by Jim Elferdink and David Reynolds

Copyright © 2000 Pogue Press, LLC. All rights reserved.
Printed in the United States of America.

Published by Pogue Press/O'Reilly & Associates, Inc., 101 Morris Street,
Sebastopol, CA 95472.

May 2000:	First Edition.
June 2000:	Second Printing.

This book is printed on acid-free paper with 85% recycled content, 15% post-
consumer waste. O'Reilly & Associates is committed to using paper with the
highest recycled content available consistent with high quality.

ISBN: 1-56592-858-X [06/00]

Table of Contents

Part Two: AppleWorks Power

Part Three: Integration

Part Four: Appendixes

TABLE OF CONTENTS

The Missing Credits

About the Authors

 Jim Elferdink owns Macs for the Masses, a Macintosh consulting company in the Redwood country of far Northern California. Before moving west to earn a journalism degree, discover the Macintosh, and meet his future wife (all at Humboldt State University), he worked as a commercial photographer, carpenter and cabinetmaker. He and his wife, Joy Hardin, share a home in coastal Humboldt County with a staff of imaginary servants and a backlog of very real chores.

He invites the overly curious to snoop around at *www.sunra.com/mac* and welcomes courteous commentary on the book by e-mail: *macintosh@sunra.com*.

 David Reynolds is executive editor at *MacAddict* magazine, where he gets to mess around with the latest Macintosh toys and gadgets. Born and raised in southern Colorado, David has worked as a gas station attendant, lumber mill resaw operator, Apple Student Representative, newspaper editor, and TV director before his current job as a magazine editor. He's very tired now.

If you'd like to reach David about the book—or anything else—send email to *dreynolds@mac.com*. If you're dying to poke fun at David's Web skills, stop by his Web site at *www.greasythug.com*.

About the Creative Team

Nan Barber (copy editor) works as a freelance writer and editor from her home near Boston. She majored in Japanese studies at Brown University and traveled throughout Asia and Europe as a jewelry buyer. Nan serves as managing editor for Salamander, a magazine for poetry, fiction, and memoirs, and marketing writer for Whole Foods Market.

Rose Cassano (cover toolbox illustration) has worked as an independent designer and illustrator for 20 years. Assignments have spanned the nonprofit sector to corporate clientele. She lives in beautiful Southern Oregon, grateful for the miracles of modern technology that make living and working there a reality. Email: *cassano@cdsnet.net*. Web: *www.rosecassano.com*.

Dennis Cohen (technical editor, author of Chapter 8), a veteran of the Jet Propulsion Laboratory, Ashton-Tate, Claris, and Aladdin Systems, has served as the technical reviewer for many bestselling Mac books, including *Macworld Mac Secrets*. He's the co-author of *AppleWorks 6 for Dummies*. His leisure activities include trapshooting, bridge, and (especially) spending time with his Boston Terrier, Spenser. Email: *drcohen@mac.com*.

David A. Freedman created the cover design for the Missing Manual series (with assistance from Marc Rosenthal, who drew the Missing Manual dog). From his studio in Carlisle, Massachusetts *(df301@aol.com)*, David also designs logos and other graphics. Prior to establishing his design business, David worked for 20 years with Milton Glaser in New York City.

David Pogue (editor), award-winning back-page columnist for *Macworld* magazine, is the creator of the Missing Manual series. He's the author or co-author of 15 computer, humor, and music books, including six books in the ...*for Dummies* series *(Macs, The iMac, The iBook, Magic, Opera,* and *Classical Music.)* Web sites: *www.davidpogue.com* and, of course, *www.missingmanual.com.*

Phil Simpson (interior design and layout) works out of his office in Stamford, CT *(pmsimpson@earthlink.net),* where he has had his graphic design business for 18 years. Experienced in many facets of graphic design, he's proud to be a long-time Macintosh user/supporter and honored to be part of the Missing Manual project.

Acknowledgments

I'd like to thank my parents for a lifetime of love and support, for raising me in a house filled with books, for making it possible for me to pursue my education in an unconventional manner, and for offering to put me through college. Thanks also to Bucky VanderMeer for encouraging me to accept that offer and to never say no to adventure; to Howard Seemann, Mark Larson, and the rest of the Humboldt State University Journalism department; and to all my clients, who have been patiently waiting for months for me to complete this project.

My wife, Joy, has been the most understanding, patient, loving, and amusing partner—and a relentless editor and thoughtful critic throughout this endeavor.

Especially, I'd like to thank David Pogue for inviting me to participate in the birth of the Missing Manuals; for teaching me the ropes of the computer-book biz as only he can; for being the greatest editor a first-time author could hope for; and for being always available and frequently hilarious.

—Jim Elferdink

I'd like to thank my wife Susan for her incredible support, humor, and patience; the faculty of Humboldt State University's English department, especially Drs. John Schafer and Karen Carlton; my parents for indulging my reading and my curiosity; Peter Ottman for sharing words; Cheryl England for giving me a gig as a magazine editor; and David Pogue for giving me the chance to help write an honest-to-goodness book.

—David Reynolds

The Missing Manual series is a joint venture between Pogue Press—the dream team introduced on these pages—and O'Reilly & Associates, one of the most respected publishers on earth. It's only because Tim O'Reilly and his team had the vision to take a gamble on this concept that this book came into existence. Tim, Cathy Record,

Edie Freedman, Allen Noren, Laura Schmier, Sue Willing, Mark Brokering, Dana Furby, Lisa Mann, and Sara Winge were especially critical to this book's birth.

Thanks, too, to my agent David Rogelberg, the Missing Manuals' first believer; Scott Thomas and DataViz for making the special discount offer described at the back of this book; and Jennifer Pogue, who makes this series—and everything else—possible.

—*David Pogue*

The Missing Manual Series

Missing Manuals are designed to be authoritative, entertaining, superbly written guides to popular computer products that don't come with printed manuals (which is just about all of them).

Here are the Missing Manuals now available or coming in 2000:

- *Mac OS 9: The Missing Manual* by David Pogue
- *iMovie: The Missing Manual* by David Pogue
- *Windows ME: The Missing Manual* by Kathy Ivens
- *Windows 2000: The Missing Manual* by Sharon Crawford
- *Mac OS X: The Missing Manual* by David Pogue
- *Quicken 2001: The Missing Manual* by Kathy Ivens and Thomas E. Barich

Introduction

Combining word processing, database, spreadsheet, and graphics capabilities in a single software package has been a worthy goal since the early days of personal computing. Back then, almost everyone was a first-timer, an early adopter willing to spend a couple grand on a computer—but reluctant to spend hundreds more assembling a collection of software.

Developing a multi-talented software package was a daunting task. Some of the early attempts—Lotus Jazz, Microsoft Works, GreatWorks—did a little bit of a lot of things, but nothing well; all of them have long since gone to the great CD-ROM in the sky. AppleWorks is the only survivor.

The AppleWorks Corps

The funny thing is, ClarisWorks/AppleWorks has been around for so long that many people don't realize that it long ago outgrew its clumsy adolescent period and is now buffed up and ready for serious work. For years, people have called it the Swiss Army Knife of software. But there's a better term for it: icebergware. A cursory examination of it doesn't even hint at the power that lurks below the surface.

AppleWorks is not just a set of six programs that can interact. Rather, it's a single unified package with six aspects that can be all integrated. This integration is so seamless that it's easy to forget that you're actually switching between modules. A corollary benefit is the fact that you're learning to use one program instead of several; Apple Works requires less time to learn and gives you more time to actually get some work done.

Over the years, the program formerly known as ClarisWorks has attracted a devoted following. These sensible souls have opted for simplicity, appropriate technology, and economy. They accept that people driving around in their Microsoft Sport-Utility Programs could crush them to dust in an auto-formatting competition, but they don't care. They've learned to make this seemingly basic program jump through all the hoops necessary to get the job done. Fans stick with AppleWorks because it's powerful, uncluttered, and dependable.

With a strong foundation in education, the AppleWorks following includes millions of home users and small businesses—and some large ones, too, such as General Motors, Sears, and Exxon. The appeal of a lean, easy-to-use, Mac-and-Windows, bargain-priced suite of productivity tools, perhaps fueled by a dash of anti-Microsoft backlash, has led many to AppleWorks.

What's New in AppleWorks 6

The leap from version 5 to version 6 was among the largest in AppleWorks history. Packed into the new version, you'll find a long list of changes like these:

- **A radical visual redesign.** AppleWorks 6 has a new face, an updated look that's designed to match the look of Mac OS X—a translucent, brightly colored realm of jumbo icons. In fact, AppleWorks 6 is the first program that is *Carbon compatible*—ready to run when Mac OS X becomes available.

- **Starting Points.** AppleWorks' Open and New document dialog boxes are now augmented by the Starting Points window (Chapter 1): an easy-to-use, tabbed window for creating new documents or opening recent documents, templates, and Assistants.

- **Internet hooks.** If your Mac is connected to the Internet, AppleWorks can access thousands of clip-art images and professionally-created template documents, all located on Apple's server computers. But that's just the beginning; AppleWorks can also transform any of its documents into Web-page (HTML) format, or *import* any Web-page document and turn it into an AppleWorks document. And you can incorporate live links to the Internet into any AppleWorks document.

- **A new Presentation module.** Now you can create and display sophisticated slide shows without investing big bucks in a program like Microsoft PowerPoint.

- **Death of the Communications module.** The old ClarisWorks Communications module, which few used, let alone understood, is gone. If you still need to connect to a local BBS, you'll have to use shareware to do it.

- **Tables.** A new table-creation tool lets you insert stretchy, highly customizable tables (for résumés, price breakdowns, and so on) into any kind of AppleWorks document. The days of cobbling together tables using tabs or spreadsheet frames are over.

- **Linked spreadsheets.** AppleWorks spreadsheets can now contain *external cell references*—active links to other spreadsheets. Make a change in Spreadsheet A, and watch the totals automatically updated in Spreadsheet B.

- **Auto-Save.** AppleWorks automatically saves your documents in the background as you work. Then, if your computer should crash or lose power while you're working, AppleWorks automatically opens your auto-saved documents when you restart.

- **Other changes.** AppleWorks contains a host of other new features, including much better AppleScript-ability, a Recent Items command in the File menu, an improved thesaurus, and expanded mail-merge capabilities.

- **New system requirements.** To support its new features and increased abilities, AppleWorks makes higher demands on your computer. To run AppleWorks 6, your Macintosh must have a PowerPC processor, at least 24 MB of memory (in Mac OS 8.1) or 32 MB of memory in Mac OS 8.5. or later, and a CD-ROM drive.

The Difficult Birth of AppleWorks 6

For years, AppleWorks (and ClarisWorks) 5 users had been looking forward a powerful new version of their favorite program. But when AppleWorks 6 finally arrived in February 2000, certain aspects of it created an uproar—a wave of irritation reminiscent of the reception given another famous version 6 program: Microsoft Word 6.

Many people complained that favorite features had been changed or removed. Others just didn't care for the new visual design. Some were upset that there was no reduced upgrade pricing for loyal AppleWorks users. But the most serious charges centered on three AppleWorks aspects:

- **Speed and stability.** Without a doubt, there were some giant-cockroach-sized bugs strolling around within AppleWorks 6 when it was released; random crashes occurred every day, and even *repeatable* crashes—ones that should have been fixed during testing—were commonplace.

  Fortunately, two software updates from Apple followed quickly on AppleWorks 6's heels, which solve most of the speed and stability problems. If you haven't downloaded the latest updater (to AppleWorks 6.0.4 or later), you're missing a great thing. These updaters (available at, for example, *www.missingmanual.com*) provide dramatic speed and stability increases. No longer do you make sacrifices to the QuickTime gods every time you embed a movie into a slide show.

- **The new Button bar.** Compared to the AppleWorks 5 Button bar, which could hold several rows of smaller buttons, the new AppleWorks 6 Button bar can hold only one row of relatively large buttons—according to many button-efficiency aficionados, a real step backward. Nor does the new Button bar offer Font and Style display boxes that, in the AppleWorks 5 Button bar, let you identify the active font and style at a glance.

- **Elimination of translators.** In an ill-conceived bout of corporate belt-tightening at Apple, the AppleWorks team dissolved its long-term association with DataViz, the makers of MacLinkPlus file-translation software. AppleWorks doesn't come with any *file translators*—formerly a standout feature of AppleWorks—which let you convert your AppleWorks documents into, for example, Microsoft Word files.

The latest AppleWorks updater (which gives you version 6.0.4 or later) helps by restoring RTF translation, an intermediary Word exchange format. But if you want to import or export files in other word processor formats directly, you must now buy MacLinkPlus yourself. (At the back of this book, you'll find a coupon that lets you get MacLinkPlus Deluxe for $40—a 60% discount.)

The unfortunate result of all this negative brouhaha was that a lot of perspective was lost. AppleWorks still offers an extremely powerful word processor, complete with thesaurus, definitions dictionary, footnotes, style sheets, multiple columns, section formatting, macros, and outlining; the only serious Macintosh spreadsheet competitor to Microsoft Excel; drawing and painting tools that can create Web-ready JPEG or PNG files; an extremely fast database with almost as much design flexibility as the $300 FileMaker Pro; and much more. At $80 (or $0, if you have an iMac or iBook), AppleWorks is, more than ever, a remarkable value.

A Note to Windows PC Users

AppleWorks' cross-platform capabilities have always been one of its most attractive features. It may come as somewhat of a surprise to Macintosh users, but AppleWorks is found on a huge number of Windows PCs, especially in education. As this book goes to press in mid-2000, the Windows version of AppleWorks 6 is, according to AppleWorks, many months away.

When AppleWorks for Windows finally appears, it will be nearly identical to the Macintosh version described in this book. Almost all the information presented in this book should apply to the Windows version—with a few "key" differences.

Macintosh and Windows keyboards have different names for a few keyboard keys, which would make the tutorials in this book confusing if you didn't have a substitution guide. The following table summarizes the keyboard differences.

Macintosh	Windows
Return	Enter
Option	Alt
⌘	Ctrl
Control-click	Right-click

By making these substitutions when working with AppleWorks 6 for Windows, you should be able to follow all the tutorials in this book. And when AppleWorks 6 for Windows does appear, you'll find more information on this book's page at *www.missingmanual.com*.

About This Book

Despite the many improvements in AppleWorks over the years, one feature has grown consistently worse since the original ClarisWorks: Apple's documentation. With AppleWorks 6, you get nothing but a slim pamphlet. To learn about the hundreds of commands that make up this application, you're expected to use one of Apple's help systems (Balloon Help or the browser-like Mac Help).

Unfortunately, as you'll quickly discover, these help systems are tersely written, offer very little technical depth, lack useful examples, and provide no tutorials whatsoever. You can't even mark your place or underline, let alone read it in the bathroom.

The purpose of this book, then, is to serve as the manual that should have accompanied AppleWorks 6. In this book's pages, you'll find step-by-step instructions for using every AppleWorks 6 feature, including those you may not even have quite understood, let alone mastered: style sheets, database reports, links, macros, and so on.

AppleWorks 6: The Missing Manual is designed to accommodate readers at every technical level. The primary discussions are written for advanced-beginner or intermediate AppleWorks users. But if you're a first-time AppleWorks user, special sidebar articles called Up To Speed provide the introductory information you need to understand the topic at hand. If you're an advanced AppleWorks user, on the other hand, keep your eye out for similar shaded boxes called Power Users' Clinic. They offer more technical tips, tricks, and shortcuts for the experienced AppleWorks fan.

About the Outline

AppleWorks 6: The Missing Manual is divided into three parts, each containing several chapters:

- Part 1, *Parts of the Sum,* covers the six modules that make up the heart of AppleWorks: Word Processing, Database, Spreadsheet, Drawing, Painting, and Presentation.

- Part 2, *AppleWorks Power,* covers the AppleWorks features that don't create documents, but serve as tools to help *you* create them. One chapter is devoted to the things that make it easier for you to get started with a project: Clippings, Assistants, and Templates. Another chapter covers AppleWorks' new Internet features, such as creating Web pages. A third covers all the ways you can customize AppleWorks, including the *macro* function that lets you turn AppleWorks into a software robot that's absolutely thrilled to do boring, repetitive tasks for you.

- Part 3, *Integration,* details how the modules with each other, with other programs, and with other computers. Finally, a troubleshooting chapter helps you to get out of trouble if you're in it, or stay out of trouble if you're not.

At the end of the book, two appendixes await. One provides a menu-by-menu explanation of every AppleWorks command; the other offers guidance in installing the program and upgrading from earlier versions.

About→These→Arrows

Throughout this book, and throughout the Missing Manual series, you'll find sentences like this one: "Open the AppleWorks 6→Starting Points→Templates folder." That's shorthand for a much longer instruction that directs you to open three nested folders in sequence, like this: "On your hard drive, you'll find a folder called Apple-Works 6. Open that. Inside the AppleWorks 6 window is a folder called Starting Points; double-click it to open it. Inside *that* folder is yet another one called Templates. Double-click to open it, too."

Similarly, this kind of arrow shorthand helps to simplify the business of choosing commands in menus, as shown in Figure I-2.

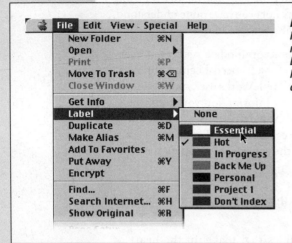

Figure I-1:
In this book, arrow notations help to simplify folder and menu instructions. For example, "Choose File→Label→ Essential" is a more compact way of saying, "From the File menu, choose Label; from the submenu that then appears, choose Essential," as shown here.

The Quest for a Term

The word processing thing, the drawing component, the spreadsheet gizmo—what's the right noun for these core AppleWorks talents? Some say *windows, modules,* or *modes. Document type* has a few fans, as does *parts*. Apple has always called them *application environments;* a clunkier term never walked the earth.

For the sake of clarity, this book uses the term *modules* to refer to the various kinds of documents AppleWorks produces: Word Processing, Database, Spreadsheet, Drawing, Painting, and Presentation.

About MissingManual.com

If you have an Internet account, visit the *MissingManual.com* Web site. Click the *AppleWorks 6: The Missing Manual* button to reveal articles, tips, and updates to the book. In fact, you're invited and encouraged to submit such corrections and updates yourself. In an effort to keep the book as up-to-date and accurate as possible, each time we print more copies of this book, we'll make any confirmed corrections you've suggested. We'll also note such changes on the Web site, so that you can mark important corrections into your own copy of the book, if you like.

In the meantime, we'd love to hear your own suggestions for new books in the Missing Manual line. There's a place for that on the Web site, too, as well as a place to sign up for free email notification of new titles in the series.

Part One:
Parts of the Sum

1

The Sneak Preview

Many people treat AppleWorks as six individual programs under one roof, shifting between them the same way you might shift between, for example, Internet Explorer, Quicken, and your email program.

But the real strength of AppleWorks, the key to unlocking its efficiency, is the *integration* of its modules—its ability to seamlessly incorporate one module within another. If it so suits you, AppleWorks can plop a photo into your spreadsheet, or a spreadsheet into a report you're typing, or a typed report into a database. AppleWorks refers to these "documents within documents" as *frames*, gateways that give you the complete features of, for example, the spreadsheet in the middle of a word processing document.

Further enhancing its versatility is AppleWorks's ability to create *links* between and within documents—"Click here to read more on this topic," for example—and its ability to automate documents so that they perform routine tasks *for* you.

For example, suppose your company's weekly newsletter features a table of the week's sales data and a chart of year-to-date sales. The table and chart are used every week in the same form—only the data changes. AppleWorks can create a live link between a spreadsheet containing the table data and a spreadsheet frame within the newsletter document. The same arrangement works for the chart.

If your Mac is connected to an office network, this arrangement can save a lot of work and steps. When the spreadsheet is revised by the accounting department downstairs, the table and chart in the newsletter—created by the art department upstairs—reflect the changes automatically.

Or maybe you're cataloging your genealogy and family history. From a list or chart of family members, a single click on a person's name can open another document containing some of their reminiscences, or a QuickTime movie of an interview with that person, or even that person's home page on the Internet.

This chapter serves as a guidebook to the rest of this book. It's a crash course in AppleWorks, a sneak preview that highlights the program's significant features and gets you ready for the productivity lessons in the chapters to come.

Starting Points

When you open AppleWorks, and whenever the program is running (but doesn't have any documents open), you're confronted with the Starting Points window. Across the bottom of this window is a series of tabs representing the various ways you can open a new AppleWorks document (see Figure 1-1).

Figure 1-1:
The Starting Points window opens to the tab you were on the last time you used the program. But you may prefer to use a template or assistant (see Chapter 9) to get a head start on your creation.

Above the Starting Points window is the *Button bar* (Figure 1-1). When no document is open on the screen, the Button bar displays six buttons representing the six AppleWorks modules (word processing, drawing, and so on). A single click on any of these buttons opens a new document of the corresponding type. If the Basics tab (of the Starting Points window) is selected, then its icons duplicate those of the Button bar (but larger and with titles to tell you what the icons represent). A single click on any of these icons also opens a new document.

Tip: If you almost always open the same type of new document, choose Edit→Preferences→General, and then click the bottom pop-up menu, "On ⌘- N, Create" and select your preferred module. From now on, when you open AppleWorks, you can ignore the Starting Points window and Button bar; just press ⌘-N to open a document of the type you specified.

Starting Points Tabs

Click any of the other tabs on the Starting Points window to reveal the assistants, templates, or recent documents used in AppleWorks.

- **Basic.** Click one of the big icons to open a new document in any of the Apple-Works modules.

- **Assistants.** An *assistant* interviews you, screen by screen, to help you create a document that contains fancy, prefab formatting, such as business cards, envelopes, certificates, and so on. For details on assistants, see page 284.

- **Recent items:** AppleWorks remembers the documents you've opened most recently; they're displayed in this tab. Click any item to open it again. Recent items can also be opened by choosing File→Open Recent, and then selecting from the list.

Tip: The Recent Items tab can be a lifesaver when you're looking for a document you created recently but you're not sure how, or where, you saved it.

But AppleWorks comes set to remember only the 10 most recently used documents—bad luck if the document you're looking for happens to be the *eleventh* most recently used one. Increase AppleWorks's short-term memory by choosing Edit→Preferences→General→Topic→Files, and then increasing the number for recent items remembered to, say, 25.

- **Templates.** AppleWorks includes 36 document *templates*—pre-designed documents like letterheads, reports, postcards, brochures, flash cards, and so on. Dozens more are available from Apple over the Internet by clicking the Web tab, and hundreds more are available from a variety of other sources. For more on templates, see page 275.

- **Web:** If your computer has Internet access, this tab is your connection to Apple's collection of AppleWorks templates on the Web. Since they're on the Internet instead of on the AppleWorks CD, Apple can continue to expand the collection of available templates. Downloading all the templates would be time-consuming and would fill your hard disk with files you may never use, so AppleWorks instead downloads two special-purpose templates: *Newsletter* and *Templates* (see Figure 1-2).

The icon titled *Templates* is a word processing document that contains short descriptions of the template categories—Home, School, Business, and so on—with blue, underlined links. Clicking a link downloads another directory template listing all the templates in that category, each with another link. Click one of those and AppleWorks automatically receives the file from the Internet, places it into its proper folder on your hard drive, and opens the template.

Figure 1-2:
When AppleWorks connects to a remote computer over the Internet and downloads documents, the Web progress window displays the familiar progress bar, the number of files to be downloaded, and how many of them are yet to be transferred.

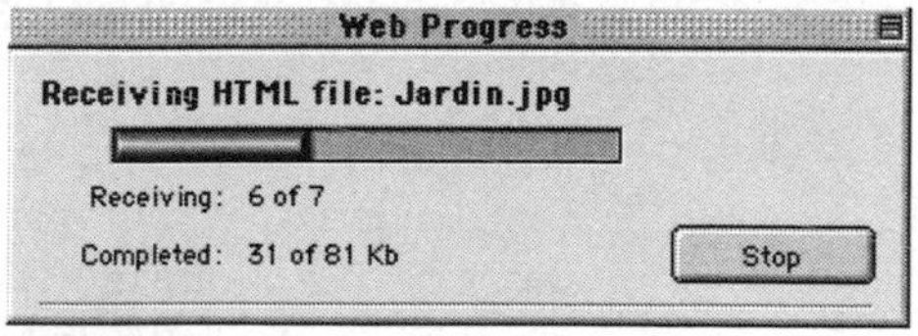

Web Progress
Receiving HTML file: Jardin.jpg
Receiving: 6 of 7
Completed: 31 of 81 Kb
Stop

The AppleWorks Newsletter is actually a template just like the rest, but it's designed to be a source of up-to-date information from Apple. The newsletter is updated monthly by Apple with news and features about AppleWorks and its users. (For more on AppleWorks's new Internet features, see Chapter 10.)

• **Add [+]**. The last tab is marked by a big plus sign—the Add tab. Clicking this tab opens the Add Tab dialog box, where you create your *own* tabs for the Starting Points window.

For example, you can make one tab for your business documents and another for household ones—or perhaps one for each member of your family. In addition using it as a launch pad for documents on your hard drive (choose My Computer in the dialog box that appears), you can also use the Add tab to link to AppleWorks documents on other computers on the Internet (choose Internet based from the dialog box).

Of course, creating a tab to hold your favorite documents is only half the battle; you must also find a way to put your document icons *onto* it. You can do so in two ways: first, by dragging the icon of an AppleWorks document (if it's visible) from the Macintosh desktop directly onto the tab you've created.

Second, you can save or drag your documents into the AppleWorks 6→Starting Points→[your tab name] folder. Anything in this folder appears automatically on your Starting Points tab.

Meet the Modules

If you've never used AppleWorks before—or even if you have—a short review of the six modules may help ease any confusion about this multi-faceted program.

Words–The Word Processing Module

When you need to get words on the page, the word processing module is the place to start. It's not just a computerized typewriter; it's a computerized typesetting department. With a word processor you create, edit, spell check, and format your words on the page. AppleWorks also makes it easy to add graphics, borders, columns, tables, and spreadsheets to spice up the text of your documents. See Chapters 2 and 3.

Facts–The Database Module

While the purposes for the word processor, spreadsheet, and graphics modules are self-evident, the database module possesses an aura of mystery for many AppleWorks users.

A *database* is a tool to collect, manage, and retrieve lots of little pieces of information. For example, your mailing list, stamp collection, invoicing system, favorite recipes, CD collection, and warehouse inventory tracking are tasks for the database module. The AppleWorks database is a simplified version of FileMaker Pro, the most popular database program for Macintosh (and an increasingly popular Windows database). For the full story, see Chapter 4.

Numbers—The Spreadsheet Module

For most people, the word *spreadsheet* conjures up an image of dreary columns of numbers being crunched by the computer—and for most people, *spreadsheet* means Microsoft Excel. But in fact, a spreadsheet can also put its crunching prowess to work on text instead of numbers, to create schedules, lists, and calendars. It can also generate attractive graphs and charts, as you'll see in Chapter 5.

Graphics—The Drawing and Painting Modules

The AppleWorks art department is divided into two modules: *drawing* and *painting*. They represent the two fundamentally different approaches to computer graphics. The Drawing module, like such programs as Adobe Illustrator, creates *objects*—lines, squares, circles, and blocks of text—that you can move, resize, or rearrange even after you've placed them on the screen. The Painting module—like such programs as Adobe Photoshop—lets you create images composed of the dots on the screen. (It's great for editing photos you've scanned.) Figure 1-3 should make this distinction clearer.

See Chapters 6 and 7 for more on these modules (and advice on when to use which).

Figure 1-3:
In a painting document, you can paint over or erase a part of your painting, but you can't remove or re-position the strokes (left). In a drawing, each object remains a distinct object (right), which you can click, drag around, retype, and so on—but you can't erase individual dots.

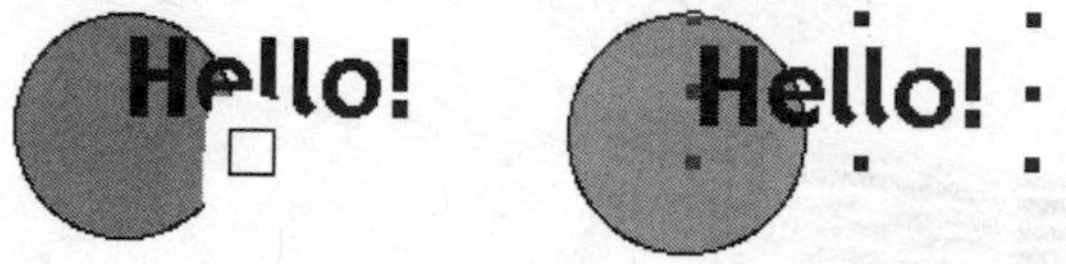

Show Time—The Presentation Module

In classrooms, meeting rooms, and board rooms, the overhead projector is going the way of the slide rule, thanks to computer-presentation software like the AppleWorks slide-show module. Like such pricey programs as Microsoft PowerPoint, AppleWorks 6 can produce very sophisticated presentations. Despite their obvious use in the boardroom, the audience for a presentation need not be a group. A salesperson's laptop can contain a presentation tailored to a particular client, or an educational presentation can be a self-paced lesson for one student. See Chapter 8 for more.

AppleWorks Grand Tour

If you've used previous versions of AppleWorks, version 6's radical visual overhaul may leave you disoriented. Actually, the beautiful but label-free buttons and toolbars may baffle anyone who's used *any* software before. In the following sections, you'll meet the core AppleWorks control palettes—and even take a whirl at creating a text-and-graphics document.

Button Bar Basics

The set of icons directly beneath the menu bar is the *Button bar* (see Figure 1-4). You can view it horizontally or vertically, rooted to the edges of the screen or as a movable bar. Buttons provide easy, one-click access to commands that you would otherwise have to locate in one of the menus. Buttons can also run *macros* (automated software robots that perform complicated sequences of steps, as described in Chapter 11), open documents, launch other programs, or open a Web page. You can customize the Button bar, adding, removing, or redesigning the buttons to your taste (also in Chapter 11).

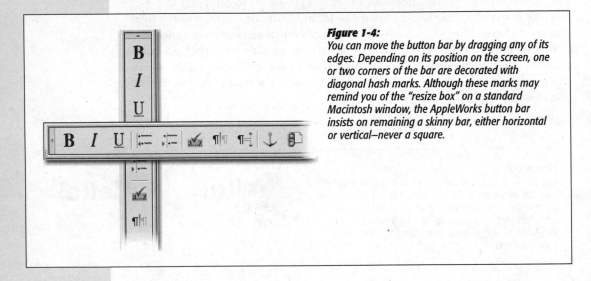

Figure 1-4:
You can move the button bar by dragging any of its edges. Depending on its position on the screen, one or two corners of the bar are decorated with diagonal hash marks. Although these marks may remind you of the "resize box" on a standard Macintosh window, the AppleWorks button bar insists on remaining a skinny bar, either horizontal or vertical—never a square.

Each end of the bar has a narrow scroll-arrow button. When this triangular arrow is black (not gray), AppleWorks is telling you that additional buttons are hidden beyond the bar's boundaries; click the arrow button to bring them into view.

Buttons are *supposed* to be easily understood iconic representations—but one person's model of clarity is another's confusing hieroglyph. Furthermore, AppleWorks comes with over *200* pre-defined buttons! In other words, you're not expected to identify these buttons just by looking at their cryptic pictures.

Instead, if you place your arrow pointer over a button without clicking, a balloon appears with a description of the button's function. (If not, somebody has turned the feature off. Use AppleWorks's Choose Edit→Preferences→Button Bar, and then check the box marked "Show tooltips.") For the rest of the story on Button bar customization, see page 309.

Tip: AppleWorks provides an easier way to open the Customize Button Bar dialog box—and to get at many other program controls: *contextual pop-up menus.* Control-click the Button bar to make this pop-up menu appear; choose Customize Button Bar from the pop-up menu.

The First Look At a Document

Whether you start with a new document or open a template, AppleWorks opens it as "untitled (WP)," or "untitled (SS)," for example. This designation conveys two things: First, it tells you which module created the document (WP for word processor, SS for spreadsheet, and so on); second, it hints that you haven't yet saved the document and given it a title.

Every Mac program offers *menus* across the top of the screen or window. Apple-Works adds a new wrinkle: Its menus *change*, depending on which module you're using. In fact, AppleWorks menus can change even within a single document—when you edit a spreadsheet you've placed into a word processor document, for example. See Chapter 12 for details on these documents-within-documents (called *frames*).

The changing menus can cause considerable confusion for the beginning AppleWorker. But once you realize the method behind this madness, these morphing menus make perfect sense.

Like the menu bar, the Button bar is also given to alarming visual changes as it endeavors to provide the appropriate set of buttons for the active module. If the button-changing disturbs you—or if you need the screen space—you can hide the Button bar entirely. Choose Window→Hide Button Bar to remove it, or Window→Show Button Bar to display it.

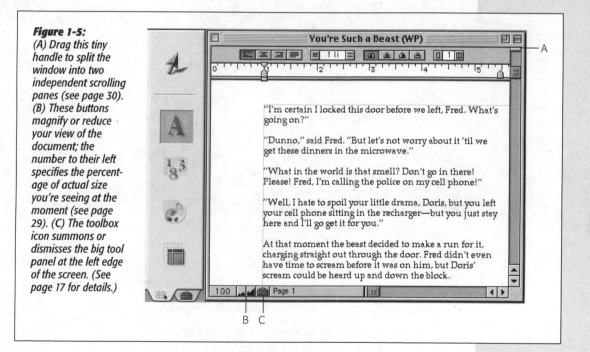

Figure 1-5:
(A) Drag this tiny handle to split the window into two independent scrolling panes (see page 30). (B) These buttons magnify or reduce your view of the document; the number to their left specifies the percentage of actual size you're seeing at the moment (see page 29). (C) The toolbox icon summons or dismisses the big tool panel at the left edge of the screen. (See page 17 for details.)

The Document Window

Overall, the AppleWorks document window itself doesn't pose much mystery. For instance, the word processing module window sports a ruler, the spreadsheet module window features a formula bar, and so on. However, lurking on the edges of all AppleWorks windows are added doodads that control how the information in your window is displayed. Figure 1-5 reveals a few of them.

Frames: A Short Tutorial

The genius of AppleWorks is its ability to combine different kinds of data on the same page. You can put a spreadsheet into your scanned photo, or a map into your typed report, and so on (see Figure 1-6). Chapter 12 contains reams of information on the possibilities—and limitations—of these combinations.

In the meantime, here's a tour—a five-minute taste of AppleWorks's potential.

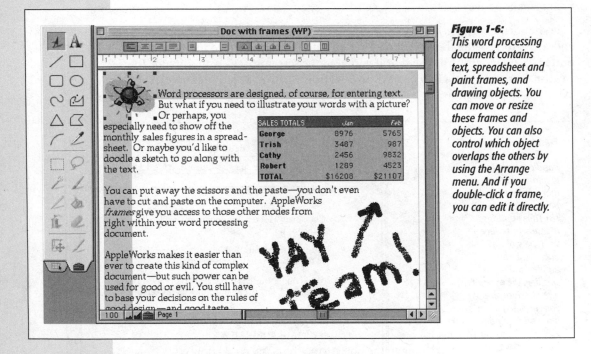

Figure 1-6:
This word processing document contains text, spreadsheet and paint frames, and drawing objects. You can move or resize these frames and objects. You can also control which object overlaps the others by using the Arrange menu. And if you double-click a frame, you can edit it directly.

1. Launch AppleWorks. In the Starting Points window, click the Basic tab (if it's not already selected) and click the Word Processing icon.

   A new, untitled word processing document appears.

2. Type a few words into the new document window.

   Your manuscript is well under way.

3. Make the tool appear by clicking the toolbox icon at the lower-left corner of the window (labeled A in Figure 1-7).

Alternatively, you can choose Window→Show Tools. The Tools window, which is usually hidden when you're word processing, appears.

4. Click the toolbox *tab* at the bottom of the Tools window (B in Figure 1-7).

Now the Tools window changes to show an array of what appear to be drafting tools.

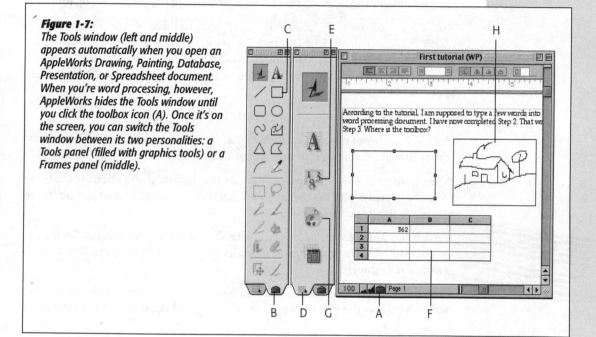

Figure 1-7:
The Tools window (left and middle) appears automatically when you open an AppleWorks Drawing, Painting, Database, Presentation, or Spreadsheet document. When you're word processing, however, AppleWorks hides the Tools window until you click the toolbox icon (A). Once it's on the screen, you can switch the Tools window between its two personalities: a Tools panel (filled with graphics tools) or a Frames panel (middle).

5. Click the Rectangle tool (C in Figure 1-7). Now drag diagonally anywhere inside the document window, creating a rectangle.

You've just added a *drawing object* to your document. Notice that the menus and Button bars change as soon as you click the rectangle tool button; now they're filled with options pertaining to the object you drew. You could now go to town with these controls, rotating or reshaping your rectangle, making text wrap around it, and so on. The point here, though, is that you've just added a drawing to what started out as a pure text document.

But that's just the beginning:

6. Click the Frames tab on the Tools window (D in Figure 1-7). Click the Spreadsheet tool (labeled E in Figure 1-6). Once again, drag diagonally across an empty area of your document window.

This time, a little spreadsheet appears in the rectangle (labeled F in Figure 1-7). You've created a *spreadsheet frame;* once again, the menus and Button bar change to reflect the newly pertinent options. At this point, you could type numbers into this spreadsheet, perform "what-if" comparisons, generate graphs, and calculate your net worth.

But that's for later. Now then:

7. **Click the Painting tool (labeled G in Figure 1-7). In yet another blank area of your document window—if you can find one—drag diagonally yet again.**

You've just added a third kind of frame to your humble memo: a canvas upon which you can paint (H in Figure 1-7). Yet again, the menus and Button bar change in readiness for the painting you could now make. To prove it to yourself, drag the cursor inside the rectangle you've just made; expressive little doodles appear wherever you drag.

8. **Click the various rectangles you've created.**

One click on any of these objects *selects* that object, which you can tell by the tiny square handles that appear at its four corners.

When a frame is selected like this, you can manipulate it in various ways: press Delete to get rid of it; drag the tiny black handles to change its shape; drag inside it to move the frame; and so on.

A *second* click within the painting or spreadsheet frame brings forth the menus and buttons associated with that module: painting tools or spreadsheet commands, for example.

As you click the various elements in this document, the menus and buttons frantically change as the various AppleWorks modules take their turns in the foreground.

AppleWorks for the Overworked (or Lazy)

You don't always have to create AppleWorks documents from scratch. This program is creaking under the weight of half-finished, gorgeous documents that you can bend to your purposes, saving a lot of time in the process.

In version 6, in fact, the traditional AppleWorks collection of clip art and professionally-designed templates has ballooned to include 25,000 clip art images and 100 new templates, many of which are available only if you have an Internet connection. Those new Internet capabilities link you seamlessly to an ever-growing collection of templates and clip art images.

Assistants

The Assistants tab in the Starting Points window puts at your disposal six software robots—interactive templates, each designed to produce a certain kind of document. Based on your answers to questions the Assistant asks, AppleWorks generates a tailor-made document, complete with graphics, formatting, borders, and so on. Some Assistants provide very basic help, like formatting an envelope properly with an address and return address. Others, like the Address List assistant, walk you through the process of creating a database for your addresses and phone numbers. (For details, see Chapter 7.)

Templates

Templates, or stationery documents, are complete, professionally designed documents, complete with gibberish text. By replacing the bogus information in these attractive documents with your own information, you can appropriate that document for your own use. For example, instead of creating a newsletter from scratch, you can select one of the AppleWorks newsletter templates that appeals to you, delete the dummy text, and use the remaining shell as a basis for your own publication. (See Chapter 9 for more.)

Clippings

AppleWorks lets you access over 25,000 clip art images (which it calls *clippings*) arranged by topic. A couple hundred of these graphics are installed on your hard drive; you can access thousands more via AppleWorks's Web link.

To see these pictures, choose File→Show Clippings to open the clippings window. Tabs on the bottom of this window organize the clippings by topic. Just like the Starting Points window, the Clippings window's tabs can contain items stored on your computer's hard drive or on the Internet.

The beauty of clippings is that you can insert them into any of your AppleWorks documents just by dragging them from the Clippings window onto your document window. Once a picture appears in your work, you can squish it, stretch it, rotate it, and otherwise tease it into submission.

Though mostly used for still images, clippings can also contain QuickTime movies, frames, or even complete AppleWorks documents. Did you thrash through those 25,000 clip-art images in the first week? No problem: you can add your own images, documents, or QuickTime movies. (See Chapter 9 for details on clippings.)

Macros

Macros are one of the AppleWorks features that separate the power users from the rest of the pack. A macro is like a tape recording of a series of your steps. The next time you need to repeat that procedure, you can run the macro instead; it dutifully plays back your actions—every mouse click, every menu command—exactly as you performed them earlier.

Macros can seem intimidating at first, but after you've made a couple, you'll discover that they're not difficult. You'll begin to notice more and more places where a macro can save you keystrokes or mouse work. Any time you find yourself repeating the same series of actions more than a few times, consider creating a macro to do that job for you. Chapter 11 contains the details.

Links

You're probably familiar with *links* from your Web browser: Click a bit of under-lined text, a button, or an image, and you're instantly taken to another Web page, possibly on a completely different computer in a completely different part of the world. Links let you move around the Internet with ease, jumping from one page to another.

In AppleWorks, you can create similar links that take you from place to place within a document, open another AppleWorks document, or open your Web browser to take you to a Web page. For example, you can create a "live" table of contents: your reader can click a chapter title to open the corresponding AppleWorks document. AppleWorks links can even open documents on other computers in your office net-work—or even on the Internet. See Chapter 3 for more.

Exchanging Files

The Tower of Babel has nothing on modern computer users. Different platforms, different software, different versions of the same program—they all have their own way of "talking." The problems created by this language barrier of file formats are brought home every time you try to send an email attachment or exchange a disk with someone who uses a different program or a different kind of computer.

You can move an AppleWorks 6 document from Mac to Windows, or Windows (if it has AppleWorks 6) to Mac, without performing any conversion or translation at all. AppleWorks 5 fans enjoyed extensive built-in file-translation abilities that allowed the program to open and save in a variety of other file formats—but unfortunately, Apple removed these features from AppleWorks 6. The only real solution to this dilemma is to purchase an accessory program that does nothing but translate files from one format to another; a 60%-off discount coupon is included with this book. (See Chapter 13 for details.)

Help

AppleWorks doesn't come with a proper printed manual; if it did, this book wouldn't exist. But it's not completely Help-less. The Help menu provides access to several electronic help mechanisms, including these:

Balloon Help

Choose Help→Show Balloons to turn on the *Balloon help* system. Once you've turned it on, this feature displays a little pop-up balloon containing a description of what-ever your cursor points to: a menu item, tool, button, or window-edge feature, for example. Getting work done with balloons popping up all over the place can be a challenge, but balloon help can occasionally be helpful in identifying a confusing icon or menu item.

AppleWorks Help

When you choose Help→AppleWorks Help, you summon the most extensive built-in AppleWorks help feature: AppleWorks Help, which runs in a separate application program called Help Viewer. (Help Viewer doesn't work with Mac OS 8.1. Instead, AppleWorks launches your Web browser to display the help files.) Like a real book, Help Viewer lets you find information either by looking up specific terms in the index, or by using the table of contents. The option of flipping through the pages until what you're looking for jumps out at you is not available—however, you can use the search function instead. You can click on hyperlinks to move through the guide by jumping to related topics.

Tip: Many dialog boxes in AppleWorks include a Help icon. Click it to open the related topic in AppleWorks Help—which remains open, so when you've finished reading the help topic, you can continue with your choices in the dialog box.

Figure 1-8:
The AppleWorks Help window (top left) is the starting point for the electronic AppleWorks manual. Enter a word or phrase and click Search, or click any of the underlined topics, to view related subtopics (middle). Keep clicking the appropriate links until you find what you're looking for (bottom). Or scroll to the bottom of the contents list to reveal the Index link.

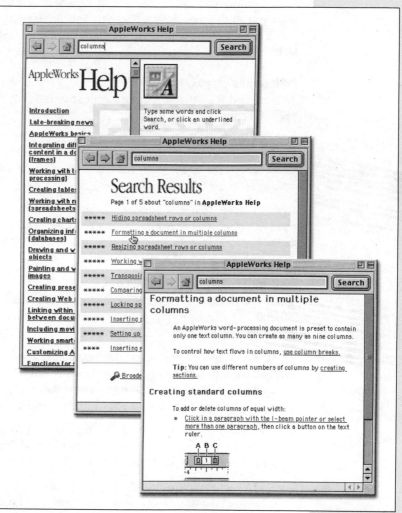

Navigating Help

The *home* button brings you back not to the table of contents, but to the Help Center: a central listing of help modules for your entire computer—Mac OS, AppleScript, AppleWorks, and perhaps others—are listed here. Click AppleWorks Help to get back to the table of contents. The back and forward arrow buttons work just like the back and forward buttons on your Web browser, taking you back, and then forward through the screens you've already viewed.

Searching Help

To search AppleWorks Help, type a word or phrase into the keyword box, and then press Return. After a moment, the Search Results window displays its findings, indicating *relevance* (what percentage of the help text matches your search request) with up to five asterisks. At the bottom of the window are links to *More results*, which takes you to the next page of results, and *Broaden my search*, which extends the search to all the Help Viewer files on your computer (instead of just the AppleWorks Help file).

Printing and copying Help

To convert this electronic help document into paper, choose File→Print. You can print only one topic at a time.

Tip: The Help Viewer application doesn't let you select or copy text. But since Help Viewer files are actually HTML files—the same format used by Web pages—you can open them in your Web browser, where you can copy text to your heart's content.

To do so, launch your Web browser. Choose File→Open, and then navigate to your System Folder→Help→AppleWorks Help folder; double-click the file called AppleWorks Help. There you are at the table of contents page for AppleWorks Help, with full copying privileges.

Still More Help on the Internet

The huge amount of AppleWorks help available on the Internet ranges from the official word from Apple to collections of templates, tips, and tutorials from AppleWorks users all over the world.

- **Apple:** From the AppleWorks Starting Points window, click the Web tab. Double-click the Newsletter to access the monthly AppleWorks newsletter directly from Apple. Or visit the official Web site—*http://www.apple.com/appleworks*—for news, updates, tutorials, resources for educators, and links.

- *www.missingmanual.com*: Go to the Missing Manual Web site and click the AppleWorks 6 button for more templates, new developments, corrections and updates to this book, and more links.

- **AWUG:** The AppleWorks User Group publishes a superb monthly newsletter. Its extensive Web site at *www.awug.com* teems with links, information, tutorials, and a huge collection of templates available for members to download.

- **The AppleWorks/ClarisWorks email list:** You can read the archives or join this very active, informative email list—essentially a discussion group conducted by email—by going to *http://listserv.temple.edu/archives/claris-works.html*. This is a great place to post a specific question about AppleWorks—you'll probably end up with more than one reply by the end of the day.

Word Processing Basics

AppleWorks gives you the ability to perform a half-dozen different tasks on your computer—without buying six different pieces of software. Depending on how you work, you may find yourself spending a lot of time in, say, the spreadsheet module, and none in the painting module. But no matter what you do, you'll probably spend a considerable amount of time word processing. You can dramatically increase your overall efficiency by learning the ins and outs of this core function.

Creating a Document

Unlike most programs, which open directly to a new document, AppleWorks 6 greets you with the Starting Points window—one of the tabbed windows that constitute the most significant visual change from earlier versions of AppleWorks. Here you choose between starting from scratch with a brand new document (by clicking the Basic tab) or from an existing document (using one of the other tabs).

You can open a new word processing document in any of four ways (see Figure 2-1):

- Click the Word Processing icon (on the Basic tab of the Starting Points window).

- Click the word processing icon in the Button bar (that is, the leftmost icon on the horizontal strip at the top of the screen).

- Choose File→New→Word Processing

- Press ⌘-N. (If ⌘-N doesn't open a word processing document, someone has altered the program's preferences. Choose Edit→Preferences→General, and then select the Word Processing module from the second pop-up menu.)

Tip: If you regularly open a document you've created by using the File→Open Recent command (or the Recent Items tab on the Starting Points window), you may lose track of *where* you actually stored a file on your hard disk. Two scripts in the Scripts menu (the scroll icon next to the Help menu) help you recover from these "senior moments."

With the document in question open, choose Scripts→Universal→Reveal in Finder; you jump to your Macintosh desktop, where your document's folder is opened and its icon highlighted. Or choose Scripts→Universal→Copy File Path to copy the *path* of the errant file to the clipboard (such as *Macintosh HD:Documents:Memos,* which you can paste into, say, a word processing document to uncover the document's icon's hiding place. (See Appendix A for details on the Scripts menu.)

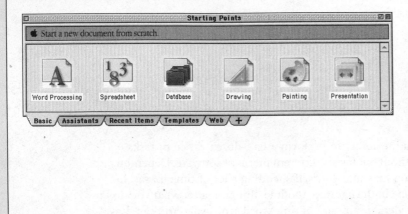

Figure 2-1:
The first of many decisions: The Starting Points window. The Basic tab is the real starting point–but Apple-Works opens to whichever tab was most recently used. So if what you want is a new document, ignore the Starting Points window altogether and use the Button bar to pick a module–or press ⌘- N to open your preferred document type.

The Document Window

A new AppleWorks word processing document is called "untitled (WP)," which reminds you that you haven't yet saved your word processing document or given it a title. The insertion point is blinking and waiting for you to begin typing.

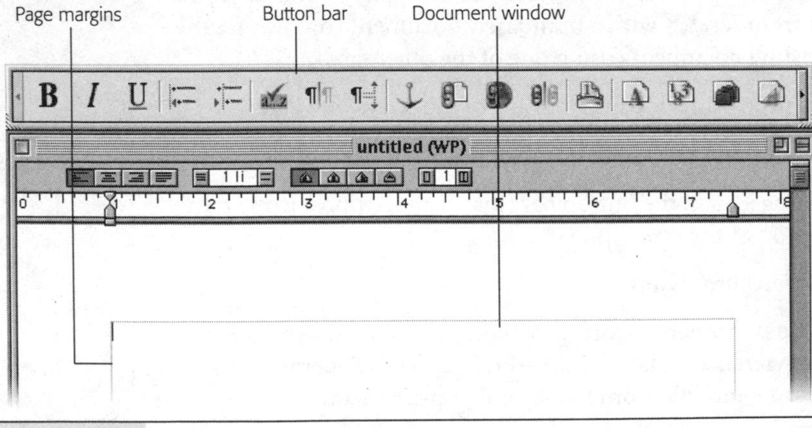

Page margins · Button bar · Document window

untitled (WP)

Figure 2-2:
As soon as you make your selection from the Starting Points window it vanishes, replaced by the new document window. Buttons associated with the selected module materialize in the Button bar, and you're confronted with that writer's nemesis: the blank sheet of paper.

AppleWorks comes out of the box with the assumption is that Helvetica is your favorite typeface (font). But, as a professional typesetter might tell you, Helvetica is a *sans-serif* font, best suited for headlines, not body text. Fortunately, it's easy enough to train AppleWorks to have better typographical taste.

1. **Choose Edit→Preferences→General.**

   The Preferences window appears. From the Topic pop-up menu, choose Text (if it's not already selected).

2. **From the Default Font pop-up menu, select a font.**

   Palatino or Times are good choices for a "normal" font.

3. **Click Make Default, and then click OK (or press Return).**

   The Preferences window closes. From now on, every new AppleWorks document will have your new default font.

The First Rule of Fonts

Serifs are the little points or lines at the ends of the strokes that form certain kinds of typefaces. They're a remnant of the time before printing presses, when all type was inscribed by hand with a broad-tipped pen and ink. Tests for readability have shown that serif-style typefaces—especially the *oldstyle* ones like Garamond, Palatino, and Times—are much easier to read in blocks of text than are *sans-serif* typefaces.

Most books, including this one, use a serif font as the primary typeface, and a sans-serif font for headlines, titles, and little informative sidebar boxes like this one.

Grab almost any book, newspaper, or magazine and you'll see the serif-for-body-copy rule in effect. Do your readers a favor by following this rule, whether you are writing a letter, a newsletter or a doctoral dissertation.

The Document Window

The thoughtful programmers at Apple have created a document window fairly bristling with tools and controls. Learn their secrets, and you'll be well on your way to mastering document formatting and viewing.

The Button bar

The *Button bar,* just below the program's menu bar, saves wear and tear on your mouse by providing one-click access to a variety of popular menu commands. The default assortment of buttons let you, among other things, bold, italicize, and underline text; check spelling; create document and Web links; print; or open new documents in any of the AppleWorks modules. You can add buttons to do almost anything you can do in the menus, or delete the ones you don't need. (For example, you can drag the underline text button to the Trash to rid the Button bar of that outmoded style of emphasis.) You can read more about these icons and the secrets of Button bar customization in Chapter 11.

The ruler at the top of the word processor window displays formatting controls that affect whatever paragraph (or paragraphs) you've selected (see Figure 2-3). You'll find all the details of paragraph formatting later in this chapter, but don't wait until then to get acquainted with these essential tools. Here's the abbreviated version:

UP TO SPEED

The Curse Of The Cursor

For such a tiny thing, your computer's mouse pointer is surprisingly intelligent. It changes shape depending on what's under it. When you have no document open, it maintains its arrow-pointer shape.

When the cursor is positioned over something you've typed in AppleWorks, however, the pointer changes into an *I-beam cursor*—so called due to its resemblance to the cross-section of a steel I-beam. The cursor is shaped this way so that you can precisely position it between two letters in a line of text. When you then *click the mouse*, the blinking insertion point jumps to that spot, so you can add or delete at that point.

When you start typing again, the I-beam cursor *disappears*, leaving only the blinking insertion point. AppleWorks makes the I-beam invisible when you're actually typing so that it's

not distracting (and so that you don't confuse it with the letter I). If you move the mouse a fraction of an inch, however, the I-beam cursor reappears. (This distinction between I-beam cursor and insertion point challenges beginners. Many first-timers feel compelled to carefully position the I-beam cursor *over* the insertion point before typing—a pointless effort.)

As soon as you move the I-beam cursor past the edge of a text window, it resumes its arrow shape, ready to manipulate scroll bars, buttons, or menus.

In AppleWorks, cursor transformation has yet another dimension: the arrow pointer changes to a big plus sign when using the spreadsheet, a crosshair (+ symbol) when using the drawing tools, a paintbrush when "painting," and so on. As the computer geeks say, cursor variety is the spice of life.

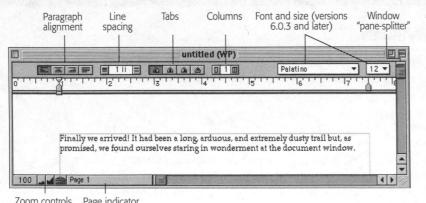

Paragraph alignment   Line spacing   Tabs   Columns   Font and size (versions 6.0.3 and later)   Window "pane-splitter"

untitled (WP)

Palatino   12

Finally we arrived! It had been a long, arduous, and extremely dusty trail but, as promised, we found ourselves staring in wonderment at the document window.

100   Page 1

Zoom controls   Page indicator

Figure 2-3:
The document window's controls. The ruler controls modify the formatting of the document: text alignment, line spacing, tab settings, and columns. The bottom-edge features adjust how the document is viewed on the screen: the zoom buttons, page indicator, and Toolbox button.

- *Paragraph alignment:* This group of four buttons controls the paragraph alignment or justification—from left to right: left-justified, centered, right-justified, and fully justified paragraphs.

- *Line spacing:* Next on the ruler is the line-spacing control, which controls how much space each paragraph has between lines: single-spaced, double-spaced, and so on.

- *Tabs:* The four tab buttons at the ruler's three-inch mark feature a house-shaped icon. The dark portion of this symbol, resembling the opening of a tent, indicates what kind of tab stop each sets: left, center, right, or decimal. See page 43 for more on using tabs.

- *Columns:* AppleWorks can create newspaper-style columns on a single page, such that your text flows automatically from one into the next. These buttons represent "fewer columns" and "more columns"; the current setting is shown in between.

Zoom and Toolbox Controls

The ruler affects how the document is *formatted*. The other controls around the edges of the AppleWorks window affect how the document is *viewed*. They don't affect the formatting or printing.

For example, you can enlarge or reduce your view of the document using the controls in the lower-left corner of the document window (see Figure 2-4). The two buttons whose icons seem to represent a graph of Apple's stock price are actually meant to be mountains—far and near. They reduce and enlarge the view, respectively, with each successive click.

To the right of the mountains is the toolbox button. When clicked, it summons or dismisses yet another AppleWorks palette: the Tools window. For everyday word processing, you don't need any of the tools on the Tools window; that's why AppleWorks generally hides the Tools window when you're word processing. (You *do* need the tools when you want to create a graphic or spreadsheet inside your word processing document.)

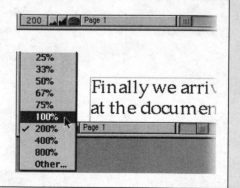

Figure 2-4:
The number at the lower-left corner of every AppleWorks document (top) tells you what percent of actual size you're seeing (200 means twice as big as the actual, printed size). This number is also a pop-up menu (bottom) that lets you jump directly to a certain "zoom level." (Choose Other to specify a particular amount of reduction or enlargement, from 3.125% to 3200%.)

Page-Number Indicator and Window Splitter

The page-number indicator displays the page you're on. It also lets you jump to another page: Double-click it to bring up a Go To Page window, type the page number you want to jump to, and click OK (or press the Return key).

There's one more easily overlooked control contained in the document window: the *pane control,* the small rectangle at the end of each scroll bar (see Figures 2-3 and 2-5). When you move your cursor over this spot, it becomes a horizontal bar with two tiny arrows. If you drag this bar, you split the window into two independently scrolling panes. For example, you can use this trick to keep the introductory paragraph of a document in sight as you write the body of the piece. Or you may want to keep a table or graph in view as you refer to it in the paragraphs that follow.

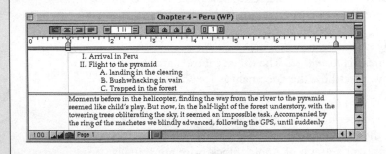

Figure 2-5:
Divide the window into panes *to show multiple views of the same document in one window. You can split the document window vertically or horizontally—or both. You can have up to three vertical and three horizontal panes, nine total. (Your confusion may well be total, too.)*

The Ultimate Alternate View

Whether your document is divided up into panes or displayed in multiple New View windows—or both—formatting changes affect the *document,* not the view. You can't display one view in, for example, Times 12, flush left, and another in Helvetica 18, justified. If such schizophrenic viewing is vital to you—for example, a side-by-side comparison of your Last Will and Testament in Palatino versus Old English—you'll need to create a duplicate document.

- Choose File→Save As, give this version a different name, perhaps add something like "test view" to the name, and click Save.

- When you do a Save As, the computer pulls a little switcheroo on you. The document on the screen becomes the new "saved as" version and the original is closed.

- Re-open the original document. The quick way to

do this is to choose →Recent Documents, and choose the document's name from the submenu.

- Rearrange the windows so you can see the two identical documents. Then modify the formatting of the "test view" document to your heart's content. Because it is a completely separate document, not just a different view, you can change fonts or margins, remove paragraphs—do anything at all—and the companion document won't be altered.

- When you've satisfied yourself with this alternate viewing session, do yourself a favor and *delete or rename the version of the document you don't want to keep.* If you don't delete it now, you'll inevitably become confused about which is which, leading to yet more sessions of alternate view comparisons as you attempt to sort out which version is the one you intended to use.

Tip: You don't have to split the window to view two parts of your document at once. Here's another approach: Choose Window→New View to open another window that shows the *same document.* Using this technique, you can adjust the magnification of each window independently. This trick can be helpful, if, for example, you're designing a page layout and want to keep an eye on the overall look of the page in a 50% view, while editing text in a 100% view.

Owners of gigantic monitors, take note: You can make as many New View windows as you need. And if splitting one window into nine panes isn't enough for you, you can make nine panes in each of nine copies of the same window!

Word Processing in AppleWorks

As in any word processor, editing in AppleWorks involves a handful of simple techniques endlessly repeated: Scroll up and down to read through the text. Click to place the insertion point where you want to insert or delete words. Type to replace characters, words, and sentences. Shift the order of passages using the Cut, Copy, and Paste commands. Use the mouse to move words and passages with *drag-and-drop* (see page 34). Improve the appearance of the document with formatting.

Navigation

The first order of editing business is just getting around in the document. That's not a problem for a one-page letter, but a challenge in a 95-page Environmental Impact Report.

Of course, you can use the vertical scroll bar at the right edge of every AppleWorks window, as in any computer program. (If you've split the window into horizontal panes, then each has its own scroll bar.) Instead of using the mouse, you can also scroll in AppleWorks using the keyboard, as shown in this table.

Press this key	To scroll
Page Up	Up a screenful
Page Down	Down a screenful
Home	To the beginning of the document
End	To the end of the document
⌘-up or down arrow	To the beginning or end of the document
Option-up or down arrow	To the beginning or end of the paragraph

You can also scroll by pressing the arrow keys: Hold down the up or down arrow key to move the insertion point up or down through your text. (When the insertion point reaches the edge of the screen, AppleWorks scrolls a half screen, putting the insertion point back into the middle of the newly scrolled screen.)

Finally, you can jump to a specific page by clicking the page number indicator at the bottom of the document window, as discussed earlier in this chapter.

Inserting

Inserting text or spaces in a document is the most basic editing task. Move the I-beam cursor to the point you want to insert text, click the mouse, and then type. Any words that follow your insertion get pushed to the right to make room.

Deleting

More word processing basics: If you've just made a typo, press the Delete key to backspace. If you have to jump back a *couple* of words to make a correction, hold down the Delete or Backspace key steadily, watching the letters disappear until you get to the word you need to correct, and then retype.

But if you find an error too far back in your typing to be worth backspacing, use the mouse to correct it in one of these two ways:

- **Click, then press Delete.** Position the *I-beam cursor* to the immediate right of the error you want to delete, click the mouse, and press your Backspace or Delete key to remove the offending letters. Type your correction. Then move the I-beam cursor back to where you left off, click, and continue typing. (If your keyboard has a Forward Delete button, marked Del on older Mac keyboards, you can click just to the *left* of the error before pressing the key.)

- **Highlight text, then retype.** If the error you want to delete is more than a few letters long, use the highlight-then-retype method. Start by dragging carefully from the beginning to the end of the erroneous text. Sometimes this means dragging perfectly horizontally, very carefully; other times it means dragging diagonally from the beginning of a passage to the end.

    In either case, once you've released the mouse, anything you now type instantly replaces whatever you had highlighted. There's no need to delete it first.

Making the Selection

To edit text, you always follow a two-step process: First *select* the text, then retype (or use menu commands) to *change* it. You can select (or *highlight*) as little as a single character, or as much as an entire document.

- **Select a word or a passage:** Position your I-beam cursor at one end of your intended selection, drag to the other end, and then release the mouse button. Everything between those two points is selected, the text highlighted.

- **Select an individual letter:** Drag across the letter.

Mass selection techniques

While selecting text with a drag of the mouse works just fine, AppleWorks offers several ways to speed up the process. You might adopt these techniques, for example:

- **Select one word:** Double-click any part of the word.

- **Select several consecutive words:** Double-click anywhere on the first word—and on the second click, keep the mouse button pressed. Drag horizontally. As you go, AppleWorks highlights the text in one-word chunks, which lets you be much sloppier (and quicker) in your dragging effort.

- **Select one line of text:** Triple-click anywhere within the line. (To select text in one-line increments, triple-click and, with the mouse button down on the last click, drag onto other lines.)

- **Select one whole paragraph:** *Quadruple*-click anywhere in the paragraph. Quadruple-click and drag to select paragraph by paragraph.

- **Select a block of text:** Click to place the insertion point at one end of the block. Then, while pressing the Shift key, click at the far end of the block you want to select, even if the far end is many pages away.

- **Select the entire document:** Choose Edit→Select All, or press ⌘-A. Use this technique when you want to make a global change, such as changing the font or the margins for the whole document.

Keyboard selection techniques

Keyboard experts take note: you can select text without letting your fingers stray to the mouse. Starting from the current location of the blinking insertion point, you can select text.

To select	**Press this keystroke**
Next/previous word	Shift-Option-right arrow or -left arrow
Next/previous paragraph	Shift-Option-up arrow or -down arrow
To beginning/end of line	Shift-⌘-right arrow or -left arrow
To beginning/end of document	Shift-⌘-up arrow or -down arrow

No matter which method you used to make a selection, your very next action is applied to the text you've highlighted. For example, if you choose a different font, size, or style, AppleWorks applies it only to that selection.

Caution: Remember that when word processing, anything you type *replaces* whatever text you've highlighted. This phenomenon can be useful when, for example, you want to replace one highlighted word in a sentence. On the other hand, this behavior can also be dangerous. If you've highlighted your entire document, for example, typing a single letter (or even the Space bar) replaces all the text in your document. (Only the Edit→Undo command can save you in that event.)

Cut, Copy and, Paste

Back in the BC era—Before Computers—cutting and pasting involved real scissors and real paste. Now, thanks to the Cut, Copy, and Paste commands, we're free to be as sloppy and disorganized as we like as our creativity pours, lava-like, over the pages—and tidy them up later.

These three commands are in the Edit menu. But you'll repeat the cut, copy, and paste routine over and over again as you use your computer. Train yourself to use the keyboard commands for these functions; you'll save time and feel powerful.

- ⌘-X cuts, or removes whatever text you'd first highlighted. Your computer socks a copy of the deleted material onto its invisible Clipboard, ready to be re-deposited when you use the Paste command.

- ⌘-C *copies* the highlighted text—leaving it as it was, but again placing it on the invisible Clipboard. (C, as in *copy*.)

- ⌘-V pastes the cut or copied text back into your document at the current location of the blinking insertion point. (V as in, *voilà, there it is!*)

Tip: You can also use the F1, F2, F3, and F4 keys on the top row of your keyboard to trigger the Undo, Cut, Copy, and Paste commands.

Clipboard Crash Course

As you may have read, the Cut, Copy, and Paste commands rely on an invisible temporary storage platter called the Clipboard. It's not an AppleWorks function; it's built into the Mac operating system.

The Clipboard is a single-minded assistant: it can only hold one thing at a time. Hand it something else, and it drops what it had been holding. It then clutches this new item, ready for your command to paste, until you shut down the computer.

Put another way, whenever you cut or copy something, whatever was already on the Clipboard is obliterated. On the other hand, you can paste whatever's currently on the Clipboard an infinite number of times without wearing it out.

Because the Clipboard is a part of the operating system it is available in all programs, serving as the conduit to transfer information between them. For example, if your grandmother sends you an anecdote in an email message that you'd like to include in the family history you're compiling in AppleWorks, just copy it out of the email and paste it into the family history document.

Drag-and-Drop Editing

AppleWorks offers a one-step alternative to the cut/paste two-step: *drag-and-drop*. Figure 2-6 shows the procedure.

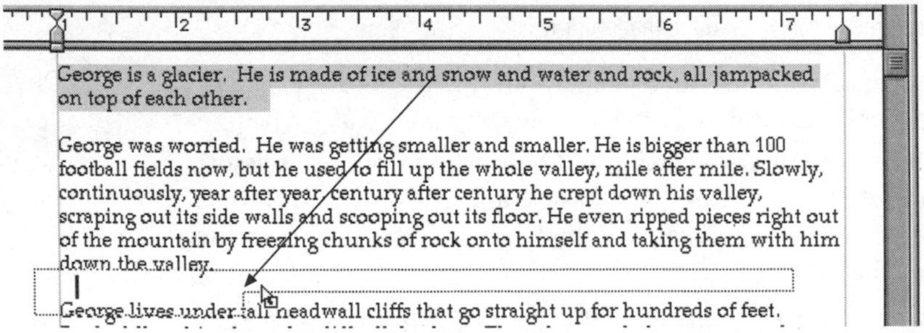

Figure 2-6:
Position your pointer over a chunk of highlighted text (top). The arrow sprouts a little box. Now you can drag that selection to another place in the document; when you release the mouse, the text you dragged appears in its new location.

You can also use drag-and-drop to *copy* a selection: hold down the Option key while performing the drag-and-drop. When you release the mouse button, you'll see that you've duplicated the original passage.

Tip: Drag-and-drop is most useful when you're dragging your selection a short distance. You can drag the arrow to the top or bottom edge of the window to scroll automatically, but even that technique can be clumsy.

Fortunately, AppleWorks offers a clever spin on the drag-and-drop method: *click-and-drop.* After highlighting some text, scroll leisurely to the destination page—and then ⌘-Option-click the new location to drop in the selected text!

The Undo and Revert Commands

The Edit→Undo command is your personal safety net, always ready to save you from your most recent error. When you choose Edit→Undo (or press ⌘-Z), AppleWorks reverses whatever your last action was.

In fact, the wording of the Edit→Undo command changes to reflect the kind of action that it will undo. For example, if you just used drag-and-drop to move a paragraph into the wrong spot, the Edit menu says Undo Move. Other possibilities for the Edit menu are Undo Format, Undo Typing, Undo Cut, and so on.

After you perform an undo (and breathe a sigh of relief), you've used up your one undo. The Edit menu now reads Redo—which *undoes* the Undo.

Caution: AppleWorks can't undo some actions, including using the File→Save As or File→Revert commands.

If you've really made a mess of your document—you've damaged it well beyond the powers of a single Undo—your last resort is the Revert command. Choose File→Revert to undo all the changes you've made since the last time you used the Save command. (Of course, doing so also discards any *good* work you've done in the meantime.)

Formatting

Computer word processing suddenly changed into *desktop publishing* when the 1985 Macintosh, coupled with the PostScript laser printer, offered the ability to create and print formatted text. No longer did you need a typesetting machine to produce beautiful (or hideous) pages containing fonts in different sizes and styles. Whether done with panache or with amateurish abandon, formatting is what separates modern computer word processing from the Remingtons and Underwoods.

Even if you don't add headlines and change fonts in your AppleWorks document, its appearance is still governed by an array of factory-installed formatting settings. AppleWorks can format your text, in fact, on four different levels: Character, Paragraph, Section, and Document.

- *Character* (or text) formatting is modifications you apply to each character: font, size, style, and color. You can apply these modifications to a single character or to entire words, sentences, paragraphs, or documents—whatever you've highlighted before using the formatting commands described below.

- *Paragraph* formatting involves tabs, indents, alignment, and line spacing within and between paragraphs. Since this formatting is applied to the entire paragraph, you need only have your insertion point *somewhere* within the paragraph before changing any of these attributes. You *can* have the entire paragraph selected, but you don't need to. (See "Paragraph Formatting," page 38.)

- *Section* formatting includes columns, page numbers, and header and footer layouts. (See "Section Formatting," page 46.)

- *Document* formatting is the page margins and footnote setup for the whole document. (See "Document Formatting," page 46.)

Tip: If you don't highlight any text before using the formatting commands described in this section, your formatting will affect whatever you type *next* (at the blinking insertion point, that is).

Character Formatting

This kind of formatting affects individual letters and words you've typed. For example:

Font

Choose Text→Font to select a typestyle for the highlighted text. (In AppleWorks 6.0.3 or later, you can use the pop-up menu on the ruler instead.) The fonts in your Font menu aren't, of course, an AppleWorks thing; they're the fonts installed in your operating system, and so are available to every program that offers a Font menu.

Size

Choose Text→Size (or use the Size pop-up menu on the ruler) to specify a new size for the highlighted text. Type is measured in *points*, with 72 points to the inch. "Normal" size for body text is usually 10- or 12-point type.

If you don't see the point size you want in the menu, choose Other. You'll be offered a dialog box in which you can type in any point size from 4 to 255.

Tip: Choose Text→Size→Larger or→Smaller to bump the size up or down one point at a time. Expert type tweakers use the keyboard shortcuts for these commands, ⌘-Shift-> or ⌘-Shift-<, to fine tune font sizes.

Style

Choose Text→Style, or click one of the equivalent buttons in the Button bar, to further modify the character of your characters. Plain Text means just what it says. You can use **Bold**, *Italic*, <u>Underline</u>, <u>Double Underline</u>, ~~Strikethrough~~, Outline, or

Shadow styles, singly or combined, to create some *really dreadful* text effects. (Choose Text→Style→Plain Text to remove these multiple stylings all at once.)

The other commands in the Style menu affect how the letters are placed in the line of text:

- Condense and Extend squeeze the highlighted letters together or s p r e a d t h e m a p a r t.

- Superscript and Subscript shift the highlighted letters $^{\text{a half line above}}$ or $_{\text{below}}$ the line.

- Superior and Inferior shift the highlighted letters a half line ^{above} or $_{\text{below}}$ the line *and* reduce their size; for anyone who writes chemical symbols or writes out exponential notation, this is a far more useful style than simple Superscript and Subscript.

Tip: Extensive formatting changes are usually part of the editing process, but it's easy to apply italics to a word or create a bold heading *as* you're typing. Immediately before the word you want to Italicize, press the keystroke for italics (⌘-I). Type the word, which now appears in italics—and then press the keystroke *again*. The first press turns italics on, the second turns it off. .

Similarly, ⌘-B turns **boldface** on and off. (⌘-U does the trick for underlining, but italics and bold are far more elegant and effective methods of expressing emphasis.)

Color

Choose Text→Text Color to change the color of the highlighted text.

Don't let the interior decorator inside you feel restrained by the 256-color assortment in the Text→Text Color palette, by the way. Choose Window→Show Accents to open the Accents window. Click the Text button and then, from the Palette pop-up menu, choose one of the 15 other palettes.

Tip: The commands in the Scripts menu (the scroll icon next to the Help menu) provide several additional features that aren't built into the regular AppleWorks menus. (See Appendix A to find out what this Scripts menu is all about.)

Three scripts change the capitalization of selected text—to small caps, title case ("Chicken of the Sea"), or every word capitalized ("Chicken Of The Sea"). Another searches for a text string in a selection and copies any paragraphs that include that text into a new document. The remaining script is designed to find accidentally repeated words in a selection, for example, *this is the the place*, or *these scripts are really really slow*. (And they *are* very slow—try them on a very small selection first.)

Return of the contextual menus

Another way to get at all the text formatting commands, as well as the Paragraph dialog box, the Spell Check, Thesaurus, and Word Count commands, is through the contextual pop-up menu. Control-click directly on your text to produce this pop-up menu, which contains an assortment of commands appropriate for a word processing document.

These mini menus are called *contextual* because their contents change depending on where you invoke them. Try clicking various AppleWorks windows in this fashion. You'll discover alternative methods to perform a variety of commands.

Un-Typewriter Class

Even though most computer users haven't touched a typewriter for years, many bad habits from that earlier technology persist. Here are a few of the more egregious examples of typewriter style that are obsolete in the computer age.

- Underlining: Although AppleWorks makes it simple to format text with underlining, don't use this style for emphasis. Use bold or *italics,* which are much more professional looking (and equally easy to apply). (When's the last time you saw something underlined in a magazine article?)

- Spacing with the Space bar: Use the Space bar only for spacing between words. Never use the Space bar for aligning successive lines of text; when printed, those spaces will cause your text to tumble out of alignment. Instead, use the AppleWorks's tab feature, as described in Chapter 3.

- Special characters and accents are easy to produce correctly on a computer. Don't write resume if you mean résumé. Are you making copies or using the Xerox™? Don't put it off until mañana—take that vacation to Curaçao today! (To find out how to produce these special markings, choose menu→Key Caps. You can then press Option—with and without the Shift key—to display these hidden characters.)

- Using two hyphens (--) to represent a dash is passé. What you want is an *em dash*—so called because it's the width of an upper-case M. Create it with the Shift-Option-hyphen key combination.

Paragraph Formatting

After reading about the font, size, color, and other formatting commands AppleWorks can apply on the *character* level, you may wonder what possible variations could remain. But some kinds of formatting make no sense unless applied to an entire *paragraph* at a time: whether your text is single- or double-spaced, for example.

Every paragraph of an AppleWorks word processing document has a set of attributes that determines how the paragraph is laid out on the screen and on the page. Most of the controls for paragraph formatting are available on the ruler (see Figure 2-7) and a few more are in the Paragraph dialog box.

In any case, before you can apply any of the paragraph formatting options described here, you must begin by first *highlighting* the paragraphs you want to affect. (You don't have to highlight a paragraph completely; if any portion of it's included in your selection, your formatting commands will apply to it.)

Tip: To select just *one* paragraph before formatting, just click inside it. You don't actually have to highlight anything.

Alignment

One of the most important decisions to be made about the appearance and readability of your documents is the style of text *alignment*. Two of the four choices look "normal" and are easily read; the other two choices are for special occasions only (see Figure 2-7). Make the choice using the four text-alignment buttons in the ruler; the currently active alignment's button is darkened. (You can also set a paragraph's alignment by choosing Format→Paragraph and using the alignment pop-up-menu in the dialog box.)

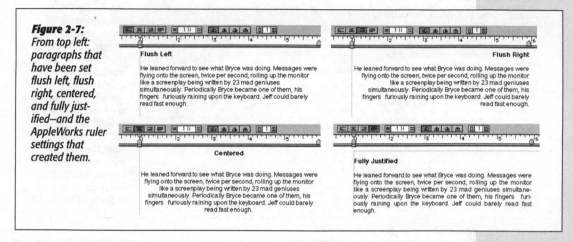

Figure 2-7:
From top left: paragraphs that have been set flush left, flush right, centered, and fully justified—and the AppleWorks ruler settings that created them.

Flush Left

He leaned forward to see what Bryce was doing. Messages were flying onto the screen, twice per second, rolling up the monitor like a screenplay being written by 23 mad geniuses simultaneously. Periodically Bryce became one of them, his fingers furiously raining upon the keyboard. Jeff could barely read fast enough.

Flush Right

He leaned forward to see what Bryce was doing. Messages were flying onto the screen, twice per second, rolling up the monitor like a screenplay being written by 23 mad geniuses simultaneously. Periodically Bryce became one of them, his fingers furiously raining upon the keyboard. Jeff could barely read fast enough.

Centered

He leaned forward to see what Bryce was doing. Messages were flying onto the screen, twice per second, rolling up the monitor like a screenplay being written by 23 mad geniuses simultaneously. Periodically Bryce became one of them, his fingers furiously raining upon the keyboard. Jeff could barely read fast enough.

Fully Justified

He leaned forward to see what Bryce was doing. Messages were flying onto the screen, twice per second, rolling up the monitor like a screenplay being written by 23 mad geniuses simultaneously. Periodically Bryce became one of them, his fingers furiously raining upon the keyboard. Jeff could barely read fast enough.

Flush left

For most text, most people use good old typewriter style: flush left, also called *ragged right* or *left aligned*. Readability experts say this style is most readable because we're used to it, every line starts at the same point, and words are separated with just one space. This is the usual style for letters and manuscripts—in fact, anything that you don't want to proclaim itself as "differently formatted."

Justified

The next on the readability scale—when properly used—is *fully justified*, or *force justified*. This style, in which the beginnings *and* ends of the paragraph lines align neatly at the margins, shows up in many magazines, newspapers, and books (including this one). It gives the columns a clean, block-like appearance—no raggedness here!

AppleWorks creates this look by inserting extra spaces between the words as necessary to fill out every line. If the columns are wide enough and the words are not too long, the system can work well, giving the page an especially orderly appearance. But if the columns are too narrow or the words too long, you can end up with a very uneven look with huge gaps between words. (Using AppleWorks's automatic hyphenation feature can help. Choose Edit→Writing Tools→Auto-Hyphenate to turn this feature on or off.)

Flush right

When you want your document to scream, "Look at me, I'm different!" consider flush-right alignment. Also known as *right aligned, ragged left, right justified,* or *weird,* a paragraph formatted in this way demands attention.

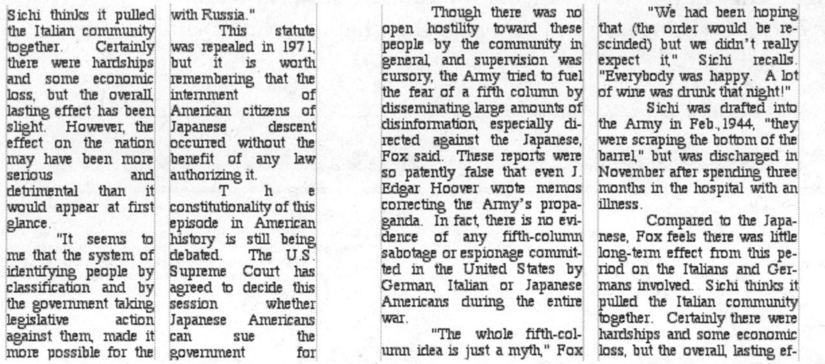

Sichi thinks it pulled the Italian community together. Certainly there were hardships and some economic loss, but the overall, lasting effect has been slight. However, the effect on the nation may have been more serious and detrimental than it would appear at first glance.

"It seems to me that the system of identifying people by classification and by the government taking legislative action against them, made it more possible for the

with Russia."

This statute was repealed in 1971, but it is worth remembering that the internment of American citizens of Japanese descent occurred without the benefit of any law authorizing it.

T h e constitutionality of this episode in American history is still being debated. The U.S. Supreme Court has agreed to decide this session whether Japanese Americans can sue the government for

Though there was no open hostility toward these people by the community in general, and supervision was cursory, the Army tried to fuel the fear of a fifth column by disseminating large amounts of disinformation, especially directed against the Japanese, Fox said. These reports were so patently false that even J. Edgar Hoover wrote memos correcting the Army's propaganda. In fact, there is no evidence of any fifth-column sabotage or espionage committed in the United States by German, Italian or Japanese Americans during the entire war.

"The whole fifth-column idea is just a myth," Fox

"We had been hoping that (the order would be rescinded) but we didn't really expect it," Sichi recalls. "Everybody was happy. A lot of wine was drunk that night!"

Sichi was drafted into the Army in Feb., 1944, "they were scraping the bottom of the barrel," but was discharged in November after spending three months in the hospital with an illness.

Compared to the Japanese, Fox feels there was little long-term effect from this period on the Italians and Germans involved. Sichi thinks it pulled the Italian community together. Certainly there were hardships and some economic loss, but the overall, lasting ef-

Figure 2-8:
Full justification can make your document look especially orderly—but beware gaps of white in narrow columns (left). Typesetters call the effect rivers, *as these gaps above one another create meandering channels of white space flowing through the column of text. The trick is to make the columns wide enough for the font size being used and make careful use of hyphenation (right).*

POWER USERS' CLINIC

Justification Meets Hyphenation

The secret to full justification is to use a long enough line, and to hyphenate long words to make them break at the right margin. A rule of thumb for column width: font size in points, divided by three, equals the minimum line length in inches. So for 12 point type, the narrowest column should be four inches.

You can easily hyphenate an entire AppleWorks document by choosing Edit→Writing Tools→Auto-Hyphenate. This setting is a toggle that is either on or off; it applies to the entire document or section (if you've broken up the document into sections).

AppleWorks divides words at the ends of your lines according to its built-in *Hyphenation Dictionary.* In order for Auto-Hyphenation to work with words *not* in its dictionary, you have to add them. To do so, choose Edit→Writing Tools→Edit Hyphenation Dictionary. The Edit Hyphenation File dialog box appears—empty, for now. Type in a new word,

five letters or longer, complete with hyphen(s)—such as *AppleWorks*—and then click Add. From now on, AppleWorks will include this word in the auto-hyphenation set.

If you don't like the way AppleWorks hyphenates a word, or if you don't want a word hyphenated at all, open the Edit Hyphenation File dialog box again. Add the word with your preferred hyphenation—or none at all. Your entry will take precedence when Auto Hyphenation does its thing.

One final note: Whether auto hyphenation is on or off, you can still manually hyphenate words as you do the final tidying up of your document. The secret: Add a *discretionary hyphen* by clicking inside the word at the appropriate spot and then pressing ⌘-hyphen. This special breed of hyphen appears *only* if the word falls at the end of a line and AppleWorks needs a break. Yet if further editing moves the hyphenated word to the middle of a line, the discretionary hyphen disappears automatically.

Remember, though, that readers have limited tolerance for such eccentricity. Like centered text (described next) and body piercing, the flush-right style can be effective when used selectively, but scary in excess.

Centered

A thousand years of wedding invitations and what seems like a thousand years of poorly-designed posters and flyers proves that people love *centered-text* alignment. Centering can bring an elegant or formal look to small amounts of text.

But use restraint. Like flush-right, this style is at the bottom of the heap for readability—every line begins and ends in a different spot, creating a real tracking problem for the reader's eyeballs. If your document is longer than a wedding invitation, think twice about centering.

Line spacing

Line spacing is the amount of space between each line of text in a paragraph. In the typewriter days, you could single-space or double-space a document; in AppleWorks, you can one-and-a-half space your paper, one-point-six-space it, and so on.

To do so, find the line-spacing control on the ruler, as shown in Figure 2-9. (If you don't see the ruler, choose Format→Rulers→Show Rulers.)

Figure 2-9:
Two line-spacing buttons on the ruler flank a display of the current setting (left). Click the left button for tighter spacing, the right button for wider. You can also double-click the current-spacing indicator ("1.5 li") to open the Paragraph dialog box (right), where you can make finer adjustments.

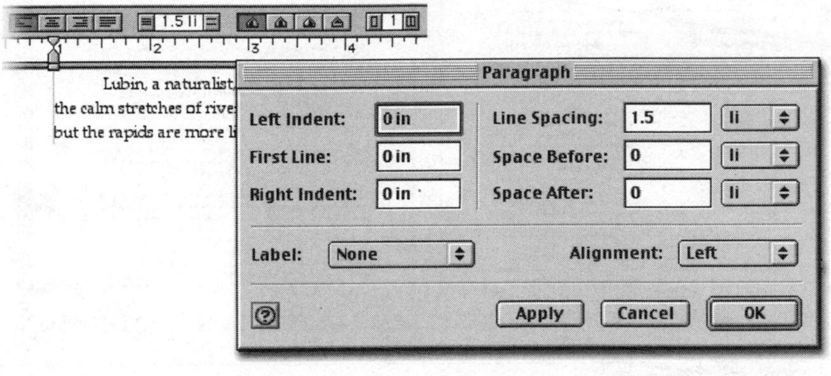

Tip: The ruler control lets you adjust line spacing only in half-line increments. Fortunately, you can adjust line spacing with more precision from within the Paragraph dialog box.

To do so, Choose Format→Paragraph, or choose Paragraph from the contextual menu. Enter a number directly into the Line Spacing box. You can choose a different measurement unit from the pop-up menu next to this box: lines, points, inches, millimeters, centimeters, or picas. The unit you designate here will be displayed next to the line-spacing buttons in the ruler.

To do so, highlight the paragraphs you want to affect—or perform the next step before typing anything. Choose Format→Paragraph to call up the Paragraph dialog box. For a blank line between paragraphs, enter a 1 in the Space After box, and make sure the units pop-up menu is set to "li" for *lines*.

If you prefer instead to indent the first line of each paragraph, read on.

Lead Between the Lines

In typesetters' lingo (and that of many desktop publishers), line spacing is still called *leading* (rhymes with "bedding").

In the days of metal type, publishers inserted thin strips of lead between the lines of type to give wider spacing.

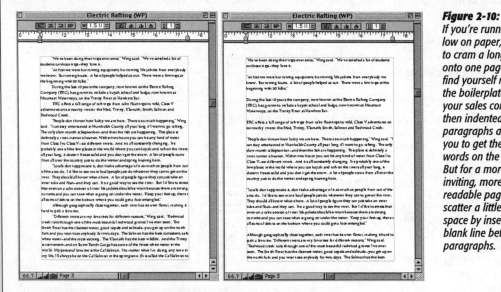

Figure 2-10:
If you're running low on paper, need to cram a long letter onto one page, or find yourself riveting the boilerplate onto your sales contract, then indented paragraphs allow you to get the most words on the page. But for a more inviting, more readable page, scatter a little white space by inserting a blank line between paragraphs.

Line indents

Why not just type five spaces as you begin each paragraph? Not only is that a lot of effort, but it's also much too wide an indent. Don't just press the Tab key, either; you'll jump to the half-inch indent provided by the first tab stop on the ruler. Again, you'll get a gaping, unprofessional first-line indent.

If you care, the correct indent for professionally typeset pages is one *em space*—the width of an upper-case M, which is about .16 inch if you're using 12-point type. To indent your first lines, therefore, choose Format→Paragraph to bring up the Paragraph dialog box. Set the First Line box to about .16 or .2 inch for a professionally typeset look. (You can also adjust the indent using the ruler, as shown in Figure 2-11.)

Tip: You may want to indent a paragraph on *both* sides. This technique, called *blocking text*, is often used to make a long quotation stand out from the body of the text.

To create this effect, drag the tiny square beneath the left indent marker (marked D in Figure 2-11). On the right side, drag the right indent marker (labeled B) the same distance.

Figure 2-11:
Select any existing paragraphs you want to indent—otherwise, the changes you're about to make apply to the next *paragraphs you type. Use the left and right margin markers (A and B) to move the margins. Drag the first-line indent marker (C) to indent the first line of the selected paragraphs. Grab the little block beneath the left indent marker (D) to drag it and the first-line indent marker at the same time.*

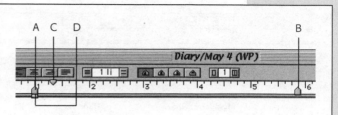

Dear Diary,

Today I learned how to indent properly—not by pressing the Space bar, honoring my grandparents; nor by pressing the Tab key, honoring my parents; but by using the automatic First-Line Indent doohickey on the ruler.

I feel liberated. It's as though the fog has lifted, the light has appeared at the end of the tunnel, and all the world's a stage. As far as I'm concerned, this is just the beginning. Now I can create outdents when necessary, block quotes when appropriate, and smaller first-line indents when space is tight.

Today, I live. Tomorrow, I fly: I'll tackle the spelling checker.

Hanging indents

By creating an "outdent," you can set off paragraphs by hanging a part of a word *into* the left-hand margin. This style is sometimes used for lists—as an alternative to bullets. To create these *hanging indents*, drag the left indent marker inward, leaving the first-line indent marker at the left margin.

Tabs

Besides showing the position of paragraph and first line indents, the ruler also lets you adjust *tabs*, or, as they're often called, *tab stops*. Tabs are invisible notches on the ruler. Each time you press the Tab key, the insertion point jumps to the next tab stop you've set up—until you reach the right margin, whereupon the insertion point jumps down to the next line.

Tabs are great for making simple tables or making sure columns line up on an invoice, résumé, or expense report. You can set as many tabs as you like for each paragraph.

Tabs come in four styles—left, center, right and decimal; each is represented on the ruler by a button bearing a house-shaped icon (see Figure 2-12).

- **Left-aligned:** This is the "normal" type of tab, familiar to former typewriter users worldwide. After you press the Tab key and begin to type, the left end of text lines up with this tab, *à la* flush left.

- **Center-aligned:** After pressing the Tab key so that the insertion point appears beneath the tab stop, your subsequent line of typing remains centered under this tab. For example, you can make sure several lines in a column are centered above one another.

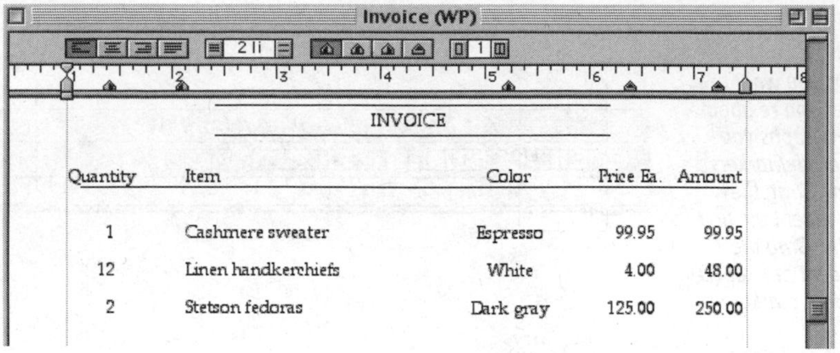

Figure 2-12:
This simple invoice uses the entire battery of tab types: right-aligned for the quantity, left-aligned for the item, center-aligned for the color, and decimal for the price and amount. Drag tabs from the appropriate tab-style button into position on the ruler. Once there, drag it back and forth to adjust its position. Delete a tab by dragging it down off of the ruler.

- **Right-aligned:** After pressing the Tab key so that your insertion point aligns with this kind of tab stop, your subsequent typing flows to the left; the right end of the text remains aligned with the tab stop.

- **Decimal or Align-On:** This tab-stop type is the secret to keeping columns of numbers under control (though you don't *have* to use it for numbers). When you've pressed the Tab key so that the insertion point aligns with this tab stop, it behaves like a *right*-aligned tab stop until you press the decimal point. The period remains directly underneath the tab stop, and now your typing flows to the *right* of the tab stop. In other words, the decimal points of subsequent lines of numbers will neatly align with the tab stop, so that they can be added together.

Tip: The period (.) doesn't have to be the symbol that lines up, line after line, beneath a decimal-point tab. If you double-click the tab stop marker on the ruler, you open the Tab dialog box; in the Align On box, you can type any symbol you like, such as an asterisk, percent sign, or even a letter. The first occurrence of symbol, when typed, will serve as the balancing point between right-and left-justified typing beneath this special kind of tab stop.

For example, if you're aligning a column of version numbers for software programs, AppleWorks will align the version numbers on the first "dot" in "version 5.6.3. "

When you create a new AppleWorks word processing document, the ruler appears devoid of tab stops. In fact, however, there are invisible default tabs every half inch. If you're in a hurry to create a paragraph indent, in other words, and don't care about typographical niceties, you can just press Tab for a quick half-inch indent.

Once you place your own tabs onto the ruler, any of the invisible default tabs to the *left* of the custom tab evaporate; to the right of the custom tab, they remain in effect.

Setting tabs

To set a tab or adjust existing tabs, begin by highlighting the paragraphs that you want to affect. (Alternatively, set or adjust the tabs *before you type* the text you want to affect.) Now, drag one of the four tab buttons down onto the appropriate position on the ruler. As soon as your cursor moves onto the ruler, a vertical, dotted guide line appears to show how the tab will line up with your text. You can also place a tab by simply clicking the lower half of the ruler; a tab stop of whichever style (of the four above the ruler) is currently highlighted appears at that spot. (To adjust a tab stop that's already on the ruler, drag it.)

You can also double-click one of the four tab buttons to open the Tab dialog box. Here you can enter the exact ruler measurement for the new tab. You can also open this dialog box by double-clicking a tab stop on the ruler (in order to specify its position numerically, for example, or change its alignment style).

Figure 2-13:
Change the tab style and position, add leader characters, or change the "align on" character from the Tab dialog box. To call forth this window, double-click a tab or tab button, or choose Format→Tabs.

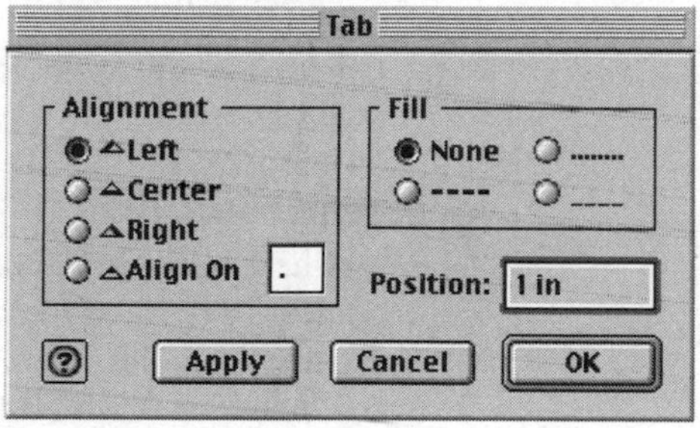

The Fill setting in the Tab dialog box lets you designate a *fill* or *leader*—dots, hyphens, or an underline—that lead the eye from one column to another, as used in menus, tables of contents, or theater programs. These characters fill the void *leading up to* the tab. Figure 2-14 shows the idea.

Figure 2-14:
Never try to create this effect by typing multiple periods. Use tabs instead. Using the Fill choices, specify what symbol you want to fill the gap between the columns. Now, each time you press the Tab key, your dots or dashes extend all the way to the second column.

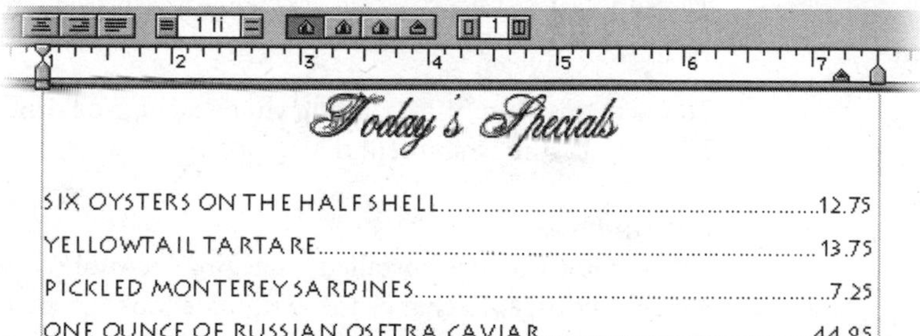

You can apply tabs independently for each paragraph; so, to adjust tab settings for one paragraph, place the insertion point anywhere within the paragraph and then make your changes. To change the tabs for more than one paragraph, first highlight the desired paragraphs.

Copying paragraph formatting

You can copy ruler settings you've created for one paragraph—indents, alignment, line spacing, outline style, and tabs—en masse to other paragraphs.

1. **Place the insertion point within the paragraph whose formatting you want to copy.**

2. **Choose Format→Rulers→Copy Ruler.**

   AppleWorks copies the paragraph formatting to the Clipboard.

3. **Place the insertion point within the target paragraph—or highlight several target paragraphs.**

   These can be in the same document or in another AppleWorks document.

4. **Choose Format→Rulers→Apply Ruler.**

   The Copy and Apply Ruler keyboard shortcuts are the same as the Copy and Paste keystrokes, with the addition of the Shift key.

Section Formatting

Somewhere between document formatting, which controls the look of the whole document (described next), and paragraph formatting, which controls the look of each paragraph, lies *section formatting*. AppleWorks lets you break up a document into sections, each with different kinds of formatting. For example, suppose you're writing a complex report that's broken down into chapters. For convenience, you want to contain it in a single file—and yet some elements, such as the page-numbering style and the headers at the top of each page—will change from chapter to chapter. Using Sections, you can have your all-chapters-in-one-document cake and eat it too. For details on sections, see Chapter 3.

Document Formatting

The layout of the whole page, the "big picture," depends on *document formatting*. This kind of formatting includes page margins, page numbering, footnotes, and endnotes.

To make this kind of formatting change, choose Format→Document. As shown in Figure 2-15, the Document dialog box appears.

Page margins

The default (factory-installed) margins in AppleWorks are one inch all the way around the page. To change the margins, choose Format→Document, and then press the Tab key to highlight the margin number you want to change. The number you type must be in decimal form: .25 = one quarter; the box won't accept fractions. Don't bother entering the "in" for inches—AppleWorks assumes that you're using its current measurement unit.

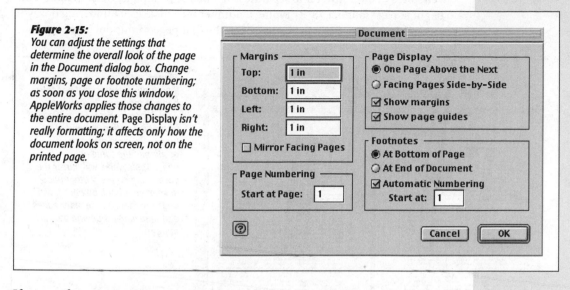

Figure 2-15:
You can adjust the settings that determine the overall look of the page in the Document dialog box. Change margins, page or footnote numbering; as soon as you close this window, AppleWorks applies those changes to the entire document. Page Display *isn't really formatting; it affects only how the document looks on screen, not on the printed page.*

If you prefer your measurements in the metric system—or points or picas—choose Format→Rulers→Ruler Settings to call forth the Rulers dialog box. Here you can not only select your favorite unit, but also how finely divided it is on the ruler scale. Choose the Text Ruler Type setting for a ruler across the top of the window with margin and tab indicators, or Graphics for rulers on the top and left side, for more accurate positioning of objects on the page.

Tip: If you open the Document dialog box to change a margin setting, you don't have to specify your margin in inches, regardless of the current Ruler Settings setting. You can just type the measurement you want *and the unit*—for example, *16 mm* or *24 pc* (for picas).

The next time you open the Document dialog box, AppleWorks shows the measurement you entered as converted back into inches (or whatever unit you've selected in the Ruler Settings dialog box). In other words, this dialog box can double as a unit-conversion calculator, when you really need to know the pica equivalent of 56 mm. (It's 13.25 picas.)

Facing pages

If you're making a document with book-style formatting—that is, printed on both sides of the page and bound—turn on "Mirror Facing Pages." With this box checked, the left and right margin settings now say Inside and Outside. Now you can create an extra-wide margin on the inside for the *gutter*, to allow room for binding.

Page Numbering

Beginning the numbering of your pages with 1 makes sense for most documents, but there are reasons to start at a different number. For example, if you've divided the chapters of your novel into separate documents, you might want Chapter Four to begin at page number 78. By typing a number into the Page Numbering box, you can specify the number that will appear on the first page of this document.

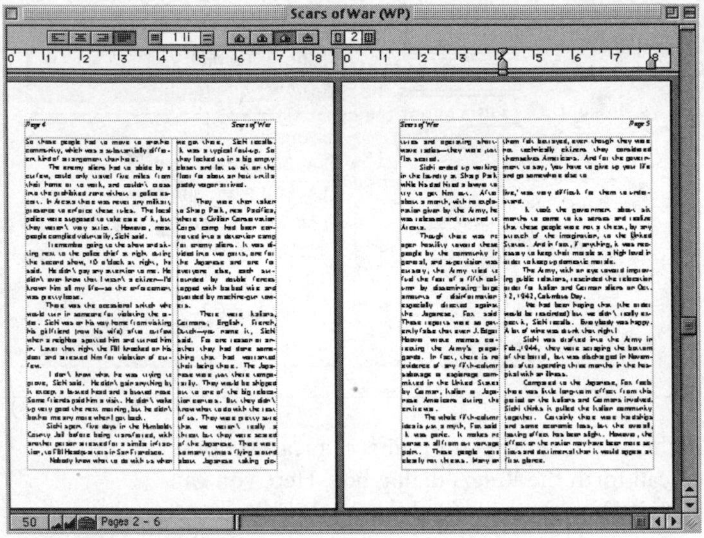

Figure 2-16:
If your document is destined for a book or magazine layout, use AppleWorks's Mirror Facing Pages formatting option. Instead of having the page elements positioned the same on every page, AppleWorks will mirror the positioning on every other page, to keep your book balanced, with page numbers on the outer edges and matching inside and outside margins.

Tip: You can even type a zero into the a "Start at Page" box. That's a useful technique if the first page of your document is a title page that you don't want numbered.

Footnotes

If you're a scholarly type, you can use *footnotes* to cite your sources or attach a note or comment to the body of your text. AppleWorks automatically numbers them; if you add or delete footnotes later, AppleWorks renumbers all the others automatically. AppleWorks also manages to keep footnotes on the same page as the text they refer to.

Note: Footnotes appear at the bottom of the page *above* the *footer*, if one is present. (See page 82 for details on footers.) You can't put footnotes inside the footer.

As with page numbering, you can adjust the number that begins the numbering of your footnotes; to do so, turn on Automatic numbering and type a number into the "Start at" box.

By turning off Automatic numbering, you can request *no* numbers on the footnotes. Thereafter, every time you insert a footnote, AppleWorks will ask you to designate a marker to use in the text—an asterisk, for example.

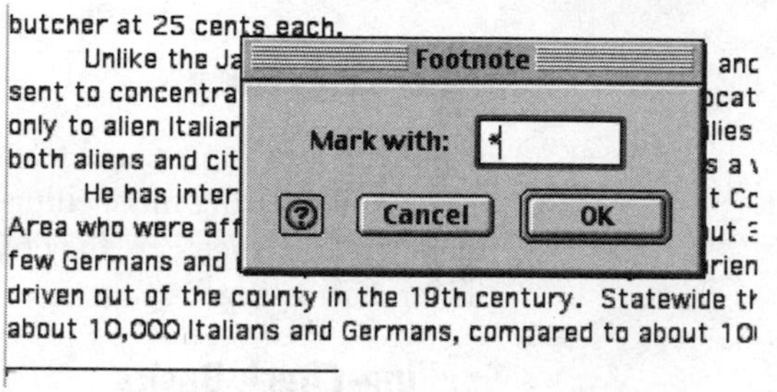

Figure 2-17:
For the occasional footnote, you don't need numbers. Choose Format→Document and turn off Automatic Numbering. AppleWorks then asks you for a footnote marker every time you insert a footnote. Unfortunately, you can't tell AppleWorks to always use an asterisk, for example. You have to specify the marker each time.

butcher at 25 cents each.

Unlike the Ja... ... anc
sent to concentra... ...ocat
only to alien Italian... ...lies
both aliens and cit... ...s v

He has inter... ...t Cc
Area who were aff... ...ut 3
few Germans and... ...rien
driven out of the county in the 19th century. Statewide th
about 10,000 Italians and Germans, compared to about 10(

Footnote

Mark with: *

Cancel   OK

Finally, this dialog box lets you choose whether to display these notes on the bottom the page—as footnotes—or collected at the end of the document, as *endnotes*.

Page Display

This section of the Document dialog box pertains only to how the document is *viewed* on the screen—not how it is formatted for printing. Figure 2-18 has the details.

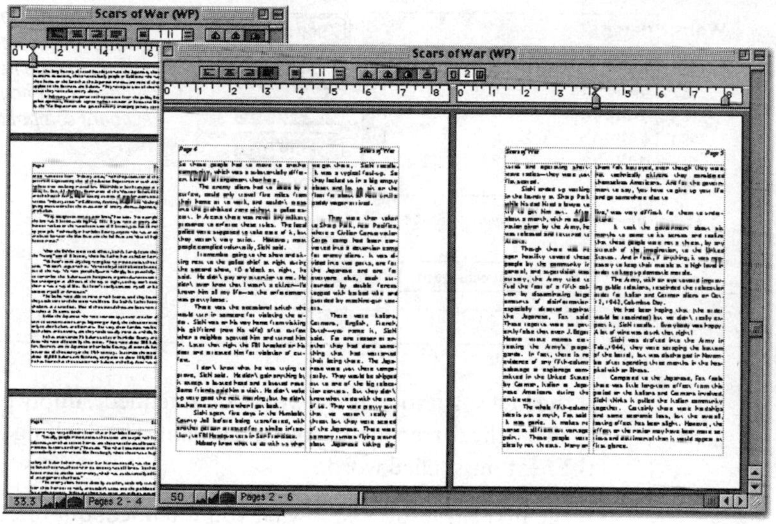

Figure 2-18:
The page display options control how the document looks on the screen while you're working on it. One Page Above the Next displays a multiple-page document like a column of pages (left), as in most word processors. The alternative, Facing Pages Side-By-Side, is appropriate if you're creating a document that will be printed like a book (right). Your monitor may not show two entire pages side-by-side when viewed at full-size, but you can use the zoom buttons to reduce the view as necessary.

The final options, "Show margins" and "Show page guides," further affect how your document looks while you're working on it. When you turn off "Show margins," AppleWorks does away with the white space on each side of your text frame. If you uncheck "Show page guides," AppleWorks removes the light gray rectangle that outlines the usable text area of your page.

Spell Checking

One of the most apreciated features of the modern word processor is its ability to correct embarassing misspellings. AppleWorks can't tell an "its" from an "it's" or a "there" from a "their" or "they're," but it certainly knows how to spell "appreciated" and "embarrassing."

Spelling-Check Basics

A spelling check should be the last stop before you consider any document finished. Even if you're a good speller, typos affect everyone on earth.

To begin, choose Edit→Writing Tools→Check Document Spelling; Control-click and choose Check Document Spelling; or just press ⌘-=, which is far quicker.

Whichever way, the Spelling window now appears (Figure 2-19), showing the first questionable word selected and the suggested replacements listed.

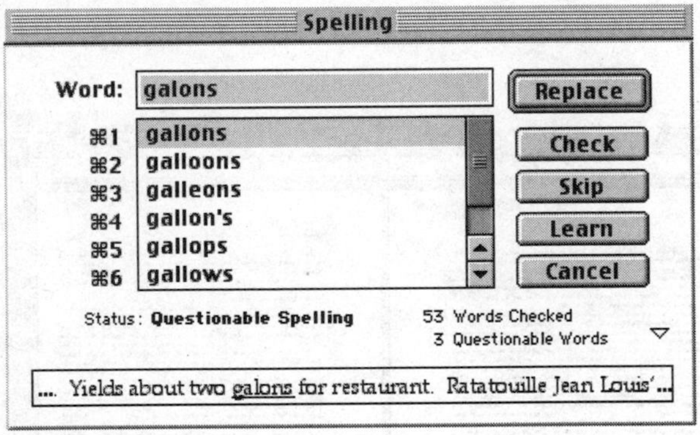

Figure 2-19:
You can view the misspelled word in context (bottom) by clicking the "flippy triangle" (lower right) to reveal the hidden pane. Use the mouse to direct the spell-checking process, or learn the keyboard commands—this window is 100% keyboard compatible.

If the first suggestion is the word you intended, simply press Return or click Replace to make the correction in your document. The Spelling window instantly shows you the next misspelled word.

If the first suggestion isn't what you intended, but one of the other listed words *is*, you can proceed in either of two ways:

- **Using the mouse:** Double-click the word you want (or click it once, and then click Replace). The clicked word replaces the misspelling in your document.

- **From the keyboard:** Press the keyboard combination for the word you want to choose, and then press Return. Alternatively, you can use the up and down arrow keys to select your choice from the list, followed by Return.

In fact, you can use commands for *all* the buttons in the spell-checking window, though you'd never know it by looking at the screen:

⌘-Return	Replace
⌘-K	Check
⌘-S	Skip
⌘-L	Learn
⌘-. (period)	Cancel

Tip: Want to uncover such secret dialog-box keyboard shortcuts yourself? When any AppleWorks dialog box is on the screen, hold down the ⌘ key. AppleWorks temporarily displays labels for all of the dialog box's keyboard shortcuts, such as those identified in the table above.

Many of the words that AppleWorks marks as "questionable" are actually perfectly spelled words and names—they're just not in the spell checker's dictionary. When AppleWorks flags such words, you can click Skip, which leaves the word untouched in your document, or Learn, which adds the word to your dictionary as a correctly spelled term. Words you add to the dictionary in this way will be viewed as correctly spelled from now on—so be sure they *are* correctly spelled before clicking Learn.

Mastering the Dictionary Files

When you check spelling with a freshly installed copy of AppleWorks, the program compares the words in your document against its 100,000-word Main dictionary, which you can't modify. The AppleWorks CD-ROM also includes UK English and Spanish dictionaries. To install them, open the AppleWorks Extras→Spanish or US and UK Dictionaries folders; copy the Spelling, Thesaurus, and Hyphenation files onto your hard drive. Put them with the other dictionary files in AppleWorks 6 folder→AppleWorks Essentials→Dictionaries folder.

If you've installed more than one Main dictionary, you can switch between them (but only one can be active at a time). To do so, choose Edit→Writing Tools→Select Dictionaries, select the Main Dictionary radio button, click Choose, and double-click the desired dictionary in the list.

When you click the Learn button while checking your spelling, you add words to a separate file called the User Dictionary. AppleWorks combines the contents of these two files, the Main Dictionary and the User Dictionary, when it checks your spelling.

AppleWorks can only use one user dictionary and one Main dictionary at any one time, but you can create several *different* user dictionaries for use in different tasks. For example, if you're writing a story that contains some words in phonetic dialect—say, baby talk—and your usual writing doesn't, you might want to create a user dictionary containing *wawa, googoo,* and so on. You wouldn't want these words to be "correct" when you are *not* writing baby talk, so you would only use the Baby Talk User Dictionary when writing in this idiom.

Selecting and Creating User Dictionaries

To create a new User dictionary, choose Edit→Writing Tools→Select Dictionaries. The Select Dictionaries window appears (see Figure 2-22). Select the User Dictionary radio button and click New to create a new User dictionary; you'll be asked to give it a title and save it. This new one becomes the active User dictionary.

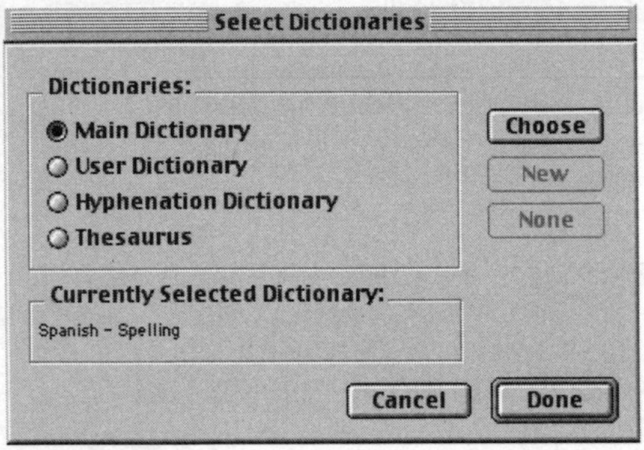

Select Dictionaries

Dictionaries:
- ● **Main Dictionary**
- ○ **User Dictionary**
- ○ **Hyphenation Dictionary**
- ○ **Thesaurus**

Choose
New
None

Currently Selected Dictionary:
Spanish – Spelling

Cancel   Done

Figure 2-20:
Choose the active Main and User dictionaries and create new User dictionaries from the Select Dictionaries window. When you click the radio buttons for the various dictionaries, the currently selected one is named at the bottom.

To switch between user dictionaries, repeat the process—Edit menu→Writing Tools→Select Dictionaries, click the User Dictionary radio button, click Choose— and double-click the desired dictionary from the list.

Editing the User Dictionary

AppleWorks's main spell-checking dictionary contains 100,000 words. That sounds like a lot, and it's certainly enough to handle the needs of the basic speller. But even *Webster's New World Dictionary*—not the most comprehensive dictionary by any standard—contains more than 170,000 words. Furthermore, *no* dictionary contains such *à la mode* expressions as *MP3, iBook, eBay*—or *AppleWorks.*

You can, of course, easily add words to your User Dictionary during everyday spell-checking. But you can also edit the User Dictionary word list more directly, like this:

1. **Choose Edit→Writing Tools→Edit User Dictionary.**

   The User Dictionary dialog box appears with a scrolling window (see Figure 2-21).

2. **To add a word, type it into the Entry field and then click Add (or press Return).**

   The word now appears in the scrolling window; AppleWorks will treat it as correctly spelled in subsequent spell checks.

3. **To delete a word, click it in the scrolling list, then click Remove (or press ⌘-R).**

The word disappears from the list, but remains selected in the Entry field—so if you have second thoughts about removing this word, you can just click Add (or press Return) to restore it to the list.

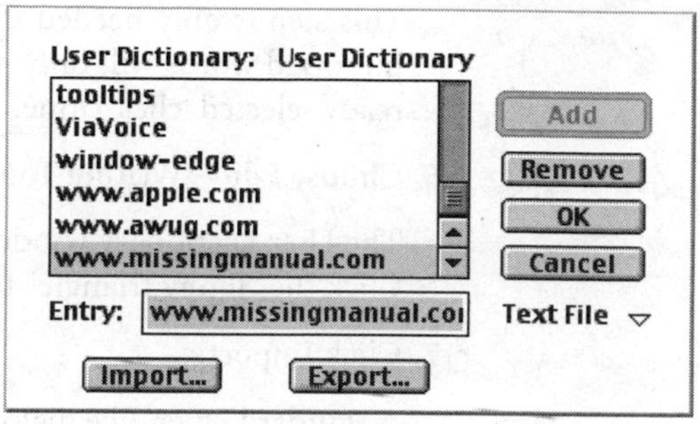

Figure 2-21:
The User Dictionary dialog box provides direct access to your customized word list. All the entries it contains are listed here, in alphabetical order. If you click Learn by accident while spell checking, locate the errant entry in this list and remove it. Click the "flippy triangle" marked text file to reveal the Import/Export buttons, the key to importing your favorite collection of jargon.

User Dictionary: User Dictionary

tooltips
ViaVoice
window-edge
www.apple.com
www.awug.com
www.missingmanual.com

Add
Remove
OK
Cancel

Entry: www.missingmanual.co   Text File

Import...   Export...

Importing and Exporting User Dictionaries

Instead of creating your own custom user dictionary one word at a time, you may want to import a large collection of words into your user dictionary all at once. Or you may want to export your carefully crafted collection for use by a colleague—whether she's using AppleWorks or another word processor.

AppleWorks can import a word list from any plain text document. In fact, it doesn't have to be a *list*; any text document works. During the import process, AppleWorks compares each word you're importing with the entries in the selected main and user dictionaries, and imports only the words that aren't already included. This means you can take an entire document—perhaps your treatise on the cultivation of *Gunnera chilensis* in the Western hemisphere—save it as a text file, import in into your user dictionary, and instantly add all those specialized words that you labored so hard to spell correctly. Or, if you find yourself in a new job with a new set of jargon, find the most jargon-rich document you can and import it into your user dictionary. Instantly you'll be letter-perfect with your buzzwords—to the amazement of your new boss and co-workers.

Here's how the process works:

1. **Open the document that contains your kind of jargon.**

   Use any word processor: AppleWorks itself, Microsoft Word, and so on.

2. **Choose File→Save As. Rename the document, perhaps adding a .txt extension to the name.**

   Specify a hard drive destination for this text file—you might consider clicking the Shortcuts button and selecting Desktop or Documents.

3. **Using the File Format pop-up menu, choose Text, and then click Save.**

4. **Close the document. Switch to AppleWorks, if you're not already there.**

5. **Choose Edit→Writing Tools→Select Dictionaries, click the User Dictionary radio button and click Choose. Select the User Dictionary you want to receive the new words.**

   This step is only needed if you have more than one user dictionary, since the imported words will only go into the active dictionary. If the correct one is already selected, click Done.

6. **Choose Edit→Writing Tools→Edit User Dictionary.**

   The User Dictionary window appears—with its import/export buttons hidden. Click the "flippy triangle" to reveal the buttons.

7. **Click Import.**

   A standard Open File dialog box appears.

8. **Navigate to the text file you saved in Step 1 and open it.**

   The import begins. When it has finished, an alert window informs you that the process is complete.

9. **Click OK.**

   The scrolling list in the User Dictionary window now displays the new and improved word list.

After performing an import—even though you're sure there were no misspellings in your source document—scroll through the user dictionary to make sure you didn't import typos.

To *export* the user dictionary word list, start with Step 4, above, but this time click Export to bring up the Save dialog box. Give the exported file a name, select a destination, and then click Save. The resulting text file can be opened by any word processor or imported into the spell checker for another program. And since it's plain text, it will be readable on either Mac or (if you add *.txt* to the end of its name) Windows.

CHAPTER 3

Advanced Word Processing

A ppearance isn't everything, but looking good has its advantages. It's just as true for term papers, manuscripts, and business letters as it is for cars and actresses. No matter how good your work, if your résumé, report, or press release isn't visually appealing, it may not get that all-important second glance. The more advanced AppleWorks techniques covered in this chapter not only make word processing easier, but help you present your work to best advantage.

Find and Change

Consider these common problems:

- You've turned in the final manuscript of your novel. Your editor loves it—except for one little thing. She thinks that in order to sell in today's competitive market, you need to change the name of your main character. There's only about 752 occurrences of Penelope to change to Casey.

- You're ready to turn in your term paper on the modern novel, but you feel apprehensive. Your English professor has promised to give a failing grade to anyone who uses an apostrophe in the possessive word *its*.

- You're fighting a losing battle with a deep-seated habit: Thanks to a typing teacher two decades ago, you automatically put two spaces after every sentence. You're fully aware that the design of modern computer typefaces eliminates that requirement, but your thumb on the space bar seems to have a mind of its own.

In each of these cases, a powerful AppleWorks automaton is at your editing service: the Find/Change command. Called find/replace in most other word processors, this tireless servant can sift through page after page of your work, searching for each occurrence of some typed term and replacing it, if you like, with a better one. You can use this obedient robot to search for a single character, a word, or an entire sentence.

Tip: In AppleWorks, the Find/Change command can replace words and phrases in every module except Painting. In the Database module, however, it starts out checking only the data you've typed into Browse mode—not the titles and field labels that you can edit only in Layout mode. To edit those elements, choose Layout→Layout before using the Find/Change command. (See Chapter 4 for details on the Database module.)

Find

Find/Change is actually two commands rolled into one: Find, and Find/Change.

Sometimes you just need to find a certain word in your long document. For example, you might want to examine every occurrence of the words "its" and "it's," in order to be sure you've used the apostrophe correctly.

Choose Edit→Find/Change→Find/Change. The Find/Change dialog box appears, as shown in Figure 3-1. Type the word you're searching for—*it's*—into the Find field. In this case, also check the "Whole word" checkbox, so that AppleWorks ignores words that *include* your search term (such as *nitwit's,* in this example). In the Change field, type the word you may want to change it to: *its.*

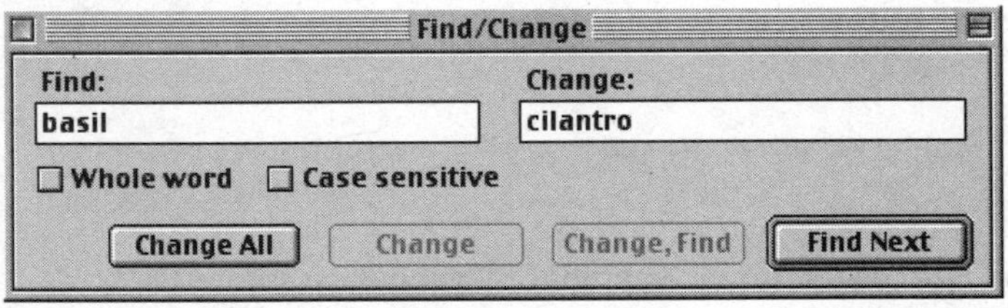

Figure 3-1:
Whether you're "just looking" or you want to change "the world"—perhaps to "the Earth"—the Find/Change dialog box gives you the power you need. The "Whole word" and "Case sensitive" options further refine your abilities. If you check the "Case sensitive" checkbox, AppleWorks finds only words that exactly match the capitalization of the word you entered in the Find field. For example, if you're searching for Fox, it wouldn't match fox or FOX.

Click Find Next, or press Return. The search begins at the insertion point; almost immediately, AppleWorks highlights the next occurrence of *it's* in your document. If this occurrence is OK, click Find Next again. By clicking Find Next again and again, you can work your way through the entire document, evaluating each *it's* for grammatical correctness.

Tip: If you don't see the found word highlighted in your document, it's probably hidden behind the Find/ Change dialog box! To avoid this unfortunate circumstance, arrange the text window and the dialog box so they don't overlap *before* you embark on a Find/Change session.

Find/Change

Instead of just *finding* a certain word or phrase, AppleWorks can also *change* every occurrence in a specific way.

Replacing text

To change a name, for example, choose Edit→Find/Change→Find /Change. In the Find/Change dialog box, type the old name in the Find field. In the Change field, type the replacement name. If you now click Change All, AppleWorks changes every occurrence throughout the entire document.

Caution: After using the Change All button, you can't use AppleWorks's Edit→Undo command to reverse the operation–so proceed with care. It's wise, for example, to turn on the "Whole word" checkbox when doing a Change All. That way, when you change *ring* to *bracelet*, the words *cringe* and *caring* won't turn into *cbracelete* and *cabracelet.*

Of course, searching for *ring* (with the "Whole word" option turned on) won't find the word *rings;* you'll have to perform a separate Find/Change cycle to catch those cases. When you're finished, take one last run through your document, clicking the Find Next button repeatedly, to guarantee that you don't miss, for example, a *ring's.*

Replacing spaces

You can remove double spaces in the same way. In the Find field, type two spaces; in the Change field, enter one space. Click Change All—and then click Change All again. (You need to click it more than once to pick up any clumps of *three or four* spaces: the first time through reduces every three-space to two, and the second time through reduces two spaces to one. Run it even more times if there are clumps of five or six spaces, and so on.)

Replacing invisible characters

AppleWorks can find more than just visible letters on the screen. It can also hunt down *invisible* characters, such as places where you pressed the Tab key or Return key, or places where you inserted a page break. You might want to use this feature when, for example, you paste a lengthy email message into a word processing document and, as often happens, it contains invisible line-feed characters. Or you discover that after adding a few new paragraphs here and there to your screenplay, the page breaks you'd so carefully added are now in the wrong places.

Of course, because these elements are invisible, how are you supposed to type them into the Find blank? Solution: Use special codes to represent them, as shown here.

To find	Enter this code
Space	Space bar
Nonbreaking space	Option-Space bar
Paragraph (Return)	\p or ⌘-Return
Line break	\n
Page break	\b
Column break	\c or ⌘-Enter
Section break	\§ (make that symbol with Option-6)
Discretionary hyphen	\- or ⌘- – (hyphen)
Tab	\t or ⌘-Tab
Automatic date	\d
Automatic time	\h
Automatic page number	\#
Backslash	\\

Making invisible characters appear

Actually, there's another way to search for these invisible characters. You can *copy and paste* them into the Find/Change dialog box. Of course, you may find it challenging to copy something that's invisible; fortunately, AppleWorks can make these secret symbols appear.

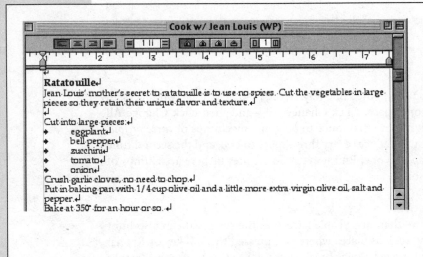

Figure 3-2:
You've got myriad invisible characters hiding in every document. Once you make them visible, you can copy and paste them into the Find/ Change dialog box. These visible invisibles are also helpful for identifying potential formatting problems before printing— for example, the places where someone used spaces instead of tabs to line up words. In fact, some formatting fanatics leave Show Invisibles on all the time.

Choose Edit→Preferences→General. In the Preferences dialog box, turn on the checkbox marked Show Invisibles. Click OK (or press Return). Now your document is festooned with dots and arrows representing spaces, tabs, returns, and so on (see Figure 3-2).

Select the symbol representing the invisible character you want, and then choose Edit→Copy.

Now open the Find/Change dialog box. Click in the Find box and then choose Edit→Paste. Instead of pasting an invisible character in this field, AppleWorks converts it to the appropriate symbol.

The Thesaurus

Before you can find and change words, you've got to come up with the right word in the first place. You might get away with using the word *awesome* once or twice, but there are plenty of other words to effectively express the same idea.

Enter that directory of alternative wording: the Thesaurus. A collection of more than 200,000 synonyms constitutes the AppleWorks thesaurus. Now your writing won't just be awesome; it'll be great, terrific, spectacular, wonderful, delightful, and so on. New to version 6: the Thesaurus provides word definitions along with synonyms.

To look up synonyms for a particular word, proceed as follows:

1. **Highlight the word in your document that you want to look up.**

   Suppose, for example, that you highlight the word *big*.

2. **Choose Edit→Writing Tools→Thesaurus.**

   The Thesaurus dialog box opens. The selected word's definitions appear in the Meaning box. (If you can't see the whole definition, drag the lower-right corner to expand the window.) In the middle of the box is the list of synonyms.

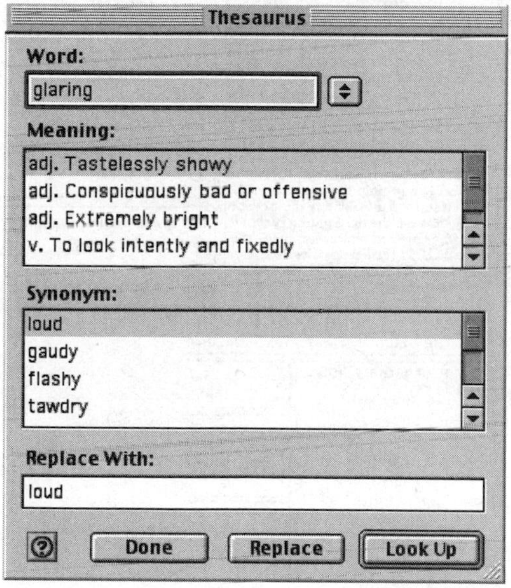

Figure 3-3:
You can consult the Thesaurus to look up mean-alike words for a highlighted term in your document. You can also use the Edit→Writing Tools→Thesaurus command without having highlighted a word first, though; just type any word you'd like to look up. Click Replace to make AppleWorks do just what you'd expect—at the insertion point.

Thesaurus

Word:
glaring

Meaning:
adj. Tastelessly showy
adj. Conspicuously bad or offensive
adj. Extremely bright
v. To look intently and fixedly

Synonym:
loud
gaudy
flashy
tawdry

Replace With:
loud

Done   Replace   Look Up

On the other hand, maybe no synonyms appear—if AppleWorks's thesaurus has no entry for the word you looked up, you're treated to a barren dialog box. In that case, you can type a different word to search for in the Word field; click Look Up (or press Enter) to find its synonyms.

3. **Click the definition in the Meaning list that matches your intended significance.**

   As you click alternate definitions, the list of synonyms changes. Use the scroll bars on both the Meaning and Synonym boxes to see all the possibilities.

   At any time, you can use the Word pop-up menu to look over all the words you've searched for so far. (AppleWorks remembers your search words—until you close the Thesaurus window.)

4. **If you see the ideal word in the list of synonyms, click it once, and then click Replace.**

   If the desired word is already in the Replace With field, click Replace to insert that word into your document, which *replaces* the word you'd highlighted in step 1.

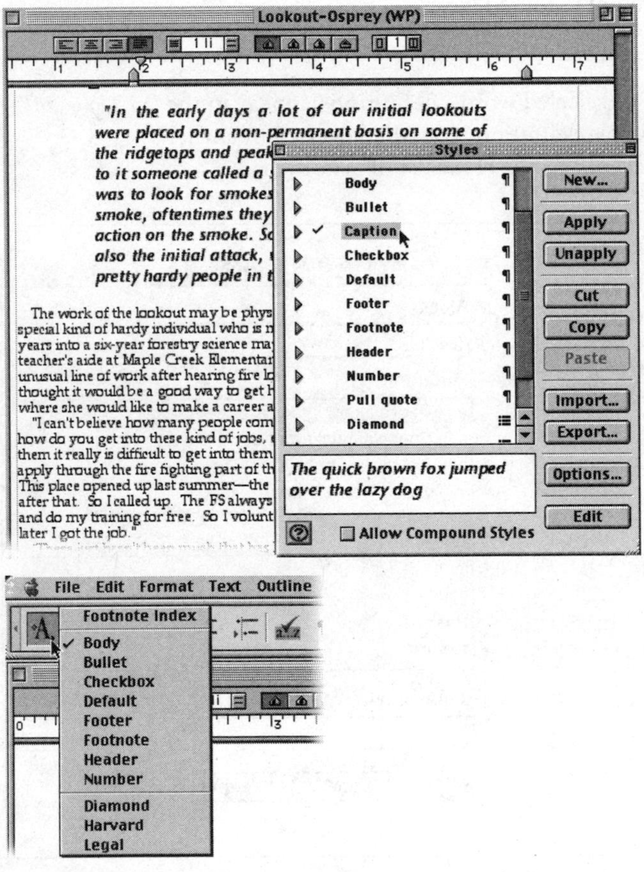

Figure 3-4:
A double-click on a style in the Styles window results in perfect, consistent formatting in your document. As you create your document, you don't have to try to remember how you formatted a picture caption the last time you used one, five pages back. Instead, choose Caption from the Styles window; AppleWorks does the remembering for you. For quicker access—and a way to switch styles without losing so much screen space to the Styles window—add the Text Styles pop-up menu to your Button bar, as shown here at bottom (see Chapter 11 for instructions on modifying the Button bar).

Stylesheets

When you create text documents, you usually use a small assortment of formatting styles, over and over again throughout the document. In a short piece, reformatting your chapter titles (for example) is no big deal; just highlight each and then use the Format menu to make it look the way you like.

But what if you had written a long document? What if your document contained 49 chapter headings, plus 294 sidebar boxes, captions, long quotations, and other heavily formatted elements? In such documents—this book, for example—manually reformatting each heading, subhead, sidebar, and caption would drive you to distraction. Thankfully, *stylesheets* can alleviate the pain.

Stylesheets: An Overview

Here's the idea: you format a chunk of text exactly the way you want it—font, paragraph formatting, margins, and so on—and then tell AppleWorks to memorize that collection of formatting elements as a *style*. A style is a prepackaged collection of formatting attributes that you can re-apply with a click of the mouse. Repeat for other styles you need: chapter headings, sidebar styles, whatever. You end up with a collection of custom-tailored *styles* for each of the repeating elements of your document. Figure 3-4 should make all of this clearer.

Once you've created your stylesheet, as you type along, you can select the styles as you need them—guaranteed that they'll be consistent throughout the document. During the editing process, if you notice you accidentally styled a headline using the subhead style, you can fix the problem by simply re-applying the correct style with a single click on the Styles palette.

Styles aren't just for word processing, either—you can also create styles for drawing objects, spreadsheets, and tables. For example, you can create one style for drawing objects with a thin black outline and a purple fill, and another style for objects with a thick red outline and a blue fill—or table styles with a specific border, cell shading, and font.

But the ease of applying several formatting attributes with one click is only half the joy of stylesheets. You'll appreciate them even more when it comes time to *change* the formatting of a particular style. If you change a style's description, AppleWorks changes *every occurrence* of that style in your document.

For example, suppose that, at 3 a.m. after a couple of espressos, the French script font you used for the section headings in your grant proposal looked stunning. But now, upon re-examination in the cold light of day, you decide to tone them down a bit. Instead of having to scroll through 78 pages, changing each heading manually, you can make one change to the Headline Style description. AppleWorks updates every headline in the document—instantly.

Using Styles

Because styles can be so powerful and flexible, AppleWorks offers correspondingly complex controls to manipulate them. The first glimpse of the Styles window strikes fear in the heart of most beginners. However, if you can steel yourself and decipher the system, your effort pays off quickly.

Choose Format→Show Styles to display the impressively endowed Styles window (Figure 3-5). The scrolling list displays the current collection of available styles and information on the active style or selection.

Much like the AppleWorks Button bars and menus, which change to display only items appropriate to the current module, the Styles window displays only styles that you can apply to the currently selected object.

AppleWorks arrives with a selection of default styles ready to use, though you'll soon want to make your own "style statement."

Applying styles

Here's how you apply a canned style to some text you've already typed.

1. **Highlight the text or paragraph you want to format.**

   For example, drag through some text or quadruple-click a paragraph to highlight it.

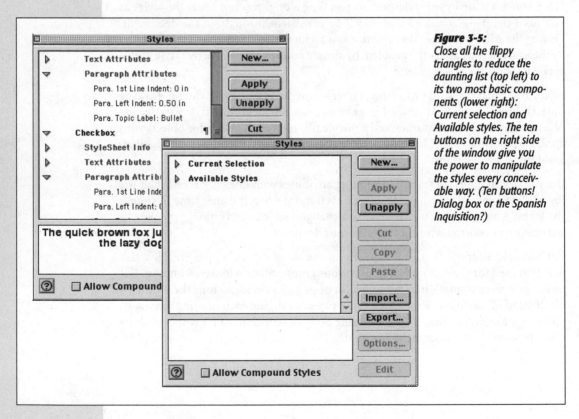

Figure 3-5:
Close all the flippy triangles to reduce the daunting list (top left) to its two most basic components (lower right): Current selection and Available styles. The ten buttons on the right side of the window give you the power to manipulate the styles every conceivable way. (Ten buttons! Dialog box or the Spanish Inquisition?)

2. **Choose Format→Show Styles.**

The Styles palette appears, as shown in Figure 3-5. (If the Format menu says Hide Styles, then the Styles palette is already open.)

3. **Under the Available Styles heading , double-click a style name.**

(Or, if you've got time to kill, click a style name once, and then click Apply.)

AppleWorks applies all of the associated formatting to the selected blob of text, graphics, or cells. (If nothing was highlighted, AppleWorks applies the style to the *next* text you type, or the next object you create.)

Just for fun, take a few minutes to double-click some of the other style names. You'll quickly get the idea: with each double-click, AppleWorks applies a canned format to whatever you've highlighted.

Compound styles

If you apply a style to an item that you've already formatted, AppleWorks replaces the first style with the new one.

Additionally, AppleWorks gives you the ability to apply more than one style at the same time. This isn't a feature that AppleWorks fans have been clamoring for, but Apple's programmers included it at no extra charge. For example, you might want to apply one style (a Basic style) that affects the font, size, and color, and then a second style (a Paragraph style) that affects paragraph indents. Check the Allow Compound Styles checkbox at the bottom of the Style window to permit this kind of layering.

Caution: If the compound styles conflict over the same property, then the *second* style's property prevails. For example, if the first style says Helvetica 18, bold, italic; and the second style says Times, bold, the styles are in conflict only over the font property. Therefore, the outcome of these two styles combined is Times 18, bold, italic.

Removing applied styles

You can remove an applied style, which makes the text or object revert to its default, or "unstyled," appearance.

1. **Select the text, paragraph, or object from which you wish to remove the style.**

If the Styles palette isn't already open, choose Format→Show Styles. A check mark in the Styles palette designates the latest applied style.

2. **Double-click the checked style.**

(For the slow-lane crowd: alternatively, you can click the style name and then click Unapply.)

You've removed the selected style from the document selection. It returns to its original appearance.

If compound styles are in effect, you can remove each individually, leaving the other style or styles in effect.

Tip: Don't waste your time opening the Style window if you just need to remove a text style—bold, italic, outline, and so on—from a selection in your document. Instead choose Text→Style→Plain Text, or press ⌘-T.

Creating styles by example

There are two ways to go about creating your own styles. You can use the Styles window to build one from scratch. Or you can "create by example"—format the text, paragraph, or object in the document the way you want it, and then copy that formatting. The second method is usually easier.

For example, suppose you want to create a style for illustration captions in your term paper. Start by typing out the caption, ending with Return to create a paragraph.

1. **Select a paragraph (by quadruple-clicking, for example).**

   Now use the formatting controls to make it look exactly like you want it:

2. **Using the Format menu and the ruler, choose the Palatino font, at 10-point size, italic, centered, indented on both sides.**

   Leave the paragraph selected. Choose Format→Show Styles to open the Style window, if it isn't already open.

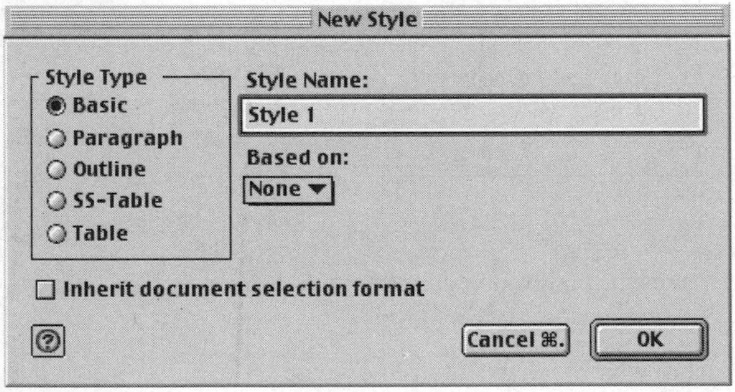

Figure 3-6:
If you're going to be a style setter, you have to start at the New Style dialog box. This is a time to be extra clear with your descriptive naming. Instead of Headline, Subhead, and Detail heading, consider Heading 1, Heading 2, and Heading 3. Choose a Style Type; if you're creating styles by example, turn on the "Inherit document selection format" checkbox.

3. **Click New.**

   The New Style dialog box appears.

4. **Give this style a descriptive name, such as *Captions*.**

   Figure 3-6 shows this step.

5. **Choose one of the style types.**

   AppleWorks gives you the choice of all five types, but for a word processing document, only some are applicable: Basic, Paragraph, Outline, and Table. (See Chapter 12 for details on tables, including table style sheets.)

   Basic style determines *character formatting* for text—font, size, style, and color.

   Paragraph style affects a paragraph at a time: indents, tabs, line spacing, alignment, and the gap above and below each paragraph—all the settings you can adjust by choosing Format→Paragraph. (Paragraph style can optionally *incorporate* the Basic-style character formatting.)

   Outline style is a variation on Paragraph style; it formats paragraphs especially for outlines, as described later in this chapter.

   In this example, you're formatting a paragraph, so click the Paragraph button.

6. **Select a "Based on" style, if desired.**

   In order to tie styles together to provide consistency throughout your document while providing for future modifications, you can base one style on another. For example, if your report uses four levels of headlines and subheads—using the same font at different sizes—you can set up the first headline style and then create subhead styles based on the headline style. Then, if you decide to change to a different font for your headline and subheads, just make that change once to the headline style; all the subhead styles you've based on it inherit the change, too.

Tip: If you base a style on an existing one, you may save time in creating the new style. But when you change the underlying style in some way, the new style reflects the change. Sometimes this can cause big problems as a change cascades from one style to another.

To prevent this auto-rippling effect, leave the "Based on" pop-up menu set to None.

---

7. **Check "Inherit document selection format."**

   AppleWorks memorizes the formatting of the selected paragraph.

8. **Click OK.**

   You return to the Styles window, which is now titled Edit Styles, reminding you that you're still in the style-editing mode. The newly-minted style is listed in the Available styles list; a sample appears in the preview at the bottom of the window. (At this point, you can further modify the style, if necessary—you're still in the editing mode. See "Editing styles," below.)

9. **Click Done.**

   The new style's definition exactly matches the selection you started with. If you now click inside some *other* paragraph, and then click the name of your new style (such as Caption), AppleWorks instantly applies the formatting to the second paragraph.

Creating styles using menus

You can also create a new style by building its attributes from AppleWorks menus—in other words, without having to start by formatting a selected text, graphics, or spreadsheet area. To do so, follow steps 2 through 5, above; click OK, and then begin editing your new style as described in Step 2, below.

Editing styles

If you ever need to make wholesale formatting changes to a long document, the time you spend learning about styles pays off handsomely.

You edit a style by modifying its properties. Instantly, those changes are updated all the way through your document, everywhere you had applied the style. (If any other styles are *based on* the style you edit, they too inherit the change.)

Start by choosing Format→Show Styles to open the Styles window, if it wasn't already open.

1. **From the list of styles, click the one you wish to edit, and then click Edit.**

   Three things change appearance to remind you you're in style-editing mode: The arrow pointer takes on an S shape, the Edit button changes to say Done, and the title of the Styles window changes to Edit Styles.

2. **Choose commands from the AppleWorks rulers, menus, and the Accents window to modify the formatting for this style.**

   For example, use the Text menu to choose a font, size and style. Click the center alignment button, increase the line spacing, and set a tab using the ruler.

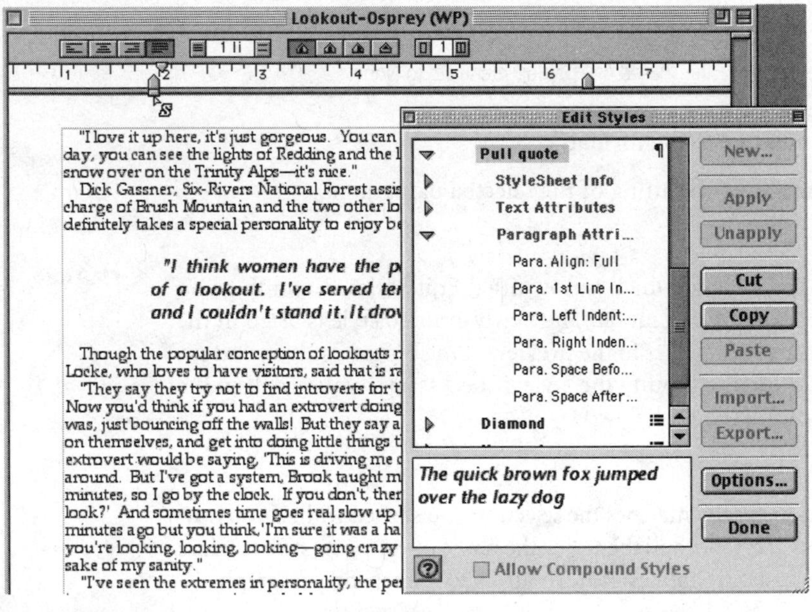

Figure 3-7:
When you build a style from scratch, each selection you make (with the "S" cursor) from the menus or the ruler is recorded as a property in the Edit Styles window. Just as with editing text, you can experiment with different fonts, sizes, alignments, and so on, until your style is just right. Then click Done to exit the style-editing mode.

As you make each selection, the Style window reflects the addition of that property to the style. If you make a mistake, choose again from the menu or ruler to override it. (You can also delete a property from the current style by clicking once to select it and clicking Cut or pressing your Delete or Backspace key.)

While in the style-editing mode, you can also copy and paste properties from one style to another. For example, if an existing style has text properties—font, size, style, color—you'd like to duplicate in your new style, select those properties and click Copy. (Don't use the keyboard shortcuts for copy and paste; they apply to the document, not the Style window.) Click the name of the style you want to inherit those properties, and click Paste.

Note: If, while editing a style, you see your S cursor revert to the regular arrow pointer when it's in the document window, then you've dropped out of the editing mode. Either you clicked in the document, or you performed another action that's not part of style formatting. Click Edit to return to the style-editing mode.

3. When you're finished editing this style, click Done.

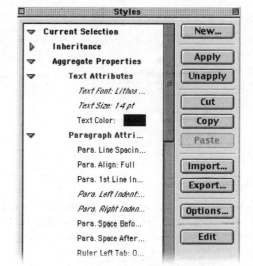

Figure 3-8:
Navigate through the flippy-triangle maze to uncover the Aggregate Properties, the sum total of all formatting properties applied to the selection. If you're troubleshooting a style, this lists everything that influences the display of a character or paragraph.

Deleting styles

You can delete a style from the stylesheet only if you haven't actually applied it to anything in your document. Just select a style in the Styles window and then click Cut. If this style *is* applied anywhere in your document—even on a non-printing line or space—an alert box warns you that it is still in use.

If you cut a style by mistake, on the other hand, choose Edit→Undo.

Columns

Columns, like paragraphs, break up a page full of text into less intimidating, more readable chunks. Designers frequently divide a page into columns so that the width of the text isn't too tiring for readers' eyes. If lines of type are too long, your eyes lose their way as they try to track from the end of one line to the beginning of the next. In other words, the wider the page, and the smaller the type, the more you need columns to reduce line length.

Creating columns in AppleWorks couldn't be much easier; see Figure 3-9.

Tip: Working with columns is much easier if you can see the margin *guidelines* , the light gray lines that show you the outline of the column on the screen. If you can't, choose Format→Document, turn on the "Show page guides" checkbox, and click OK.

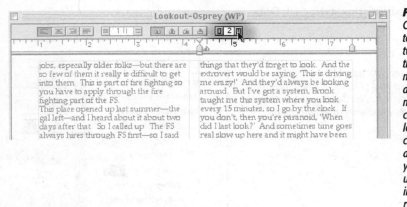

Figure 3-9:
Click the Add Column button in the ruler to produce two columns. Keep clicking that button to create as many additional columns as you need—up to the maximum of nine. The companion button, on the left side of the number-of-columns indicator, removes a column with each click. If you've created columns of unequal widths, then clicking the column buttons restores equality.

Adjusting column widths with the mouse

The Add Column button creates columns of equal width. If having equal width columns offends your sense of design, adjust their width with the mouse, as shown in Figure 3-10.

Adjusting the number of columns

You can vary the number of columns from place to place in your document, but only if you divide your document into different *sections,* as described in the following discussion. (Each section can have a different number of columns.) Therefore, if you want to change from two columns to three columns part way through your document, insert a section break (by choosing Format→Insert Section Break).

Adjusting column number and widths numerically

If precise measurements are important to your column setup—if you have to match the width of some existing artwork, for example—click in the section whose columns you want to adjust (if you have more than one section, of course). Now choose Format→Section to open the Section dialog box (see Figure 3-11). Using the Number of Columns box, specify how many columns you want in this section.

If you want the freedom to specify a different width for each column, turn on the on Variable Width Columns checkbox. Now use the Settings for Column pop-up menu to select a column; then specify the amount of Space Before, Column Width, and Space After. Use the Settings for Column pop-up menu to choose the next column number and repeat the process. (If Variable Width Columns is not selected, then you have just two measurements to deal with: Column Width and Space Between Columns.)

If you're going to print the document on both sides of the page, to be bound like a book, turn on the Mirror on Facing Pages checkbox, too. AppleWorks will automatically create "left" and "right" pages that mirror each other's layout. This option lets you create, for example, a narrow column on the insides of each two-page spread and a wide one on the outside.

Tip: You're not stuck with calculating the size of your columns and column gaps in *inches,* as AppleWorks initially suggests. You can also do your computations in picas, points, centimeters, or millimeters; just type the appropriate abbreviation into the Section dialog box (use *in, cm, mm, pc,* or *pt* for inches, centimeters, millimeters, picas, or points, respectively).

On the other hand, if you do *all* of your measuring in one of those other units, you may as well change AppleWorks's master measurement unit. To do so, close the Section dialog box (if it's open). Then choose Format→Rulers→Ruler settings to change this preference.

Figure 3-10:
To change the width of a column: While pressing the Option key, move your cursor over the column margins. The arrow cursor becomes a double-headed arrow flanking two vertical lines (top). Drag the margin to reposition it. You can move every column margin independently this way. To adjust both columns simultaneously, press the same key while dragging the space between them (bottom).

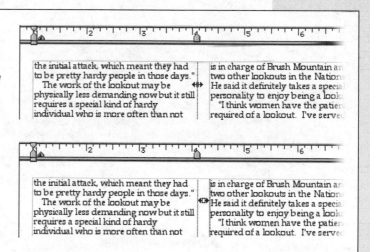

Sections

When you create lengthy, complex word processing documents—books, reports, dissertations—you may find it handy to break them up into chapters, one per file. Once that's done, you can format each file in different ways to reflect the different kinds of information they contain. Furthermore, you don't put all your eggs in one basket this way—if one of your chapter files should become corrupted, God forbid, you won't lose your entire manuscript.

There are some equally good arguments, however, for keeping your entire manuscript in *one* file. For example, you can use the Find or Find/Change commands to search your entire manuscript at once. Using the AppleWorks *sections* feature, you can break up your single document into individual chapters. AppleWorks can divide a document into as many sections as you like, each with distinct formatting.

POWER USERS' CLINIC

Stylesheet cheat sheet

Styles come with a lingo all their own. Here's a glossary of terms. You can create and use styles without ever looking at this stuff—but it does come in handy when you edit styles. You'll see these items listed in the Edit Styles dialog box, as shown in Figure 3-8.

Style: A collection of formatting attributes that you can apply to an element of a document. You might create one called, for example, Bullet List Style that indents the paragraph on both sides and adds a bullet paragraph label.

Stylesheet: A document's *collection* of styles is called a stylesheet. (Each document has its own private stylesheet.)

Basic Style: A style that determines *character formatting* for text—font, size, style, and color—or *object formatting* for graphics: line, fill, and color.

Paragraph Style: This kind of formatting affects a paragraph at a time: Indents, tabs, line spacing, alignment, and the gap above and below each paragraph. (Paragraph style can include Basic-Style character formatting elements.)

Outline Style: This kind of paragraph formatting affects outlines, as described later in this chapter.

Spreadsheet Style: You can use stylesheets in spreadsheets, too. With one click, you can affect the cell color and shading, thickness and colors of cell borders, fonts, and other attributes of a selection of cells, a spreadsheet frame, or an entire spreadsheet.

Table Style: A style can affect a selection of cells in a table, or an entire table frame.

Properties: These are the individual formatting components that make up a style. The font is one property, font size is another.

Attributes: AppleWorks groups the collection of properties of each type together as *attributes:* text attributes, paragraph attributes, drawing attributes, table attributes, and spreadsheet attributes. A paragraph style contains both text attributes and paragraph attributes, while a text style contains only text attributes.

Aggregate properties: The complete list of properties that define a style. For example, the aggregate properties for a paragraph include the font, size, and style, as well as the paragraph line spacing, alignment, indents, and so on. Styles—including the default styles—can assign some of these properties, and you might manually apply others.

Inheritance: A style can *inherit* properties copied from another style or from a document selection.

Based on: A style linked to, or based on, another style; if the base style is modified, the style linked to it changes, too.

For example, you may write a business report that contains an introductory narrative; a section with lots of facts and figures, tables and footnotes, set in two columns; another section featuring customer endorsements with photographs set in three columns; and a concluding narrative. For this type of job, divide (into sections) and conquer!

To create a new section, place the insertion point where you want the first section to end. Choose Format→Insert Section Break. (Keyboard shortcut: Option-Enter.) AppleWorks responds by displaying a thin gray line to show the section break. (If you don't see the gray line, choose Format→Document and turn on the "Show page guides" checkbox.)

Figure 3-11:
The Section dialog box controls how a section will differ from the one that precedes it. The Start Section and Page Numbers portions pertain only to a new section, but the Headers and Footers and Columns parts apply either to a new section or to a document that contains only one big section.

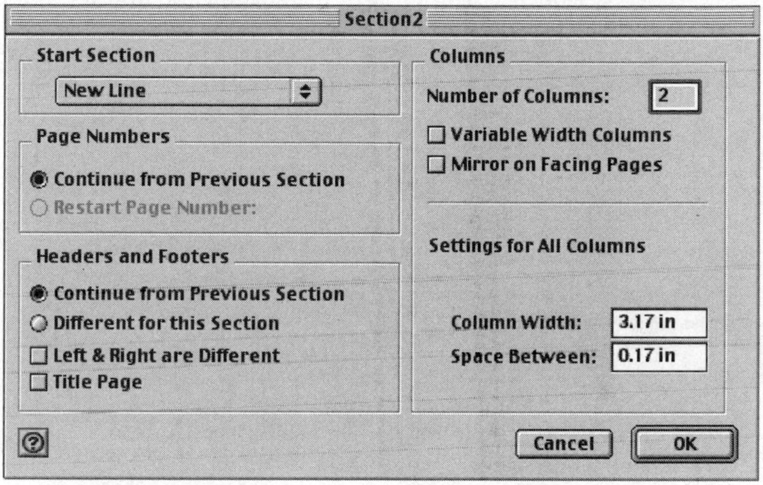

Section2

Start Section
New Line

Page Numbers
◉ Continue from Previous Section
○ Restart Page Number:

Headers and Footers
◉ Continue from Previous Section
○ Different for this Section
☐ Left & Right are Different
☐ Title Page

Columns
Number of Columns: 2
☐ Variable Width Columns
☐ Mirror on Facing Pages

Settings for All Columns

Column Width: 3.17 in
Space Between: 0.17 in

Cancel   OK

The first time you create a section break, AppleWorks starts the new section on the next line of your document; by looking, you can't even tell that you've inserted a section break. That's a neat system: it lets you change major formatting (such as the number of columns) right smack in the middle of the page.

Often, however, you may find it more useful to begin the new section on a new page, such as when you're beginning a new chapter. In that case, choose Format→Section to open the Section dialog box (Figure 3-11). Here, the Start Section pop-up menu determines where the section begins. Your choices are:

• **New Page.** The new section will begin on the next page. Use this option if you're using the Sections feature to divide your document into chapters.

• **New line.** The new section will start on the next line of the same page. Use this to switch from two columns to three columns (for example) part way down the page.

• **New Left Page** or **New Right Page**. In most published books, including this one, every chapter always begins on the *right-side* page, even if that means that the left-side page is blank. Use this choice to create that same effect.

Tip: If you're working in a section that you've designated as beginning on a new page, any subsequent section breaks you insert will *also* begin on new pages. (Furthermore, you don't see the light gray line that appears when you *first* make a section break—the gray line designates only "new line"-type section breaks.)

Page Numbers

How much of an individual identity do you want for your new section? AppleWorks can continue page numbering from the previous section, carrying the numbering sequence right through the document. However, you may sometimes want the sequence to start over, as shown in Figure 3-12.

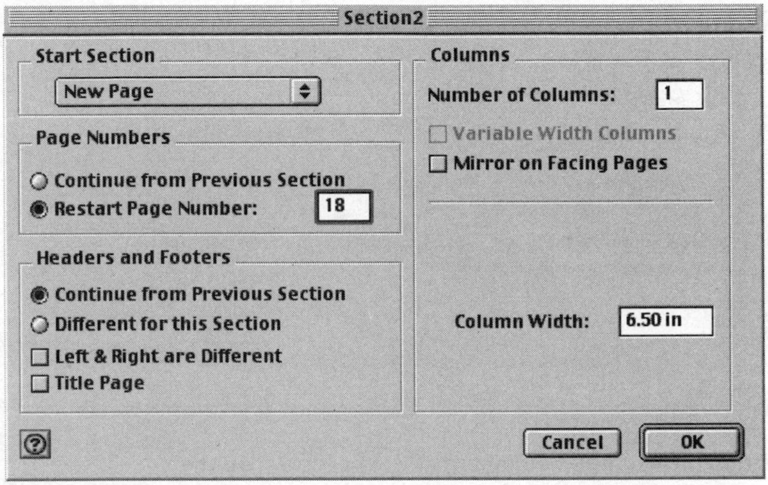

Figure 3-12:
By starting a new section on a new page, you can initiate a new page numbering sequence. You'd use this ability if, for example, your new section marks the beginning of a chapter and you want chapter-relative page numbering—for example, 3-1. This dialog box is where you'd restart the numbering sequence at 1 for the new chapter.

To begin a new numbering sequence, choose one of the New Page options from the Start Section pop-up menu, turn on the Restart Page Number button, and, if necessary, enter a restarting page number other than 1. See "Page-Number Placeholders," page 84, for the rest of the page-numbering story.

Tip: You can't choose the Restart Page Number option if you've used the Start Section pop-up menu to choose New Line. AppleWorks can't very well apply a new page number to a section that begins on the *same page!*

Headers and Footers

You can change your headers and footers when you change sections, too. That's fortunate if your aim is to simulate a book like this one, where the footer changes in every chapter. For a complete discussion, see "Headers and Footers" on page 82.

Section and Page Breaks

By inserting a *section break,* as described in the preceding discussion, you can vary the page number styles, header and footer layout, or number of columns within a document. But AppleWorks provides two other important kinds of breaks to further control the layout of your document.

Page breaks appear automatically in your document every time your typing reaches the bottom margin of the page. Occasionally, however, you may want to begin a new section or chapter at the top of a fresh page—without completely filling the page you're on. Resist the temptation to press Return enough times to push your insertion point to the next page. (Doing so almost certainly guarantees formatting chaos later, when you add or remove material during editing.)

Instead, insert a page break manually. Choose Format→Insert Page Break, or press Shift-Enter. The insertion point jumps to the top of the next page, ready to begin the next chapter. No matter how much text you add or delete later on, your new chapter will always start on a new page.

If you've formatted your document with columns, AppleWorks provides yet another kind of break: the *column break.* Column breaks behave just the same as page breaks, except they begin a new column instead of a new page. You might want to introduce a column break when, for example, you come to the end of a topic and you want to start the next topic at the top of the next column.

Choose Format→Insert Column Break, or press Enter, to create a column break.

Tip: If you haven't created multiple columns in your document, you still have one column. In other words, in a one-column document, the Insert Column Break and Insert Page Break commands have exactly the same effect.

FREQUENTLY ASKED QUESTION

The Laptop Lovers' Lament

Hey, what's the story? I'm typing along on my laptop, and I wind up with column breaks everywhere!

Laptop users beware—the keyboard command for Insert Column Break is the Enter key. Due to the Enter key's unfortunate position next to the space bar on some laptop models, it's easy to inadvertently hit the Enter key in the heat of typing, resulting in a surprise column break.

Worse, if you're typing up a document that *doesn't have* multiple columns (only one column, that is), then each accidental press of the Enter key generates a *page* break, which is certain to alarm the unaware. There's no solution, really, except to press Delete or Backspace to eliminate the accidental break.

Outlining

You may not have made an outline since high school, but give it a try. The benefit to your writing can be profound.

Outlining imposes order on your thoughts. Once you get your framework of ideas on the screen, AppleWorks makes it easy for you to reorganize and reprioritize them. You can collapse an outline to hide subtopics when you just want to see the "big picture," and expand it to show more detail. (Figure 3-13 illustrates the point.) Then, when your outline is finished, you're all set to begin writing, fleshing out the outline topics as you go. When you're done, your document should be well organized— whether it's a progress report, short story, or Dear John letter.

Lists, a related AppleWorks feature, are in the same formatting category as outlines. They aren't as precisely organized as outlines, but they share the basic feature: a hierarchy of topics and subtopics with some kind of a paragraph label.

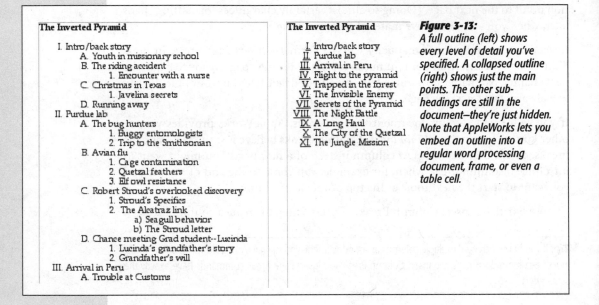

The Inverted Pyramid

I. Intro/back story
    A. Youth in missionary school
    B. The riding accident
        1. Encounter with a nurse
    C. Christmas in Texas
        1. Javelina secrets
    D. Running away
II. Purdue lab
    A. The bug hunters
        1. Buggy entomologists
        2. Trip to the Smithsonian
    B. Avian flu
        1. Cage contamination
        2. Quetzal feathers
        3. Elf owl resistance
    C. Robert Stroud's overlooked discovery
        1. Stroud's Specifics
        2. The Alcatraz link
            a) Seagull behavior
            b) The Stroud letter
    D. Chance meeting Grad student--Lucinda
        1. Lucinda's grandfather's story
        2. Grandfather's will
III. Arrival in Peru
    A. Trouble at Customs

The Inverted Pyramid

I. Intro/back story
II. Purdue lab
III. Arrival in Peru
IV. Flight to the pyramid
V. Trapped in the forest
VI. The Invisible Enemy
VII. Secrets of the Pyramid
VIII. The Night Battle
IX. A Long Haul
X. The City of the Quetzal
XI. The Jungle Mission

Figure 3-13:
A full outline (left) shows every level of detail you've specified. A collapsed outline (right) shows just the main points. The other sub-headings are still in the document—they're just hidden. Note that AppleWorks lets you embed an outline into a regular word processing document, frame, or even a table cell.

Creating an Outline

Outlines are most commonly used as the blueprint guiding you from *tabula rasa* to *magnum opus*, but you can also insert an outline anywhere within a word processing document or frame. (In "real" word processors like Microsoft Word, by contrast, a document must be either *all* outline or *all* prose.) AppleWorks can do this because outlines are actually just carefully formatted *paragraph styles,* as described in the previous section.

All outlines are variations on a common hierarchical layout (see Figure 3-14).

Select the outline style

Begin an outline in a word processing document (or frame, as described in Chapter 12). Click to place the blinking insertion point where you want the outline to begin.

Choose Outline→Label Style; select an outlining *style* from the submenu. (Some of the available styles are shown in Figure 3-14.) Here's what you can choose:

- **Harvard.** This style (and Legal, described next) produce clearly numbered outlines, making it easy to understand the hierarchy of topics and subtopics. Harvard-style outlining is what you learned in high school, where you see Roman numerals for each main heading. Use it for any outlines you have to turn in to an English professor. This style makes it very easy to follow the hierarchy—at least until you get five or six levels deep, at which point you might prefer Legal style.

- **Legal style** uses only numerals for labels, with each subtopic level adding a decimal point and another number to the label (2.2, 2.2.1, and so on). This method of labeling is easier to keep straight when your outlines become complex and detailed. This form is favored by lawyers, scientists, and government bureaucrats.

Figure 3-14:
*All outline label styles create outlines in the indented format to show hierarchy, but only Harvard and Legal provide a numbering system to tell you what's going on. The main styles are **Harvard** (top left), which uses the traditional combination of numbers and letters for the different levels; **Legal** (top right), which uses a multiple-decimal approach to defining the levels; and **Diamond** (middle left), which puts a diamond-shaped bullet in front of each item. Use list styles for simpler outlines, checklists, or numbered paragraphs. For example, **Numeric** (middle right) uses the same number series for topics and subtopics, **Bullet** (lower left) uses the same marker for everything, and **Checkbox** (lower right) creates a list with checkable boxes, which is ideal for to-do lists and progress reports.*

The Inverted Pyramid

    I. Intro/back story
        A. Youth in missionary school
        B. The riding accident
            1. Encounter with a nurse
        C. Christmas in Texas
            1. Javelina secrets
        D. Running away
    II. Purdue lab
        A. The bug hunters
            1. Buggy entomologists
            2. Trip to the Smithsonian
                a) Birds in the basement
                b) Professor Fix

The Inverted Pyramid

    1. Intro/back story
        1.1. Youth in missionary school
        1.2. The riding accident
            1.2.1. Encounter with a nurse
        1.3. Christmas in Texas
            1.3.1. Javelina secrets
        1.4. Running away
    2. Purdue lab
        2.1. The bug hunters
            2.1.1. Buggy entomologists
            2.1.2. Trip to the Smithsonian
                2.1.2.1. Birds in the basement
                2.1.2.2. Professor Fix

The Inverted Pyramid

    ◆ Intro/back story
        ◇ Youth in missionary school
        ◆ The riding accident
            ◇ Encounter with a nurse
        ◆ Christmas in Texas
            ◇ Javelina secrets
        ◆ Running away
    ◆ Purdue lab
        ◆ The bug hunters
            ◇ Buggy entomologists
        ◆ Trip to the Smithsonian
            ◇ Birds in the basement
            ◇ Professor Fix

The Inverted Pyramid

    1. Intro/back story
        1. Youth in missionary school
        2. The riding accident
            1. Encounter with a nurse
        3. Christmas in Texas
            1. Javelina secrets
        4. Running away
    2. Purdue lab
        1. The bug hunters
            1. Buggy entomologists
            2. Trip to the Smithsonian
                1. Birds in the basement
                2. Professor Fix

The Inverted Pyramid

    • Intro/back story
        • Youth in missionary school
        • The riding accident
            • Encounter with a nurse
        • Christmas in Texas
            • Javelina secrets
        • Running away
    • Purdue lab
        • The bug hunters
            • Buggy entomologists
        • Trip to the Smithsonian
            • Birds in the basement
            • Professor Fix

The Inverted Pyramid

    □ Intro/back story
        □ Youth in missionary school
        □ The riding accident
            □ Encounter with a nurse
        □ Christmas in Texas
            □ Javelina secrets
        □ Running away
    □ Purdue lab
        □ The bug hunters
            □ Buggy entomologists
        □ Trip to the Smithsonian
            □ Birds in the basement
            □ Professor Fix

- **Diamond and leader style.** These outline styles don't have detailed labeling. If a topic has subtopics, its diamond-shaped bullet is solid black; if not, the diamond is empty. Leader style uses a "+" if an item has subtopics, and a "−" if not.

These styles are useful for making simple outlines that don't need to be very precise. They also show whether a topic contains any subtopics, even when compressed. These styles are also wildly popular in *presentations*—the slide shows described in Chapter 8.

The diamonds alternate, solid black and hollow, in each successive level of the outline. (When you collapse a topic, as described later, the diamond turns gray.)

- **Numbered lists: Letter Caps, Letter, Numeric, Roman Caps, and Roman.** These are *list* styles. They feature the same letter or number series for topics *and* subtopics. You'd use this style for simple outlines or for numbered lists where all topics are at the same level.

- **Bullets and checkbox lists.** In this kind of list, you don't get any hierarchy other than the indenting—just a bullet or checkbox before each item. Use this style when creating to-do lists or presentations. These checkboxes are more than just fancy bullets—you can actually click them to place or remove a checkmark.

Tip: You can also apply Outline styles via the Styles window, described in the previous section. Choose Format→Show Styles, and then choose from the list of Available Styles.

Entering your headings

After specifying what outline style you want, type the first major heading. AppleWorks creates a main topic—or Level 1—label in the outline style you selected.

To enter another topic at this same level, just press Return. But to enter an indented subheading, *don't* press Return. Instead, choose Outline→New Topic Right, or press ⌘-R. Figure 3-15 makes this process clearer.

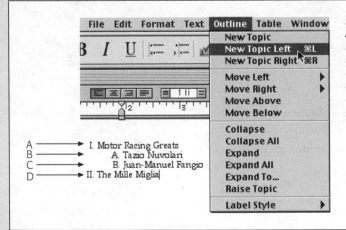

Figure 3-15:
An outline in progress. (A) You type the first heading. (B) When you choose Outline→ New Topic Right, you get a subhead. (C) Press Return for the next subhead at the same level. (D) To make the next level-1 heading, choose Outline→New Topic Left— and continue the process.

You can create a new topic at a higher level—that is, a main heading farther to the left—by choosing Outline→New Topic Left. If you need your new topic to be more than one level to the left, you can continue to move it leftward by choosing Outline→Move Left→With Subtopics. Repeat until you arrive at the correct level—or until you reach the top level, the end of your leftward movement. If you're mouse-averse, you can do all of this just by pressing keystrokes, as outlined in the following table.

Action	Menu Command	Keystroke
Create a new topic (at the same level)	None	Press Return or Enter
Create a subtopic (indented)	Choose Outline→ New Topic Right	⌘- R
Create a topic at a higher level (after you finish entering a set of subtopics)	Choose Outline→ New Topic Left	⌘- L
Move a topic up or down (at the same level)	Choose Outline→Move Above (or Below), or drag with the mouse	
Move a topic up or down without its subtopics (Use this when you decide your topic doesn't apply to its subtopics; the subtopics will become associated with the next topic above them.)	Select the topic only, press Option, and then choose Outline→Move Above (or Below)	
Move a topic right (demote)	Choose Outline→Move Right→ With or Without Subtopics	⌘-Shift-R
Move a topic left (promote)	Choose Outline→Move Left→ With or Without Subtopics	⌘-Shift- L
Collapse a topic	Choose Outline→Collapse, or double-click label	
Expand a topic	Choose Outline→Expand, or double-click label	
Expand or collapse a topic to a certain level	Select topic and choose Outline→Expand To	
Collapse entire outline	Select the whole outline and choose Outline→Collapse All	
Expand entire outline	Select the whole outline and choose Outline→Expand All	
Select a topic with subtopics	Click its label	
Select a topic without subtopics	Click in the topic's text	

Editing outlines

Once you've created your outline, AppleWorks provides a variety of ways to rearrange, edit, and view it. You can rearrange topics, carrying their subtopics along with them. You can move a subtopic up a level—to promote it—or demote it down a level. You can expand or collapse topics to reveal more or less detail in the outline. The table below shows how to make it all happen.

Moving topics with the mouse

Click the topic *label* to highlight the topic and all its subtopics. Now you can drag this selection up or down in the outline. To drag a topic without its subtopics—if you're doing a major rethinking of your purpose—highlight just the text of the topic you want to move, then drag it to its new position.

Note: You can't move topics left or right–to promote or demote them–with the mouse. You can only move topics up and down at the same level. To move a topic left or right, choose Outline→Move Left or Move Right, or use the keyboard commands (see the table on page 77).

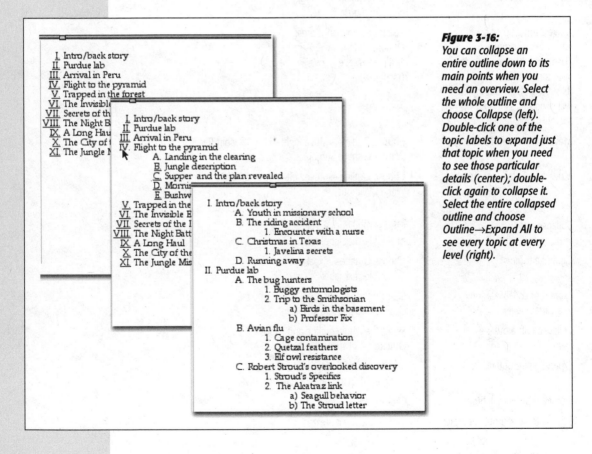

Figure 3-16:
You can collapse an entire outline down to its main points when you need an overview. Select the whole outline and choose Collapse (left). Double-click one of the topic labels to expand just that topic when you need to see those particular details (center); double-click again to collapse it. Select the entire collapsed outline and choose Outline→Expand All to see every topic at every level (right).

Collapse & Expand

When you create a long or very detailed outline, you can easily lose track of the "big picture." By collapsing some or all of these topics, you can "zoom out" to get your bearings—and then expand, or unfold, the topics again as needed to see the detail. If you move or delete a collapsed topic, its subtopics move or disappear along with it.

You can collapse or expand individual topics by double-clicking the label. Or select the whole outline and choose Outline→Collapse All or Outline→Expand All to affect the entire outline.

Tip: When you double-click a topic label, AppleWorks expands or collapses that topic. But if you double-click a checkbox in a checkbox style outline, you get only a checkmark. The trick to collapsing and expanding checkbox outlines is to double-click just to the *left* of the checkbox.

You can also expand or collapse an outline to a designated level by choosing Outline→Expand To. The "Expand to" dialog box appears, in which you can specify the level of subtopics you wish to reveal by entering a number (up to 16, the maximum for an AppleWorks outline). For example, if you have collapsed your outline to show only the main topics, set this dialog box to "Expand to 3"; AppleWorks reveals the first three levels of the outline, keeping the deeper levels hidden.

Tip: Even though AppleWorks calls the command "Expand to," it will also "collapse to." For example, to zoom in on your six-level-deep outline, choose Outline→Expand To and set the dialog box to "Expand to 2." AppleWorks responds by *collapsing* the outline to level 2, showing you just the two most important levels.

Customizing Outline Styles

For your everyday outlining needs, the selection of styles AppleWorks provides should be adequate. But when you require something fancier or just different, AppleWorks allows you to edit the existing outline styles or even create new ones of your own.

Custom labels

If the extreme rigidity of the Harvard style becomes too stifling—for example, when you need to insert a section of subtopics that aren't numbered or lettered—you can change the label style for just that section of the outline.

1. **Select a topic by clicking in its text, or select several topics by dragging through their text.**

2. **Choose Format→Show Styles to open the Styles window.**

3. **Select a new style from the list of available styles and click Apply.**

If you chose one of the non-outline styles—for example, plain Body style, in order to provide a few paragraphs of description to go along with a topic—your selection will jump out of its indented order back to the left margin. Use the Move Right command to jog the selection back into position.

Tip: Each outline topic is, as far as AppleWorks is concerned, a paragraph. It can be any length. Try using outline style to write a report, speech, or presentation, and take advantage of the automatic bulleting, rearranging, and collapsing features.

Custom Styles

If you aren't satisfied by AppleWorks's set of standard outline styles, you can create your own from scratch or modify one of the existing styles. See "Creating styles using menus" and "Editing styles" on page 66.

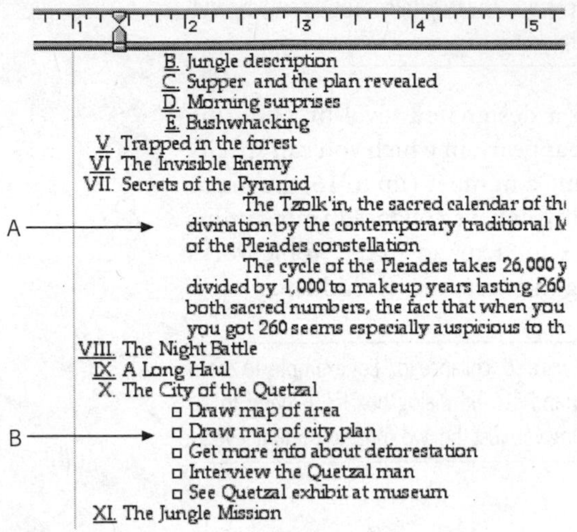

Figure 3-17:
You can create subtopics in an outline that are styled differently than the rest of the outline in order to, for example, provide several paragraphs of description for a topic (A), or to provide a checklist in the midst of the outline (B). To do this, select the topics you want to restyle, choose Format→Show Styles, choose a style from the list of available styles, and then click Apply.

The Insert Command

AppleWorks lets you insert another entire document from your hard drive into the current document—a feature you'll find handy when you find yourself using the same lengthy project summary or product description over and over again.

This feature works in all of the AppleWorks modules. In other words, you can incorporate—into whatever document is open—any word processing, spreadsheet, graphics, or database information from another file. The source file can be an AppleWorks document or any file that AppleWorks can translate (see Chapter 13 for details on file translation).

In the word-processing module, you can use the insert command like a supercharged copy and paste.

1. **Place the insertion point in your document at the place you want the inserted text to appear.**

2. **Choose File→Insert.**

   The Open File dialog box appears.

3. **Navigate to the document you wish to insert; double-click its name (see Figure 3-18).**

   If you're inserting an AppleWorks file, it pops instantly into your document at the insertion point. If you selected a different file type, but it's one that AppleWorks knows how to convert, AppleWorks does so and *then* inserts it into your text.

Figure 3-18:
When inserting one AppleWorks file into another, you can simplify your choice of files by choosing the appropriate file format from the pop-up menu, such as AppleWorks or (if you have the DataViz translators described in Chapter 13) Microsoft Word. Doing so hides all other files, making it easier to find what you're looking for.

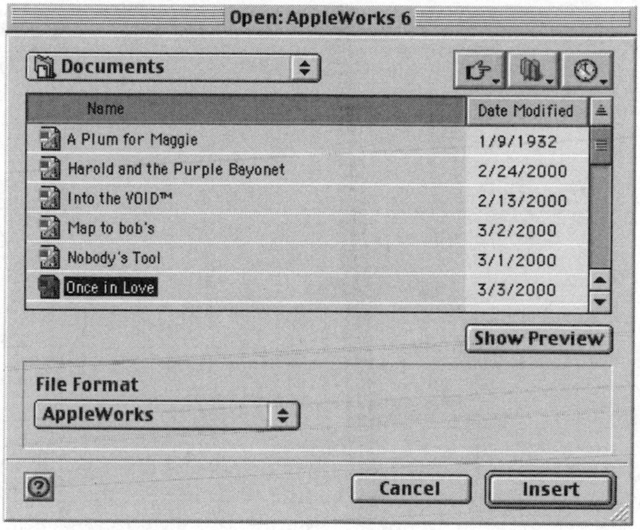

Drag and Insert

You can also insert a file using drag-and-drop, thereby avoiding the Open File dialog box entirely. Use the mouse to drag the icon of the file you wish to insert from the desktop into the proper position in your document (see Figure 3-19).

The same rules about file type noted above apply: as long as AppleWorks can open or convert the file, it drops right into your document.

Tip: If you drag-and-drop an AppleWorks spreadsheet or database document into a word processor document, the program inserts just the *contents* of the cells or fields—as if you had saved the file in text format.

If you'd rather preserve the spreadsheet or database's field or cell structure, start by creating a spreadsheet *frame* (see Chapter 12) in your word processor document first, and then drop the file into *that.* You'll end up with a real spreadsheet (or database data in spreadsheet format).

No matter which method you use to insert a file, AppleWorks copies it from the source document and pastes it into your current document.

Note: AppleWorks doesn't link the two files; if you delete the source document, you don't affect the inserted text.

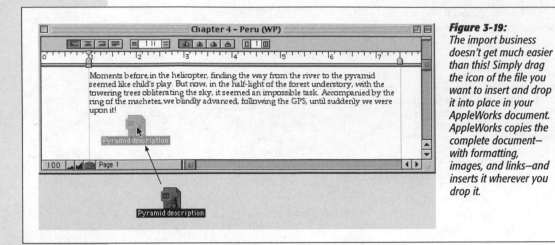

Figure 3-19:
The import business doesn't get much easier than this! Simply drag the icon of the file you want to insert and drop it into place in your AppleWorks document. AppleWorks copies the complete document—with formatting, images, and links—and inserts it wherever you drop it.

Headers and Footers

Headers and footers are the areas at the top and bottom of each page where you might see the title of a book, or the current chapter number. In a header or footer, you put information you wish to repeat on every page; you can see an example of a footer at the bottom of this very page.

Most books—including this one—use footers or headers as a place to display page numbers, the book title, and the chapter. Often, the left and right headers are different: the book title appears on the left-side page, and the chapter name shows up on the right, for example.

Headers and footers are also common in much shorter documents; even on a one-page memo, you might use a header to store your letterhead or return address. Headers and footers can also show the date or time you created the document, the name of the file, and so on.

Note: One thing that you can't include in the footer, ironically, is a footnote. Footnotes appear *below* the body text, but *above* the footer. See page 48 for more on footnotes.

If you've split your document into sections, as described on page 46, you can make the headers and footers different for each section. Put another way, if you *don't* want your headers and footers to be the same throughout your document, you *have* to divide the document into sections.

Adding Headers and Footers

Choose Format→Insert Header or Format→Insert Footer to create a header or footer
in the current document or section. AppleWorks divides the body of the page from
the new header or footer with a gray guide line, as shown in Figure 3-20. (If you
don't see the gray guide line, choose Format→Document and turn on the "Show
page guides" checkbox.) All headers and footers start life as a single line, but you can
add as many lines to these areas as you need—up to about a third of the page height.

AppleWorks creates headers and footers with *center-text alignment.* But you can use
any of usual AppleWorks text-formatting options and ruler settings to affect what
appears here.

Once you've created a header or footer, you need only click in that region—on any
page in the document or section—to edit it. Changes you make on one page carry
through to every page. For example, suppose you added a header to your short story
containing your name and the title. If you later decide to use a pen name, just replace your real name with your *nom de plume* on any page of the story; every page
header reflects your affectation.

Inserting Placeholders

AppleWorks offers you three special characters that are in a class by themselves:
placeholders. Create them by choosing Edit→Insert Date, Insert Time, or Insert Page #.
Once you understand how placeholders work, they can make your writing life much
easier.

Inserting the date or time

The Insert Date and Insert Time commands consult the computer's system clock to
report the correct time and date.

You can insert date and time placeholders in two ways: as *fixed* or as *auto-updating.*

- **Fixed dates and times** don't change—they show the current date or time as of the
  moment when you inserted them. You'd use a fixed date, for example, when keeping a journal that you add to day after day. When you open it and begin today's
  writing, you can insert a fixed date for today's journal entry. You can always look
  back and see when that entry was made.

- **Auto-updating dates and times** *change* every time you open the document. You'd
  use this option, for example, to create a fax cover sheet or a daily press release, so
  that the date on it is always current. They're handy, in other words, for throw-away,
  one-shot items, but lousy for record-keeping (because the date never stays put).

To insert a date or time, choose Edit→Insert Date (or Time)→Fixed or Auto-updating. AppleWorks inserts the date or time at the blinking insertion point. You'll quickly
discover that you can't edit an auto-updating time or date; it appears in your document as a solid, unbreakable block of text that resists your efforts to click inside.

Tip: You control how the date or time is formatted (8/9/00 vs. "August 9, 2000," for example) using the AppleWorks preferences. Choose Edit→Preferences→General, and then select a date format from the pop-up menu.

Time formatting, on the other hand, is determined by the system clock preferences. To edit it, choose →Control panels→Date & Time→Time Formats.

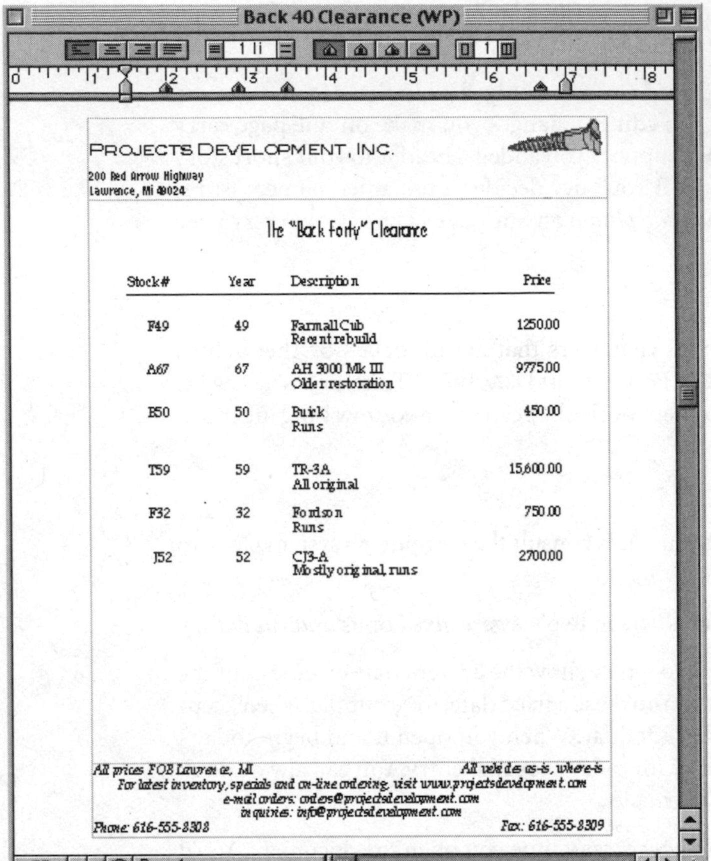

Figure 3-20:
Headers and footers can give your document a "framework" that's consistent from page to page. For example, a footer repeated on every page of your product list can repeat ordering information and shipping restrictions, while the header displays your logo and address. When you're word processing, headers and footers are the places to insert graphics if you want them to show up on every page.

Page-Number Placeholders

The placeholder you'll probably include most often in a header or footer is the page number.

You can't tell by looking at the screen, but behind the scenes, the Edit→Insert Page # command creates an automatically-updating page-number *calculator*—not just an ordinary typed number. In other words, if you add a few pages at the beginning of your document, the page-number placeholder changes to reflect each page's new position in the document.

In order to know where to begin the page numbering sequence, AppleWorks refers to the Document dialog box. If you've divided the document into sections, then AppleWorks begins the section page numbering according to your settings in the Section dialog box. But unless you've changed these settings, the first page of the document is numbered 1.

Adding Page Numbers to a Header or Footer

Technically, you can insert a page number anywhere in your document. If you find it useful, you can insert a sentence in your term paper that says, "By the way, we're already up to page 23."

Far more often, however, you'll want the page number to appear in the header or footer, as it does in any other book or magazine.

1. **Insert a header or footer, if you don't already have one (see page 82).**

2. **Click to place the insertion point in the header or footer.**

   If you're adding a page number to a new, empty header or footer, AppleWorks sets it up with center alignment. If you prefer, choose left or right alignment using the paragraph alignment buttons in the ruler.

   If you want the page number to say "Page 24" (instead of just "24"), type *Page* and a space.

3. **Choose Edit→Insert Page #.**

   The Insert Page Number dialog box appears, giving you four choices for the type of number to insert.

   Page Number numbers the pages as you'd expect: 1, 2, 3, and so on.

   Section Number inserts the current Section number (if, indeed, your document is divided into sections). Use this option for chapter numbers.

   Section Page Count inserts the total number of pages for the current section (again, only if you've divided your document into sections).

   Document Page Count inserts the total number of pages in the document. By inserting both a Page Number and Document Page Count into the same header, you could create a header that says, for example: *Page 5 of 97*. Similarly, using both the Section Number and Section Page Count choices, you could create a header that says, *Chapter 3—page 22*.

4. **Using the Representation pop-up menu, specify whether your numbers (or letters) will be Arabic, Roman numerals, or alphabetical.**

   When preparing the Preface for your book, for example, you may want the "i, ii, iii, iv…" numbering style; you could use the "a, b, c, d…" style for an inserted addendum; and so on. (Remember: you can use different page-numbering styles within the same document only if you've divided it into sections.)

5. **Click OK.**

   The numbers appear in your document.

6. **Format the text and numbers.**

   Highlight the contents of the header or footer and format the text with the Text menu commands. Use the Ruler settings to adjust alignment, line spacing, and indents.

Tip: As noted earlier, the Insert Page Number command functions just as well in the body of a document. For example, if you've divided your document into sections that don't always begin at the top of the page, use Insert Page Number→Section Number to display the section number in a section title (such as *Chapter 34: The Beginning of the End*).

Word Count

If you're paid by the word, need a 2,000-word term paper to pass your class, or want to make sure your letter to the editor is within the 400-word limit, you'll appreciate AppleWorks's word-count feature.

Choose Edit→Writing Tools→Word Count to display the Word Count window. Revealed within are the statistics for not only the number of words, but also the number of characters, lines, paragraphs, pages, and sections, as shown in Figure 3-21.

Tip: The word-count dossier provides statistics on the entire document. If you want to evaluate just a part of the document, highlight the appropriate chunk of text before opening the Word Count window. Then, in the Word Count window, turn on the Count Selection checkbox to reveal the stats for the selected chunk of text.

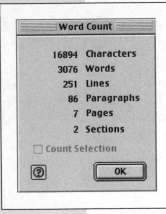

Figure 3-21:
If you want to reduce your exertions at the keyboard to cold statistics, refer to the Word Count window. If you think two pages of text is not much of an accomplishment, how does 4096 characters sound? Word Count tracks all these statistics, but it can't tell you if what you're saying really adds up.

CHAPTER 4

The Database

You're already all too familiar with *databases*. "I don't show that in stock; would you like us to back-order it?"; "Thank you for shopping at Safeway. May I scan your card?"; "Welcome back to Amazon.com, Chris!"

This is the Information Age, and the quantity of information on file is mushrooming at ever-increasing rates. Database software keeps all these facts and figures under control, permanently stored, and easily accessible—for better or for worse.

But databases don't have to be big, secretive, and impersonal. In fact, that's the beauty of the AppleWorks Database module: It lets you corral your *own* data. You can use it to make the address book of your dreams, to track your collection of anything, to score tests or sports. You can use it to make guest lists, grocery lists, or to-do lists.

And best of all—this *is* AppleWorks, after all—you can incorporate your data with the other AppleWorks modules. You can use the graphics tools to add your logo to the top of your invoices, for example, or merge your address book into the word processor to crank out very personal-looking form letters (see Chapter 12).

Database Basics

To understand *computer* databases, consider a paper one—a little drawer filled with cards, one for each person in the database. Each card has pre-printed blanks for name, address, phone number, fax number, email addresses, pager number, favorite food, shoe size, and so on. Very few cards in the collection will have *all* of these blanks filled in. But every card has, at the very least, a name, and most have a phone number and address.

You add a person to this database by filling out a blank card—and you can delete people from this database by removing their cards. You can retrieve information about any person in the database easily, because the cards are filed alphabetically by name.

Now suppose that this tiny file cabinet has other drawers, filled with similar index-card databases: one for a record collection, one for recipes, and one for business invoices.

If you can understand this example, then you've already grasped the idea behind the AppleWorks database.

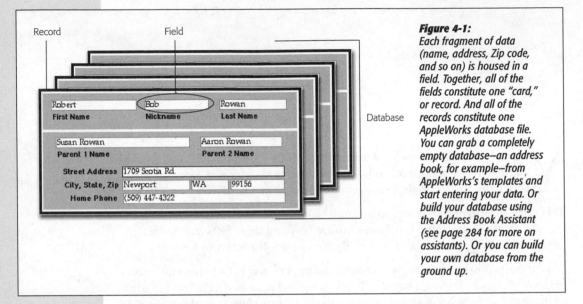

Figure 4-1:
Each fragment of data (name, address, Zip code, and so on) is housed in a field. Together, all of the fields constitute one "card," or record. And all of the records constitute one AppleWorks database file. You can grab a completely empty database—an address book, for example—from AppleWorks's templates and start entering your data. Or build your database using the Address Book Assistant (see page 284 for more on assistants). Or you can build your own database from the ground up.

Computer Databases

But instead of *blanks, cards,* and *file drawers,* AppleWorks (and all other computer databases) have loftier terminology:

- In AppleWorks, the electronic "cards" are called *records.* (That term can get confusing when you're using the database to catalog your music collection of old 45s, 78s, and LPs, but otherwise, it's a useful term.)

- Each blank on a card (such as Name or Phone) is called a *field.* The same fields appear in every record in the database, although you don't have to fill in every field for every person.

- Each collection of cards (records) is one AppleWorks *database* file—the electronic version of that file drawer (see Figure 4-1).

Electronic databases have some distinct advantages over paper ones. For example, suppose you wanted to sort your paper address cards by Zip Code instead of name, or see a list of people who have email addresses. Either way, you'd have a nightmare of a chore on your hands. Electronic databases, however, excel at re-sorting and finding data, instantly and easily.

If you're traveling to Alabama, you can print out a list of all your Alabama contacts, complete with addresses and phone numbers. You could even use a *mail merge* to generate "personally addressed" form letters alerting those friends of your imminent arrival, and print mailing labels for the envelopes.

The key difference between electronic and paper versions of the database is flexibility. Both can contain exactly the same bits of data attached to records. But the electronic database can find, sort, and display that data in all kinds of ways, and share it with other programs.

AppleWorks Database Preview

This chapter offers a unique, patented Parallel Structure: After reading about each database concept, you can put it to use in a tutorial project that's woven all the way through the chapter.

But first, here's an overview of the most important AppleWorks database concepts: *Layouts* and *Modes*.

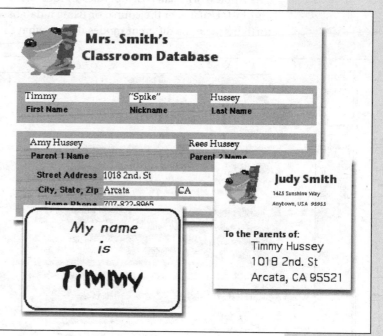

Figure 4-2:
Layouts allow you to examine and present the data in your database in an endless variety of ways—they each draw from the same pool of information, but can perform radically different functions. An address list database, for example, might have three different layouts: One that has fields for recording everything you know about each person. A second layout may show only the name and phone number, so that you can print yourself a little take-along phone book. And a third layout, for use at your summer picnic, might be designed for printing name tags saying nothing but, "Hello, I'm ROBIN."

Layouts

In your file drawer, there's only one way to view the data in the database: pull the file card and look at it. The best part of the AppleWorks database, though, is that you can, if you wish, design different views—or *layouts*—of the same data. You type in the information *once* for each person, and then you can re-use that information in dozens of different kinds of printouts.

For example, suppose your address book database has dozens of fields pertaining to each person. As shown in Figure 4-2, you might want to create three different layouts of this information.

If you like, you can design one layout for data entry, one for viewing on screen, and one for printing. Since layouts are just different ways of looking at the same set of data, you can create new layouts, or delete unused layouts, as often as you like, whenever your needs change.

Read this twice: No matter how you fiddle with layouts, they never, ever affect the information you've actually typed in. Even in a layout that shows nothing but "Hello, I'm ROBIN," all of the phone, address, and salary-history data is still in the database—it's just hidden for the moment.

Modes

The AppleWorks database operates in four *modes,* or views: Browse, Find, Layout, and List. Usually, in the course of using a database, you regularly switch back and forth between the different modes. Here's what they do:

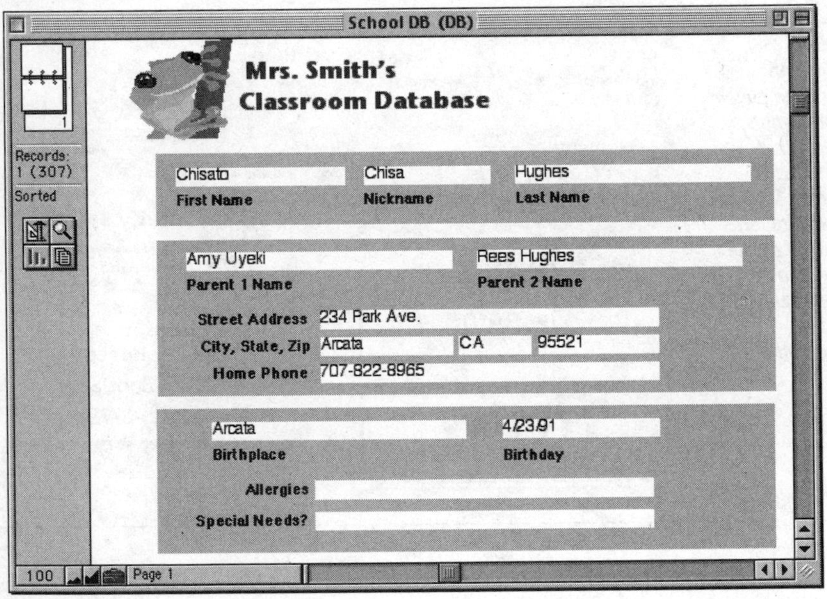

Figure 4-3:
AppleWorks uses Browse mode to display the fields you've set up to hold all your information, and the information you've entered into them. You create new records, add information, and edit the information you've previously entered. And then, to get your valuable information out of the database, you can go on to print out records, lists or labels.

Browse mode

Browse means "use my database." In this view, you look at, type in, delete, sort, and print your information. Browse mode looks something like Figure 4-3.

List mode

The *List mode* is a specialized browse mode. It displays your data like a spreadsheet: every *record* is a row across the screen, and every *field* is a column, as shown in Figure 4-4. Every field you've added to your database, in other words, shows up as a column in this mode—which can make for a *very* wide page.

Figure 4-4:
No matter what shape your other layouts are in, you can always turn to the List mode to see every single one of your fields displayed in spreadsheet fashion.

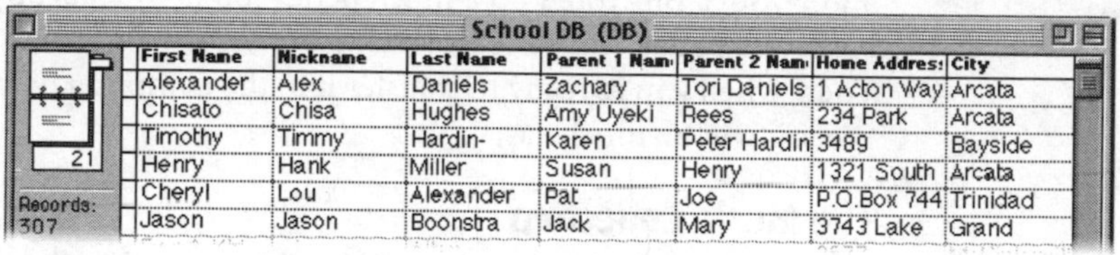

First Name	Nickname	Last Name	Parent 1 Nam	Parent 2 Nam	Home Addres:	City
Alexander	Alex	Daniels	Zachary	Tori Daniels	1 Acton Way	Arcata
Chisato	Chisa	Hughes	Amy Uyeki	Rees	234 Park	Arcata
Timothy	Timmy	Hardin-	Karen	Peter Hardin	3489	Bayside
Henry	Hank	Miller	Susan	Henry	1321 South	Arcata
Cheryl	Lou	Alexander	Pat	Joe	P.O.Box 744	Trinidad
Jason	Jason	Boonstra	Jack	Mary	3743 Lake	Grand

School DB (DB)

Records: 307

Find mode

Find mode is your search engine: you type what you're looking for and then, in a fraction of a second, AppleWorks grinds its way through the entire database and shows you all the records that match your criteria.

After finding, Find mode deposits you back in *Browse* mode—with all the records that didn't match your search request temporarily *hidden*. A Find operation produces a subset, in other words, of your database, which you can then sort, browse, print, or manipulate. For example, from your CD-collection database, you can find all the works of Debussy, and print a list of just those recordings.

When you're finished fooling with this subset of information, another command (Organize→Show All Records) brings back all of the hidden records, so that you're once again viewing your complete database.

Layout mode

The Layout mode is AppleWorks's design department. It's here that you design new views of your data: choosing fonts, styles, and colors for the various fields; choosing which fields you want to show up in each layout; and make all the behind-the-scenes adjustments to make your database function properly.

Phase 1: Design the Database

The next part of this chapter guides you through the creation of a typical AppleWorks database, step by step. In the process, you'll meet each of the primary AppleWorks database tools.

Tip: Chances are good that whatever you're about to organize, someone else has organized it before. Many of their databases have been published as *templates*—complete AppleWorks database shells. All you do is add data.

The AppleWorks Starting Points Web tab connects you, via the Internet, to a variety of prefab database templates that may fill the bill. Another source is the AppleWorks User Group Web site (*www.awug.com*), home to hundreds of freeware and shareware database templates.

Plan Ahead

It's very tempting to sit right down at your computer and begin churning out fields and layouts. But you'll do a much better job if you start by plotting out your database with paper and pencil. Sketch every screen and printed report; list every field. Then, when you're ready to transfer it to the computer, you'll have a clear guide; the process will be much easier.

The Music Collection

To illustrate, here's how you might go about creating a music collection database: a catalog of records, tapes, and CDs.

First, examine a CD to decide how many fields of information you want to include. For example, every recording has a catalog number; but unless you're running a record store, you probably don't need to include it in your database.

Suppose that you end up with a list of these fields:

- **Title.** The name of the CD or record.

- **Artist.** The band or singer.

- **Recording Label.** The record company.

- **Category.** What kind of music it is: rock, classical, rock/classical fusion, whatever.

- **Format.** Is this a CD, record, or tape?

- **Cost.** Soon you'll know just how much of your money you've sunk into this music collection.

- **Date Purchased.** From now on, you can record the date each new recording enters your collection.

- **Notes.** It's always handy to have a blank where you can type your own random notes about each recording.

- **Song Titles.** Think carefully about this one. Will you really take the time to type in the names of every song on every CD? If you have that kind of discipline, great—otherwise, remember that you can always add new fields to your database, even after you've been using it for a while.

As you look at the fields and continue examining the problem, you may come up with new ideas for ways to improve the function of the database. For example, if one of your design goals is to separate the good music from the bad, then you could add a "Rating" field to the list.

Sketch the Layouts

Now it's time to imagine what your database will look like. A database like this might have several different layouts: a full-screen design to use when typing information into the database, a much more compact one designed for printing, and so on. (See "Phase 4," later in this chapter, for illustrations of what these might look like.)

Refer to the list of fields; sketch out what each layout should include and how it should be displayed. AppleWorks can also incorporate text, graphics, background colors, and clip art into each layout—elements to make your database more attractive and easier to use.

Phase 2: Build the Database

After you've figured out which fields your database will include, and how you might like them arranged on the screen, the time has come to begin construction.

Note: The following discussion goes into great depth exploring the options you can use when creating a database of your own. If you've decided to use one of the built-in database templates provided with AppleWorks, or a template you've found online, you can jump directly to "Phase 3: Fill in the Blanks" on page 111.

Open a New File; Create a Field

You create a new database the way you create any AppleWorks file—using the Starting Points window, the Button bar, or the File→New command.

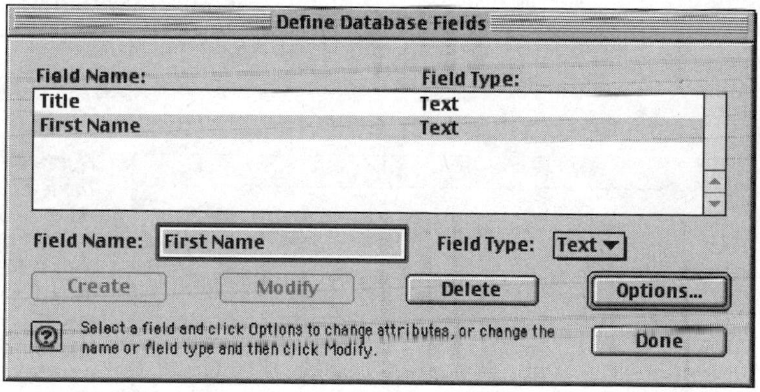

Figure 4-5:
Every database needs at least one field—and databases with 50 or more fields aren't unusual. This dialog box appears when you first create an Apple-Works database; when you want to return to it—to create more fields, for example—choose Layout→ Define Fields. Fields that you've already created are listed here along with their type in the scrolling list.

Create the file

From the Starting Points window, click the Basic tab, and then click the Database icon. Alternatively, you can click the database icon in the Button bar, or just choose File→New→Database.

Either way, the Define Database Fields dialog box opens (Figure 4-5). Now you're about to make a list of the fields you want to include. You'll make one field for every field on your paper list, beginning with *Title*.

Type the first field name

Type the name of the first field you want to create; in this CD-collection example, it would probably be *Title*.

Choose a Field Type

AppleWorks offers 14 different *kinds* of fields—some designed to hold only numbers, others for times or dates, and so on. By cleverly choosing the correct kind of field for each nugget of information in your database, you can make AppleWorks perform useful tasks automatically—doing math, offering multiple-choice lists, and otherwise saving you time and effort.

Each time you create a field, in other words, you must choose one of these field types from the Field Type pop-up menu:

Text fields

A *text field* is the world's most popular database field. You can type any kind of text into it, including numbers or symbols. (A text field is ideal for numbers like Zip Codes; if you used a number field instead to hold the Zip Code, every time you typed *06902*, AppleWorks would try to do you a favor by chopping off the initial 0. Creating the Zip Code as a text field solves the problem.)

A text field can contain a maximum of about 1,000 characters—a page of double-spaced text. As in a word processing document, you can format all or part of the text in any font, size, style, or color, and you can press the Return key to break up the text into paragraphs.

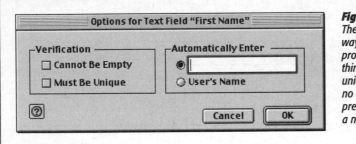

Figure 4-6:
The Text Options dialog box fine-tunes the way AppleWorks handles a text field. The program can require you to enter something in the field or enter something unique (that is, something that's found in no other record); and it can automatically pre-enter some text every time you create a new record.

Tip: The limit for a text field is *about* 1,000 characters because AppleWorks invisibly includes *character formatting* in the field, too. If AppleWorks warns you that you have exceeded the limit for a text field, removing any formatting (such as bold, italic, or text colors) may permit you to type in a few more words.

Text Options

After you've typed a name for your field and specified a field type, you can click the Options button. The Options dialog box appears (see Figure 4-6), presenting settings that pertain to this kind of field—Text, Number, or whatever.

The Text Options dialog box gives you these options:

- **Cannot Be Empty.** When you turn this checkbox on, AppleWorks will object if the data-entry person leaves this field empty. If he tries to skip over the Title field, AppleWorks will beep and warn him that he's supposed to enter *something* in this field. He'll be offered the chance to leave the field empty, or to go back and type something into it. You won't want to turn this option on for every field—for example, you may not have a first name for every singer in your collection, so you'd be foolish to require one—but you'll probably want to insist that each CD listing include a title.

- **Must Be Unique.** If you use this option, AppleWorks checks to make sure that the data in a field is *unique* (not duplicated in your database)—for example, a serial number or a name you don't want duplicated.

  Suppose you turn this on for the Title field in your music database, for example. When somebody tries to enter the name of a CD that has already been cataloged, AppleWorks will beep, alert them that this field is supposed to contain unique values, and ask if they're sure they want to allow this duplicate title.

- **Automatically Enter.** Using this choice, you can specify something that you want AppleWorks to enter *automatically* every time you create a new record. If you're about to type in 50 CD names into your music database that are all by Duke Ellington, for example, you can set up AppleWorks to type *Duke Ellington* into the Artist field of each new record you create, saving you endless typing. (You can always return to this Options dialog box to delete *Duke Ellington* from the Automatically Enter box, or replace it with the name of the next artist for whom you own 50 CDs.)

- **User's Name.** If you turn this option on, then every time you create a new record, AppleWorks will type in the name of the person who owns this computer. (To find out this name, AppleWorks consults the name in the →Control Panels→File Sharing control panel.) This option is primarily useful if you are on a network in an office, where several people are working on the same database. In such a case, you might create a field called "data entered by," so that AppleWorks would make a note of who created each record, so that the boss would know who to blame if some information got really fouled up. (On the other hand, even then you'd be better off using the more powerful Record Info field for this purpose—it's described later in this chapter.)

Number fields

Number fields can contain *only* numbers. If you try to type anything else, even a hyphen or a parenthesis, AppleWorks beeps its displeasure at you. Use this kind of field to hold quantities, prices, and so on—but not Zip codes, as described above, and not phone numbers, which usually include hyphens and parentheses.

As you'll discover later in this tutorial, AppleWorks can perform *calculations* on the contents of your number fields (and other kinds of fields), making them even more useful. For example, AppleWorks could multiply the number in a Price field by the number in your Quantity field—and display the result automatically in a third field.

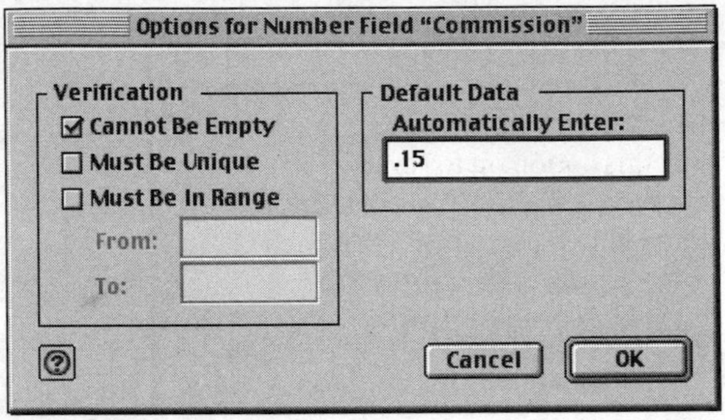

Figure 4-7:
The Number Options dialog box (left) allows you to control verification options to make certain, for example, you enter the sales commission rate; or you can tell AppleWorks to enter it for you (right).

Number Options

The Number Options dialog box (Figure 4-7) gives you three verification options and a default data entry option:

- **Cannot Be Empty.** This option functions exactly the same as it does in the Text Options dialog box. You'd turn this option on for the Cost field, for example, so that AppleWorks will remind you to specify how much you paid for a CD.

- **Must Be Unique.** This option functions exactly the same as it does for text fields. In a number field, you might want to insist that each number in a serial number, stock number, or employee number field is unique (not duplicated) in the database.

- **Must Be In Range.** Turn on this option if you want AppleWorks to check the number you type, confirming that it falls within a certain range. For example, a field that tracks student grades must be in the range from 0 to 4; a field for Olympic athlete scores must be in the range from 0 to 10; and so on.

- **Default Data.** Fill in the Automatically Enter box with a number you want entered by default (that is, automatically when you create a new record). For example, in the "Number of doors" field of your car-dealership file, you might want AppleWorks to enter "4" for each car-sales record you create. Sure, you might sell a few two-doors—but in the meantime, the other 90 percent of your fields will have been filled automatically by the number 4, saving you a little bit of typing each time.

Date fields

Into a *date field*, AppleWorks lets you type only dates, such as *February 6, 2001*, or *2.6.01*, or *2/6/01*. (Later in the database creation process, you can tell AppleWorks which format you prefer.) You can enter dates manually, or AppleWorks can enter the current date in this field automatically. If you try to type anything else into such a field, AppleWorks will beep and show you an error message.

Tip: If you're entering a date for the current year, you don't have to type any numbers for the year—AppleWorks assumes you're referring to *this* year. If it's the year 2000, you can type *9/15* to represent September 15, 2000.

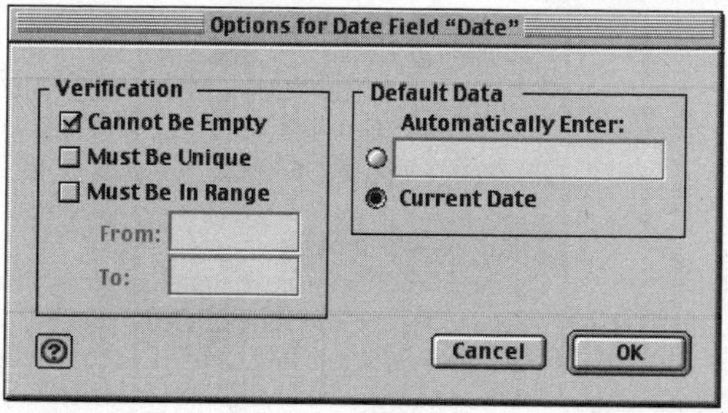

Figure 4-8:
The Date Options dialog box lets you control the usual validation options and can also cause AppleWorks to enter the current date—or any other date you choose—in the field for you.

Date Options

The date-field options are similar to those for number fields—but you're also offered the option to have your field filled automatically with the current date (that is, the date that's current at the moment the record is created).

Time fields

A *time field* is exactly like a date field—except that it displays hours, minutes, and seconds instead of days, months, and years. You'd use a time field to list, for example, the times classes begin and end for a school's class list.

In the Time Options dialog box, you'll see that AppleWorks can automatically enter the current time (as of the moment the record is created). That could be a helpful option for the Time of Call field in the Community Help Line's call-log database.

Name fields

When creating a database, millions of people have, for decades, created two different fields to enter each person's name: First Name and Last Name. The AppleWorks *Name* field is designed to eliminate that hassle—it lets you type each person's first *and* last name in a single field. Then, when you ask AppleWorks to sort your list of names, it's smart enough to sort your database by the last word in this Name field.

Unfortunately, this system breaks down if you have names like Walter van der Ley, Alicia de Larrocha, and Al Unser, Jr. in your list; they wind up sorted far out of alphabetical order. An even worse problem, however, emerges if you want to do a mail merge—combine names from your database with a word processing document to create a personalized form letter. Instead of being able to write, "Dear Karen," or "Dear Ms. Jones," you're stuck with "Dear Karen Jones"—not a good way to begin a letter. Unless you're certain you'll never need to create such a form letter, avoid the Name field. Use two individual Text fields—called First Name and Last Name—instead.

Tip: If you press Option-space (a *nonbreaking space*) between words instead of a regular space, AppleWorks treats the two separate words as one, which works around the two-name sorting problem.

Name Options

Since the name field is simply a text field enhanced with name-sorting abilities, its Options dialog box offers the same assortment of options found in the Text Field options box.

Pop-up menu fields

One of the database designer's principal goals is consistency of information. If you like to record the state of California as *CA*, you don't want your spouse to confuse AppleWorks by using *Calif.* If you provide a limited range of choices for the person who's going to be typing in information, you enjoy two blessings: you ensure consistency, and you save that person from having to type things out. AppleWorks provides *pop-up menu fields, radio buttons, value lists,* and *checkboxes* to aid in this process, as shown in Figure 4-9.

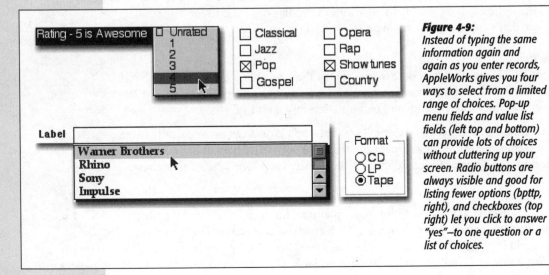

Figure 4-9:
Instead of typing the same information again and again as you enter records, AppleWorks gives you four ways to select from a limited range of choices. Pop-up menu fields and value list fields (left top and bottom) can provide lots of choices without cluttering up your screen. Radio buttons are always visible and good for listing fewer options (bpttp, right), and checkboxes (top right) let you click to answer "yes"–to one question or a list of choices.

Pop-up menus let you provide a finite list of alternatives to choose from when recording your information. For example, when you're creating the Format field for your record collection, you could create a pop-up menu offering only three choices: *CD, LP,* or *Tape.* From now on, you'll find it very easy to record this information—just choose it from a pop-up menu. Doing so prevents people from confusing the issue by typing, for example, *compact disc, vinyl,* or *cassette.*

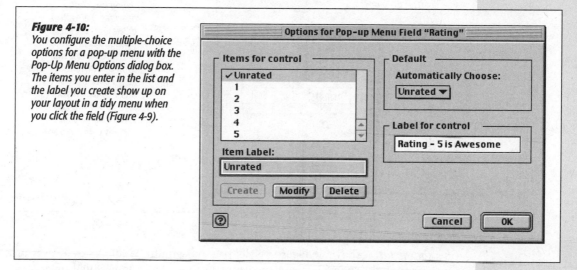

Figure 4-10:
You configure the multiple-choice options for a pop-up menu with the Pop-Up Menu Options dialog box. The items you enter in the list and the label you create show up on your layout in a tidy menu when you click the field (Figure 4-9).

Pop-up Menu Options

When you type the name for your pop-up menu and then click Create, you get the dialog box shown in Figure 4-10. Here you assign the items for your menu by typing them one at a time in the Item Label box and clicking Create; now they appear in the "Items for control" list. You can reorder the items as they'll appear in the pop-up menu by dragging them up or down in the list.

Using the Automatically Choose pop-up menu, you're supposed to specify which of your choices comes up first when you create a new record. In other words, if you have mostly vinyl in your collection, make *LP* the automatically chosen choice.

Finally, "Label for control" is where you can enter a new label for this field to show on your layouts—if you prefer something other than the field name. For example, instead of being labeled Format, you could enter *Media Type.*

Radio button fields

Radio buttons work just like pop-up menus—they offer a multiple choice. Radio buttons have one advantage over the pop-up menu, however: All of the multiple choices are visible simultaneously on the screen. (On the other hand, a pop-up menu is more compact.)

Radio Button Options

First cousin of the pop-up menu field type, radio button fields share the same range of options.

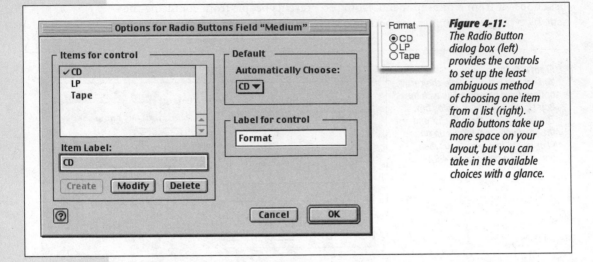

Figure 4-11:
The Radio Button dialog box (left) provides the controls to set up the least ambiguous method of choosing one item from a list (right). Radio buttons take up more space on your layout, but you can take in the available choices with a glance.

Checkbox fields

Checkbox fields, as shown in Figure 4-9, let you make multiple choices by answering a question—unlike pop-up menus and radio buttons. (Most often, you'll create several checkboxes in a group.) For example, in the music library example, you might create several checkboxes to indicate musical style: Classical, Jazz, Rock, Pop, Rap, Gospel, Instrumental, and Vocal. You can check off as many as you like for a particular recording—for an especially versatile singer, you could even check all of them. (Now *that's* fusion.)

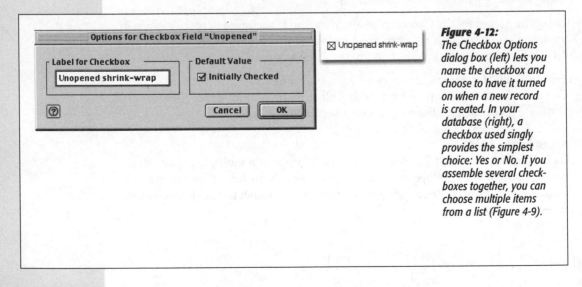

Figure 4-12:
The Checkbox Options dialog box (left) lets you name the checkbox and choose to have it turned on when a new record is created. In your database (right), a checkbox used singly provides the simplest choice: Yes or No. If you assemble several check-boxes together, you can choose multiple items from a list (Figure 4-9).

You can also create a checkbox that stands alone—it might say, for example, "Unopened shrink-wrap."

The Checkbox Options dialog box presents you with only two settings. You can specify a *label* for the checkbox—that's usually the field name, but you can change it if you like; and you can select whether the checkbox should be Initially Checked (that is, displaying a checkmark when you create a new record).

Serial number fields

The *serial number field* makes AppleWorks assign a unique serial number to every record—another must-have field for careful database designers. Because serial numbers go up (usually by 1) with each new record, you can use them to track the order in which you created your records. At any time, you can sort your database by serial number to return the records to the order in which you created them, and any gaps in the serial number sequence reveal where you deleted records. Serial numbers can also be used to number invoices, customers, or students.

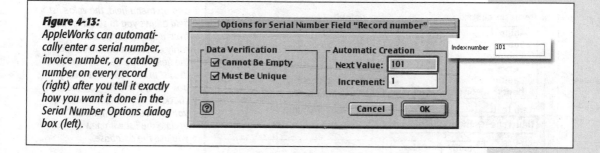

Figure 4-13:
AppleWorks can automatically enter a serial number, invoice number, or catalog number on every record (right) after you tell it exactly how you want it done in the Serial Number Options dialog box (left).

Serial Number Options

In the Options dialog box (Figure 4-13), you should always turn on both verification options, Cannot Be Empty and Must Be Unique—if you're creating serial numbers, you certainly want each record to have a unique number. You determine where you want your number series to begin with the Next Value box: The next record you create will bear that serial number. If you're converting from a paper invoice system to AppleWorks, you can set this number to pick up where the paper invoices left off. Only numbers are allowed in this field, no letters or punctuation.

The Increment setting determines how AppleWorks counts from one record to the next. For example, if the member numbers for your Oddfellows Association must be odd, you can set the Next Value to an odd number and increment by 2.

Value list fields

A *value list* is similar to a pop-up menu, but it has some important differences. When you click a value list field, a list of possible selections drops down, as shown in Figure 4-14. If the data you want to record isn't listed in the drop-down list, you can type it in. (You can't make up your own answers like this when you're using a regular pop-up menu.) AppleWorks then asks if you'd like your entry added to the value list, so that the *next* time you create a record, your newly typed answer will show up as a choice.

Value lists are great for fields like cities or products. If your customers are mostly from the local area, for example, your value list will slowly grow to include all of the nearby cities. Each time you create a record for a new customer in one of these cities, you won't have to type the city name—just choose it from the list.

Tip: Unfortunately, as you add new choices to your value list, they appear in the list in the order in which you added them—not in alphabetical order. If you find it easier to scan the choices here in order, choose Layout→Define Fields, double-click the field name, and re-order the value list choices by dragging them up or down in the list shown in Figure 4-14.

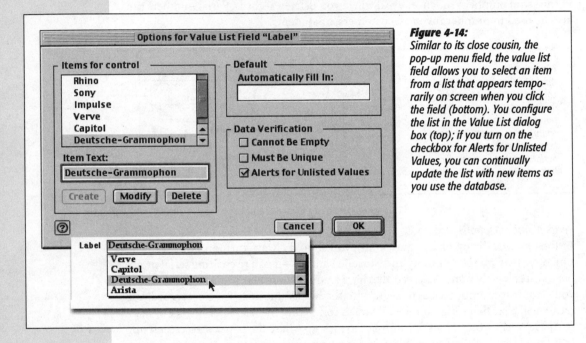

Figure 4-14:
Similar to its close cousin, the pop-up menu field, the value list field allows you to select an item from a list that appears temporarily on screen when you click the field (bottom). You configure the list in the Value List dialog box (top); if you turn on the checkbox for Alerts for Unlisted Values, you can continually update the list with new items as you use the database.

Value List Options

As you might expect given its similarity to the pop-up menu field type, the value list options are almost the same. One difference is the Data Verification section of the dialog box (see Figure 4-14), which gives three options: Cannot Be Empty, Must Be Unique, and Alerts for Unlisted Values.

The first two options are described under "Pop-up menu options," earlier in this chapter; Alerts for Unlisted Values is unique to this field type. If you turn on this option, AppleWorks will beep whenever you type an entry into this field that's not one of the choice you've already set up. A dialog box then gives you three choices:

Continue (which means, "Return to the field and try again"); Accept (which means, "Accept what I've typed for this one record"); and Add to List (which means, "Accept the entry I've typed, *and* add it to the drop-down list of choices, so it will be available the next time I create a record and click this value list").

You'll see how all of this works in the Music Database tutorial later in this chapter.

Multimedia fields

You can use a *multimedia field* when you want to attach sounds, pictures, or movies to a record. You can use this field to store employee ID photographs, product pictures, sound clippings for your music database, scans of stamps for your collection, or movies of the kids' trip to the pumpkin patch. (A note to the technical: The multimedia field is really a QuickTime field, so sounds, pictures, and movies must be in QuickTime format. Fortunately, AppleWorks converts many kinds of multimedia files into QuickTime automatically—often slowly.)

You can add pictures, sounds, and movies to a multimedia field in three different ways: By *pasting* copied sounds, graphics, or movies into one of these fields; by *dragging* them in from another AppleWorks document, another program, or from the desktop; or by choosing File→Insert to locate a file on your hard drive, which then pops into the multimedia field.

The multimedia field has no Options dialog box.

Record info fields

You can't type anything into a *record info field;* only AppleWorks can put information into this kind of field.

Still, this feature can be very useful. For example, it's often important to know when each record was created or modified. Record Info fields can provide an automatic time or date stamp, or keep track of who created and modified it.

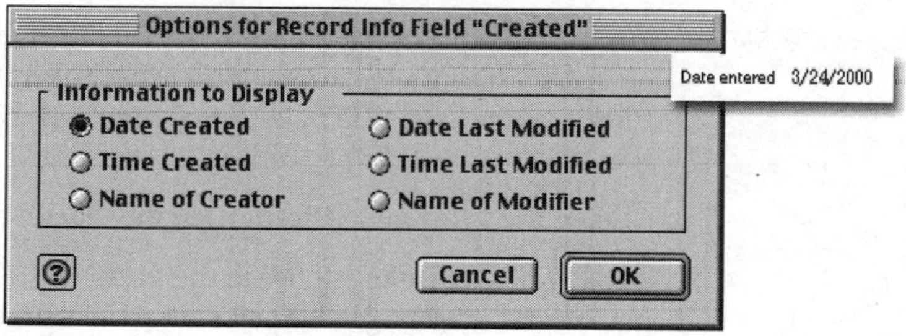

Figure 4-15:
The Record Info dialog box (left) lets you select one of six factoids to be automatically inserted into a Record Info field (right). If you need to know more than one of these tidbits about your records, you can create additional fields, each with a different option.

Record Info Options

When you click the Options button, you'll see that AppleWorks can automatically record any of these pieces of information (see Figure 4-15): the date or time the record was created; the date or time the record was last changed; or the name of the person who created or last modified the record. (AppleWorks gets this name from the →Control Panels→File Sharing control panel.)

Calculation fields

You can't type anything into *calculation fields,* either. AppleWorks fills them in by performing math or other operations on the contents of *other* fields. Figure 4-16 shows an example.

Sometimes these equations can be simple—for example, you could create a calculation field called Total Tax using this formula: *Income * Tax Rate,* where Income and Tax Rate are two number fields in your database. The asterisk tells AppleWorks to multiply them.

Sometimes these equations can be fantastically complicated, involving mathematical, logical, geometric, and financial calculations, and requiring a head like a programmer's. For a complete description of the various AppleWorks functions, see the Functions Appendix on this book's page at *www.missingmanual.com.*

To perform a simple calculation, for example, one that figures the sales tax for an invoice, you begin by creating a new field to hold the results of your calculation.

1. **Choose Layout→Define Fields.**

   AppleWorks displays the Define Database Fields dialog box.

   You can open this dialog box in other ways, too. For example, you can Control-click any blank area of the screen and then choose Define Fields from the contextual menu.

   Suppose, for the sake of this example, that your database already contains a field called Sale Total.

2. **Enter *Sales Tax* in the Field Name box, choose Calculation from the Field Type pop-up menu, and then click Create.**

   The Formula dialog box appears (Figure 4-16), listing all the fields in the database, the list of mathematical (and other) operators, and the list of Functions. Click the Sale Total field in the Fields list. AppleWorks enters it into the Formula box.

3. **Choose the * (for multiplication) in the Operators list.**

   AppleWorks adds the asterisk to the formula. (In computerese, * means "multiply by" and / means "divide by." The – and + mean exactly what you think.)

4. **Complete the formula by entering your local sales tax rate, such as .075 (for 7.5 percent).**

   The "Format result as" pop-up menu should be set to Number.

5. **Click OK.**

The Formula dialog box closes, leaving the Define Database Fields dialog box, with the newly created field and its calculation, highlighted in the list.

6. **Click Done.**

AppleWorks adds the new field to the layout and displays the amount of sales tax (see Figure 4-16).

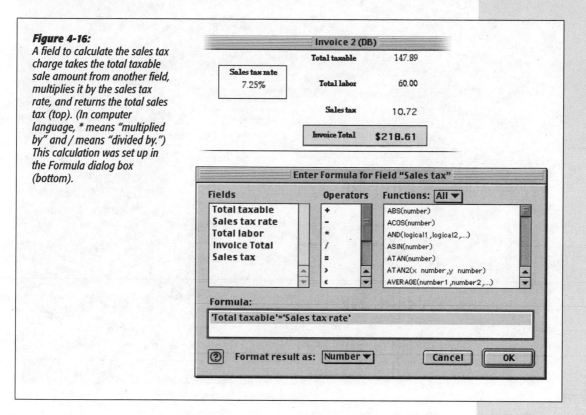

Figure 4-16:
A field to calculate the sales tax charge takes the total taxable sale amount from another field, multiplies it by the sales tax rate, and returns the total sales tax (top). (In computer language, * means "multiplied by" and / means "divided by.") This calculation was set up in the Formula dialog box (bottom).

You can also use calculation fields, weirdly enough, for *text calculations.* For example, if you've created a First Name field and a Last Name field, you can use the calculation field to combine, or *concatenate,* the two into a full name. The formula would be:

```
"First Name" & " " & "Last Name"
```

The ampersands (&) tell AppleWorks to join the fields together, and the space surrounded by quotation marks provides a space between names (to avoid a result like *BobDylan*).

Summary fields

Summary fields are the "bottom line" of your database. They're similar to calculation fields—AppleWorks puts information into a summary field automatically, based on a calculation that you establish. But instead of calculating fields within a single record, summary fields draw from *many* records to provide an answer for the whole database.

POWER USERS' CLINIC

Date Calculation Example

Calculation fields can perform their magic with times and dates—for example, you can create a field that displays how many days are left until Christmas.

To do so, choose Layout→ Define Fields to open the Define Database Fields dialog box. Enter *Days until Christmas* in the Field Name box, choose Calculation from the Field Type pop-up menu, and then click Create.

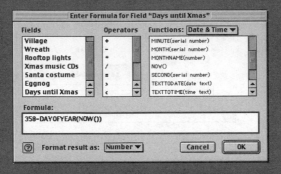

Now the Formula dialog box appears, listing all the fields in the database, the list of mathematical operators, and the list of Functions. Christmas is usually the 358th day of the year, so enter *358* and a minus sign (hyphen) in the Formula box.

Choose Functions→Date & Time; click DAYOFYEAR. (This function is described in the Functions Appendix at *www.missingmanual.com.* It calculates how many days have elapsed in the year for a given date.)

AppleWorks adds the function to the formula and highlights its parenthetical *argument*—that is, what you want the function to operate on. In this example, the argument is a placeholder for, "You want to see how many days have elapsed in the year until *what* date?"

Scroll down the function list and click NOW, which means whatever date your computer thinks it is right now. AppleWorks adds this second function to the formula, which is now complete: 358-DAYOFYEAR(NOW()).

Click OK, and then Done. The dialog box closes and Apple-Works adds the new field to your layout, performs the calculation, "Start with 358; then subtract today's date in the form of days elapsed in the year," and displays the correct number of days left until Christmas.

Figure 4-17:
This report layout uses a Trailing grand summary to calculate summarizing information about a music collection: the total value, the total investment, and the net value.

For example, a summary field in your CD collection database could keep a running tally of the money you've spent on music; it would do so by totaling the Price Paid field for every record in your database. Or you can use this field to provide a total for just the Elvis holdings in your collection. Summary fields are often used in printed reports to show totals, averages, medians, and so on. (Figure 4-17 shows an example.)

Tutorial: Designing the Music Collection

If you've slogged through the previous discussion of field types, then you'll understand exactly what's going on in this tutorial, and you'll appreciate how useful the field types can be.

Start by creating a new AppleWorks database file (for example, by choosing File→New→Database. The Define Database Fields dialog box appears, as shown in Figure 4-5.

1. **Type the name for your first field—in this case, *Title*. Choose a field type from the pop-up menu—*text*—and click Create (or press Enter) to create the new field.**

   The field name and type appear in the list window, as shown in Figure 4-5.

   At this point, you could create the next field by typing its name; you'd be starting over at Step 1. It's worth using some of the special Options for this text field, however.

2. **Click Options (or press Enter).**

   The Options dialog box appears, as described earlier in this chapter.

3. **Turn on the Cannot Be Empty checkbox; click OK (or press Enter).**

   You've just made sure that whoever types your record collection information into the database—even if it's you—can't accidentally leave the Title field empty.

   The Options dialog box closes. The Define Database Fields window is still open, ready for you to enter the next field name and repeat the definition process. (You could also click Options to return to the Text Options dialog box, Delete to remove a field, or Done if you're finished defining fields.)

4. **Type *First Name,* and then click Create (or press Enter).**

   You're about to divide the Artist field into two text fields: first name and last.

5. **Type *Last Name,* and then click Create (or press Enter) again. Click Options, turn on Cannot Be Empty, and then click OK.**

   If your recording was made by a singer with a person's name, such as Elton John, you'll put those names into the first and last name blanks; if it's a band name, such as the Rolling Stones, you'll record that in the Last Name field. Either way, the Last Name field will never be empty.

   Now it's time to create the Recording Label field.

6. Type *Recording Label* (or just *Label*). From the Field Type pop-up menu, choose Value List. Click Create.

The Label field could be a plain text field. But if you make it a value list, like the one illustrated in Figure 4-14, you'll make it much easier for yourself when it comes time to type in all of your CDs. Why type *Warner Brothers* or *Deutsche Grammophon* over and over again if AppleWorks can enter the words for you?

In any case, the Options for Value List Field dialog box is now before you, like the one shown in Figure 4-14. This is where you're supposed to type the list of choices that will appear whenever you try to fill in the Recording Label field. Grab a stack of your CDs and prepare to type in some of the popular labels.

Tip: AppleWorks can't automatically alphabetize the order of the choices you stash in your value list, but you can manually rearrange the items in the list—just drag them up or down.

---

7. In the Item Text blank, type the name of the first label and then click Create (or press Enter). Type the next recording label and then press Enter again. Repeat until you've built up a useful list.

Make sure you enter these names with correct spelling and capitalization—you'll use these entries over and over again in the database.

8. Turn on Alerts for Unlisted Values.

If a majority of your recordings are from one label, for example, enter that name in the Automatically Fill In box. AppleWorks will propose that recording label every time you create a new record.

In step 7, you created a list of the recording labels you might want to specify when filling in your database. But what about the occasional CD that was produced by a little-known recording company? There's no telling what musical preoccupations you might succumb to in the future—you may start accumulating a lot of Motown or Stax/Volt recordings, for example. Fortunately, AppleWorks can accommodate you—but only if you turn on the checkbox called Alerts For Unlisted Values.

9. Click OK to close the Options box.

Now it's time to create a Category field. This field, too, could be a simple text field in which you'd enter *Jazz, Classical,* and so on. But you can save time and ensure consistency by creating a canned list of categories.

In the previous steps, you created a value list; you could use the value list to represent the choices of category, too. Trouble is, you can make only one choice from a value list—which could be a problem when classifying the occasional gospel rap CD.

If you design a group of checkboxes, however, you'll be able to choose as many categories as you like for each recording. To make this work, you must define a separate checkbox field for each category—Classical, Jazz, Rock, Folk, and so on.

10. In the Field Name box, type *Classical;* from the Field Type pop-up menu, choose Checkbox; click Create. Type *Jazz,* and then click Create. Type *Rock,* and then click Create. Repeat until you've exhausted the possibilities of your collection.

Notice that you don't have to keep choosing Checkbox from the Field Type pop-up menu; AppleWorks maintains whatever you last selected from this pop-up menu as you create new fields.

To be sure, creating a set of checkboxes means that you vastly expand the list of fields in your database; by now, you probably have to use the vertical scroll bar in your fields list to see them all. That's perfectly OK. Having a lot of fields doesn't slow AppleWorks down or make the file much bigger.

Next stop: creating the Format field, where you'll specify whether a particular recording is a CD, vinyl album, or cassette.

11. Type Format. From the Field Type pop-up menu, choose Radio Buttons. Click Create, and then click Options.

The Format field is well suited to radio buttons. An Options for Radio Buttons dialog box now appears.

12. Type labels for each of the buttons you'll want to appear in your database: for example, *CD, LP, Tape, 8-track*, and so on. After typing each label, click Create (or press Enter).

What you see now resembles Figure 4-11 at left; what you'll see later, when filling out your database, is shown there at right.

From the Automatically Choose pop-up menu, you might also want to select the format most of your recordings share. That way, AppleWorks will automatically select the most common format, saving you one step every time you fill in a new record.

Now you'll create the Cost field, where you can record how much you spent on each recording. Next year, when you're selling your Britney Spears CDs on eBay, you'll be grateful that you did so.

13. Click OK to close the Options window. Type *Cost;* from the Field Type pop-up menu, choose Number; click Create.

You may also want to track when you bought each new recording:

14. Type *Date Purchased;* from the Field Type pop-up menu, choose Date; click Create.

Finally, most databases benefit from the field called Notes or Comments—a catch-all field into which you can type miscellaneous information—"signed by Tony Bennett at the Indianapolis Airport, 8/21/99," for example.

15. Type *Notes.* From the Field Type pop-up menu, choose Text. Click Create.

To finish up, consider creating a Ratings field. You could create it as a pop-up menu, containing choices 1, 2, 3, 4, 5, and Unrated.

You might also consider creating a Serial Number field, so that you can see where you've deleted records or conjure up the original data-entry order of the records. To make one, type Record Number; choose Serial Number from the Field Type list. When the Options window opens, turn on both Cannot Be Empty and Must Be Unique (so that you don't wind up with two identical serial numbers).

In the Automatic Creation section of this dialog box, you can set the Next Value at 100 or 1000 to make your database look like it's a bit more established than it actually is. Leave the Increment set to 1, so that each new record will have a serial number one greater than the previous one.

Finally, you might consider creating a *Creation Date* field that AppleWorks automatically fills in with the date you enter each album's information. Make a field named *Created*; give it the field type called Record Info. In the Options window that appears, choose Date Created.

16. **When you're finished creating your fields, click Done.**

    You've just created an extremely powerful and fairly sophisticated database—in 16 easy steps. It looks like Figure 4-18—for now. The beauty of the AppleWorks database is that you can rearrange these fields on the screen to make them look any way you like. You'll find out how in "Phase 4: Design New Layouts," later in this chapter.

Tip: You've just put in a lot of work defining fields, even though you haven't yet typed in a single piece of *data* about your music collection. It's a good idea to save your new file just after defining the fields, before you even begin to type in new data.

Editing Field Definitions

Setting up your fields isn't a first-day, one-time opportunity. You can create new fields whenever you want as your needs change, delete ones you no longer use, or even set up new options for existing fields.

To do any of this, choose Layout→Define Fields. The now-familiar Define Database Fields dialog box appears, as shown in Figure 4-5. To change a field's type, select its name in the list, choose a new field type from the pop-up menu, and click Modify (or press Return).

At this point, a message warns that you may lose some information when you convert a field from one type to another. For example, if you transform a text field into a number field, you'll lose any *words* you've typed into those fields (because regular alphabet letters aren't allowed in the number field).

Tip: The Undo command doesn't work after you've made changes to the name, type, or field options of your fields. Particularly if you already have data entered in the database, therefore, be especially careful when making such changes. One way to protect yourself: Make a backup copy of the database file before making such changes. Then, if your changes backfire, you can always go back to the unaltered file.

To rename a field, click its existing name in the list, type a new field name, and then click Modify. To change the options for a particular field, double-click its name in the list. Modify the options as needed, and click OK.

Deleting field definitions

Sometimes you create fields—and then, as you work with the database, you realize you really don't need them. The safest way to get rid of such a field is to delete it from your layouts, as described in the next section. Doing so removes the fields from the screen, but not from the database—in case of future emergency, you can put them right back onto your layouts, with the data still intact.

However, you *can* remove a field once and for all, so that it's irretrievable. In the Define Fields dialog box, click its name in the field list and then click Delete. An alert box appears to ask you if you really know what you're doing: permanently deleting the field *and* all information you may have typed into this field in all of your records. You can't undo this move, so be sure of your decision before clicking OK.

Phase 3: Fill In the Blanks

As soon as you click Done after defining fields, you get your first view of the database window—in the Browse mode. AppleWorks automatically creates a generic layout of these fields—titled Layout 1 (Figure 4-18).

Entering Data

A brand-new database contains only one record—empty. You are ready to start typing information into the fields you've so intelligently set up.

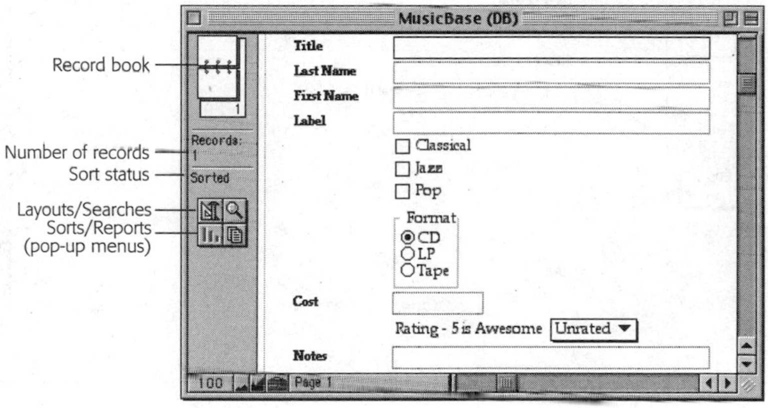

Figure 4-18:
This layout shows in one column all your new fields and their default labels. Your database is ready to go. The controls at the left side of the screen let you navigate your database; for example, you can click the "pages" of the Record book to view the previous or next record (or click, and type a new number over, the record number just beneath it to jump elsewhere in the database). The four clustered icons are pop-up menus that control layouts, searches, sorts, and reports, all described later in this chapter.

Data-entry basics

To do so, notice which field has the *darkened outline*—in the case of the sample music collection database, the Title field (the first one you created)—is outlined. When you start to type, this is where your typing will go. Here are the basics of filling in AppleWorks database records:

- When you've finished typing the information into one field, you can jump to the next field by clicking there—but you may find it more convenient to press the Tab key. Doing so automatically highlights the next field. (In a newly created database, the Tab key highlights fields in the order you created them. In the next section, you'll learn how to change the tab order to whatever you prefer.)

- To jump back into the previous field, press Shift-Tab.

- Once you've highlighted a particular field, you can replace its contents (if it has any) by backspacing over what's there. It's usually faster, however, to highlight the existing contents by a triple-clicking it, by choosing Edit→Select All, or best of all, to use the Select All keyboard shortcut: ⌘-A. Once you've highlighted the contents of the field, just type to replace it.

- If you have more information than will fit within a field—an especially long album title, for example—just keep typing. The field grows automatically to contain all your data. When you move to another field, don't be alarmed—the expanded field contracts to its previous size. But everything you type is still there, which you can prove to yourself by clicking the field again.

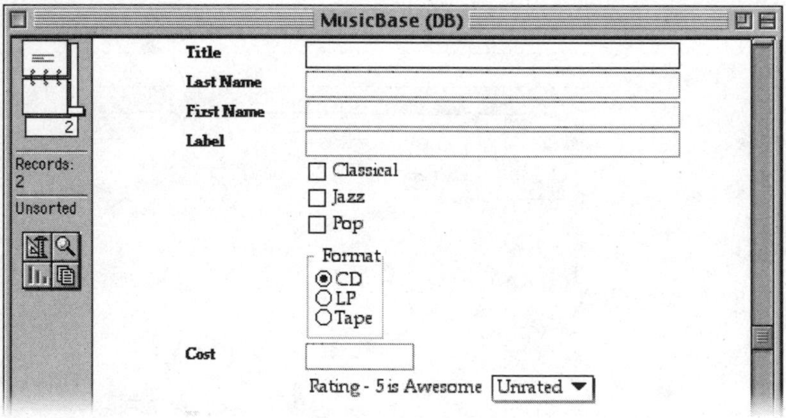

Figure 4-19:
The new record appears, looking identical to the last one, except it's devoid of data—except for any automatic entry options that you may have specified when defining field options. In the database tools panel, the Record book tells you you're looking at record 2, and below it, AppleWorks shows the total number of records in the database is now also 2.

- When you've finished filling out as many fields as you want in the first record, you'd be wise to save your work by choosing File→Save.

Now it's time to create a new, blank record. You do that by choosing Edit→New Record (or by pressing its keyboard equivalent, ⌘-R; or by choosing New Record from the contextual menu). AppleWorks responds by producing an exact, blank duplicate of the set of fields you've just filled in, as shown in Figure 4-19. You can begin the field-filling process anew.

Tip: If you need to create several duplicate database records–for example, one for each of the Project Mercury stamps in your stamp collection–you can create several copies at once (and then change only what's different in each record). To do so, use the Scripts menu (the scroll icon in your menu bar). Choose Scripts→Database→Duplicates Record Multiple. Enter the number of duplicate records you need and then click OK. AppleWorks cranks through the duplication, adding the number of records you specified.

Moving between records

AppleWorks provides several ways to move back and forth through your records once you've created them. The Record book in the database tools panel (see Figure 4-18) displays the number of the current record and serves as a navigation tool: click the top half of the book to scroll backward through your records, click the bottom half to scroll forward, or drag the protruding "bookmark" to move rapidly through your records. You can also use the vertical scroll bar to scroll through your records.

AppleWorks also provides a complete range of keyboard commands to help you move through your records.

Keyboard Shortcut	Action
Tab	Move to next field
Shift-Tab	Move to previous field
⌘-Return or ⌘-Down Arrow	Move to next record
Shift-⌘-Return or ⌘-Up Arrow	Move to previous record
⌘-G	Go to a record by number, as identified by the number underneath the little book icon (at the upper-left corner of the screen).

Tutorial: Filling in the Music Collection

If you've been following the music database example, you've put a good deal of time into setting up the fields. Here's a typical example of how you might input the information from the first two CDs.

These instructions assume that you're staring at the screen shown in Figure 4-19, a blank set of fields before you.

1. **Type the name of the first recording**—*Kind of Blue,* for example. **Press Tab.**

   Learning to press the Tab key is essential to your mastery of the AppleWorks database.

   Now your cursor is blinking in the Last Name field.

2. **Type the artist's last name, or the name of the band**—*Davis,* in this case. **Press Tab.**

The Last Name field is the one required name field in the database, so use it for one-name artists, like Sade, Madonna, or Sting; or groups, like the Rolling Stones, the Kronos Quartet, or the Birmingham Symphony Orchestra.

Tip: If a name or title begins with "The," don't type that part. If you do, when you sort your collection alphabetically, all such groups will be listed under "The."

The cursor is now waiting for your next entry in the First Name field.

3. **Type the artist's first name (if any) such as *Miles*, and then press Tab.**

   If you're typing the name of a group, don't type anything; just press Tab.

   If the artist uses his middle name or a nickname, you can enter it here along with the first name—for example, *Julian "Cannonball" (Adderly)*.

   Now the cursor is blinking in the Recording Label field, and the drop-down menu appears.

4. **Choose one of the names in the list, or type a new one.**

   There are several ways to choose from the value list (see Figure 4-20).

   - Scroll through the list with the mouse, and then double-click your selection. Press Tab to move to the next field.

   - Use the up- and down-arrow keys to choose an item in the list; then press Enter. Press Tab to move to the next field.

   - Type the first letter or two of your choice to select it in the list, then press Enter. Press Tab to move to the next field.

   - If the value list doesn't contain the name you want, press Esc, Return, or Enter as soon as you tab into the field. AppleWorks hides the list, so that you can type in your entry and then press Tab to move to the next field. (The Esc key also means, "oops." That is, if you've already begun to scroll through the value list, or you've already typed to highlight one of the canned choices, Esc collapses the list so that you can manually type a new entry.)

     Suppose, for example, that your album was made by Columbia Records; just type *Co.* If Columbia isn't in your list, the list jumps to the closest match—for example, *Capitol.* To enter a name not on the list, press Esc, and then type.

5. **Press Tab to highlight the first Category checkbox.**

   Remember that each checkbox is actually a separate field. In other words, you'll have to press Tab repeatedly until the checkbox you want is selected.

6. **Keep pressing Tab until the desired category is outlined—in this case, Jazz. Then press the Space bar, or any letter or number key, to put an X in the checkbox.**

   If you tab too far, press Shift-Tab to move through the fields (checkboxes) in reverse. And if you check the wrong checkbox, press the Space bar—or any other key—to remove the X. (Of course, you can also *click* a checkbox to add or remove an X.)

7. **Continue pressing Tab until you highlight the Format field.**

   Radio buttons aren't the same as checkboxes—all the radio buttons are part of the same field. Instead of Tab, therefore, you press the *Space bar* repeatedly to highlight the radio buttons in turn.

8. **Press the Space bar repeatedly to cycle through the radio buttons, or use the arrow keys to do the same. When the correct button is turned on—*CD*, in this example—press Tab.**

   You can, of course, also use the mouse to make your radio button selection.

9. **Type the price you paid for the recording into the Cost field: *15*. Press Tab.**

   Don't type a dollar sign, and don't bother with the decimal point if it's a round dollar amount. In the next section you'll learn how to format the field so that it automatically adds the dollar sign, the decimal point, and the zeros.

10. **Enter the date you acquired this disc in the Date Purchased field. Press Tab.**

    If you got it this year, dispense with the year and just enter the month and day—for example, *3/21*. In fact, you can enter the date in a variety of formats—*3/21, 3-21, March 21, Mar 21*; AppleWorks re-formats it for you to match the date format you prefer. You'll learn how to specify that format in the next section.

11. **Type any notes you want to for this selection: the names of other musicians in the band, the date it was recorded, whatever. Press Tab.**

    If you created a Rating pop-up menu, use any of the four arrow keys to cycle through the choices, or click the pop-up menu and make your selection. (On a scale of 1 to 5, *Kind of Blue* is definitely a 5.)

    Congratulations! You've completed data entry for your first CD. Choose File→Save to preserve your work.

12. **Press ⌘-R to create a new record for your next recording.**

    Before AppleWorks allows you to move on to another record, it warns you if any of your entries don't meet the requirements you set using the verification options.

    For example, suppose you added a new recording label that wasn't one of the choices in the value list. AppleWorks displays an alert message that offers three choices, as shown in Figure 4-20.

List Mode

As described earlier in this chapter, AppleWorks offers four different *modes* of operation in its database. Whether you realize it or not, you're now in Browse mode, where you can type actual information into your database. (To check your current mode, open the Layout menu and see which of the first commands has a checkmark.)

You can add data to your database only in the Browse or List modes. You can switch between modes using the commands in the Layout menu, the buttons in the Button bar, using keyboard shortcuts, or by Control-clicking anywhere in the database window. (A pop-up contextual menu appears, whose commands you can use to switch modes.)

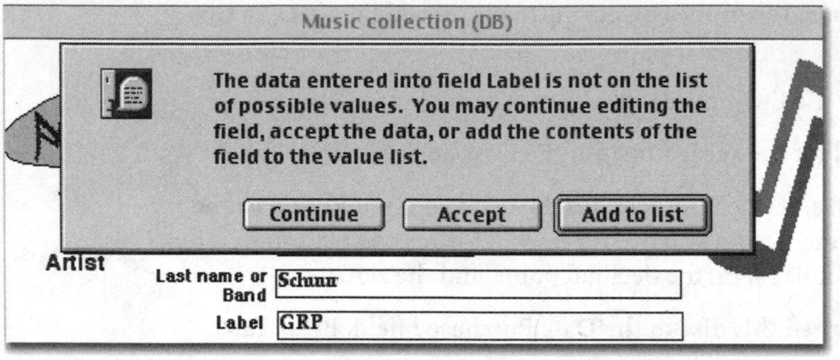

Figure 4-20:
When you type a value that isn't one of the value-list choices, AppleWorks offers you three courses of action. You can choose from the value list (Continue), accept what you typed, or add what you typed to the list of choices, so that in the future, it will appear in the list (Add to List).

Although Browse mode so far looks like a vertical list of the fields you set up, it's easy to switch to a horizontal, sometimes equally useful view of your data—List mode. Choose Layout→List to reveal this view, which looks like a giant spreadsheet. You can think of this view as a master directory that includes every field and every bit of data you've ever recorded in the database, as shown in Figure 4-21.

Figure 4-21:
The unloved and un-lovely—yet essential—List mode. By reducing your database to this spreadsheet format, AppleWorks provides access to every fragment of data associated with the database. In other words, List mode offers a master layout that shows every field of every record, even those that may be hidden on your other layouts.

You can fiddle around with List-mode fields—changing their width or order, for example—just by dragging them. (You don't have to switch into Layout mode to do so, as you do when adjusting other kinds of database views.)

That's fortunate, because every list view requires a little bit of adjustment; when List mode first opens, the fields appear in the order in which you created them, and every column is the same width. Here's how you go about adjusting the list view to your satisfaction:

Change column order or width

When your cursor approaches the title region of a column, it becomes a little box with double arrows, as shown in Figure 4-22. You can drag a column anywhere else in the list to reposition it.

When your cursor approaches the dividing line between two columns, it sprouts double arrows. At this point, you can drag a divider line horizontally to make the column to the cursor's left wider or narrower, also shown in Figure 4-22.

Note: AppleWorks won't allow you to hide columns by reducing their width to zero (as you can in a spreadsheet). Columns always remind you of their presence by showing at least a sliver.

Figure 4-22:
As shown here by the highlighted cursors, you can adjust the List mode columns in several ways. You can drag a column heading to move that entire column horizontally relative to other columns (top). You can adjust a column's width by dragging the dividing line between it and the next column (middle). Likewise, you can make a row taller or shorter by dragging the horizontal dividing line beneath it (bottom). If you Shift-click several row or column heads before performing these moves, you can operate on several columns simultaneously.

Change row height

You can make the rows of this display taller, too. Move the cursor carefully into the narrow margin to left of the columns, as shown in Figure 4-22. When the cursor touches one of the horizontal dividing lines, its shape changes yet again. Drag downward to make the upper row taller, or upward to make it shorter. (If you make the row tall enough, you can see more than one line of text, which can be useful when your text fields contain more than a few words—like the Title field in the music-collection database, for example).

Phase 4: Design New Layouts

The generic layout, where all of the fields appear in a tidy stacked column, is functional, if lacking in elegant design. The fields are arranged in the order you created them—which isn't always the most efficient arrangement for entering data. They all use a boring font, and all appear equally important.

Fortunately, you can drag these fields around into a different order, move some of them to the top of the screen, make some bold, make some blue, change the typeface, add borders and arrows, and otherwise give your database a visual kick. But to do any of this, you must switch into yet another database mode—a special graphic design window called Layout mode.

Note: The terms *layout* and *Layout mode* can be confusing. A layout is the view of your database—the way you see you data in Browse and Find modes. AppleWorks creates a new database with just one layout, but you can create as many others as you need. Layout *mode* is where you create new and modify existing layouts by choosing which fields to include and how to display them.

In Layout mode, you're not "using" the database—you can't even see your data. Instead, you're at the drawing board where you control how the database looks. The beauty of the AppleWorks database (and its more expensive, more professional big brother, FileMaker Pro) is that you can create multiple layouts for any one database file—so that one collection of data can be displayed in many different ways, for different purposes.

A layout can show all your fields, but it doesn't have to. For example, a database of student school records might have one layout with class and grade information, another just for attendance, and a third for printing mailing labels.

The Layout mode resembles the AppleWorks drawing module: you manipulate objects on the screen, draw or import new objects, and set up the document for printing. The difference, however, is that in the database Layout mode, some of those objects are *fields* that are associated with the storehouse of information in your database.

For the music-collection database, it will be helpful to create three layouts for three different tasks.

- **A data-entry layout.** This is the view you'll use when you sit down with the latest shipment from the record club and enter all the information about each recording into the database.

- **A search layout.** This is the layout you'll routinely use to *retrieve* information from the database—to see if you have the Bartók Violin Concerto No. 2 in your collection, or to find the correct title of that Charles Mingus album that has something to do with Tijuana.

- **A report layout.** This layout will be designed to print a list of records from the database and to provide a total of your monetary investment in the collection. You'll be able to print a master list of all your recordings, or sort out a subset of the database in order to print, for example, a list of all your Ice-T discs.

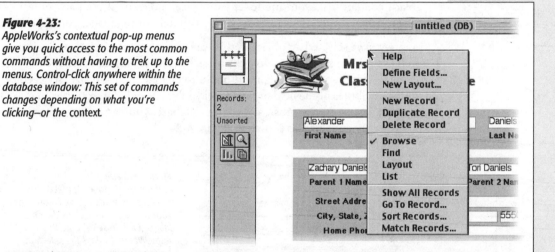

Figure 4-23:
AppleWorks's contextual pop-up menus give you quick access to the most common commands without having to trek up to the menus. Control-click anywhere within the database window: This set of commands changes depending on what you're clicking—or the context.

UP TO SPEED

Switching Modes

You'll be doing a lot of mode switching during the database design and testing phase. There are several ways to accomplish this chore.

Choose Layout→and select a mode from the menu.

Use the contextual pop-up menu and select the mode from the menu.

Use the Button bar buttons—although only Browse and List mode are installed in the default Button bar set. You can customize the Button bar to include Layout and Find modes.

Use keyboard commands. This is the quickest way to switch modes, once you memorize the key combinations: ⌘-Shift plus the first letter of the mode: Browse, Layout, or Find. Most people rarely use List mode—they ignore it, and so its keyboard shortcut is ⌘-Shift-I—for "Ignore."

1. **Switch to the Layout mode by choosing Layout→Layout.**

   Of course, you can switch instead using any of the other methods described in the "Switching Modes" sidebar.

   Layout mode looks almost like Browse mode—except instead of data, each field shows only the field name and a rectangle (see Figure 4-24). The database tool panel disappears, and layout grid lines show in the background.

2. **Click a field or its label.**

   When you do so, you see the tiny black handles around its edges. You'll get to know these black handles very well in AppleWorks—they're *everywhere* in the Drawing module described in Chapter 6. Exactly as in that Drawing module, the black handles in Layout mode let you resize, move, or stretch any object—but their primary purpose is to show you which field or field label you've selected.

   Once you've selected an object in this way, you can press Delete or Backspace to remove it from the screen. Drag the black handles to resize or reshape the object. Use the commands in the Format menu to change the font, size, style, color, or other attributes of the field or field label you've clicked. For example, to make the title stand out in the music collection database, you can enlarge the field and increase the font size, as shown in Figure 4-24.

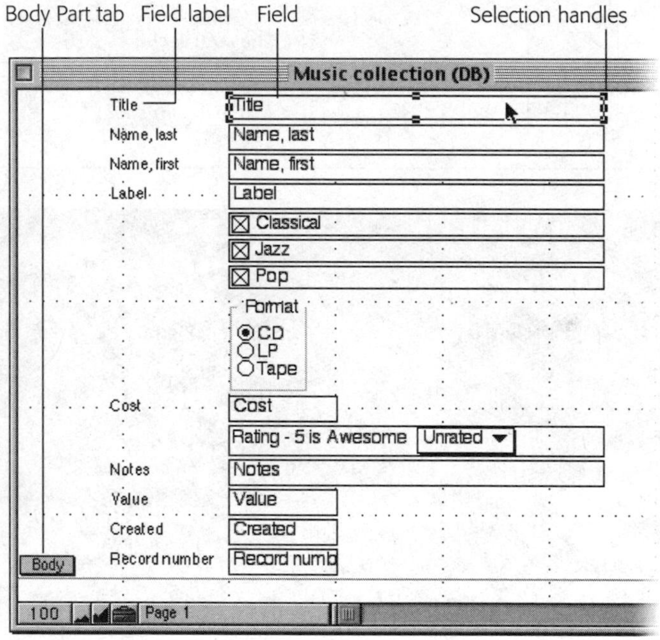

Figure 4-24:
In the Layout mode, AppleWorks displays the fields you've created for your database, as well as the field labels. Click to select a field; AppleWorks displays the selection handles, which you can drag to resize the field or field label. You can change the font of any selected field or label using the font controls in the Format menu. Making its first appearance is the Body Part tab and dividing line, described in this section. The layout shown here has only one part.

Note: The size of a field on the layout determines the amount of text AppleWorks will *print*. Even if you've typed a whole page's worth of text into a text field, in other words, only two words of it will print out if that's how big the field is on the *layout*. Adjust the size of the field in order to print as much of it as you need.

Layout Parts

AppleWorks lets you divide a database layout into *parts*—that is, different broad horizontal bands that subdivide the page. Every layout contains a Body part, which holds most of your fields; creating other parts is optional. When you create a new layout, it begins life with just a Body part.

Header and Footer parts

You can add a *Header* or *Footer* part to a layout, too—recurring stripes of information that appear at the top or bottom of every page. These headers and footers appear only on the layout in which they were inserted—on screen and in print. They may include, for example, the column headings for a list report, or the database name, the date and time, and so on (see Figure 4-25).

You can also drag *fields* into a Header or Footer part. For example, a fund-raising database header could say, "So far, 364 people have donated a total of $4,682.59 toward our goal of $12,000," where the number of donors and the total donated are summary calculation fields.

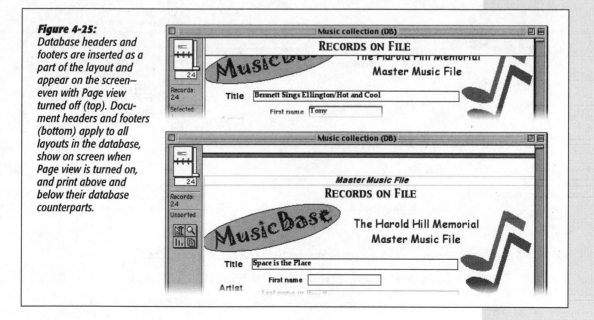

Figure 4-25:
Database headers and footers are inserted as a part of the layout and appear on the screen— even with Page view turned off (top). Document headers and footers (bottom) apply to all layouts in the database, show on screen when Page view is turned on, and print above and below their database counterparts.

Document headers and footers

In addition to the database-specific Header and Footer *parts* described above, AppleWorks allows you to also use regular *document* headers and footers—the kind you use with word-processing and other AppleWorks modules. These appear on every page of a database document, no matter which layout you're in. Document headers and footers can only contain text, so can't include database fields.

You can use both kinds of headers and footers at the same time in an AppleWorks database. Document headers appear above a database Header part and document footers appear below a database Footer part. On the fund-raising example, a document header could contain the agency name and address that prints on all pages, regardless of which layout is in use (see Figure 4-25).

Summary parts

AppleWorks provides three other parts you can add to a layout: *Leading* and *Trailing grand summaries*, and *Sub-summaries*. These parts provide totals, averages, and other summary information calculated from all the records in the database. When you create printed reports from your database, summary parts come in especially handy. For all the details on summaries and summary reports, see "Reports" on page 130.

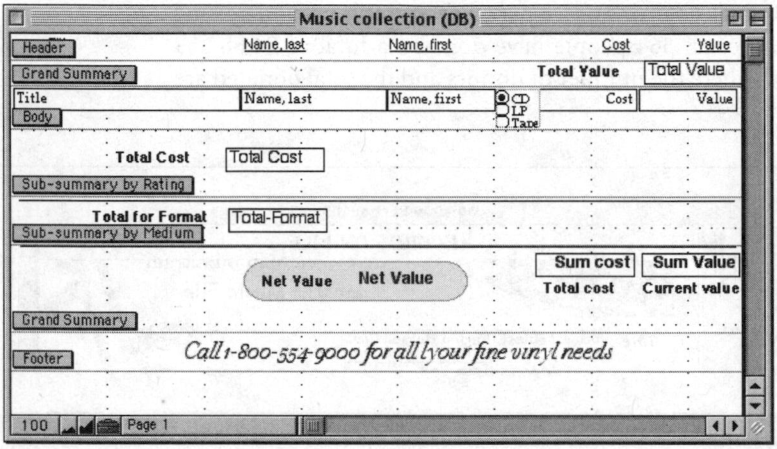

Figure 4-26:
For illustration purposes, all the possible parts are included in this one layout. You can drag the dividing line of a part label to resize any part. You can also include regular document headers and footers in addition to the layout headers and footers shown here. Insert them in the Browse mode; they'll print at the very top and bottom of every printed page. Remove an unwanted part by removing its contents, then dragging the part up to the top of the window, where it disappears.

How to create a part

Inserting any of the parts follows the same basic procedure.

- Make sure you're in Layout mode. Choose Layout→Insert Part.

- Choose the part type using the radio buttons in the Insert Part dialog box.

- Click OK. AppleWorks closes the dialog box and inserts the new part in the layout.

Tutorial Layout 1: the Data-Entry Layout

AppleWorks created a basic layout for the music collection database, as shown in Figure 4-24. It's functional, but definitely not pretty. By making a few changes to this layout, you can not only make it nicer to look at, but also easier to use. This will be the data-entry layout, the one you'll use every time you come home from the record store.

To create a new layout, you can modify the default layout, create a new layout completely from scratch, or start with one of AppleWorks's other prefab layouts.

In this example, you may as well create a new layout, thus preserving the basic starter layout in case you ever need to refer to it.

1. **Choose Layout→New Layout.**

   The New Layout dialog box appears, as shown in Figure 4-27.

2. **Give the layout a descriptive name and choose a Layout Type.**

   Data Entry wouldn't be a bad choice for a name. Leave the Layout Type set to Standard—or select Duplicate. (Since our existing layout *is* the standard style, either choice produces the same result.)

3. **Click OK.**

   You are now looking at the newly created Data Entry layout. Yes, it looks just the same as the original layout.

Figure 4-27:
The New Layout dialog box is where you begin your layout artistry. After naming the layout choose Standard to create a default layout like the one in the background; Duplicate to make a clone of the current layout; Blank to provide a completely empty canvas; "Columnar report" to create a list style, with the fields arrayed in columns; and Labels to set up for printing labels.

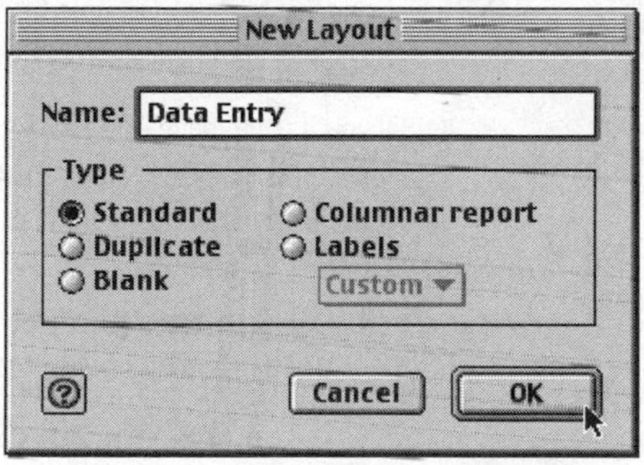

New Layout

Name: Data Entry

Type
- ● Standard   ○ Columnar report
- ○ Duplicate   ○ Labels
- ○ Blank   Custom ▼

Cancel   OK

Tip: When you have similar or identical layouts—as you do now—the only way to determine which layout you're looking at is to examine the list of layouts at the bottom of the Layout menu. You should see *Layout 1* and *Data Entry;* the checkmark indicates the layout you're now viewing.

---

4. **Choose Layout→Layout to return to Layout mode. Drag the Body tag downward about an inch to increase the size of the body part.**

   It would be nice to create a bold headline at the top of this layout that identifies your database as, for example, MusicBase. At the moment, however, there's no room for such a headline. You'll need to move all the fields and labels out of the way.

5. **Choose Edit→Select All.**

   Selection handles appear on every item in the layout.

6. **Drag any one of the highlighted objects downward about an inch to give yourself some space at the top.**

   Instead of using the mouse, you can also press the down-arrow key repeatedly (or simply hold it down). Pressing the arrow keys is a very useful trick—it shifts any highlighted objects in Layout mode in the corresponding direction. (If, using the Options menu, you've turned on the Autogrid, the arrow key nudges the object by one ruler notch; if the grid is off, by one pixel.)

7. **Click outside of the selected objects to deselect them.**

   The little black handles disappear.

   If the AppleWorks tool panel isn't sitting there to the left of the window, click the red toolbox icon at the bottom of the window (next to the words "Page 1").

8. **In the Tool panel, click the big A, which is the Text tool.**

   A gray background appears behind the big A icon, indicating that the Text tool is selected.

Tip: Clicking the Text tool (or any AppleWorks tool) selects it for *one-time* use. As soon as you're finished using that tool—for example, after you type something with the Text tool—AppleWorks thinks it's doing you a favor by automatically re-selecting the Arrow tool.

If you'd rather have AppleWorks leave your selected tool alone—for example, if you want to create several text blocks in a row, without having to click the Text tool each time—just *double-click* the Text tool to lock it on. Now it stays active until you click another tool.

---

9. **Click in the space you just created above the fields. Type a name for the database—for example, *MusicBase*.**

   If you like, you can click the Text tool again, click below the title, and type in a subtitle or credit line, such as *My First Database, Copyright 2000.*

10. **Click the Arrow pointer on the Tools window, click the title you just created, and use the Format menu to make the title more impressive.**

    When you click the title you typed, AppleWorks displays the selection handles around it. Now you can choose Format→Font and Format→Size to specify a more interesting font in a larger size. Repeat this process for the subtitle, if you made one.

    Now that you've got a classy headline, your next job is to rearrange the fields, resize them, and remove any that are not needed, all in the effort to make this data-entry layout clear, logical, and attractive. Think about the order that will work best for data entry. For example, when you're typing in the information from a CD you've just bought, a reasonable order might be: Title, Artist, Label, Format, Category, Cost, Notes.

11. **Drag the Record Number field and its label to a bottom corner of the body, as shown in Figure 4-28. Do the same with the Created field and *its* label.**

These fields store administrative details about each record that AppleWorks automatically enters for you. You could, of course, remove them entirely from this layout and not miss them most of the time, but instead tuck them into a corner, and reduce their size. This way you'll still be able to see at a glance how many recordings you've entered into the database.

***

Tip: If you've deleted a field from your layout, you can bring it back by choosing Layout→Insert Field; when the list of all your fields appears, double-click the one you want.

You can even create entirely *new* fields for your database, even when you're in the Layout mode. Just choose Layout→Define Fields, and proceed as you did when you were first setting up your database. When you exit the Define Fields dialog box, you'll find your new field automatically added to the current layout. (If you want the new field to appear on any other layouts, you must do it yourself.)

***

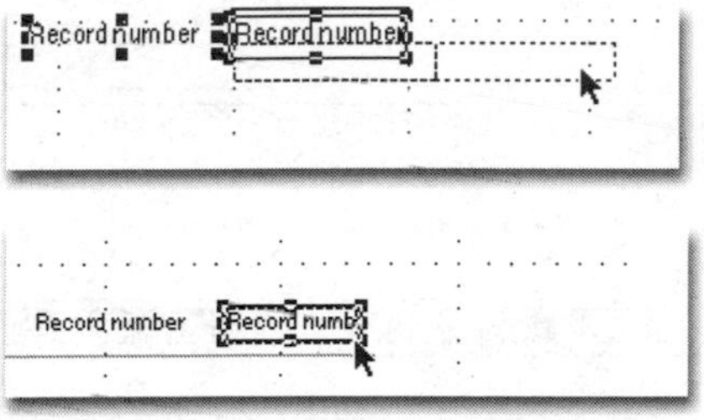

Figure 4-28:
To highlight both the Record Number field and its label, click the field, and then Shift-click its label. (Shift-clicking, in AppleWorks, means add to this selection.) Now drag either one of the highlighted objects to move it to a remote corner of the layout; both go along for the ride (top). Then, after shrinking the point size, drag the lower-right black handles to make the fields themselves smaller (bottom).

12. **Shift-click all four of the objects you just moved. Choose Format→Size→9 Point to change their font size to 9 point.**

You want to make these administrative records seem less important, yet still readable. After making the font so much smaller, you can shrink the fields to a more appropriate size using the resizing handles (see Figure 4-28, bottom).

13. **Continue to reposition the rest of the fields and labels until you have them rearranged to your liking—or until it resembles Figure 4-29.**

You can jazz up your layout by using colored text, drawing background objects, pasting clip art from Clippings (Chapter 9)—in other words, all the standard AppleWorks drawing tools and techniques (Chapter 6) are available to you.

Don't feel bound to keep the field labels that AppleWorks provides. Each field label is an object—you can rename or delete it as you like. For example, you might decide to change the label for the Last Name field from "Last Name" to "Last name (or group name)."

Tip: To change a field's font, size, or style, double-click the field to bring up the Style formatting window. Doing so is the same as choosing Edit→Field Info—but much quicker. In this one window you can adjust all the text formatting attributes for the field. (This trick works only for fields, not field labels. To format a label, you must click it and then use the commands in the Format menu.)

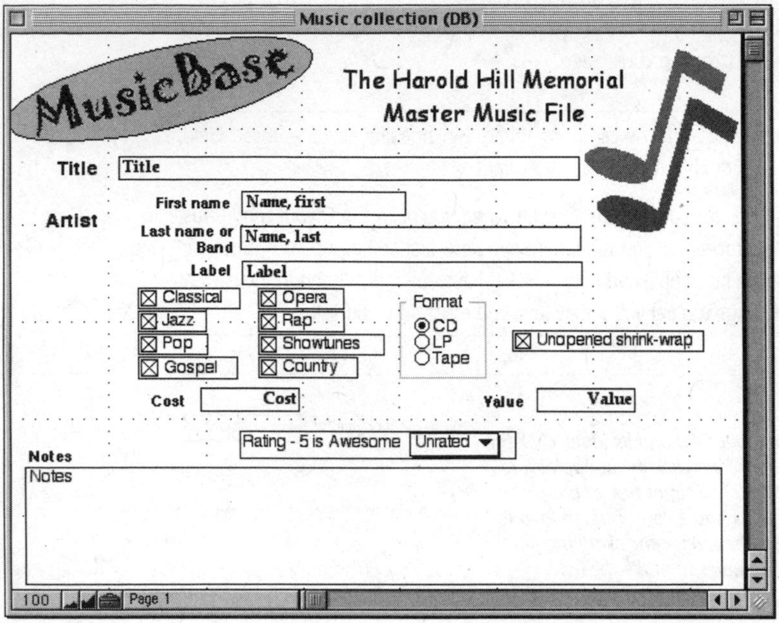

Figure 4-29:
If you or the users of the database are going to spend much time working with the database, spend some time on the layout designs. Make the window large enough to fill most of your monitor. Use the same good design principles you'd use on paper: Don't go wild with fonts—strive for readability. Use plenty of white space. Group fields logically. Use graphics sparingly.

Set tab order

When you're typing information into your database, pressing the Tab key propels your cursor into the next field, in the order they were created. That isn't always the way you want to fill things out, however. After you rearrange the placement of fields on the layout, you may require a different order—or, as shown in Figure 4-29, you may sometimes want to fill in a little cluster of fields out of sequence.

Fortunately, AppleWorks makes it easy to define a new *tab order*—a new sequence that AppleWorks will follow each time you press the Tab key.

1. **Choose Layout→Tab Order.**

    The Tab Order dialog box appears, with all the fields included in the layout listed in creation order in the scrolling Field List on the left. (See Figure 4-30.) On the right is the Tab Order list. Unfortunately, you can't rearrange the order of fields in this list by dragging; you must rebuild the list item by item.

2. **Click Clear to remove all the entries in the Tab Order list.**

   You can also select one field at a time, and then click Move to remove each one from the list.

3. **Scroll through the Field List. Double-click the fields in the order in which you'd like to fill them in (such as the sequence shown in Figure 4-30).**

   Refer to your layout as you think about the order you'd like; you may have to reposition the Tab Order window—by dragging its title bar—so that you can see both it and the layout simultaneously. Imagine the process of entering data from a CD; create the tab order to match the logical order for filling out the form. Include all the fields you may need to enter data into, even those fields you don't use every time (such as the Notes field).

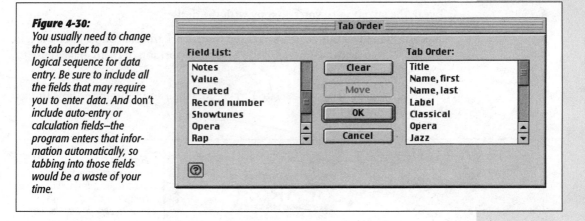

Figure 4-30:
You usually need to change the tab order to a more logical sequence for data entry. Be sure to include all the fields that may require you to enter data. And don't include auto-entry or calculation fields—the program enters that information automatically, so tabbing into those fields would be a waste of your time.

4. **Click OK (or press Enter).**

   From now on, when you're back in Browse mode, pressing the Tab key makes the cursor jump to the fields in the order you've specified. You've taken another step toward making data entry as easy as possible.

Tutorial Layout 2: The Search Screen

The second layout for the music collection will be a variation on the data-entry layout. This is the layout that will appear when you want to *look up* information in the database. Of course, you can actually perform searches using *any* layout; but for practice, suppose that you want a Search screen that's not cluttered by unnecessary fields.

Instead of creating this layout from scratch, use the data-entry layout as a starting point.

1. **With the data-entry layout on the screen, choose Layout→New Layout to bring up the New Layout dialog box. Type a name for the new layout—*Search*—select the Duplicate radio button and click OK.**

You return to whatever mode you were using.

2. **Choose Layout→Layout. Delete any fields that aren't required for music searching.**

   For example, you'll probably rarely need to search for a CD by its cost or record number. To delete one of these fields, click it and then press your Delete or Backspace key. (To delete several fields simultaneously, Shift-click them before pressing Delete or Backspace.)

3. **Make the Title and Artist fields larger so they stand out.**

   Shift-click the Title, First Name, and Last Name fields to select all three of them. Choose Format→Size→18, for example.

   You may need to drag the small black handles to make the field boxes themselves large enough to accommodate the new font.

4. **Tweak the layout until you're happy with the design.**

   Dress it up with additional titles, colored fonts, background colors, or clip art, if you wish. Drag fields around until the order and position of them make sense to you, as shown in Figure 4-31.

As you modify layouts, switch back to Browse mode periodically, to see how things look with real data in the fields.

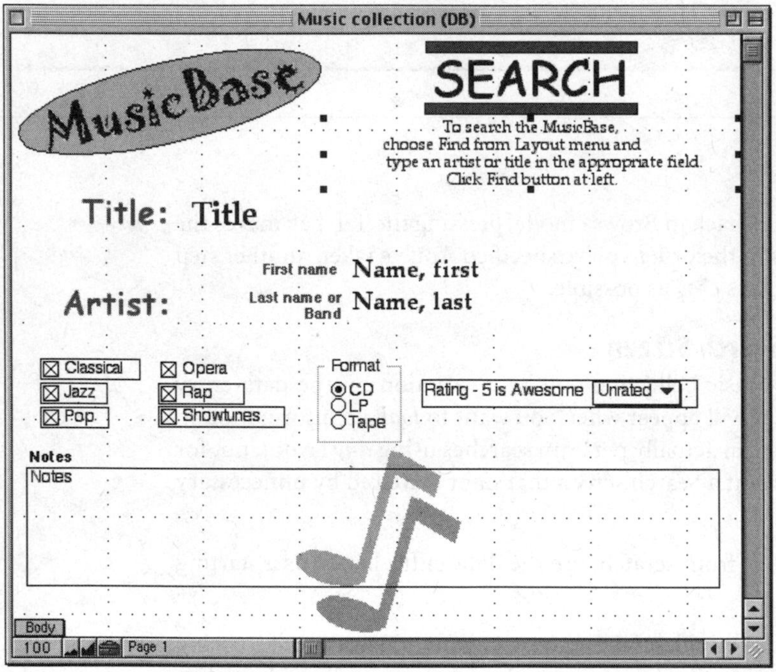

Figure 4-31:
If you're not the only one to be using this database, consider adding instructions to explain how to search for a title or artist. Click the text tool and click a spot in the layout near the place you want your instructions. Type the instructions, then reformat and reposition the text as needed to make this layout easier for other people to understand.

Create a layout from the ground up

If you need to make a layout that is not at all similar to any that you already have, start from square one: a blank screen.

1. **Choose Layout→New Layout.**

   The Label Name dialog box appears.

2. **Type a name for your new layout, such as** *Search by Recording Label.* **Click the Blank radio button, and then click OK.**

   A completely blank layout appears.

3. **Choose Layout→Insert Field.**

   The Insert Fields dialog box appears, listing all the fields you've defined in the database.

4. **While pressing the ⌘ key, click the fields you want to include in the layout.**

   Pressing that key lets you highlight more than one item simultaneously, even if they aren't adjacent in the list.

5. **Click Insert (or press Return).**

   AppleWorks inserts the fields into the layout. You may need to drag the Body separator line downward to make the layout big enough to accommodate all the fields.

   Now go to town repositioning, formatting, and resizing the fields. Add any other text, graphic elements, or colors, if you're feeling creative, using the graphics tools described in Chapter 6. If you forgot to include a field, choose Layout→Insert Field to get back to the Insert Fields dialog box.

FREQUENTLY ASKED QUESTION

Formatting List View

I'm confused—how do I adjust the List mode layout? I want to change the fonts, but List mode doesn't seem to show up my list of layouts.

The List mode *is* a bit peculiar. First of all, it isn't *really* a mode—it's a fixed, list-view layout forever stuck in the Browse mode. It's designed as a safety net: no matter how badly you may have mangled the other layouts, by deleting all fields from them, for example, you can always switch to List mode to see all your fields, with all their data.

Unlike other layouts in Browse mode, you can change the display of the List mode directly. You can format individual words or fields by selecting them and using the font commands in the Format menu. Click the field name in a column heading to select the column; click the little box on the left end of a row to select the entire row. Then use the Format menu commands to change the font, size, style, or color. See "List Mode," earlier in this chapter, for more information about this singular mode.

Tutorial Layout 3: the List Report

The final layout for this database is a list view for printing, otherwise known as a *Report,* like the one shown in Figure 4-17. Reports usually provide more information than just a printout of some of your data. You usually want to include some kind of summary information—totals, averages, and so on—to make the listing of data more meaningful. For your valuable record collection, for example, you might want to calculate the total cost and number of recordings in the collection.

In this example, you'll create a new layout—this time of the Columnar Report variety—that includes only the Title, Names, Cost, and Value fields. Refer to Figure 4-17.

1. **Choose Layout→Layout to switch to Layout mode, then choose Layout→New Layout.**

   The New Layout dialog box appears.

2. **Type *Music Summary Report;* click the Columnar Report radio button. Click OK.**

   The New Layout dialog box disappears, replaced by the Set Field Order dialog box (see Figure 4-32). Move the fields—in the order you want them to appear—from the left side to the right.

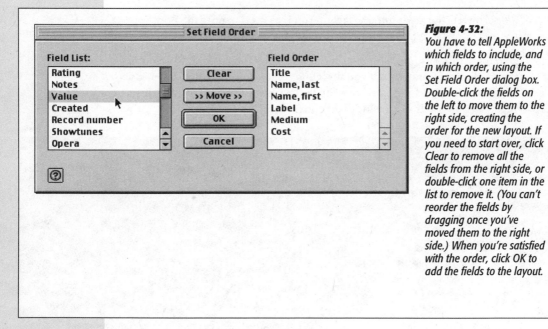

Figure 4-32:
You have to tell AppleWorks which fields to include, and in which order, using the Set Field Order dialog box. Double-click the fields on the left to move them to the right side, creating the order for the new layout. If you need to start over, click Clear to remove all the fields from the right side, or double-click one item in the list to remove it. (You can't reorder the fields by dragging once you've moved them to the right side.) When you're satisfied with the order, click OK to add the fields to the layout.

3. **Click OK.**

   The Columnar Report style layout appears. It features a Header part that contains labels for the columns. These labels are positioned directly above the Body of the layout, which contains a row of fields (see Figure 4-33). What you can't see at this moment is that when you print the report, or when you look at this layout in Browse mode, this Body part will repeat over and over again, creating columns of information (see Figure 4-33). Switch to Browse mode to see the effect, if you like.

Even though this is a simple list display, you can improve its appearance by formatting the cost and value columns and aligning them properly.

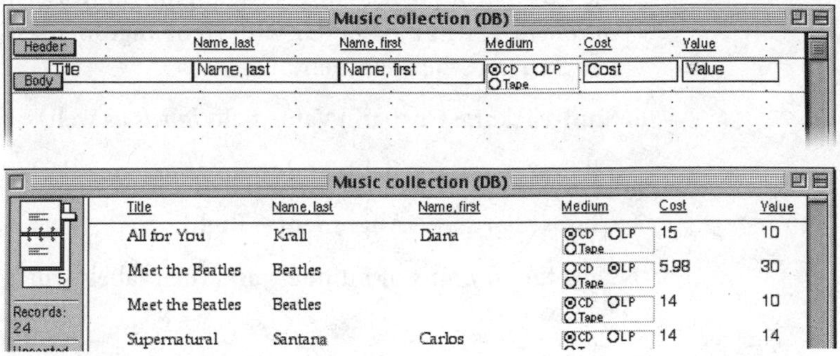

Figure 4-33:
The columnar report style In Layout mode (top), shows as just the header and one row of fields. When you switch back into Browse mode (bottom), every record of the database shows as one row, the fields lined up in columns.

4. In Layout mode, Shift-click to select the Cost and Value fields. Then double-click one of them to open the Number Format dialog box.

You could choose Currency, which would force AppleWorks to insert a dollar sign ($) in front of each number (or whatever currency your localized computer recognizes). However, in a long list of prices like this, the dollar sign would be a distracting and repetitive element. Instead, format the fields like this:

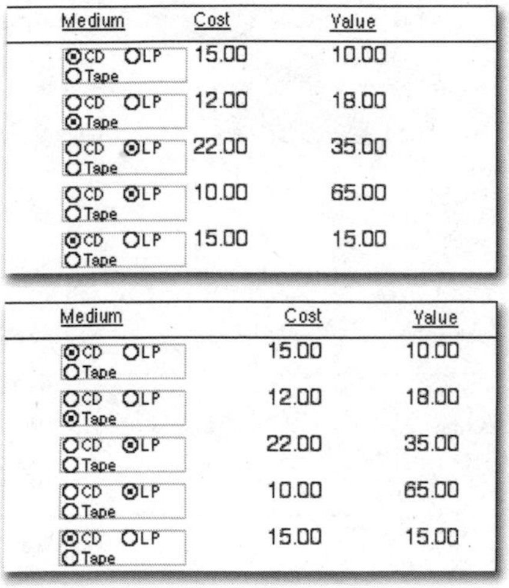

Figure 4-34:
You can greatly improve the appearance and readability of a list by changing number fields from AppleWorks's default left alignment (top) to right alignment (bottom). Be sure to do the same for the field labels.

5. **Click the Fixed radio button. Set the Precision to 2, and then click OK.**

The Precision setting means, "how many decimal places do you want?" Since these are to be monetary amounts, two decimal places is appropriate.

The dialog box disappears, leaving the two fields still selected. AppleWorks formats fields with *left alignment* by default—that is, the text inside a field begins at the left edge of the field box. That alignment works fine for text fields, but not for numbers, which look better with right alignment, so in the following two steps, you'll change the alignment.

6. **Shift-click the Cost and Value field *labels* as well.**

All four items, the fields and their labels, are selected.

7. **Choose Format→Alignment→Right.**

Now the columns of numbers and their labels will line up properly, as shown in Figure 4-34.

Summary parts

The list report layout contains a Header as well as a Body part. These are two of the six kinds of layout *parts* described earlier. The Footer is another part type, one that behaves exactly like the Header except that it appears beneath the body.

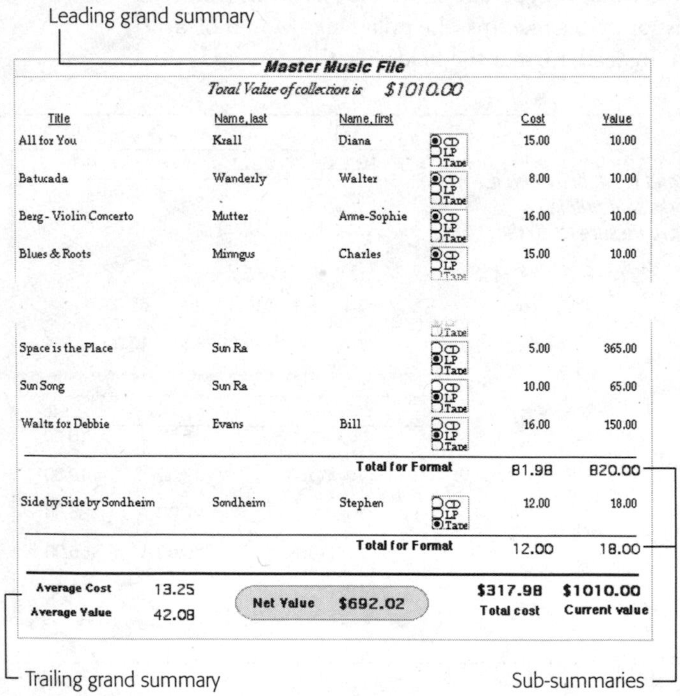

Figure 4-35:
A Leading grand summary displays an impressive figure: the total value of the collection (top). A Trailing grand summary shows a set of perhaps more meaningful totals: the amount invested and the net value of the collection. A Sub-summary calculates a total for CD, LP, and Tape when the database is sorted by Format.

The remaining types of parts aren't terrifically easy to understand. But when carefully used, they add valuable summary information at the bottom of your report pages. They include *Leading* and *Trailing grand summaries*, and *Sub-summaries*.

- **Leading and Trailing grand summaries** (Figure 4-35) display totals, averages—that is, summaries—of information from all the records visible in the database. Leading grand summaries appear at the beginning of the report, and Trailing grand summaries come at the end. They function the same way, calculating from all visible records.

  Use the Leading part type when you just can't wait to get the news out to your readers. The Trailing style is for when you want to finish with a bang—or when you want to put off the bad news as long as possible. (That's why the Amount Due field on your phone bill—the classic example of a Trailing grand summary—appears at the bottom.)

- **Sub-summaries** (Figure 4-35) perform calculations on a subset of the database—to create subtotals of each cluster of records, much the way your phone bill gives you one subtotal beneath the list of domestic calls you've made, and another that follows the international calls. For example, you can set up a Sub-summary to subtotal the value of the LPs in your music collection according to their format. Then, when you sort your database by Format, AppleWorks displays a subtotal for each kind of recording. (In fact, Sub-summaries work *only* when you've sorted your database, as shown in Figure 4-35.)

Summary fields in summary parts

Summary *fields* are a special variety of calculation field. They add up, or find the average of, or perform other functions on a particular field, making them great for creating subtotals and grand totals. If you put a summary field in a Sub-summary part, you get a subtotal; if you put a summary field in a Grand summary part, you get a grand total. (Summary fields don't work at all when you put them in any other kind of part, such as the Body.)

If you've never worked with a database before, this summary concept can be overwhelmingly confusing. The following tutorial, however, should make everything clear.

Tutorial: Create a Grand Summary

Suppose that you want to make your music collection report more informative by revealing the total amount you've spent on your music. The summary field would be just the ticket. Remember, however, that summary *fields* can appear only in Summary *parts;* therefore, adding a Summary part to your layout is the first step.

Before you begin, make sure you're viewing the appropriate layout—in the case of this music-collection database, choose Layout→Music Summary Report.

1. **Choose Layout→Layout. Then choose Layout→Insert Part.**

   The Insert Part dialog box appears.

2. **Click the "Trailing grand summary" radio button, and then click OK.**

   AppleWorks closes the dialog box and inserts the new part at the bottom of the layout. There's nothing in this part yet—in fact, you don't even have any summary fields to put into it yet. Your next step, then, is to define a new field called, for example, Total Cost.

3. **Choose Layout→Define Fields.**

   The Define Fields dialog box appears.

4. **Name the field *Total Cost,* choose Field Type→Summary, and click Create (or press Enter).**

   The Enter Formula for Field "Total Cost" dialog box appears, as shown in Figure 4-36. This is where you're going to tell AppleWorks, using a function, how to calculate the total cost of your collection.

   This function is one of the most often used—and easiest to remember. You're telling AppleWorks to add up—or sum—the contents of the "Cost" field in every record with the formula: SUM('Cost'). The first part—SUM—is one of AppleWorks's built-in functions. The second part of the formula—('Cost')—is the *argument* that tells AppleWorks what you want to sum up.

5. **Choose SUM from the Functions list.**

   AppleWorks inserts *SUM(number1,number2,...)* in the Formula box. You next have to replace the contents of the parentheses with your arguments.

6. **Select the argument placeholders in the formula (everything between the parentheses) and choose *Cost* from the field list.**

   AppleWorks replaces the selection with the chosen field, properly formatted with single quotes, completing the formula: *SUM('Cost').*

   Instead of taking the mouse route with the Functions and Fields lists, you can also just type the formula—being careful to use the proper punctuation.

Note: When typing formulas, it isn't necessary to capitalize. AppleWorks converts formulas to all capital letters for you.

---

7. **Make certain the "Format result as" pop-up menu is set to Number, and click OK.**

   The Formula dialog box closes, returning you to the Define Database Fields dialog box. At this point you could create more summary fields, to total or average other fields, for example. Otherwise, click Done to close the dialog box and return to your layout.

   Now it's time to put your brand-new summary field into the layout.

8. **Choose Layout→Insert Field.**

   The Insert Fields dialog box appears, listing all fields. The newly created field is at the bottom of the list.

Tip: In this example, you'll insert only one field into your layout. But you can insert several fields at a time by holding down the Shift key to select consecutive items in an AppleWorks list. To select random, non-consecutive items scattered through the list, hold down ⌘ as you click.

---

9. **Insert the Total Cost field by double-clicking it in the list.**

   AppleWorks inserts the new field in the Body of the layout, where it will do you absolutely no good. Summary fields work only in Summary parts.

10. **Shift-click to select both the Total Cost field and its label, and drag to the Summary part.**

    Align this field in the Summary part under the Cost field in the Body part. Then when you switch to Browse mode, it appears at the bottom of the Cost field column—the way a total should.

11. **With the field and its label still selected, choose Format→Alignment→Right, and then Format→Style→Bold.**

    To make the Total Cost line up with the Cost field, you must change the alignment to match. And to make the total stand out in the report, you can change it to bold.

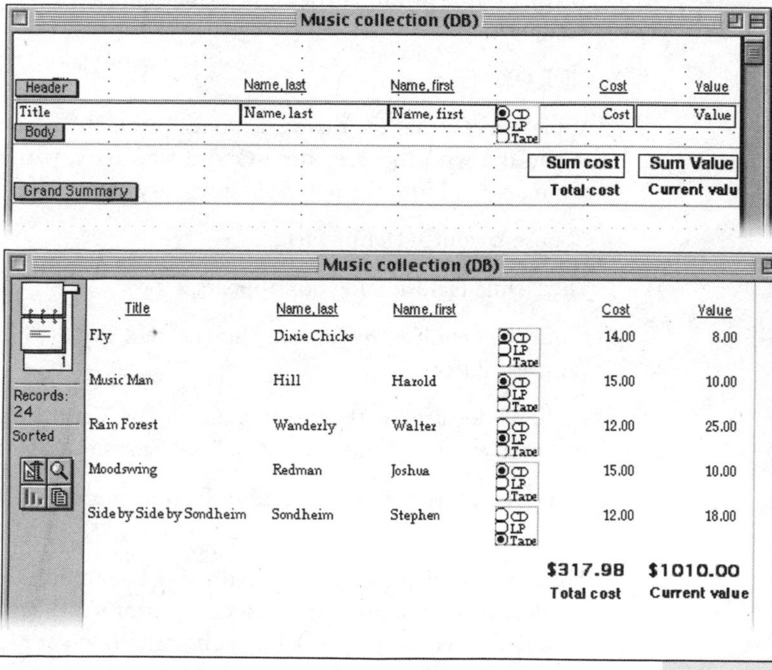

Figure 4-36:
After you move summary fields into the Summary part in Layout mode (top) and switch to Browse mode (bottom), the report displays the grand total amount that you've invested in your music collection.

Switch to Browse mode to see the Total Cost displayed at the bottom of the report, as shown in Figure 4-36. (If you don't see the Summary parts displayed, someone has turned off Page View. Choose Window→Page View to turn it back on.)

Tutorial: Create a Sub-summary (Subtotal)

To break out subtotals for the amount you've invested in CDs, LPs, and tapes, you can create a *Sub-summary* part to hold the summary fields.

1. **Choose Layout→Layout, and then choose Layout→Insert Part.**

   The Insert Part dialog box appears.

2. **Click the "Sub-summary when sorted by" radio button, and then select Format from the list of fields.**

   A Sub-summary field, by definition, is a subtotal that summarizes your records according to the way they're *sorted.* If your database isn't sorted, Sub-summary fields, like subtotals, go haywire and don't work. In the phone bill example, for example, you get a subtotal when the phone bill is sorted by kind of call—domestic or international.

   In the music database, your subtotal will appear beneath each group of recordings when sorted by *format* (CD, cassette, and so on). That's why you selected Format in the list of fields here.

   If you like, you can also turn on "Page break after part," which will ensure that each group of recordings will begin on a new separate page when printed. If you want the summary information to appear at the top of a new page *above* its corresponding group of sorted information, check "Page break before part" instead.

3. **Click OK.**

   AppleWorks closes the dialog box and inserts the new part into the layout. Just as you did with the preceding Grand summary, you now define and insert a summary field into the new Sub-summary part.

4. **Choose Layout→Define Fields.**

   The Define Fields dialog box appears.

5. **Name the field *Cost by format,* choose Field Type→Summary, and click Create (or press Enter).**

   AppleWorks displays the formula dialog box. Create the same formula here that you used for the Grand summary Total Cost field: SUM('Cost').

6. **Make certain the "Format result as" pop-up menu is set to Number, and click OK.**

   The Formula dialog box closes, returning you to the Define Database Fields dialog box. At this point you could create more Sub-summary fields. Otherwise, click Done to close the dialog box and return to your layout.

Now it's time to put your brand-new summary field into the layout. You'll notice that, except for its name, you defined this field exactly the same as the Total Cost Grand summary field. Its *placement* in a Sub-summary part is what makes it subtotal the field instead of total it.

7. **Choose Layout→Insert Field.**

   The Insert Fields dialog box appears, listing the newly created field at the bottom of the list.

8. **Select the "Cost by format" field by double-clicking it in the list.**

   AppleWorks inserts the new field in the Body of the layout, where it can't do any summarizing at all.

9. **Shift-click to select both the "Cost by format" field and its label, and drag them to the Sub-summary part.**

   Align this field in the Sub-summary part under the Cost field in the Body part. Then when you switch to Browse mode, it appears as a subtotal in the Cost field column.

10. **With the field and its label still selected, choose Format→Alignment→Right, and then Format→Style→Bold.**

    To make the Total Cost line up with the Cost field, you must change the alignment to match. And to make the subtotal stand out in the report, you can change it to bold.

11. **Choose Layout→Browse.**

    AppleWorks switches back to Browse mode, displaying the records with the Grand summary, as shown in Figure 4-35.

    Remember, however, that Sub-summaries don't appear until the database is *sorted*.

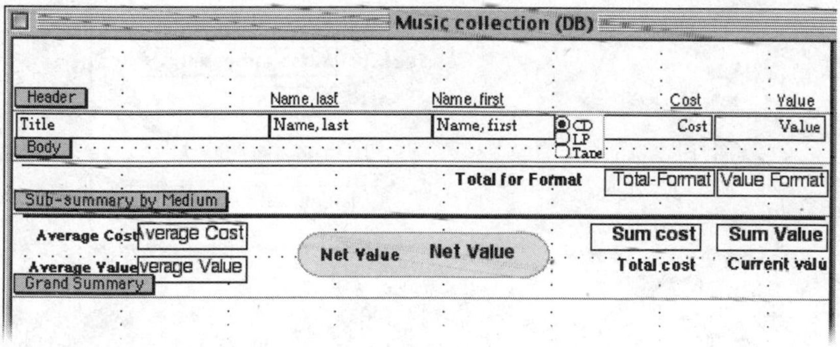

Figure 4-37:
By including Sub-summary and Grand summary parts in the layout, each containing summary fields (shown here in Layout view), the resulting report viewed in Browse mode after sorting reveals subtotals by category, as well as the grand totals. You can see the result in Figure 4-35.

12. **Choose Organize→Sort Records.**

    The Sort Records dialog box appears.

13. **Click Clear to erase whatever sorting criteria appears there already. Double-click Format.**

    The Format field name jumps to the right side, indicating that AppleWorks will sort your database by recording format. Click Ascending or Descending order, if you wish, to control which direction the sorting takes place—alphabetically or reverse alphabetically.

POWER USERS' CLINIC

Saving Reports

In a typical educational or corporate environment, preparing a decent report requires more effort than simply choosing a layout in AppleWorks. You'll often want to include only a subset of your records—only the last month's data for a monthly sales report, for example—and you'll often want to sort it in a particular way.

You can read about sorting your records later in this chapter, and you can read about extracting only subsets of information in the Searching and Matching Records sections of this chapter. Fortunately, once you've gone to the trouble of finding exactly the records you want, sorting them into the order you want, and switching to the layout you want for your report, AppleWorks can memorize all of this effort—and duplicate it instantly later, thanks to the feature called *saved reports*.

To save the report, begin by creating the layout you'll want to use, creating and saving the search you'll want to use (see page 144), and saving the sorting method you'll want to use (see page 149).

Now choose New Report from the Reports pop-up menu in the database tool panel, as shown here. The New Report dialog box appears. Name the report, and then, from the pop-up menus, choose a layout, a saved search, and a saved sort.

This dialog box also contains the checkbox called Print the Report. If you turn it on, then whenever you choose your finished report's name from the Reports pop-up menu (shown here), AppleWorks will print the report automatically. That's a great time-saver if you frequently have to print updated versions of the same report—but a great paper-waster if you haven't set the whole thing up quite correctly. Finally, click OK.

Saved reports are great for monthly sales reports or attendance records. You can also use this feature solely for its ability to find, sort, and switch to a particular layout all at once. For example, as an active Patsy Cline-on-vinyl collector, you can create a report that searches just for Patsy Cline LPs, sorts them according to value and title, and prints them out using the Monthly Report layout.

---

14. Click OK.

AppleWorks closes the dialog box, sorts the database, and now, at last, displays the layout with three Sub-summaries—one for each recording format—and the Grand summary. Figure 4-35 shows the idea.

Find Mode

AppleWorks's Find mode searches for and retrieves information you've stored in the database. It's actually only one of two different ways AppleWorks can call up individual records from your pile of data; see also "Matching Records," later in this chapter.

You can open the Find mode in any of the usual mode-switching ways:

• Choose Layout→Find.

• Control-click and choose Find from the contextual pop-up menu.

• Press ⌘-Shift-F.

The Find mode opens with what appears to be a blank record in the current layout—which often alarms the AppleWorks beginner who is accustomed to seeing data displayed in the layout. In fact, however, it's a *Find request form* (see Figure 4-38). The fields are blank because that's where you enter the information you're searching for.

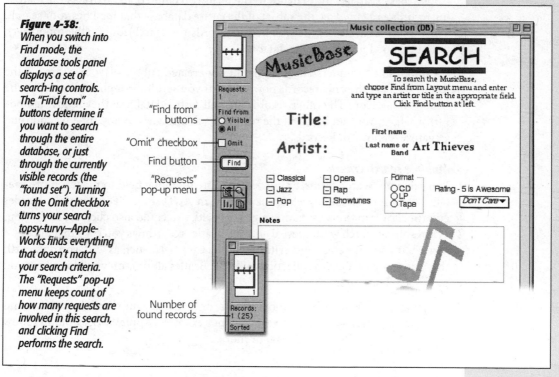

Figure 4-38:
When you switch into Find mode, the database tools panel displays a set of search-ing controls. The "Find from" buttons determine if you want to search through the entire database, or just through the currently visible records (the "found set"). Turning on the Omit checkbox turns your search topsy-turvy–AppleWorks finds everything that doesn't match your search criteria. The "Requests" pop-up menu keeps count of how many requests are involved in this search, and clicking Find performs the search.

"Find from" buttons

"Omit" checkbox

Find button

"Requests" pop-up menu

Number of found records

When you switch to Find mode, AppleWorks presents you with a Find request form that exactly matches your current layout, giving you the ability to perform a search using any of the included fields. This carbon copy of your familiar layout view allows you to use the same subset of fields you were browsing. Radio buttons, checkboxes, pop-up menus, and value list fields operate in their usual way. If this layout doesn't contain the fields you require for your search—that is, if you want to search your address-book database for a particular phone number, but you're looking at a layout that says only "Hello, my name is [First Name]," choose a more inclusive layout from the Layout menu.

How Searching Works

Enter the information you're searching for in the appropriate field. For example, if you're looking for all the Beatles recordings in the database, enter *beatles* in the "Last name (or group name)" field. Capitalization doesn't matter. Then press Enter—or click the Find button in the database tools panel.

Tip: When searching a database, don't be any more specific than absolutely necessary when entering your search term. For example, in the Beatles search, searching for *The Beatles* would not have turned up entries for Beatles. Conversely, entering *beat* would turn up *other* bands that had the word beat in their names. But entering *beatl* or *beatle* would snag Beatles, The Beatles, Beatle—and ignore The Deadbeats.

AppleWorks searches for matches to the term you entered and extracts the matching records as a *found set*, the subset of the entire database that matches your search. The tool panel indicates the number of records the search found (the found set), out of the total number in the database.

It's important to understand that the newly created subset of your records—the found set—are the only records now visible if you scroll through them or click the Record-book icon. The other records are still in the database; they're just temporarily *hidden*. You can bring all the records back into view at any time by choosing Organize→Show All Records.

Multiple search criteria

You can enter search terms, or *criteria*, in more than one field to make a more specific search. In database geek-speak, this is an *AND search*. For example, besides entering *beatle* in the "Last name or group" field, you could also click the LP button. The resulting search would reveal *only* the Beatles recordings you own that are in LP format. If you entered a third criterion in the Cost field, such as ≥50, you'd unearth the cream of your Beatles collection: only the Beatles albums on vinyl for which you paid $50.00 or more.

The more terms you enter, the more specific or focussed your search becomes—and the fewer the results returned. In the previous example, AppleWorks wouldn't show you any Beatles *CDs* worth $50.00 or more.

Omit

Instead of searching for what something *is*, you can search for what it *is not*. In the Find mode AppleWorks provides the *Omit* option in the database tool panel (see Figure 4-38). Put a check here to perform a search that finds all the records that *do not* match the search criteria. For example, if you entered *Elvis* into the First Name field, checked the Omit checkbox , and then clicked Find, AppleWorks would locate all the recordings that are *not* by The King.

Find from

Above the Omit checkbox are the "Find from" buttons: Visible or All. This choice is an important one to make after you've already performed a search. At this point, only some of your records are visible; the rest are hidden. Select the Visible option to search again, but among only the visible records. If you choose the Find from All button instead, AppleWorks searches the entire database, just as though you were starting fresh.

You may be wondering what, exactly, is served by this ability to search the results of the previous search. After all, it certainly seems like it's little more than a more complicated way of searching for two criteria at once, as in the Beatles/more than $50 example.

But sometimes you lack the foresight to do the search right the first time; instead of starting over, it's sometimes necessary to perform a second search as an afterthought.

Furthermore, the "Find from Visible" option permits a specialized kind of search that you can't achieve in any other way—that's a search where you want to *omit* one set of records from only one of the two searches. Suppose, for example, that you want a list of all your gospel recordings that *weren't* made by Elvis. You could achieve this complicated search in two steps—first, search for *Elvis* in the First Name field; by clicking the Omit button, you get a list of every recording Elvis *didn't* make. Then search again (by choosing Layout→Find)—but this time, click the Visible button. Click the Gospel checkbox, and click Find. AppleWorks searches the list of recordings Elvis didn't make on its quest to find gospel albums.

Multiple Simultaneous Requests

You may have considered the searches described in the previous section complex—but you haven't seen anything yet. Suppose, for example, that you want to be shown a list that matches two criteria *in the same field*—for your comparative study of jazz trumpeters, you want to locate all your recordings by Louis Armstrong or Miles Davis.

To pull that off, you'd perform the following search:

1. **Choose Layout→Find.**

   AppleWorks presents the empty Find layout, otherwise known as the Find request form.

2. **Enter the first search request.**

   In the First Name field, type *Louis;* in the Last Name field, type *Armstrong.*

3. **Instead of clicking Find, choose Edit→New Request.**

   AppleWorks remembers the first Find request and displays *another* blank layout. Figure 4-39 illustrates this setup.

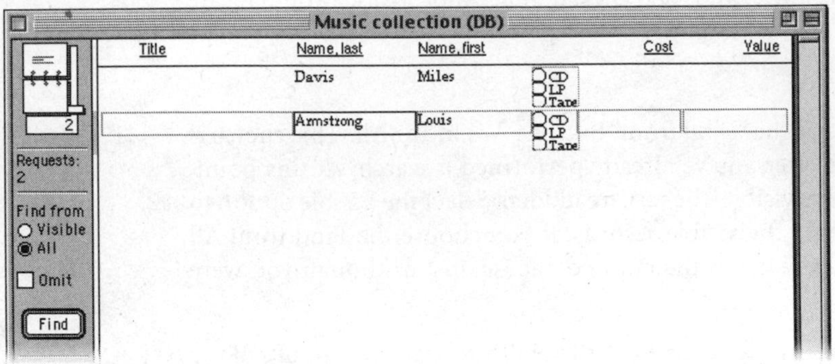

Figure 4-39:
AppleWorks remembers multiple find requests by creating a new request form for each. This is obvious in a list style layout; each new request appears as a new line. With larger layouts, you'll have to scroll up to see the prior requests. .

4. **In the First Name field, type *Miles*. In the Last Name field, type *Davis*.**

   On the database tool panel, you could, at this point, define the scope of the search by clicking either All or Visible. Unless you're adding this search on to an existing search, choose All.

5. **Click Find (or press Enter) to perform the search.**

   Congratulations! Now you can tell your nerd buddies that you're an old hand at what they would call *OR searches*. AppleWorks displays the records that satisfy any of the Find requests, showing you the recordings by Louis Armstrong *and* the recordings by Miles Davis.

   You can use the same technique on *different* fields. For example, for your thesis about the wide-ranging influence of Miles Davis on popular music, you could search for Miles Davis in the Name fields, and in a second request, search for Miles Davis in the *Title* field. This way AppleWorks finds not only all the Miles Davis releases, but also recordings titled, *A Tribute to Miles Davis* and *101 Strings Plays the Music of Miles Davis*.

Save That Search

Sometimes you'll find yourself performing the same search repeatedly. For example, if you trade albums with other collectors, one of your trading partners may call you every month to see what LPs you have in stock by her favorites, Holly Near and k. d. lang.

Instead of performing the searches manually each month, you can *save* the search. Next month, you won't have to set up a Find request—you can simply choose "Holly and k. d. LPs" from your list of saved searches, as shown in Figure 4-40. This feature is especially useful if you frequently have to create the kind of complex searches described in the previous sections. Here's how you'd go about it.

Note: Unfortunately, AppleWorks doesn't allow you to get to the end of a complex search and *then* decide to save it. You have to plan ahead—you must name and save a search *before* you set it up.

Boolean Logic

Each of your multiple requests can contain more than one criterion—that is, even when searching for albums by several different artists simultaneously, you can still specify both First Name and Last Name for each search request. Propeller-heads call these wheels-within-wheels *nested AND searches*.

For example, imagine that you want to find all albums by Miles Davis, John Coltrane, and Charles Mingus. You'd set up the first search by filling in the First Name and Last Name fields with *Miles* and *Davis;* then you'd choose Layout→Find again and specify *John* and *Coltrane;* finally, you would choose

Layout→Find yet again, this time to type in *Charles* and *Mingus.* Going to this trouble would ensure that you get the records you want—because you specified both first and last name on each search request, you won't see any albums recorded by Mac Davis, Alice Coltrane, or Mingus Amungus.

(This AND and OR business is an entire area of study unto itself called *Boolean logic.* If you've followed along this far, you already know all you'll need to search your databases. If you thirst for more Boolean knowledge, use a search engine to look for *Boolean* on that mother of all databases, the Internet.)

1. **Choose New Search from the Search pop-up menu in the database tools panel (see Figure 4-40).**

   The Search pop-up menu actually looks like a magnifying-glass icon. The Search Name dialog box appears.

2. **Enter a descriptive name for your search in the Search Name dialog box; click OK (or press Enter).**

   You enter Find mode.

Figure 4-40:
Use the magnifying-glass pop-up menu—the only way to create a saved search. Click the same icon when you want to summon a saved search.

3. **Enter the search term(s) in the form.**

For example, enter *Holly* and *Near* in the First Name and Last Name fields, and turn on the LP radio button.

4. **If you need multiple Find requests, choose Layout→Find, and specify the additional search target.**

You'd do so if, for example, you also wanted to call up all k. d. lang albums on LP.

At this point, you could theoretically click All or Visible to determine the scope of the search, as described earlier. In practice, however, you'll probably want to store searches that always search *all* records. That way, your stored search isn't dependent upon your having previously performed another, manual search to get the desired results.

5. **Click Store (or press Enter).**

The button on the database tool panel that usually says Find now reads Store.

6. **Click Store.**

AppleWorks saves this search, no matter how complex it was.

To recall and run a saved search, choose its name from the Search (magnifying glass) pop-up menu in the database tools panel. AppleWorks performs the search automatically, without requiring any additional input, and displays the results.

If you need to rename, delete, or modify a saved search, choose Edit Searches from the magnifying-glass pop-up menu.

Figure 4-41:
The Match Records command highlights the records that meet your search request. Non-matching records still appear on screen—they're just not highlighted (blackened). Since all your records are still visible, the results of a match are very easy to see in a columnar layout or in the List mode.

Tip: Create a search called Find All (set up such a search by leaving all of the fields empty before clicking Store). Running this search is equivalent to choosing Organize→Show All Records, but saves you the mouse trip to the Organize menu.

Matching Records

If the previous methods of searching don't satisfy your urge for absolute control, fear not—there's still the Match Records command. Match Records allows you to invoke the entire range of AppleWorks's mathematical, statistical, and logical functions in your quest to extract precisely the desired information from your database.

An important difference between Find and Match Records: instead of hiding the records that don't match your search, Match Records *highlights* all the records that *do* match (see Figure 4-41).

After matching the records, AppleWorks can *then* hide the non-matching records, if you like—just choose Organize→Hide Unselected. On the other hand, you can also, at this point, do the opposite: choose Organize→Hide Selected. Performing a Match Records command and then using Hide Selected is a lot like clicking the Omit checkbox when using the Find command, as described in the previous section.

Tip: You can select AppleWorks records manually, too. Select one record by clicking anywhere within it except on a field. Select multiple records by Shift-clicking (if they're consecutive) or ⌘-clicking if they're not consecutive.

After manually highlighting records in this way, you can use the Organize→Hide Unselected and Hide Selected commands; these commands aren't exclusive to the Match Records process.

Tutorial: A Complex "Match Records" Request

Suppose, in your endeavors to wring every last shred of usefulness out of your music collection database, you want to see a list of recordings that cost you between $7 and $20. A moment's reflection should convince you that such a search would be impossible using the regular Find command. The Match Records command, however, is up to the task.

1. **Choose Organize→Show All Records.**

   AppleWorks displays all the records in the database. Match Records searches only *visible* records—so choosing Show All Records is a good first step.

2. **Choose Organize→Match Records.**

   AppleWorks displays the Match Records Condition dialog box (Figure 4-42).

3. **In the Formula box, type** *AND ('Cost'>7, 'Cost'<20).*

   You can also choose AND(logical1,logical2,…) from the Functions list. AppleWorks inserts it into the Formula box, and you have to replace the placeholder words *logical1* and *logical2* with your own little sentence-like equations (called *arguments*).

In this case, the first argument is *'Cost'>7*. This tells AppleWorks, "find records where the number in the field *Cost* is greater than 7." The second argument, *'Cost'<20*, tells AppleWorks, "find records where the *Cost* is less than 20."

The AND function tells AppleWorks, "find records that satisfy *both* of these arguments."

When you enter formulas, you can use spaces to make them easier to read if you like—they have no effect on the calculation. When a field appears in a formula, it must be in single quotes (such as 'Cost'); text that *you* type in a formula must be in double quotes.

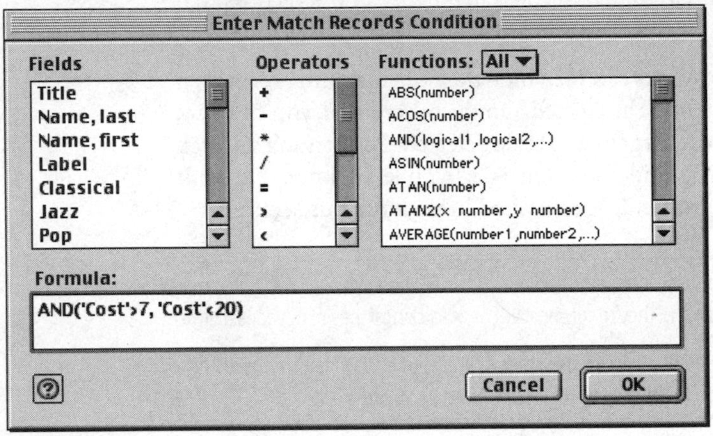

Figure 4-42:
The Match Records Condition dialog box looks exactly like the Calculation dialog box you may have encountered when setting up your fields for the first time. You specify how you want your records matched by typing in a formula or by building it using the various choices in this dialog box. Punctuation is important: surround field names with single quotes, text with double quotes—and don't forget to close your parentheses on the way out.

4. **Click OK.**

   AppleWorks closes the dialog box, performs the match, and highlights the matching records—those that cost you more than $7 and less than $20.

Here are some other formulas you could use in the Match Records dialog box of your music-collection database:

- *AND ('Cost' > 7, 'Cost' < 20, 'Last Name' = "Byrne", 'First Name' = "David")*. This formula would produce a list of recordings by David Byrne that cost between $7.00 and $20.00.

   The first two arguments are the same as the previous example, but the third and fourth arguments tell AppleWorks to find fields that contain certain text: the field *Last Name* is equal to *Byrne* and the field, *First Name*, is equal to *David*.

- *OR(AND ('Cost' > 7, 'Cost' < 20, 'Last name' = "Krall", 'First name' = "Diana"), AND('Last name' = "Sondheim", 'First name' = "Stephen"))*. This formula, believe it or not, finds recordings costing between $7.00 and $20.00 by Diana Krall, *or* by Stephen Sondheim at any price.

This formula has two AND functions similar to the previous examples, nested within an OR function. This tells AppleWorks, "find records that satisfy *either* of these two AND functions."

The complexity you can build into a Match Records formula is limited only by your imagination—and your understanding of finance, logic, algebra, geometry, and statistics. For details on AppleWorks's built-in functions, consult either the built-in AppleWorks Help or the Functions Appendix at *www.missingmanual.com*.

Match Record buttons

As described in Chapter 11, it's easy to customize AppleWorks's Button bar. If this business of using the Match Records command becomes a favorite activity of yours, you may enjoy the six AppleWorks buttons that give you one-click matches—without ever having to go near the Enter Match Records Condition dialog box.

To add these buttons to your Button bar, start by choosing Edit→Preferences→Button bar to open the Customize Button bar dialog box. Scroll down the list of Available Buttons to the Database buttons; drag the ones you want directly onto your Button bar (more in Chapter 11). The pertinent Matching Records buttons are:

- **Match Equal** (=). Selects records with values that match what's in the current field. (See below for some examples.)

- **Match Not Equal** (≠). Selects records that don't match what's in the current field.

- **Match Less** (<), **Match Greater** (>). Selects records with values *less than* or *greater than* what's in the current field.

- **Match Less/Equal** (≤), **Match Greater/Equal** (≥). Selects records with values *less than or equal to* or *greater than or equal to* what's in the current field.

Once you've installed these buttons on your Button bar, you use them like this:

1. **In Browse mode, click a field.**

   In the music collection database, for example, you might click in the Last Name field. Suppose, for example, that the one you click contains the name *Armstrong*.

2. **Click the "Match Equal" button on your Button bar.**

   AppleWorks instantly highlights all the records in your database containing *Armstrong* in the Last Name field.

Another example: Suppose the Cost field on a particular record says $20.00. If you click that field and then click the Match Greater/Equal button, AppleWorks selects all the records with a cost of $20.00 or more.

Sorting Your Data

There are plenty of reasons why you might want to sort the records in your database. For example, you might begin your phone and address database by transcribing from your Rolodex in alphabetical order—but as you add more people, they get tacked on the end of the list, ruining the order. And even if you had everyone carefully entered in the correct order, what if you wanted to look at the list by company name? Or group all the names by city or state? AppleWorks's sorting capabilities can easily reorder your database in any of these ways.

Or perhaps you're down to the wire with preparations for your kid's school's Harry Potter theme party, and the expenses are mounting faster than you can say "Dumbledore!" You've created a database, of course, to keep track of which parents are doing what, and how much everybody is spending. The other parents are asking for an accounting, subtotaled by activity, so they can decide whether an activity needs to be cut to keep expenses under $300. If you create a Sub-summary field to subtotal expenses, you can sort by activity. Then you can decide whether to economize on supplies for the broom-making activity, or if you'll have to cut the entire invisible-ink workshop.

To sort, begin in Browse or List mode. After you perform a sort, the new order applies to all the layouts, not only the current one.

You can sort your data by Last Name, City, State, or any field you like. Text and number fields (including radio-button and value lists) get sorted alphabetically and numerically; checkbox fields get sorted into "checked" and "not checked" groups.

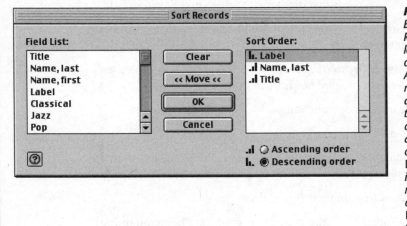

Figure 4-43:
By setting up the Sort Records dialog box for three levels of sorting, each with its own Sort Order, you can tell AppleWorks to sort this report by recording label, artist, and title. For each of these sub-sorts, you can determine whether you want an ascending or descending order. For example, Apple-Works can sort artist and title in ascending order and sort recording label in descending order—in order to keep those Windham Hill releases near the top of the list.

Sorting Using the Button Bar

The Button bar offers the easiest, quickest way to sort.

1. **If the Button bar isn't showing, choose Window→Show Button Bar.**

    The default button set for the database module includes "ascending sort" and "descending sort" buttons (the fourth and fifth icons from the left). *Ascending* sorts from A to Z (if it's text) or from zero on up (for numbers). *Descending* sorts from Z to A or down to zero for numbers.

2. **Click the field by which you want to sort (Last Name, for example).**

You can sort in any layout, as long as you're in the Browse or List mode.

3. **Click one of the sort buttons in the Button bar.**

AppleWorks reorders the records based on the field you selected.

More Complex Sorting

The Button-bar sort is great—if you want to sort only on one field. Often, however, one field isn't nearly enough. For example, you might want to sort your music collection by recording label (so that all the Columbia recordings are grouped together), then by artist (so that the singers are listed alphabetically within the Columbia group), then by title (so that the albums are listed alphabetically within each singer cluster). See Figure 4-43 for an example.

Saving a sort

If you get into the habit of sorting your data in complex ways, you can *save* a canned sorting setup. Here's how:

1. **Choose New Sort from the Sort pop-up menu in the database tools panel (see Figure 4-44).**

The Sort Records dialog box appears.

2. **Enter a descriptive name for the sort.**

You might call it, for example, *Sort by Label & Artist.*

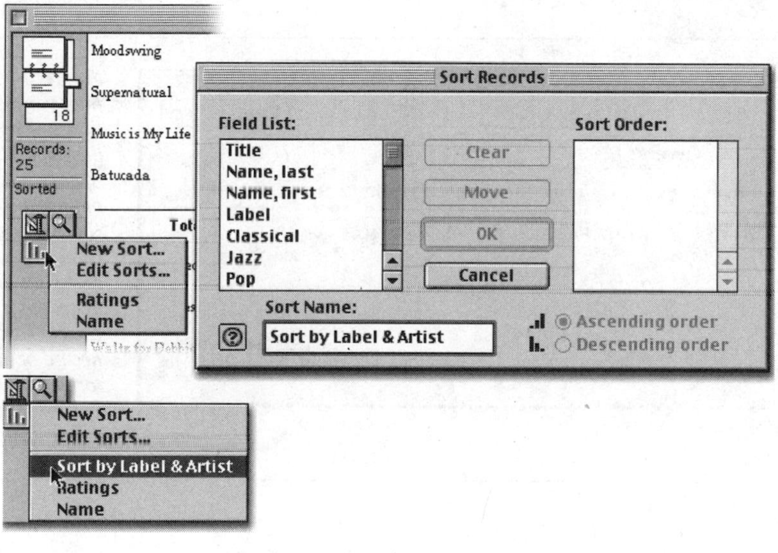

Figure 4-44:
The database tools panel's Sort button pop-up menu (top) gives you access to the New Sort Command and to previously saved sorts. The Sort Records dialog box (middle) now includes a box for the Sort Name and allows you to determine which fields and in what order AppleWorks will sort. When you're finished, the save sort appears in the Sort button pop-up menu (bottom).

3. **Double-click the primary sort field, or select it and click Move. Repeat for the secondary sort field.**

In the music collection example, your primary sort field would be the Label field. Within each record company's grouping, you'd want the singer's names sorted alphabetically—the "Last Name" field, in other words, would be your secondary sort field.

AppleWorks sets each field to sort in ascending (alphabetical) order. If you need it to sort in *descending* order, take this opportunity to highlight the field name and click the appropriate button beneath the list.

4. **When the setup is complete, click OK (or press Enter).**

AppleWorks saves the sort, but doesn't execute it.

5. **To run a saved sort, choose its name from the Sort pop-up menu in the database tools panel (see Figure 4-44).**

AppleWorks performs the sort without any further effort on your part.

Printing

Getting information out of the database when you need it and in the correct form is often the final hurdle for your data management system. For example, from the music collection database, you might want to print a list report every month to keep tabs on your growing collection.

In many respects, printing from the database is no different from printing from, for example, a word processing document. But you have an additional choice to make in the Print dialog box, as shown in Figure 4-45.

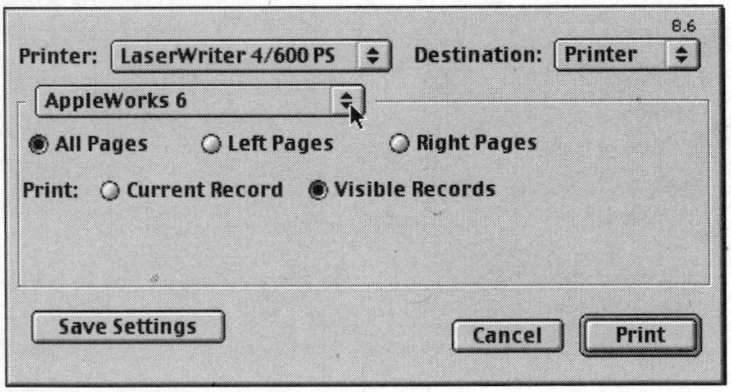

Figure 4-45:
After you choose File→Print command, the familiar Print dialog box appears. In the AppleWorks 6-specific printing options (which, if you're using a laser printer, may be accessible only by choosing from a pop-up menu), you can choose to print left or right pages— if you're printing on both sides of the page. More vital for daily use is the choice of what to print: Print Current Record or Print Visible Records. The former prints just the selected record. The latter prints all records in the visible set—which could be the entire database.

Printing Labels

Printing mailing labels is the classic database task—but labels can be used for lots of other purposes, from inventory or price labels to name tags for the company picnic.

The easiest way to generate labels is to use the Create Labels Assistant. This special-purpose Assistant doesn't show up on the Assistants tab of the Starting Points window like its fellow assistants (page 151)—only from within the Database module.

Tip: When you go to the office-supply store to buy labels, you'll be confronted with a bewildering array of computer labels, most made by Avery. There are dozens of sizes, styles, and colors to choose from. More important, some are designed for laser printers and others for inkjets–get the correct kind for your printer.

Using the Label Assistant

AppleWorks's automatic label-creation feature is designed to walk you through setting up a label layout—you just have to answer the questions it asks you.

1. **Choose Layout→New Label Layout.**

   The AppleWorks Assistant Welcome window appears, describing the help it is about to give you. Click Next to move on to your first question

   First you'll be asked whether you're using Avery labels or you want to create custom labels and specify the dimensions manually.

   If you're using Avery brand labels, check the package to find out the label-style number you bought. Then find that number in the list of Avery label styles on the screen. If you bought a different brand, look at the fine print on the package—it usually says "same size as Avery 5160" (or another number). If not, you'll have to use the custom label setup.

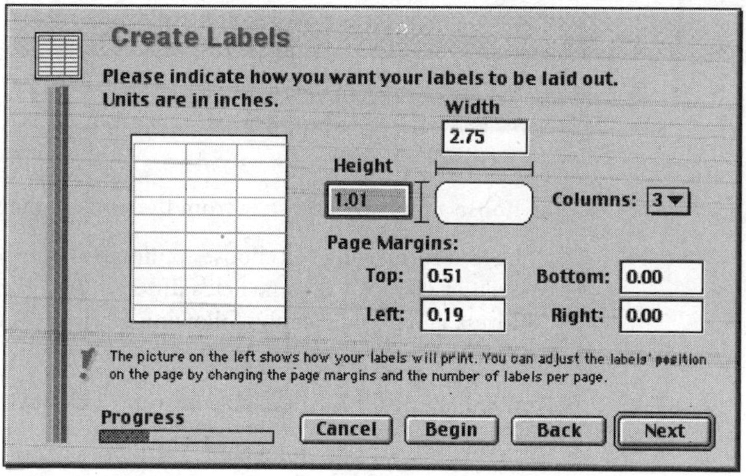

Figure 4-46:
If you can follow simple instructions, the Label Assistant is a sure-fire way to set up a layout for label printing. This assistant prefers to do all the work, however, so if you want to do any customization, you'll have to set up the labels manually–without assistance.

2. **Choose Avery labels or "create custom labels" and click Next.**

   If you choose "create custom labels," you'll have to specify the dimensions of the labels and page margins—information which should be on the label package. Otherwise, make those measurements with a ruler in order to enter them in the Assistant window (see Figure 4-46). When you've entered all the information, click Next.

   If you chose Avery labels, select the Avery style number from the pop-up menu and click Next.

3. **Choose the number of lines you want for your label—from one to six—from the pop-up menu. Click Next.**

   The Assistant displays another window with an array of pop-up menus.

4. **Select the fields to include on the labels, choosing them in order from the pop-up menus. Include any spaces or punctuation required between fields by typing in the boxes (see Figure 4-47). Click Next.**

   AppleWorks provides you with enough pop-up menus to completely crowd your label, but you only need to include essential fields.

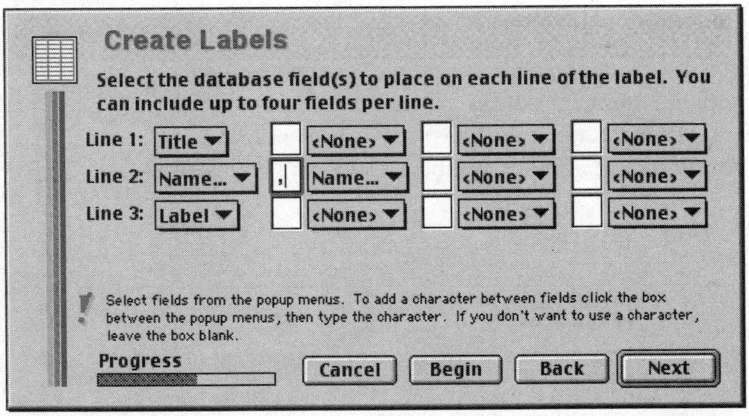

Figure 4-47:
You choose the fields to include on the labels, and their position, using the Assistant's pop-up menus. If you want any spaces or punctuation between fields—for example, a comma and space between the City and State fields—you enter them in the boxes between fields.

5. **Choose a font size and style from the pop-up menus. Click Next.**

   The font formatting you choose applies to all the fields in the label—the assistant won't let you format some fields differently. For example, make the name of an address label bold. See the following section, "Setting Up Labels Manually," to create that kind of label. Click Next to take you to the next step of the Assistant.

6. **Enter a name for the new label layout. Click next.**

   AppleWorks suggests for a name the number of the Avery label you used for this setup. If you used the custom setup, or if you want a different name, enter it here.

7. **Use the Back button to go back and make any changes; or use the Begin button to start over. Otherwise, click Create.**

An alert box appears on your screen, reminding you to select "No Gaps Between Pages" in Page Setup. (As you can read in the box below, this message is largely irrelevant, and you should ignore it.) Click OK and you're back to your database window—now displaying the new label layout. Switch to Browse mode to see your data filling the labels.

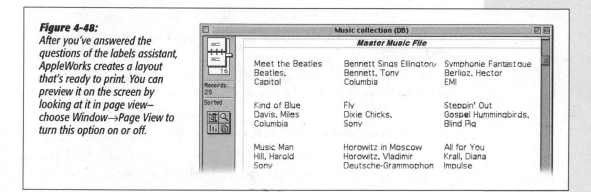

Figure 4-48:
After you've answered the questions of the labels assistant, AppleWorks creates a layout that's ready to print. You can preview it on the screen by looking at it in page view—choose Window→Page View to turn this option on or off.

Setting Up Labels Manually

The Label Assistant creates labels using the same font for all fields. If you want to be more creative with your layout—for example, to print the first line of an address label in bold, or to use a variety of fonts to produce an eye-catching "Hello, my name is JAIME" label—you have to create a custom label layout.

1. **Choose Layout→New Layout.**

Alternatively, choose New Layout from the Layout pop-up menu in the database tools panel. Either way, the New Layout dialog box appears.

FREQUENTLY ASKED QUESTION

No Gaps Between Pages

I can't find "No Gaps Between Pages" in my Page Setup. What's up?

The Alert box you see during label setup that reminds you to select "No Gaps Between Pages" in Page Setup is a throwback to the days of dot-matrix printers and continuous-feed paper—or, put another way, it's an AppleWorks bug. If you're still using an ImageWriter, or another printer featuring tractor-feed paper, you'll see the "No Gaps" checkbox on your Page Setup dialog box. It tells the printer that you don't want a margin at the top and bottom of each page, because you've threaded an endless ribbon of labels into the machine.

When using most modern inkjet or laser printer models, however, there *is* no "No Gaps Between Pages" option in the Page Setup box! The AppleWorks message that refers to it is the computer equivalent of: "If the light is low, trim the wick."

---

2. **Enter a name for the layout and click the Labels radio button. Select the Avery label style number from the pop-up menu.**

   To create the label layout completely from scratch, leave the pop-up menu set to Custom and see the next section, "Creating custom labels."

3. **Click OK.**

   An alert box appears on your screen, reminding you to select "No Gaps Between Pages" in Page Setup. (Do so only if you're using tractor-feed labels.) Click OK and the Set Field Order dialog box appears.

4. **Double-click fields in the Field List in the order you want them to appear on the label.**

   As you double-click, the field name will jump across to the Field Order box. You'll do the final arrangement in Layout mode, so just get the fields in the approximate order here.

5. **Click OK when you've included all the needed fields.**

   AppleWorks closes the dialog box and displays the new layout—in whichever mode you were in when you began the new label process.

6. **Choose Layout→Layout.**

   In Layout mode, the Body part is the size of one label. A vertical guideline marks the right edge of the label in which AppleWorks has positioned your selected fields.

7. **Modify the layout, if necessary.**

   Resize, format, rearrange, or delete fields on the label layout—just as you would on any other layout. Leave a little free space all the way around the label to accommodate any slight inaccuracies in the printer.

   AppleWorks measures labels from the top edge of one label to the top edge of the next, and from the left edge of one to the left edge of the next. In other words, the margins between labels (if any) end up occupying the right and bottom edges of your layout—a fact to keep in mind when positioning the fields.

Creating custom labels

When you don't have an Avery number to go by, you can start your label design from scratch.

1. **Choose Layout→New Layout.**

   Or choose New Layout from the Layout pop-up menu in the database tools panel. Either way, the New Layout dialog box appears.

2. **Enter a name for the layout and click the Labels radio button. Leave the Labels pop-up menu set to Custom.**

   If you're using an Avery label style number, see the previous section, "Setting Up Labels Manually."

3. **Click OK.**

   Now the Label Layout dialog box appears.

4. **Enter number of labels for one row across the page and the dimensions for your labels. Click OK.**

   The Set Field Order dialog box appears.

5. **Double-click fields in the Field List in the order you want them to appear on the label. Click OK.**

   The new layout opens, as seen in Figure 4-49.

6. **Modify the layout, if necessary.**

   Resize, format, rearrange, or delete fields on the label layout—just as you would on any other layout. Leave a little free space all the way around the label to accommodate any slight inaccuracies in the printer.

Tip: If you're clever and have some time to kill, open the AppleWorks 6→AppleWorks Essentials folder. Inside is a word processing file called AppleWorks Labels. It lists each Avery label and its dimensions—and it provides the info AppleWorks uses to build its pop-up list of "known" labels. You can edit this document, therefore, to edit the AppleWorks label pop-up lists.

Figure 4-49:
The Label Layout dialog box allows you to configure labels of any size at all. Like all AppleWorks dialog boxes that deal with measurements, you can enter dimensions in other units, as long as you use the correct abbreviation, for example, cm for centimeter.

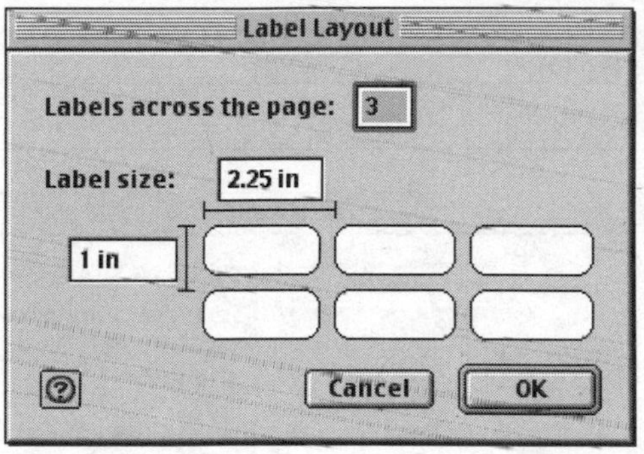

Sliding

As shown in Figure 4-50, blank lines in an address are a common hallmark of amateur label-printing. For example, some of your addresses may have a company name, some may have a two-line address, and some might just have a name and a city and state.

Fortunately, AppleWorks can shift fields during printing to close up such awkward gaps. For example, if you have a First Name field followed on the same line by a Last Name field, a less powerful database might print every Last Name exactly one inch from the left side of its label. Such labels may look fine when the name is *Anne-Sophie Mutter,* but produce a ridiculous gap after the first name on *Al Green's* mailing label. AppleWorks can solve the problem by sliding the last name to the left on every single label.

When you create a label layout, AppleWorks automatically turns on this sliding feature. You may sometimes want to turn this feature off for label layouts, however, or *on* for non-label databases you create yourself. The key, in Layout mode, is to choose Layout→Edit Layouts; click the name of the layout you want to edit; and then click OK. The dialog box shown in Figure 4-51 appears.

Robert   Hardy
104 S. Williams Ave.
Klamath Falls   OR   97601

Heidi & Tim   Harper
1902 Warren St.; Apt. 102
Mankato   MN   56001

Suzi   Hendry
3117 Prospect Ave
Eureka   CA

Bonnie   Tillotson
PO Box 76
Arcata   CA   95521

Figure 4-50:
You can avoid embarrassing breaches in your labels (top) with the careful use of AppleWorks's intelligent sliding fields. Fields can slide left, as in the last-name example, or upward, when (for example) the Company Name line in the mailing address is blank. They shift up or over to close any unsightly gaps (bottom).

Robert Hardy
104 S. Williams Ave.
Klamath Falls OR 97601

Heidi & Tim Harper
1902 Warren St.; Apt. 102
Mankato MN 56001

Suzi Hendry
3117 Prospect Ave
Eureka CA

Bonnie Tillotson
PO Box 76
Arcata CA 95521

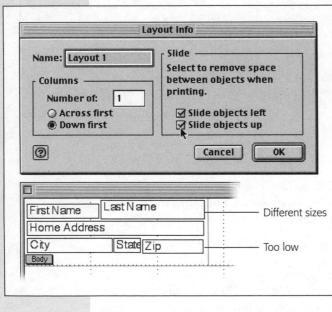

Figure 4-51:
The Edit Layouts dialog box lets you control when AppleWorks slides fields to close up empty space (top). Bottom: In order to slide, the field doing the sliding must be the same size or smaller than, and aligned with, the field it's sliding into. If the sliding field is too large or not aligned with the top or left edge of the other field, it won't slide. Resizing or realigning the fields solves the problem.

Layout Info

Name: Layout 1

Columns
Number of: 1
○ Across first
● Down first

Slide
Select to remove space between objects when printing.

☑ **Slide objects left**
☑ **Slide objects up**

Cancel   OK

First Name   Last Name ———— Different sizes
Home Address
City   State Zip ———— Too low
Body

Sliding only works if the following rules are followed when you're arranging fields in Layout mode:

- Field borders cannot touch.

- To slide left, the top edges of the two fields must be aligned.

- To slide up, the left edges of the two fields must be aligned.

- The field that is doing the sliding must be the same size or smaller than the field it is sliding into.

If you adhere to these rules, AppleWorks will close up any gaps while printing—but you'll never see the effect on the screen, not even with Page View turned on. You must print a sample sheet to make certain your fields are sliding correctly.

Tip: When you're ready to print your labels, first print out a test sheet on plain paper. Then stack it with a sheet of labels, hold them up to the light, and make sure the printing lines up with the labels. If not, you can make adjustments to the layout—and you've wasted one cent on a sheet of paper instead of one dollar on a sheet of labels.

The Spreadsheet

reen eyeshades and sleeve protectors are long gone, but the need to manipulate column after column of numbers is here to stay. Computerized *spreadsheets* take the place of paper ledgers for working with all these numbers. And although the spreadsheet's forte is working with numbers, you can use them for text, too; because they're actually a specialized database, you can also turn spreadsheets into schedules, calendars, wedding registries, address books, and other simple text databases.

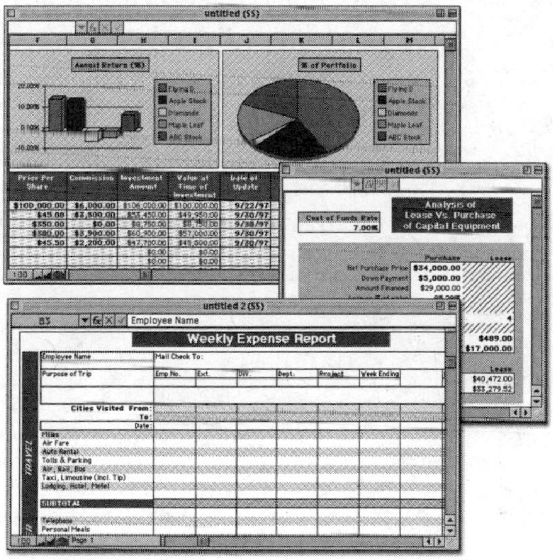

Figure 5-1:
Spreadsheets can present a lot of information in a small amount of space, keep track of lists, perform calculations, and create graphs. You can format the spreadsheet to display this information in myriad ways; the only common denominator is that the data takes the form of a table or matrix.

Spreadsheet Basics

Spreadsheets share the look of their ledger-paper counterparts, but that's where the resemblance ends. When you open a new spreadsheet document, AppleWorks fills the screen with a grid that looks a lot like a ledger page (see Figure 5-2).

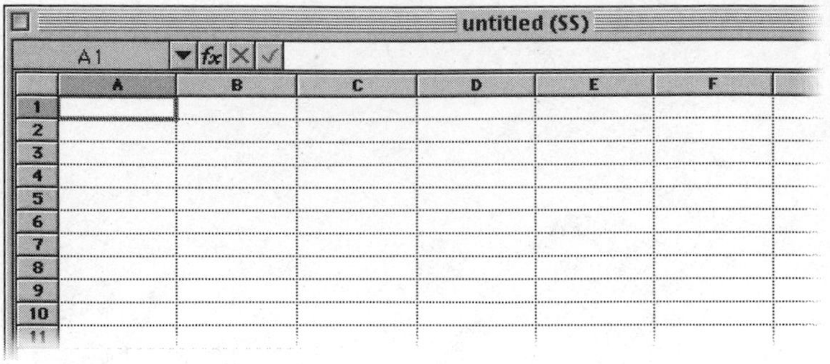

Figure 5-2:
AppleWorks creates a new spreadsheet document that features a grid of cells bordered by row headings and column headings; and along the top of the window, several features that are unique to spreadsheets. These documents are officially called worksheets—but most people just call them spreadsheets.

This grid is composed of *cells* running in horizontal rows and vertical columns. Though you see only a small corner of it on your screen, a new AppleWorks spreadsheet document is 40 columns by 500 rows. (The maximum size for an AppleWorks spreadsheet is 256 columns by 16,384 rows—a total of over four million cells. And if *that's* big not enough to accommodate your business, sell it to Microsoft.)

Each spreadsheet cell is a container into which you can put a number, a date or time, some text, or a formula. Numbers and text just sit there in their little pigeonholes, but formulas give spreadsheets the power to *do* something with all that information. A formula can grab data from other cells in the spreadsheet, perform calculations, and display the answers.

Each cell in a spreadsheet is identified by coordinates (see Figure 5-3). Each *row* is labeled with a number, and each *column* is labeled with a letter or letter pair, as in the game of Battleship. For example, the first cell in the upper left-hand corner of a spreadsheet is A1. When you open a new worksheet, cell A1 is selected—it's the *active cell*—and anything you type will wind up there. Figure 5-3 explains all.

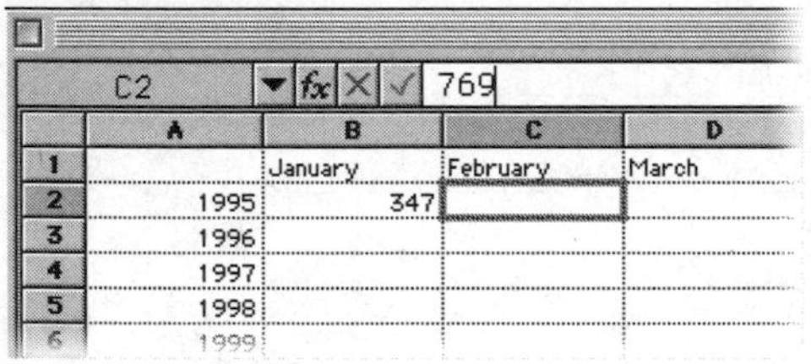

Figure 5-3:
There can be only one active cell at a time, indicated by a dark outline; its address appears at the left end of the Entry bar at the top of the window. Whatever you type goes into the Entry bar first; then, when you move to another cell the contents of the Entry bar are transferred to the active cell—and the next cell becomes active.

Note: When you type into a selected cell, you'll quickly discover that your typing doesn't actually appear there. Instead, it appears in the *Entry bar* at the top of the window. Only when you move on to another cell or press Enter does that information actually appear in the spreadsheet cell.

Navigating the Grid

As you use a spreadsheet, you enter information into one cell, move to another cell, enter more information—and repeat *ad infinitum*. You move from one cell to another either by clicking with the mouse, by choosing Options→Go To Cell, or by using keyboard commands, as shown in this table.

Mouse or keyboard action	Result
Esc, Cancel button	Cancel entry and stay in current cell (Deletes new typing in the Entry bar)
Accept button, Enter	Accept entry (transfers typing from Entry bar to active cell) and stay in current cell
Return, Option-down-arrow	Accept entry and move to cell below
Tab, Option-right-arrow	Accept entry and move to cell to the right
Shift-Tab, Option-left-arrow	Accept entry and move to cell to the left
Shift-Return, Option-up-arrow	Accept entry and move to cell above
Click cell	Accept entry and move to cell clicked
Click first cell and drag to last cell, or Shift-click last cell	Select a range of cells
Click row or column heading	Select entire row or column
Click the unlabeled box at intersection of row and column headings, or press ⌘-A	Select entire spreadsheet
Option-click the unlabeled box at intersection of row and column headings	Select active area of spreadsheet: cells that contain data or have formatting applied

Selecting a Range

Sometimes you need to select more than one cell at once—a *range* of cells. You might want to do this, for example, to indicate which information you'd like to view as a graph or chart.

Whenever you select more than one cell, the range of cells must be in the form of a rectangle—a row, a column, or a block of cells. To highlight a block of cells, click a cell in one corner of the range, scroll if necessary, then Shift-click the cell at the diagonally opposite corner of the block. You can also drag diagonally with the mouse to select them; if they don't all fit on one screen, the window scrolls automatically as you drag.

Tip: When you highlight a block of cells, AppleWorks identifies that range by its two *anchor cells*, the first (upper left) in the range and the last (lower right). In formulas, the cell range is identified by its diagonally opposite corners, such as B3..G8. You'll see this notation appear in the entry bar, in fact, whenever you're building a formula and drag to identify such a range.

To select one entire row or one entire column, click the row or column *heading*, as shown in Figure 5-4.

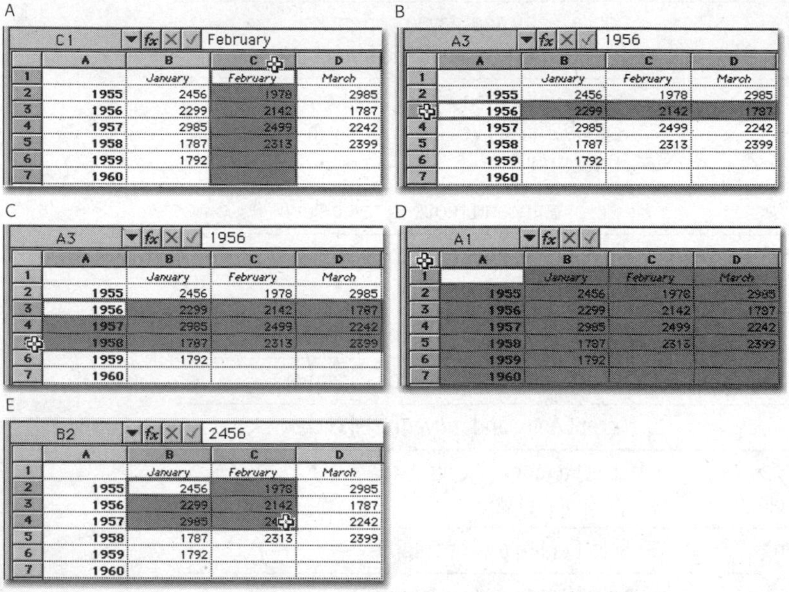

Figure 5-4:
Click a column heading to select the entire column (A), click a row heading to select the entire row (B), drag through (or Shift-click) row or column headings to select more than one (C), or click the box at the intersection of the row and column headings (D) to select the entire spreadsheet. Select a range of cells by dragging from one corner to the opposite corner (E), or by clicking one corner and Shift-clicking the opposite one.

Tutorial: Creating a Spreadsheet

Suppose you're remodeling your house. You'd like to estimate costs and keep track of expenses over many months as the project drags on (and it *will* drag on). Grab a pencil and your *Do-it-Yourself Guide to Home Remodeling*—or better yet, grab a good contractor—and jot down the expense categories you want to track.

1. **Create a new spreadsheet document by choosing File→New→Spreadsheet.**

   Alternatively, click the spreadsheet icon in the Button bar or in the Basic tab of the Starting Points window.

   Either way, AppleWorks fills your screen with the spreadsheet grid; the first cell, A1, is selected as the active cell. The top of the window contains the Entry bar and other controls (see Figure 5-5).

AppleWorks also changes the Button bar assortment to include spreadsheet-related buttons; furthermore, the menu bar now contains a Calculate menu.

2. **Begin by typing the title of your home-remodeling spreadsheet in cell A1.**

   A Living Hell might be a good choice. As you type, the characters appear in the Entry bar.

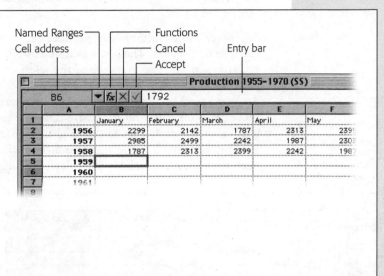

Figure 5-5:
The control center for spreadsheet creation is at the top of the window. You work on one cell at a time—the active cell—and Apple-Works displays its address at the top left. You can type new information into a cell, or edit an existing one, only in the Entry bar—you can't edit cells directly on the spreadsheet. The Named Ranges pop-up menu lets you create, edit, and select Named ranges. The Functions button calls up the Insert Function dialog box, the Cancel button deletes an entry in the Entry bar, and the Accept button accepts an entry in the Entry bar, inserting it into the active cell.

3. **Press Tab.**

   AppleWorks inserts the contents of the Entry bar into cell A1 and moves the active cell frame one cell to the right: cell B1.

4. **Type *January*.**

   You need to track expenses over time, so if you want to track the project by calendar year, begin by naming the first column January. You could now tab to the next cell, enter *February*, and work your way across the spreadsheet—but there's an easier way.

   One spreadsheet chore you'll find yourself doing repeatedly is creating a *series* of numbers, dates, times, and so on. In this case, the series is months of the year. Fortunately, AppleWorks can create a series automatically for you, saving you the effort of typing *February, March* and so on—you just have to start it off with the first entry or two.

5. **Starting with the active cell, drag directly to the right through 11 more cells.**

   If you're guessing how many cells you'll need for your series, drag a bit farther than you need to; you can always trim your series later. (Hint: if January is in column B, December will end up in column M.)

   AppleWorks highlights the cells you dragged through.

6. Choose Calculate→Fill Special.

AppleWorks displays the Fill Special dialog box, showing the contents of the currently active cell in the Start box (Figure 5-6). In this case, that item is a month name, so AppleWorks pre-selects the Month radio button. If you leave the "Increment by" box set to 1, AppleWorks displays every month. (If you were to change that setting to 2, AppleWorks would automatically generate cell labels for every *other* month.)

The other radio buttons here produce series of numbers, times, dates, days, months, or quarters. The last selection, Pattern, repeats an arbitrary series that you've typed into the first cells of the selection. For example, when creating a gradebook, you might want to repeat a set of four class names—English, Math, Art, and Science—three times, once for each term of the year. Begin by entering those items once, in four successive cells of a row. Then select those four cells, plus the eight empty cells to their right. Choose Calculate→Fill Special, set the Fill Special dialog box to Pattern, and click OK; AppleWorks automatically repeats the pattern enough times to fill all the highlighted cells.

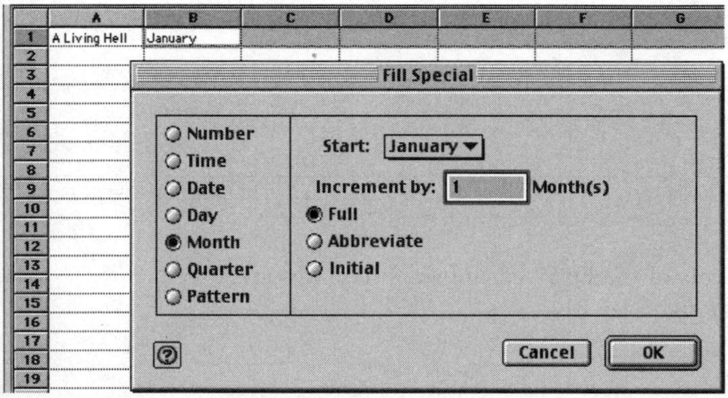

Figure 5-6:
In order for AppleWorks to do the work of creating a series for you, you have to tell the program what kind of a series you desire by choosing the appropriate radio button. AppleWorks guesses what kind of a series you want based on the contents of the first cell or cells in your selection. For all the radio buttons except Pattern, you can set a Start and "Increment by" value to determine how AppleWorks counts off the series. The Day, Month, and Quarter buttons also have options for abbreviating their names. The Pattern button requires you to indicate how many cells you want to repeat for your pattern.

7. Click OK.

AppleWorks fills in the rest of the selected cells with the names of the months.

Now it's time to list expense categories that will soon be making your life miserable, such as framing, windows, electrical, plumbing, and so on.

8. **Click cell A2 to select it. Type *Framing* and press Return.**

AppleWorks enters the first item into cell A2. Your press of the Return key highlights the cell below it, ready for you to type the second item.

9. **Type *Electrical* and press Return.**

Repeat this process as you enter each of the other remodeling expense categories: Windows, Plumbing, Roofing, Cabinets—whatever your project requires—until you've filled column A with useful construction categories (see Figure 5-7).

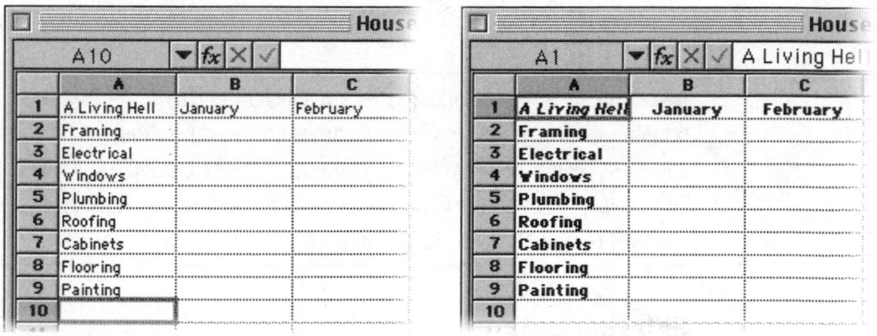

Figure 5-7:
After creating row and column headings, the skeleton of your new spreadsheet is complete (left). You can make the headings stand out from the data you'll soon put in the cells by changing the font style and alignment (right). Finally, change the style of the spreadsheet title in cell A1 to make it unique.

Formatting Cells

You want your labels to stand out from the body of the spreadsheet; fortunately, it's easy to format them. Though you can format cells individually, it's often more efficient to format a row, column, or range in one fell swoop. For example, you can set your category labels in boldface (see Figure 5-7).

1. **Drag across the occupied cells in the top row to select all the months.**

You *can* select an entire row or column by clicking the row or column heading—but dragging avoids formatting empty cells.

Note: A new AppleWorks spreadsheet is composed of empty cells. If you add text, numbers, or a formula to a cell—or even if you apply *formatting* to an empty cell—AppleWorks regards that cell as occupied. For on-screen viewing, it doesn't matter if you've formatted blank cells. But when you print, the program thinks those empty cells have something in them, and prints out any pages that contain them.

For example, suppose you have a *one-page* spreadsheet, but you chose Select All to change the font. When you print, if you don't specify that you want to print only a portion of the sheet, AppleWorks diligently prints out the entire spreadsheet, page after page of blank cells, until your printer cartridge runs out or you've printed the entire 40 columns by 500 rows, whichever comes first.

---

2. **Choose Format→Style→Bold, and then choose Format→Alignment→Center.**

AppleWorks applies bold formatting and centers the contents of the selected cells. While the cells are still selected, you can go on to change font, size, or color if you wish.

Repeat the process for the expense categories column. Because Cell A1 is already bold, the first time you use the bold command, AppleWorks *removes* the bolding from that cell, repeat the command and AppleWorks bolds all the cells in the selection.

Cell A1 is the title of the spreadsheet, so you may want to select it alone, and give it a unique look with, for example, italics. (More on formatting cells later in this chapter.)

Note: Because AppleWorks makes a distinction between the *contents* of a cell and its *formatting,* the program gives you a choice when it comes time to delete material. If you highlight a cell or range of cells and press Delete, you remove the contents of the cell, but the cell formatting remains. But if you choose Edit→Clear (or press the Clear key on your keyboard), you remove contents *and* formatting. (Edit→Cut removes cell contents and formatting, too.)

Entering Data

Now that the basic framework of the spreadsheet is in place, you can begin typing in actual numbers. For example, if you already have some expenses for January you can enter them now.

1. **Click Cell B2,** *Framing/January.*

Enter a figure for your January framing expenses. If you don't have any real figures yet, make something up—you'll be doing a lot of that if you try to predict expenses for this project!

2. **Press Return or Option-down arrow.**

AppleWorks enters the framing expenses and moves the active cell frame to the next cell down.

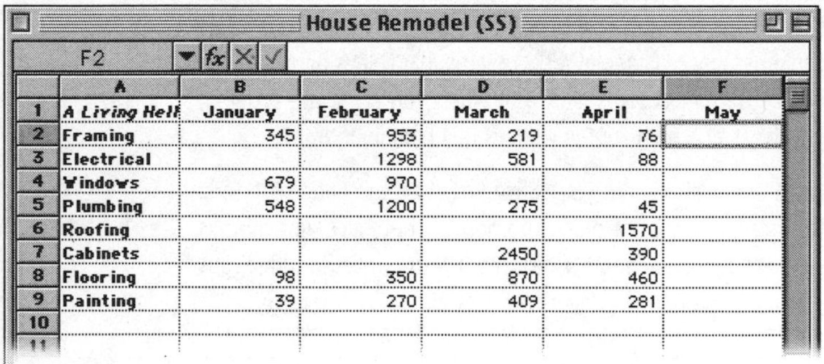

	A	B	C	D	E	F
1	A Living Hell	January	February	March	April	May
2	Framing	345	953	219	76	
3	Electrical		1298	581	88	
4	Windows	679	970			
5	Plumbing	548	1200	275	45	
6	Roofing				1570	
7	Cabinets			2450	390	
8	Flooring	98	350	870	460	
9	Painting	39	270	409	281	
10						
11						

Figure 5-8:
Fill in as many expenses as you can so that AppleWorks has some numbers to crunch. In some months you won't have expenses for every category—on the other hand, in some months you'll have expenses for categories you haven't yet dreamed of!

3. **Type another number to represent your Electrical expenses for January; press Return. Repeat steps 2 and 3 until you get to the bottom of the January column.**

For this experiment, the exact numbers to type don't much matter, but Figure 5-8 shows one suggestion.

Tip: If you want AppleWorks to handle the *year* correctly when calculating and displaying dates, type out all four digits (*3/1/1996,* not *3/1/96*). Also visit your →Control Panels→Date & Time control panel, click Date Formats, and turn on "Show Century." Doing so ensures that AppleWorks won't make silly Y2K-related errors when crunching your years numbers.

WORKAROUND WORKSHOP

Return vs. Enter

In most Mac situations, the Return and Enter keys behave identically. But when you're entering a column of numbers, there's a big difference. If you press Return, or Option-down arrow key, after each number, you enter your number in the current cell *and* advance to the next cell down. If you press Enter, on the other hand, AppleWorks enters the number in the cell, but *doesn't* advance to the next cell. If you enter another number at this moment, you *replace* your first entry.

This syndrome presents a real problem, because the Enter key is what you're tempted to use because of its location on your keyboard's number pad—which most people use when they have many numbers to enter. (If you don't already know how to do it, take a half hour to teach yourself to use the "Ten-key" pad without looking. The time you'll save over

the years can be spent enjoying the retirement savings you're calculating with your new spreadsheet.)

One solution is to drag from the top to the bottom of a column, highlighting it, before starting to type. Now, each time you type a number and then press Enter, AppleWorks highlights the next cell in the *selection*, allowing you to let your fingers fly over the number pad, pressing Enter between numbers. (This trick also works for a highlighted *row* or *range* of cells; AppleWorks proceeds across the top row, cell by cell, and then wraps to the next row, each time you press Enter.)

Another solution is to choose Edit→Preferences→ General→Spreadsheet; as described on page 307, you can change the Enter key's effect using the options in the resulting dialog box.

Totaling Columns

Continue entering numbers in your spreadsheet until it looks something like Figure 5-8. (When you reach the bottom of the first column, click in the top of the next one to continue typing.)

Now that it has some data to work with, AppleWorks can do a little work. Start with one of the most common spreadsheet calculations: totaling a column of numbers. First create a row heading for totals.

1. **Make one more row label at the bottom of column A: *Total*.**

This row will contain totals for all the monthly expenses. You can set it apart from the other rows by leaving an empty row between it and the expenses (Cell A11 in Figure 5-9).

2. **Drag from the top of the January column down to, and including, the Total row to highlight the entire column.**

   AppleWorks is adding up *numbers* here, so including "January" in your selection won't make any difference. You must, however, be sure the last cell in your selection is the cell in the Total row where you want your sum to appear (see Figure 5-9).

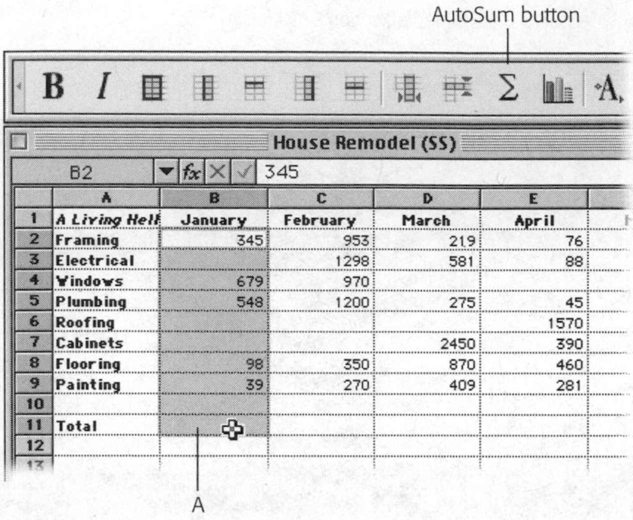

AutoSum button

Figure 5-9:
You have to tell AppleWorks what you would like it to total by selecting a column of cells. Drag through the cells, being sure to include the empty cell at the bottom for AppleWorks to insert the total into (A). You can drag from the top down or from the bottom up—either way, AppleWorks puts the total at the bottom after you choose Calculate→Auto Sum or click the AutoSum button (Σ) in the Button bar).

3. **Choose Calculate→Auto Sum, or click the AutoSum button (Figure 5-9).**

   In the bottom cell of the selection, AppleWorks automatically inserts a *formula* for totaling the column of numbers. (It's "=SUM(B2..B10)," meaning "add up the cells between B2 and B10.") You see the results of that formula in the cell—the total expenses for January.

4. **Click the cell containing the total.**

   AppleWorks displays the formula in the Entry bar. You could have manually entered the formula in this cell, but the Auto Sum command makes the process a lot easier and less prone to error.

   Now if you unearth another receipt for January expenses—for example, for that time you had to call the electrician after you accidentally cut through a wire—you can add that number to the spreadsheet.

5. **Enter an amount in the Electrical row for January (Cell B3 in Figure 5-9) and press Enter or click another cell.**

   This is why you're going to love spreadsheets: AppleWorks instantly updates January's total to reflect the change you made to the column of numbers.

Tip: The Auto Sum feature works in a similar fashion on *rows* of cells. Select a range of cells in a row, with an empty cell at the right-hand end for the total. Choose Calculate→Auto Sum; AppleWorks totals the cells from left to right, inserting the total in the rightmost cell.

On the other hand, if you've highlighted a rectangular *block* of cells, the Auto Sum command, AppleWorks tallies up the numbers in the rightmost *column* only.

The second-most-used spreadsheet calculation is *averaging* a column of numbers. Just for kicks, repeat the steps above on the February column—but in step 3, choose Calculate→Auto Average. Sure enough, AppleWorks averages the numbers in the column, ignoring cells that are empty or contain text, performing the calculation "divide the total of this range of cells by the number of cells that contain numbers."

Fill Right

You could continue selecting the cells in each month and using Auto Sum to create your totals until you'd completed the whole year. Instead, you can use the Fill command to avoid a lot of repeated effort. You can tell AppleWorks to create a calculation similar to the January total for the rest of the columns in the spreadsheet.

1. **Starting with the cell containing January's total, drag to the right, all the way over to the December column.**

   You've highlighted the range of cells for column totals, as shown in Figure 5-10.

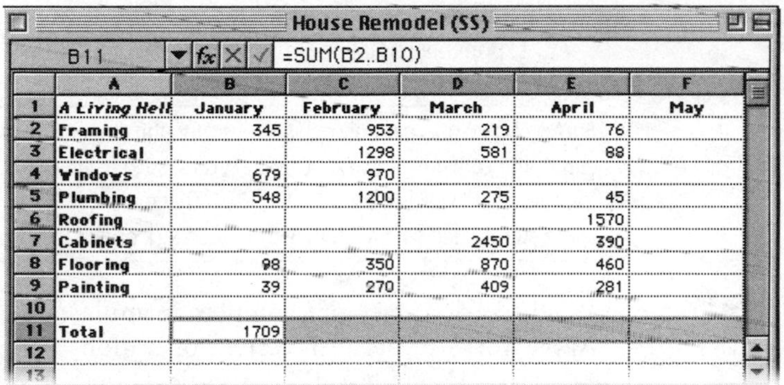

Figure 5-10:
In order to quickly total all the columns of the spreadsheet, drag from the cell containing the total for the first column (B11) all the way over to the last cell in the row that you need a column total for. When you choose Calculate→Fill Right, AppleWorks creates a total for each of the selected columns.

	A	B	C	D	E	F
1	A Living Hell	January	February	March	April	May
2	Framing	345	953	219	76	
3	Electrical		1298	581	88	
4	Windows	679	970			
5	Plumbing	548	1200	275	45	
6	Roofing				1570	
7	Cabinets			2450	390	
8	Flooring	98	350	870	460	
9	Painting	39	270	409	281	
10						
11	Total	1709				
12						
13						

B11 =SUM(B2..B10)

House Remodel (SS)

2. **Choose Calculate→Fill Right.**

   The Fill Right command copies the contents of the first cell and pastes it into every other cell in the selection. In this example, the first cell contains a *formula*, not just a total you typed yourself. So instead of pasting the exact same formula, which would place the January total into each column, AppleWorks understands that you want to total each column, and enters the appropriate formula in each cell of your selection. The result is monthly totals calculated right across the page.

This spreadsheet now functions as a monthly expense adding machine. As you enter your new expenses, AppleWorks instantly adjusts the totals.

3. Enter some figures in the column for May.

The May column was empty before, with a total of zero. After making entries in the column, AppleWorks fills in the correct total. As an added experiment, you might try *changing* one of the numbers you've typed, and then marveling as AppleWorks instantly re-calculates the total at the bottom of the column.

Formulas and Functions

You can use the Auto Sum feature to total rows or columns, but you're not limited to performing math on neat lines of adjacent cells. A formula can perform calculations using numbers from other cells anywhere in the spreadsheet—or even to cells in *other* spreadsheets.

Every formula starts with the = sign, which tells AppleWorks to display in this cell the results of the formula you're about to type. You can write your own formulas using standard mathematical operators, entering cell references by clicking the cell or by typing the cell address (see Table 5-7).

Operation	Symbol	Example
Addition	+	B7+9
Subtraction	-	C12-C4
Multiplication	*	G9*.06
Division	/	H4/C3
Exponential notation	^	E5^3

Note: AppleWorks has only one *text* operator: the ampersand (&). You can use it to combine—or *concatenate*—the contents of two or more text cells, such as a first name and a last name. In such a case, the formula would look like this: *=E7 & " " &D7.* That means: "Put whatever word is in cell E7, then a space (the space surrounded by quotation marks), then tack on the word in cell D7."

When you create more complex formulas, you can use parentheses to force AppleWorks to perform certain operations before others, for example, 3+((7-5)*(9+6))/12. AppleWorks starts calculating with the innermost sets of parentheses and works its way outward. In this example, then, it would think to itself: 7-5=2, 9+6 =15, 2*15=30, 30/12= 2.5, and finally, 3+2.5=5.5.

To make the monthly totals in the tutorial example more meaningful—and to help figure out how long it's going to take you to pay off this project—calculate an overall total for the year.

1. Skip a line below the Total row and enter another row heading: *Grand Total.* **Press Tab.**

AppleWorks moves the active cell frame to Cell B13.

To calculate an annual total for the spreadsheet, you need to tell AppleWorks to add together all the monthly totals. In this case, the cells to be added are separated from the cell for the total, so AutoSum won't work. Instead, you need to use a formula to tell AppleWorks what to add up.

One way to do this would be to type a formula in the entry bar. You could write the formula as "=B11+C11+D11+E11+F11+G11" and so on, all the way out to M11.

A far easier way is to use an AppleWorks *function* on this range of cells. Functions are pre-designed formula "templates." You're about to use one of the easiest-to-understand functions: the SUM function. AppleWorks offers 103 built-in functions that fall into eight categories: business and financial, numeric, date and time, statistical, logical, trigonometric, information, and text. (These functions are each described in the built-in AppleWorks Help. For more detail, visit *www.missingmanual.com,* where you can download a free 65-page Functions Appendix that provides a description and examples of each.)

You can enter functions into a cell in three ways. First, select the cell where you wish to place the function and, if you know its *exact* format, type it in directly. Or, click a cell and then choose Edit→Insert Function. Finally, click a cell and then click the Function button (see Figure 5-5) to display the Insert Function dialog box.

2. **Click the Function button in the Entry bar (see Figure 5-5).**

   The Insert Function dialog box appears.

3. **Scroll down the list and double-click** *SUM(number 1, number 2…).*

   AppleWorks inserts the Sum function into the Entry bar. Like all of the AppleWorks built-in functions, this one is divided into two parts: the function name ("SUM") and the parenthetical *arguments,* or independent variables, upon which the function is acting.

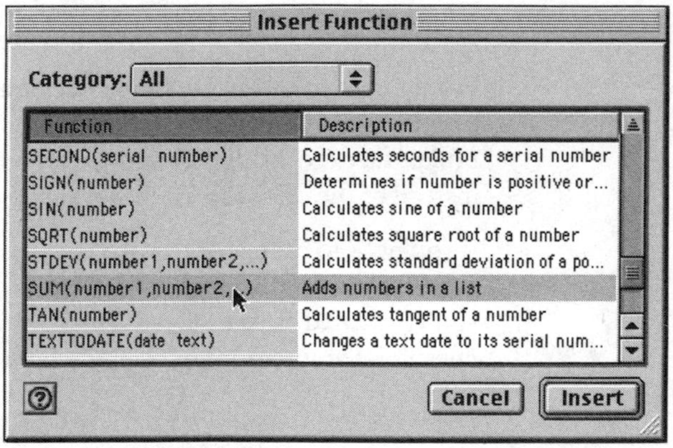

Figure 5-11:
You can choose to view just one category of functions, or the entire collection, using this window's pop-up menu. Double-click a function to paste it into the Entry bar. Descriptions of what the cryptic function names actually mean are listed on the right. For more detailed function descriptions, click the help icon and then click "Select a function" in the help window—or download the free Functions Appendix from this book's page at www.missingmanual.com.

Insert Function
Category: All

Function	Description
SECOND(serial number)	Calculates seconds for a serial number
SIGN(number)	Determines if number is positive or...
SIN(number)	Calculates sine of a number
SQRT(number)	Calculates square root of a number
STDEV(number1,number2,...)	Calculates standard deviation of a po...
SUM(number1,number2,)	Adds numbers in a list
TAN(number)	Calculates tangent of a number
TEXTTODATE(date text)	Changes a text date to its serial num...

Cancel   Insert

The freshly inserted function contains placeholders for its arguments ("number 1, number 2…") that you must replace with real numbers or cell addresses. Be sure you remove any ellipses (…), but preserve the parentheses around the arguments. If you make a mistake with function formatting, AppleWorks displays an error message in the cell when you press Enter or try to move to another cell.

In this example, you're directing AppleWorks to sum up all the monthly totals, so the range of cells containing those totals needs to go between the parentheses.

4. **Select everything between the parentheses, and drag through all the monthly totals.**

   As you drag across the cells, AppleWorks inserts the cell range within the parentheses. In this example the function now reads, =SUM(B11..M11)—in other words, "add up the contents of the cells B11 through M11, and display the result."

5. **Click the Accept button in the Entry bar, click any other cell, or press Tab.**

   AppleWorks performs the calculation and displays the result in cell B13, the grand total for the year.

Named Ranges

As you create formulas, you may find yourself referring over and over to the same cell or range of cells. For example, in the remodeling spreadsheet, you may need to refer to the Grand Total in several other formulas. So that you don't have to repeatedly type the cell address or click to select the cell, AppleWorks lets you give a cell, or range of cells, a *name*. After doing so, you can write a formula in the form of, for example, "= Grand total – Jan. Flooring" (instead of "= B13 – B9").

To create a named cell or range, simply select the cell or range, and from the Names pop-up menu in the entry bar, choose Define Name. In the resulting dialog box, enter a name for your cell(s) and click Define.

Note: No two cells can have the same name. Other requirements: the first character of a cell name must be a letter, names can't contain punctuation marks or operators (+, =, and so on), and they can't take the form of a cell reference (such as B5) or a function (such as SUM).

From now on, the cell's or range's name appears in the Named Ranges pop-up menu (Figure 5-5). The next time you want to go to that cell or range, or use it in a formula, you need only select it from this pop-up menu. AppleWorks displays the name instead of the cell address whenever you create a formula that refers to a named cell.

If you need to change or remove a name, choose Edit Names from the Named Ranges pop-up menu to display the Edit Names dialog box. AppleWorks shows all the names you've created in the spreadsheet, and makes the Delete button available—but it doesn't let you remove or change a name that's being used in a formula.

Tip: You can use named cells as a quick way to navigate a large spreadsheet. By naming cells at key points in the spreadsheet, you can select them from the Names pop-up menu and jump to the corresponding cells.

References: Absolute and Relative

When you create a formula by typing the addresses of cells or by clicking on a cell, you've created a *cell reference*. AppleWorks generally considers cell references in a *relative* way—it remembers those cell coordinates by position relative to the selected cell, not as, for example, "B12." For example, a relative reference thinks of another cell in the spreadsheet as "three rows above and two columns to the left of this cell" (see Figure 5-12).

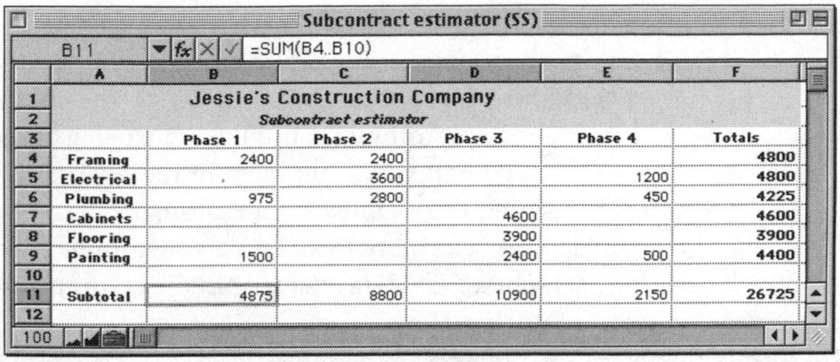

	A	B	C	D	E	F
1		Jessie's Construction Company				
2		Subcontract estimator				
3		Phase 1	Phase 2	Phase 3	Phase 4	Totals
4	Framing	2400	2400			4800
5	Electrical		3600		1200	4800
6	Plumbing	975	2800		450	4225
7	Cabinets			4600		4600
8	Flooring			3900		3900
9	Painting	1500		2400	500	4400
10						
11	Subtotal	4875	8800	10900	2150	26725
12						

***Figure 5-12:** When the formula for cell B11 [=SUM(B4..B10)] is Filled Right across the row to cell F11, AppleWorks pastes relative cell references into all those cells that say, in effect, "display the total of the numbers in the cells above this cell." That way, each column's subtotal applies to the figures in that column.*

Relative references make it possible for you to insert a new row or column into your spreadsheet without throwing off all the formulas you've already stored. They make the Fill Right command possible, too (see Figure 5-12). They also make formulas portable: when you paste a formula that adds up the two cells above it into another spreadsheet location, the pasted cell adds up the two cells above *it* (in its new location).

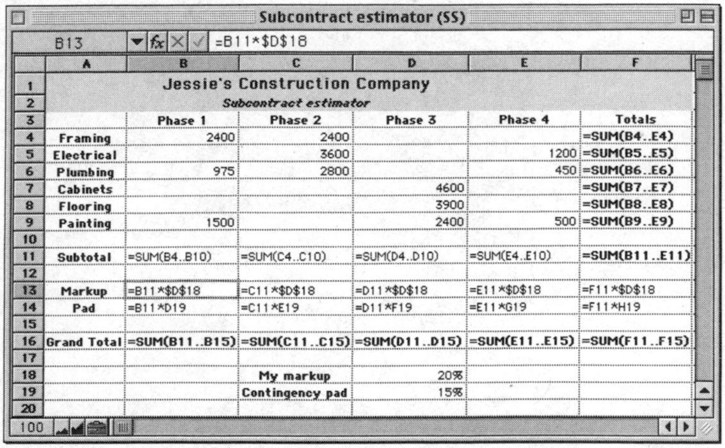

	A	B	C	D	E	F
1		Jessie's Construction Company				
2		Subcontract estimator				
3		Phase 1	Phase 2	Phase 3	Phase 4	Totals
4	Framing	2400	2400			=SUM(B4..E4)
5	Electrical		3600		1200	=SUM(B5..E5)
6	Plumbing	975	2800		450	=SUM(B6..E6)
7	Cabinets			4600		=SUM(B7..E7)
8	Flooring			3900		=SUM(B8..E8)
9	Painting	1500		2400	500	=SUM(B9..E9)
10						
11	Subtotal	=SUM(B4..B10)	=SUM(C4..C10)	=SUM(D4..D10)	=SUM(E4..E10)	=SUM(B11..E11)
12						
13	Markup	=B11*D18	=C11*D18	=D11*D18	=E11*D18	=F11*D18
14	Pad	=B11*D19	=C11*E19	=D11*F19	=E11*G19	=F11*H19
15						
16	Grand Total	=SUM(B11..B15)	=SUM(C11..C15)	=SUM(D11..D15)	=SUM(E11..E15)	=SUM(F11..F15)
17						
18			My markup	20%		
19			Contingency pad	15%		
20						

***Figure 5-13:** The formula in B13 multiplies the subtotal by the markup, using an absolute reference to D18: "=B11*D18." When the B13 formula is filled right across the row, AppleWorks uses the absolute reference for the markup percentage, and the relative reference for the column subtotal. By contrast, the formula in row 14 was incorrectly entered without the absolute reference, so when it is filled right, an incorrect result will be displayed in each of the filled cells.*

Absolute references, on the other hand, refer to a specific cell, no matter where the formula appears in the spreadsheet. They can be useful when you need to refer to a particular cell in the spreadsheet—the one containing the sales tax rate, for example—for a formula that repeats over several columns. Figure 5-13 gives an example.

You designate an absolute cell reference by including a $ in front of the row and/or column reference. (For the first time in its life, the $ symbol has nothing to do with money in this context.) For example, A7 is an absolute reference for cell A7.

Tip: When you're creating a formula, you can ⌘-Option-click a cell to create an absolute reference to it, saving you the trouble of typing $ symbols. AppleWorks inserts its address in the formula, complete with the dollar signs.

You can also create a *mixed reference* in order to lock the reference to either the row or column—for example, G$8, in which the column reference is relative and the row is absolute. You might use this unusual arrangement when, for example, your column A contains discount rates for the customers whose names appear in column B. In writing the formula for a customer's final price (in column D, for example), you'd use a *relative* reference to a row number (which is different for every customer), but an *absolute* reference to the column (which is always A).

POWER USERS' CLINIC

Linking Spreadsheets

A new feature of AppleWorks 6 is the ability to link cells in one spreadsheet to those in other spreadsheets or spreadsheet frames. For example, you can create a spreadsheet called Net Worth that adds up data from several *other* spreadsheets—your stock portfolio, checking account, mortgage, and antique-spoon collection spreadsheets. Then, when the value of a referenced cell in one of these other spreadsheets changes, the total in the Net Worth spreadsheet changes, too.

You can create references either to external spreadsheets on your hard drive or on your office network. In other words, the accounting department, the marketing department, and the PR department could reference spreadsheets on one another's computers.

As you build your formula in the spreadsheet before you, you create a reference to another spreadsheet in this form: "name of spreadsheet, exclamation point, cell address." For example, to reference cell C14 in a spreadsheet titled *Mortgage,* write the formula: *=Mortgage!C14.* Or, to total a range of values in the *Portfolio* spreadsheet, write *=SUM (Portfolio!B7..H7).*

If the spreadsheet name includes spaces, characters other than A–Z, and numbers, or itself *resembles* a cell address or function name, you must enclose it in quotation marks—for example, *="Spoon Collection"!G54.*

You can combine these external cell references with "internal" references (that is, cells in the current spreadsheet) as you create formulas. For example, *=("Spoon Collection"!G5+B7)/3* adds cell G5 of the Spoon Collection spreadsheet to cell B7 (of the open, Net Worth spreadsheet) and divides the total by 3.

To reference a spreadsheet *frame* in another document or the current document, first name the frame. To do so, select the frame, choose Edit→Frame Info, and then type a name.

Create a reference to a frame in the *same* document in the form, "name of frame in brackets, exclamation point, cell address." For example, *[Sterling Silver Spoons]!E9.*

Create a reference to a frame in a *different* document in the form, "name of spreadsheet, name of frame in brackets, exclamation point, cell address." For example, *"Spoon Collection"[Sterling Silver Spoons]!E9.*

Caution: If you create cell references that refer to cells containing other formulas, beware of the *circular reference*. This is the spreadsheet version of a Mexican standoff: the formula in each cell depends on the other, so neither formula can make the first move. For example, the formulas J6=R5 and R5=J6/3 contain circular references because the two cells refer to each other. If you create one of these impossible equations, AppleWorks surrounds the cell contents with bullet dots and displays an error message. (You can turn off this warning, if you like, in the Edit→Preferences→General→Spreadsheet dialog box.)

Copying and Pasting Cells

It's fairly easy to move cells around on the spreadsheet—in fact, AppleWorks offers four ways to do so.

- **Drag-and-drop.** Simply drag a cell or range of cells to a new locale (see Figure 5-14).

Caution: When you move or paste cells, the transferred material *replaces* any information that may be in your destination cells. Be sure your target cells have enough room for the material you're moving. (For example, if you highlight ten vertical cells, copy them, and then paste them into an area with only eight empty vertical cells, AppleWorks wipes out the contents of two already filled cells.)

If you make a mistake, choose Edit→Undo Move.

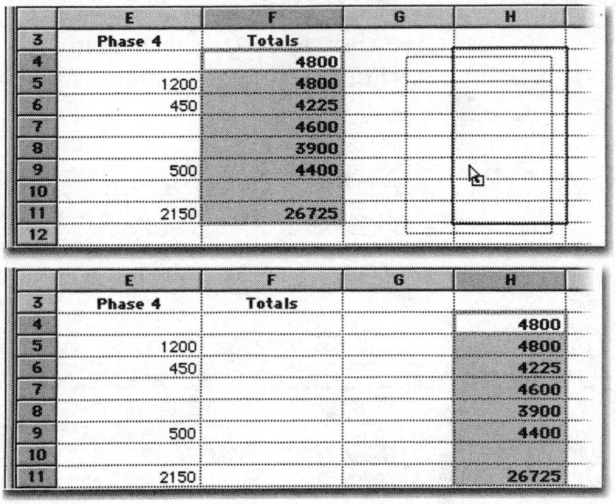

Figure 5-14:
Select the cell or cells you want to move. Position the cursor inside the highlighted area (or if only one cell is selected, on the border around the selection). The plus-sign cursor changes to the little-box-with-arrow cursor, indicating you're in drag-and-drop mode. Now drag to a new area of the spreadsheet (top). Double-check the dotted-line outline of the cells you're moving, to be certain you're not about to overwrite anything important. Finally, release the mouse button; AppleWorks deposits the cells into their new location and performs any re-calculations caused by the move (bottom).

- **Click-and-drop.** Highlight some cells. Scroll to wherever you want to move them. (This method is sometimes more convenient than drag-and-dropping when the target is extremely far from the original selection, saving you from a long drag-and-scroll operation.) While pressing ⌘-Option, click the first cell of your destination. AppleWorks instantly transports the selected cells into the location you clicked.

Be careful with this method, however; unlike the drag-and-drop method of moving cells, it doesn't provide a dotted outline of the cells you're moving to show you which cells will be overwritten.

- **The Move To command.** Here's another means of moving some cells "way across town" to the other side of a huge spreadsheet. After highlighting the cells you want to move, choose Calculate→Move to summon the Move dialog box. Enter the coordinates of the top-left cell of your destination, and then click OK. Your selection—and your view—move to the new location.

- **Cut and Paste.** First highlight the cells you want to delete. Then choose Edit→Cut. Scroll to the place where you want the highlighted material to reappear, click a cell, and choose Edit→Paste. (The original cells are now empty.)

Moving cells around in a spreadsheet can sometimes be a delicate operation, because cells containing formulas with *relative* cell references can end up referring to the wrong cells. When you cut and paste, AppleWorks *updates* the relative cell references, meaning they now refer to different cells (but in the same positions relative to the new location of the formula). If you instead use the Move command, drag-and-drop, or click-and-drop, the relative cell references don't change: the formulas refer to the same cells no matter where you move the selection. Figure 5-15 illustrates the point.

Adjusting Rows and Columns

If you have more to say than fits in a cell, if you need room for more decimal places, or if you just want to use larger fonts, AppleWorks provides several tools to adjust cell size.

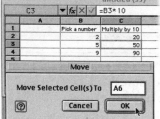

Figure 5-15:
*The cut-and-paste difference: Following this example (and any example involving cell references) requires a good deal of concentration, but it's an essential exercise for anyone who moves cells. Suppose that cell B3 contains "5" and C3 contains the formula "=B3*10." As a result, cell C3 displays "50" (top left). If you cut and paste C3 into, for example, cell D7, then the formula changes to "=C7*10" (top right)—that is, it re-computes its relative reference, and remembers that it's supposed to be multiplying 10 by the cell to its left. But if you instead use the Move command (lower left) and place that cell anywhere in the spreadsheet, the formula remains "=B3*10" (lower right), still referring to the original cell.*

Text Wrap

If you have more than a few words in a cell, AppleWorks reacts in one of two ways. If the cell or cells to the right are empty, the text can extend across several columns—which can be useful for a heading above several columns. If the cell to the right is occupied, then the overrun text is simply hidden. If you press Return to try to get a second line in a cell, you find yourself booted down to the cell below, since AppleWorks uses Return to make your entry and move to the next cell.

Fortunately, AppleWorks can *wrap* text, automatically creating more lines in the cell so all the text fits in the narrow column. Just select the cell containing the text, and then choose Format→Alignment→Wrap. AppleWorks wraps text to the width of the column—but it doesn't change the height of the row, which you'll have to do next to see your newly wrapped text.

Tip: If you let your text run wild over adjoining empty cells—to create a section headline, for example—the direction it takes depends on the text alignment setting for the cell. Flush left overwrites cells to the right, flush right overwrites cells to the left, and centered text spreads out equally in both directions.

Adjusting Row Height and Column Width

AppleWorks can automatically adjust the height of a row and the width of a column so the dimensions are just large enough to display the cell contents. Just select the overly full cell, and then choose Format→Autosize Rows (or click the Autosize Row button in the Button bar).

The row height expands enough to display the contents of the selected cell, or if the row is selected, the tallest cell in the row. If you had selected several rows before choosing Autosize Rows, AppleWorks adjusts the height of all the selected rows equally.

Note: The Autosize feature sets the size of the row, but doesn't *keep* it adjusted. If you add or remove text from your tallest cell, you'll have to re-apply the Autosize command.

The Autosize Column command (or button) works exactly the same way for column width.

Figure 5-16:
If you change font sizes or wrap text to create more than one line per row, you'll have to adjust the cell size. AppleWorks can Autosize the dimensions for you, but if you prefer more direct control, position the cursor in the row or column headings and drag the dividers manually. If you select several rows or columns at once then when you adjust one of them, they all assume the new dimension—a handy way to tidy up a spreadsheet after too many manual adjustments.

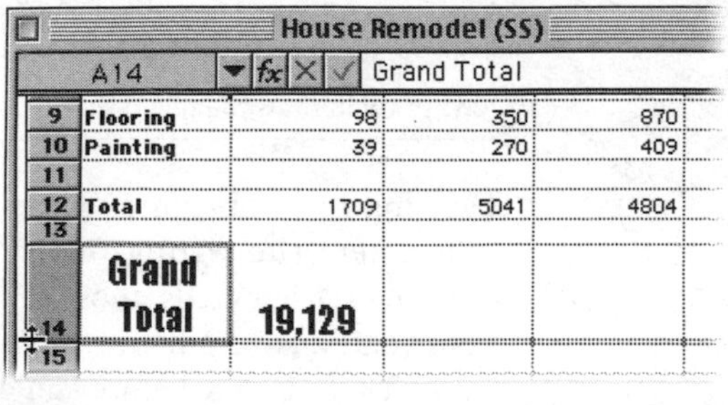

You can also adjust the size of rows and columns manually, using the mouse. Move the plus-sign cursor onto the row or column heading. When you move across the dividing line between two rows or columns, the plus sign turns into a bar with two arrows. When it does, drag the dividing line to make the row or column any size. Or, if you double click when your cursor assumes the bar shape, you trigger the Autosize command, automatically adjusting the row or column above or to the left of your cursor.

If you have a penchant for precision—or if you have chosen to hide row and column headings for a cleaner look—you can adjust the row and column dimensions numerically, using a dialog box.

1. **Choose Format→Column Width (or Row Height) to display the dialog box.**

   Alternatively, choose Column Width or Row Height from the pop-up menu that appears when you Control-click a cell.

2. **Enter a new measurement, in points.**

   Actually, you can use any unit of measurement if you use the correct abbreviation: in (inches), mm (millimeters), cm (centimeters), pc (picas), or pt (points). Or turn on the default checkbox if you want AppleWorks to return the cells to their default size.

3. **Click OK.**

   AppleWorks makes the requested adjustment, leaving it up to you to re-evaluate and repeat—or move on to your next formatting target.

Inserting or Removing Rows and Columns

Plan ahead as carefully as you can, but if something comes along—a new expense category, a recalled product, a new member in the Scout troop, or triplets when you were expecting twins—it's time to insert or delete a row or column in your spreadsheet.

To insert a row or column, click the row or column heading and choose Format→Insert Cells. AppleWorks wedges in the new row *above* the row you selected, or the new column *to the left* of the selected column. The program also adjusts any formulas containing cell references—relative or absolute—to account for the presence of this new row or column.

Tip: To insert several rows or columns at once, select the appropriate number of rows or columns, even if they already contain numbers—and *then* choose Format→Insert Cells. AppleWorks inserts as many new rows or columns as you had selected.

Deleting a row or column is almost too easy, considering the damage you can do if you delete the wrong one! Click the row or column heading and choose Format→Delete Cells; those cells—and the data they contain—are history. (Is that your *final* answer? If not, you've got one chance to change your mind: Choose Edit→Undo Delete before you do another thing.)

Inserting or Deleting Cells

You can also insert new, blank *cells* into existing rows and columns. Select one cell or a range of cells in the location you need the new cells, and choose Format→Insert Cells.

The Insert Cells dialog box appears, containing two choices: Shift Cells Down or Shift Cells Right. This choice determines what's to become of the currently selected cells. If you choose to shift down, the new cells appear at the selection, the selection slides down, and anything below in the affected column or columns also shifts down. Shift Cells Right performs a similar maneuver, sliding the rows to the east.

Caution: If the columns or rows that you send shifting across the spreadsheet by inserting cells already contain data, you can mangle the entire spreadsheet in short order. For example, data you entered in the debit column can suddenly end up in the credit column. Proceed with extreme caution.

You can also delete selected cells; use the same Format→Delete cells command. Re-read the above Caution, and make sure you wouldn't rather delete or clear the *contents* of the cells (using Edit→Clear), thereby leaving the surrounding cellular neighborhood unaffected.

Advanced Formatting

Don't let the fact that AppleWorks opens to this dreary grid of Geneva type lead you to believe that spreadsheets *have to* look so drab. AppleWorks is willing to let you format each cell of the spreadsheet to show off your design genius. Unlike word processing, where you can format each *letter* of a word differently, in the spreadsheet, you can give a unique look to each *cell*.

Figure 5-17:
If you give some cells a larger font size, AppleWorks doesn't enlarge the cells themselves to accommodate the larger type (left). The result: chopped-off numbers and letters. This is a good time to use the Autosize feature. With the cell selected, choose Format→Autosize Rows (or Autosize Columns), to produce the result shown at right.

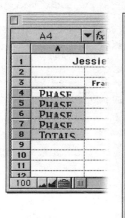
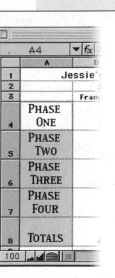

In addition to the normal word processing text formatting options—fonts, sizes, styles, and colors—you can add or remove cell borders, hide column or row headings, adjust the height and width of rows and columns, and apply colored or patterned backgrounds to cells.

Tip: If you want to save a lot of time doing this kind of formatting, check out the Starting Points Templates and Web tabs for an assortment of prefab spreadsheet templates. Begin your project with one of those and leave the graphic design to the pros.

Font Formatting

You can change text characteristics—font, size, style, color, and alignment—by choosing Format and selecting the appropriate submenu. AppleWorks applies the formatting change to the active cell or the range of selected cells. (But doing so can be tricky: see Figure 5-17).

You can also change the ho-hum Geneva font that AppleWorks favors to something better. To change the font for a spreadsheet you're working on, choose Options→Default Font, and then specify a different font in the list. If you also want to change the size, type a new size in the Size box.

As soon as you click OK, AppleWorks applies the new font to every cell of the spreadsheet, changing the font of everything you've entered—*except* cells you've formatted with another font or size.

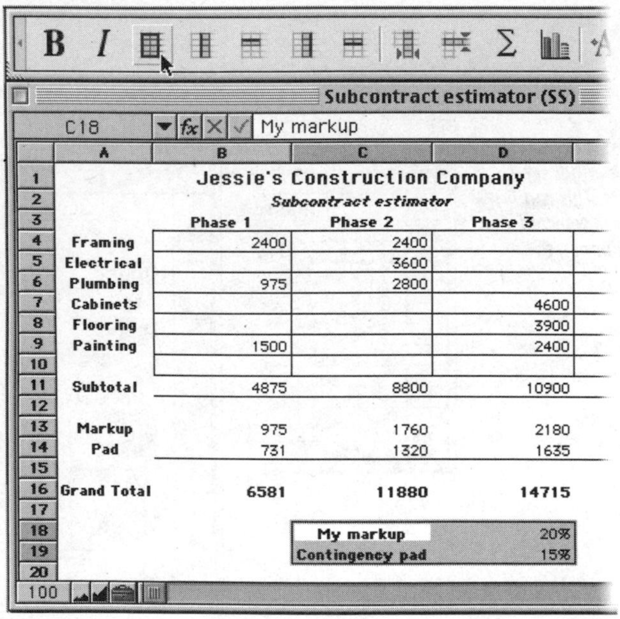

Figure 5-18:
You can use borders to create a line to separate totals from a column, create a grid to make it easier to read rows, or make a box around a group of cells to set them apart, as shown here. The border controls on the Button bar make applying borders to different sides of your cells very easy.

This default font setting applies only to the open spreadsheet. To redefine the *real* default font—the one that applies to all new spreadsheets—you need to create a new default spreadsheet document. See page 278.

Tip: AppleWorks can automatically color the negative numbers in a spreadsheet red, a common practice in accounting and business. Select a range of cells and choose Scripts (the scroll menu on your menu bar)→Spreadsheet→Negative Cells Red.

Cell Borders

You can accentuate or separate cells in your spreadsheet by using borders. For example, you can add a border to the top side of cells containing column totals, to separate the column of numbers from the total (Figure 5-18).

To add a border, select a cell or range of cells, and then click one of the five cell-border buttons in the default Button bar (see Figure 5-18). Four of these buttons add borders to any side of a cell or range; the outline button puts a border around all sides of the cell or range. These buttons are toggles: Click once to add, and again to remove, a border.

You can also select a cell or range of cells and then choose Format→Borders (or choose Borders from the contextual pop-up menu) to display the Borders dialog box. Use the checkboxes to designate which sides of the cell selection get the borders.

When AppleWorks adds individual borders to a range of cells, each *cell* receives the border—unless you choose Outline, which outlines the entire selected block of cells without affecting the inter-cell borders. If you click the buttons or turn on the checkboxes for Left, Right, Top, and Bottom, AppleWorks applies a border to each cell in the range.

Tip: The trouble with the built-in cell-border feature is that you can't *format* the borders AppleWorks adds; you can't change their color, thickness, or pattern.

Fortunately, the Scripts menu (the scroll icon in your menu bar) offers a Spreadsheet→Draw Cell Borders command. It draws borders around each cell in your selection, too. But it works by drawing actual, free-floating lines on your spreadsheet that just *look* like borders. The good news is that if you click carefully, you can select these line segments and then change their thickness, color, or pattern (using the Accents palette).

The bad news is that if any column widths or row heights change, you'll be left with line segments floating on your spreadsheet that don't align with any cells at all. For this reason, postpone using the Scripts→Spreadsheet→Draw Cell Borders command until your spreadsheet is otherwise complete.

Number Formats

When AppleWorks creates a new spreadsheet, it formats any numbers you enter exactly the way you type them—it doesn't automatically add commas, dollar signs, or decimals worked out to eight places. Often, however, you'll want to format the numbers in a certain way, perhaps as currency or in scientific notation.

To do so, open the Format Number, Date, and Time dialog box, as shown in Figure 5-19.

Tip: To format the numbers in just one cell, double-click the cell to open the Format Number, Date, and Time dialog box.

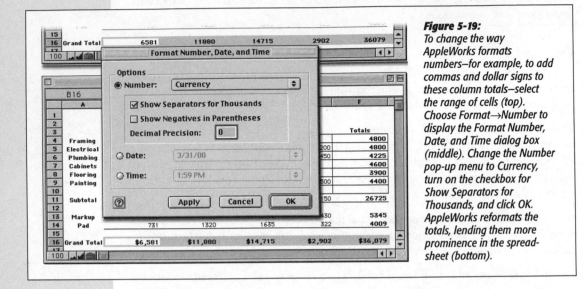

Figure 5-19:
To change the way AppleWorks formats numbers—for example, to add commas and dollar signs to these column totals—select the range of cells (top). Choose Format→Number to display the Format Number, Date, and Time dialog box (middle). Change the Number pop-up menu to Currency, turn on the checkbox for Show Separators for Thousands, and click OK. AppleWorks reformats the totals, lending them more prominence in the spreadsheet (bottom).

The Format dialog box also lets you indicate whether this cell contains a number, a date, or a time using the radio buttons; choose a format (such as *2/21/01*, *Feb 21, 2001*, or *Wednesday, February 21, 2001* for dates; *3:31 PM, 3:31:45 PM,* or *15:31:45* for times) using the pop-up menus. For number formatting, you also can opt to have AppleWorks automatically insert commas for thousands or put negative numbers in parentheses, as accountants do. You can also tell AppleWorks just how precise you want it to be—up to eleven decimal places—using the Decimal Precision setting. (If you specify that you want, say, four decimal places, then whenever you type *7* into a cell formatted that way, AppleWorks will write "7.0000.")

Tip: If you create a spreadsheet that deals with money, the dollar signs tend to clutter things up if they appear in every cell. So instead of formatting these cells as Currency, consider formatting them as Fixed numbers with a Decimal Precision of 2, as shown in Figure 5-19. Turn on the checkbox for Show Separators for Thousands; your spreadsheet will have a much cleaner appearance. Then you may want to format just the totals as Currency so that the dollar signs appear in only those cells.

If you format numbers as Currency, your computer's system settings for currency determine which currency sign—$, £, ¥, and so on—AppleWorks displays. Choose →Control Panels→Numbers to adjust your currency formatting.

Caution: Currency formats are not attached to your spreadsheet document. For example, if you prepare a spreadsheet detailing your holiday expenses in Norway, you'd change the currency setting in the system Control Panel to display Norwegian kroner. Later, when you change the settings back to display dollars, the Norwegian spreadsheet simply slaps dollar signs in front of the unchanged numbers. (No, AppleWorks doesn't automatically calculate the exchange rate.)

Adding Colors and Patterns

You can dress up your spreadsheets, emphasize certain cells, or set off clusters of numbers by adding a color or pattern to their cell backgrounds. As usual, begin by selecting the cell or cells to modify. If the Accents window isn't showing, choose Window→Show Accents. You can choose from either—or both—of the two first tabs: colors or patterns. Click the Fill button; the color or pattern you choose from its palette is applied to the selected cells. Click the Pen button to change the cell-border line color or pattern.

Style Sheets

After you create formatting that involves several steps—Palatino 14-point bold, light yellow background, blue text, black border—consider saving it as a *style,* a canned set of attributes that you can re-use on other cells with a single click. (Creating and saving new styles in the spreadsheet works exactly as it does in the Word Processing module; see Chapter 3 for details.)

As with text styles, the easiest way to create a new spreadsheet style is to format a spreadsheet cell exactly as you want it. Select the cell. Choose Format→Show Styles and click New in the Styles dialog box. AppleWorks displays the New Style dialog box. Give the style a name, turn on the checkbox for "Inherit document selection format," click the "SS-Table" radio button, change the "Based on" pop-up menu to None, and click OK.

Now you can apply that same formatting to other selected cells by choosing Format→Show Styles and double-clicking your new style, or by choosing from the Styles button pop-up menu in the Button Bar.

Tip: AppleWorks comes with a selection of handsome, ready-to-use spreadsheet styles that save you the trouble of creating your own. To see them, highlight some cells and then choose Format→Show Styles. The Styles dialog box appears. Click once on any of the styles to see a preview; double-click to apply that style to your selection.

As you might suspect with these "off the rack" styles, some alterations are required for a perfect fit, but they make a great starting point for dressing up a drab spreadsheet.

Copying and Pasting Cell Formats

With font formatting, color and pattern, and number formatting, tweaking a complex spreadsheet into submission can be a tedious process. AppleWorks provides a helpful feature to relieve some of that tedium: the ability to copy *just* the formatting of a cell or cells and apply it to another part of the spreadsheet—or even another spreadsheet.

To do so, highlight the cells whose formatting you want to copy. Then choose Edit→Copy Format. Now select the cells that you want to inherit the same formatting; finally, choose Edit→Apply Format.

Locking Cells

Accidentally deleting or changing a line or paragraph in a word processing document can certainly cause problems, but you'll usually catch the error by proofreading. But if you delete or accidentally change a formula in a *spreadsheet*, the results can be disastrous—if, for example, that formula calculates your sales tax rate, sales projections, or tithe percentage. Such errors in the basic structure of a spreadsheet can be extremely difficult to detect by proofreading, and if left undetected, can lead you to draw wrong conclusions from the data.

To help prevent this problem, AppleWorks lets you *lock* individual cells, or ranges of cells, to keep them safe from alteration. (Fortunately, locking a cell doesn't prevent the formula within it from working; the number a locked cell displays, in other words, may still update itself as you edit related cells in your spreadsheet.) To use the locking function, select the cell or cells, and then choose Options→Lock Cells.

If you try to change or delete a cell you've locked in this way, AppleWorks warns you about the cell's locked status. In order to make changes to a locked cell, you must first unlock it: select the cell or range and then choose Options→Unlock Cells.

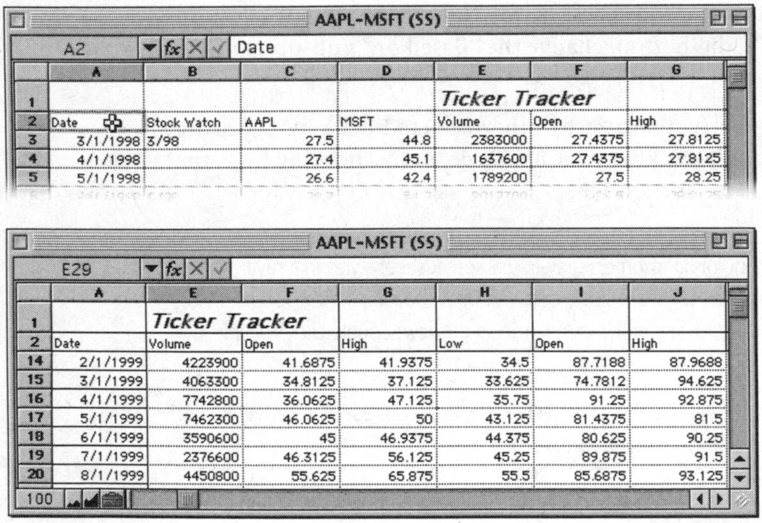

Figure 5-20:
If your spreadsheet is larger than your screen, once you start scrolling, you're lost—the column and row titles are off the screen. To keep them in view, AppleWorks offers locking titles. To lock column titles, select the bottom row of the titles; to lock row titles, select the rightmost title column; to lock both row and column titles, select the cell that both intersect (such as A2, top). Then choose Options→Lock Title Position. No matter how far you scroll, those titles remain locked on your screen (bottom)—you'll never lose your way again.

Locking Titles

Usually the first row and first column of a spreadsheet contain headings. Once your spreadsheet outgrows your screen, the headings disappear from view as you scroll down or to the right, leaving you without headings for the grid of cells now in view. AppleWorks provides *locking titles* to solve this problem.

You can lock row or column titles—or both. Then you can scroll far and wide in your spreadsheet and the titles remain locked in place in the window. Figure 5-20 illustrates how this works.

Tip: *If you need to compare widely separated parts of the spreadsheet, for example, the very last entries in Row 89 with the first entries in Row 2, split the window into* panes. *Drag the horizontal pane control (at the very top of the vertical scroll bar) downward. Then you can scroll independently within the two panes. The same trick works for columns using the vertical pane control.*

***

Sorting

To examine the data you've put into a spreadsheet, it's sometimes helpful to sort it based on one or more criteria. For example, if you've created a spreadsheet to record grades for a class full of students, you'd probably want to be able to sort it by name alphabetically, by attendance, by grade for individual tests, and by overall grade. By setting up sort operations, you can create all these lists from one spreadsheet.

Suppose you've got a gradebook spreadsheet like the one shown in Figure 5-21. To sort the gradebook by last name, begin by highlighting the entire spreadsheet except for Rows 1 through 3, which contain the column headings (Figure 5-21, left). (The easiest way to do so is to click on the label for row 4 and drag straight downward.)

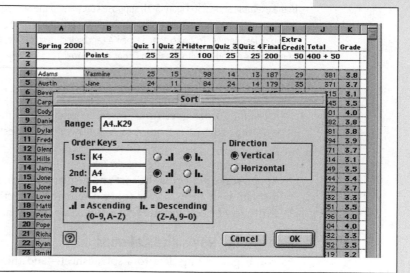

Figure 5-21:
Select all the cells in the rows you want to sort—but not the column headings. If the first cell of the selection is not in the column you want to sort on, enter a cell address from any cell in that column; choose Ascending or Descending for the sort order. For example, to sort this gradebook document by grade-point average, highlight all the cells; in the Sort dialog box, type K4 (a cell in the Grade column); and then click OK. AppleWorks instantly sorts the spreadsheet rows by grade-point average.

CHAPTER 5: THE SPREADSHEET

Caution: Be sure to select *all* your cells of data before sorting. Otherwise, you can change the row order of some of your columns and not others, destroying the *rows* of data you so carefully entered. In the above example, if you forgot to include the students' names in the selection before sorting, the grades would now be aligned with the wrong names.

1. **Choose Calculate→Sort.**

   AppleWorks displays the Sort dialog box (Figure 5-21). The cell range you selected is listed in the Range box—which you can change if it's not correct.

2. **Click the Vertical Direction radio button.**

   Doing so tells AppleWorks that you want to sort the *rows* (because you're moving them up and down); use the Horizontal button to sort *columns* (because you're moving them horizontally).

3. **Enter a cell address from the column you wish to sort in the 1st Order Keys box, if it's not the one AppleWorks proposes.**

   For example, to sort by last name in Figure 5-21, you'd type the address A4. (You can usually skip this step if the first column you highlighted contains the sorting information. For example, in Figure 5-21, the first column contains the student last names, so you wouldn't have to bother typing the cell address; AppleWorks has already proposed to sort by the A column.)

Tip: AppleWorks can sort your rows or columns into sub-clusters. For example, you can sort a list of business addresses by company, and alphabetically by name within each company group.

That's the purpose of the *Order Keys* boxes (1st, 2nd, and 3rd); to specify up to three criteria for each sort. In the example shown in Figure 5-21, suppose you wanted the spreadsheet sorted by grade (A's, B's, and so on), and then alphabetically by last name within each grade clump, and then by first name within each clump of last names. To do so, you'd type K4 (and select descending, so the highest grades are at the top of the list), A4, and B4 into the three Order Keys boxes.

---

4. **Choose a sort order—Ascending or Descending—for each order key.**

   Ascending order goes from lowest to highest number, followed by A to Z. *Descending* order goes from Z to A, followed by highest number to lowest.

5. **Click OK.**

   AppleWorks performs the sort and displays the rearranged spreadsheet. The information in each row or column remains perfectly aligned, even though the entire row or column may have moved up or down.

Transposing Rows and Columns

As you begin adding data to a spreadsheet—and think more carefully about the information you're trying to present—you may discover you made a major error in your layout: the row headings should really be the column headings, and vice versa.

Fortunately, AppleWorks provides for this kind of topsy-turvy spreadsheet modification with its ability to *transpose* a range. When you transpose a block of cells, columns and rows switch places, the cells of data realign, and you save yourself a lot of time and trouble. Figure 5-22 shows this effect.

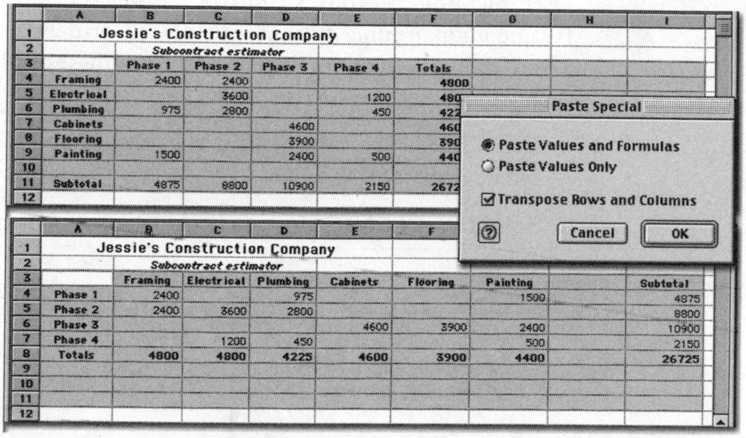

Figure 5-22:
To re-orient your spreadsheet so that the rows change places with the columns, begin by selecting a range that contains the same number of rows as columns (top). Choose Edit→Copy and then Edit→Paste Special; in the resulting dialog box (middle), select Paste Values and Formulas, turn on the Transpose Rows and Columns checkbox, click OK—and AppleWorks flip-flops the cells (bottom).

You can transpose the axes like this in either of two ways. You can copy or cut a selection and paste it—transposed—into another area of the spreadsheet, or you can transpose cells in place, overwriting the earlier data.

1. **Select the range you wish to transpose.**

   If you are transposing in place, select the same number of columns as rows—a perfect square selection.

2. **Choose Edit→Copy (or Cut).**

   Click the first cell of the destination range if you're pasting to a different location. If you're transposing in place, leave this selection as it is and continue with step 3.

3. **Choose Edit→Paste Special.**

   AppleWorks displays the Paste Special dialog box. If your selection contains formulas, choose the Paste Values and Formulas radio button. Turn on the Transpose Rows and Columns checkbox and click OK. AppleWorks performs the switch.

If the transposition doesn't work out quite as planned, choose Edit→Undo Paste before doing anything else.

Display Options

AppleWorks contains a host of spreadsheet options that can make your job much easier during spreadsheet design, but which you may prefer to hide when displaying your finished product. For example, column and row headings are essential tools during the layout process, but serve no real purpose when it's time to display or print the spreadsheet. Similarly, the gridlines that separate your cells can clutter up a carefully designed spreadsheet when it's projected on the screen during your marketing presentation.

Choose Options→Display to invoke the Display dialog box (see Figure 5-23). This assortment of checkboxes controls the way the spreadsheet appears *on the screen.* (Companion *printing* options—Print Cell Grid, Print Column Headings, and Print Row Headings—function independently of these display settings; they're in the Print dialog box described on page 199.)

- **Cell Grid.** If you turn off this checkbox, AppleWorks displays a clean, uncluttered, grid-free spreadsheet.

- **Solid Lines.** If the Cell Grid checkbox is turned on, you can turn on this check-

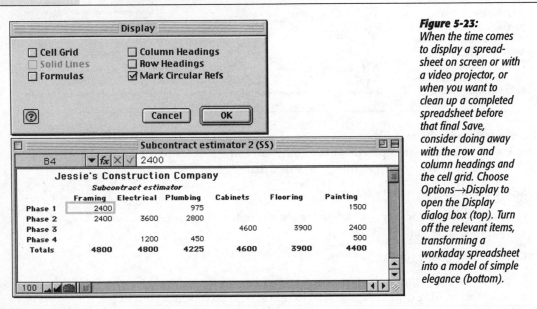

Figure 5-23:
When the time comes to display a spreadsheet on screen or with a video projector, or when you want to clean up a completed spreadsheet before that final Save, consider doing away with the row and column headings and the cell grid. Choose Options→Display to open the Display dialog box (top). Turn off the relevant items, transforming a workaday spreadsheet into a model of simple elegance (bottom).

box as well, to display the cell grid as solid lines instead of dotted lines. (As a bonus side effect, doing so makes spreadsheets print much faster on PostScript laser printers.) If this option is on, any black borders you've applied to cells become invisible—colored borders, however, still show up.

- **Formulas.** When you turn on this checkbox, something fascinating happens. In every spreadsheet cell where you've inserted a formula, AppleWorks displays the *formulas themselves* instead of the results of those formulas. (You see "=D6+F6" instead of "12.") This feature is extremely helpful for troubleshooting and proofreading your spreadsheet.

- **Column Headings.** You can turn off this checkbox to do away with the column headings (A, B, C, and so on).

- **Row Headings.** You can turn off this checkbox to stifle the display of the row headings (1, 2, 3).

- **Mark Circular Refs.** Turn off this checkbox if, for some hard-to-imagine reason, you don't want AppleWorks to alert you to circular-reference errors. When this checkbox is on, AppleWorks draws your attention to such cells by surrounding the cell data by bullet characters—for example, •0•.

Headers and Footers

AppleWorks can print repeating header or footer information on every page of a spreadsheet. For example, you might want a header on each page to read, "Remodeling estimate for Stagecoach Road house," and a footer that says, "Prepared by Jessie's Construction, 9/1/00."

To insert a header or footer, choose Format→Insert Header or Format→Insert Footer. AppleWorks switches to Page View, ready for you to begin typing into the header or footer. If you later decide you'd rather not include a header or footer, choose Format→Remove Header or Format→Remove Footer.

Unlike headers and footers in a word processing document, you can't divide a spreadsheet into Sections. Therefore, headers and footers apply to the entire spreadsheet. See page 88 for the complete story on headers and footers.

Tip: Actually, if you want various pages of your spreadsheet to show different headers and footers, the workaround is devilishly simple: Insert the spreadsheet chunks as *frames* in a word-processing document, as described in Chapter 12.

Manual Calculation

If you change one cell in a spreadsheet, AppleWorks goes to work immediately and re-calculates any formulas that depend on that cell. This process takes only a split second for most spreadsheets. But when spreadsheets become large and complex, containing layers of nested formulas—or if your computer is slow or your RAM is limited—you end up waiting for AppleWorks to complete its calculations every time you make a new cell entry.

Often you're not interested in the spreadsheet results at this point anyway; you just need to enter data without being held up by AppleWorks's accounting department. In such a case, you can turn off auto-calculation by choosing Calculate→Auto-Calculate to remove its checkmark from the menu. With Auto-Calculate turned off, AppleWorks leaves you to complete your data entry chores as quickly as possible. Then, when you're ready to see some results, choose Calculate→Calculate Now. AppleWorks promptly re-calculates every formula in your spreadsheet and updates all cells accordingly.

Charts and Graphs

The only reason many people put up with the chore of creating a spreadsheet is to produce *charts*. Charts and graphs are graphical representations of lots of little bits of data—data that must first be organized in a spreadsheet. Once those numbers are in place, the stage is set for a modern miracle: from the stultifying columns of numbers springs a gorgeous chart, dramatically revealing the hidden pattern behind the numbers. Not all charts are gorgeous, but they all reveal patterns and trends in the data that can be impossible to see in other ways.

If you've prepared your spreadsheet properly, creating a chart in AppleWorks is a quick and easy process. AppleWorks provides seven basic chart types, with several variations each, giving you the ability to create hundreds of different looks. The key to creating great charts is picking the right type for the kind of information you're presenting. Good charts can tell a complicated story at a glance—and poorly designed charts can confuse and mislead.

Chart Parts

Most charts share the same set of features to display your spreadsheet information. Refer to Figure 5-24.

- **Axes.** An *X axis* and a *Y axis* are the horizontal and vertical rulers that provide a scale against which to plot or measure your data. One axis corresponds to these row or column headings—in Figure 5-24's example, the row headings for date intervals. The other axis is the scale determined by the data *series*—in this case, dollars.

- **Series.** Each set of data—the prices of Apple stock, for example—is a *data series*. Each datum (or data point) in the series is plotted against the X and Y axis of the chart. On a line chart, each data point is connected to the next with a line. In a bar chart, each data point is represented by a bar. In Figure 5-24, column C of the spreadsheet con-

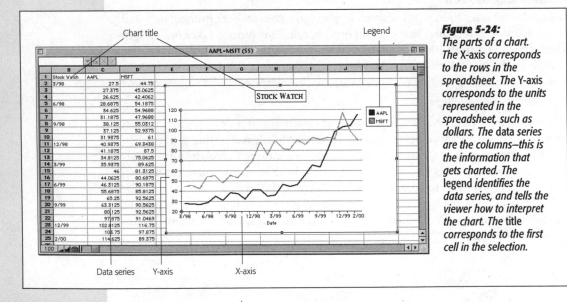

Chart title   Legend

Data series Y-axis   X-axis

Figure 5-24:
*The parts of a chart.
The X-axis corresponds
to the rows in the
spreadsheet. The Y-axis
corresponds to the units
represented in the
spreadsheet, such as
dollars. The data series
are the columns—this is
the information that
gets charted. The
legend identifies the
data series, and tells the
viewer how to interpret
the chart. The title
corresponds to the first
cell in the selection.*

tains the data series for Apple, and column D contains the series for Microsoft. The chart data series can be drawn from either columns or rows of a spreadsheet.

- **Legend.** Just like the legend on a map, this legend shows what the lines or symbols represent. The legend displays the headings of the columns containing the data series and can also display the symbol used for the data points on the chart.

Creating a Chart

To create a chart, begin with the spreadsheet that contains the desired data. For example, Figure 5-24 shows some sample data for Apple and Microsoft stock prices over two years.

1. **Select some cells that contain row labels for the X-axis, and column headings for the data series.**

   Figure 5-24 shows an example: cells B1 through D25 have been highlighted. Usually you don't want to include column totals, if they are present in the spreadsheet, because a chart presents the totals of the number series graphically.

2. **Choose Options→Make Chart, or click the Make Chart button in the Button bar.**

   If you're a keyboard fan, you can also press ⌘-M.

   AppleWorks displays the Chart Options dialog box (Figure 5-25). Choose one of the chart types from the Gallery by clicking its icon.

Tip: If you find yourself frequently using one particular graph type, you can add an icon for it to your Button bar. See Chapter 11 for Button bar customization tips.

Figure 5-25:
As you click the various chart type icons you can view the variations available for each through checkboxes below the Gallery. These options change for the different chart types. The Modify buttons allow you to further customize the chart display.

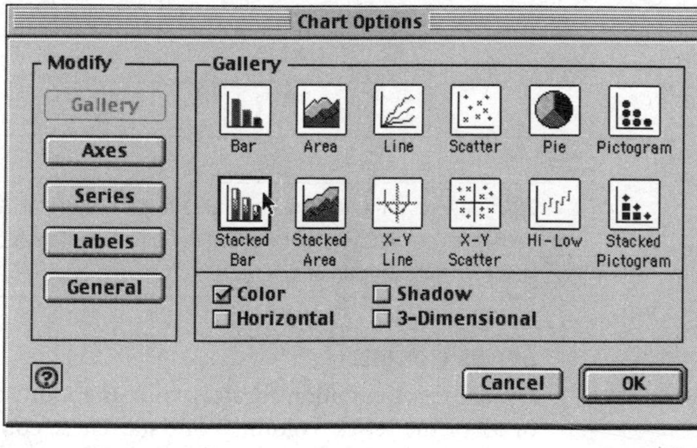

3. **Click OK.**

AppleWorks creates the chart, which appears as a drawing object that's floating on top of the spreadsheet. You can drag the graph to an unoccupied part of the spreadsheet, or drag the black handles to resize it. (See Chapter 6 for details on moving, deleting, or resizing drawing objects.)

If this first draft of a chart looks perfect, you're done. It's more likely, however, that you'll need to modify it in some way—or decide to pick another chart type.

4. **Double-click the chart to return to the Chart Options dialog box.**

You can repeat this process to preview how the other chart types display your data. Or try out the checkboxes at the bottom of the Gallery to sample the variations on a theme.

Axis Options

The chart *axes* are the vertical and horizontal scales that indicate the units of measurement for what the chart displays. Clicking the Axes button in the Chart Options dialog box allows you to add labels or grid lines and adjust the scale, as shown in Figure 5-26.

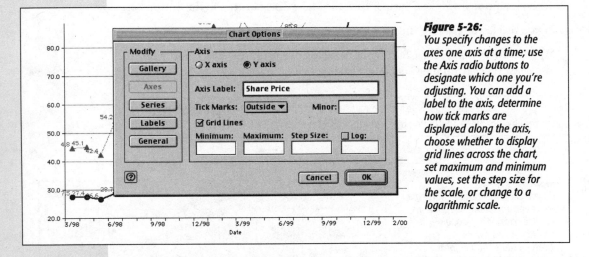

Figure 5-26:
You specify changes to the axes one axis at a time; use the Axis radio buttons to designate which one you're adjusting. You can add a label to the axis, determine how tick marks are displayed along the axis, choose whether to display grid lines across the chart, set maximum and minimum values, set the step size for the scale, or change to a logarithmic scale.

Tip: The X axis is the horizontal axis; the Y Axis is the vertical. (Only the Pie charts don't have axes.) Having trouble remembering? Remember that the letter Y has to stand upright, or vertically. The letter X looks like an X even if it's lying on its side.

Series Options

Using the Series option controls, you can modify the way AppleWorks displays some or all of the series (columns) of data. These controls give you the ability to create combination charts; for example, you can create a bar chart in which one of the series displays as a pictogram or an area chart. Figure 5-27 shows some of these possibilities. (Start by choosing a series to edit from the Edit Series pop-up menu; then choose how to display the series from the "Display as" pop-up menu.)

Label Options

You can change how labels for the chart title and the legend appear by using the Labels section of the Chart Options dialog box (Figure 5-28). The chart title is copied from the first cell in your spreadsheet selection. If that cell was blank, or if you want to change the title, enter a new one in the Title box.

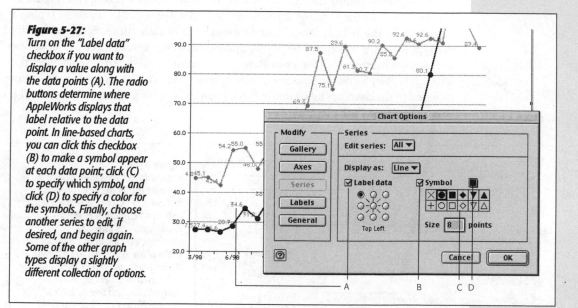

Figure 5-27:
Turn on the "Label data" checkbox if you want to display a value along with the data points (A). The radio buttons determine where AppleWorks displays that label relative to the data point. In line-based charts, you can click this checkbox (B) to make a symbol appear at each data point; click (C) to specify which symbol, and click (D) to specify a color for the symbols. Finally, choose another series to edit, if desired, and begin again. Some of the other graph types display a slightly different collection of options.

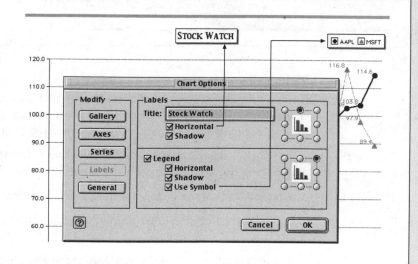

Figure 5-28:
You control the position of the title and legend in relation to the chart with the array of radio buttons. If you don't want titles to appear, you have to clear the first cell in your spreadsheet selection; if you don't want a legend, just turn off the Legend checkbox. You can orient the labels horizontally or (if you turn off the Horizontal checkbox) vertically. The Shadow checkbox adds a drop shadow behind the title or legend. The Use Symbol checkbox adds the symbol used by some chart types, such as scatter charts, to the legend.

The legend labels are determined by the column and row headings in the spreadsheet selection. You can't change them in this dialog box; you must change them, if necessary, in the spreadsheet itself.

General Options

General options occupy the final section of the Chart Options dialog box (Figure 5-29). You can reset the range of spreadsheet cells that AppleWorks charts by typing a new entry in the "Chart range" box (although it's usually much easier to specify what cells you want graphed by highlighting them in the spreadsheet). Choose one of the radio buttons for "Series in Rows (or Columns)" to determine whether the series data is in a row or column on the spreadsheet. The headings for the series included in the chart are listed in the "Series names" scrolling window. These are the names displayed in the legend.

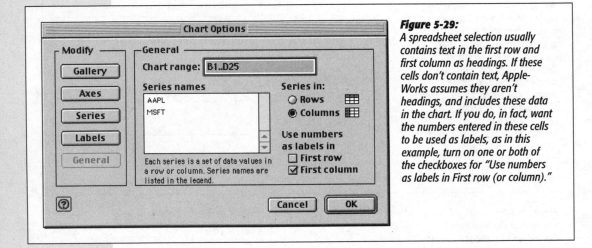

Figure 5-29:
A spreadsheet selection usually contains text in the first row and first column as headings. If these cells don't contain text, Apple-Works assumes they aren't headings, and includes these data in the chart. If you do, in fact, want the numbers entered in these cells to be used as labels, as in this example, turn on one or both of the checkboxes for "Use numbers as labels in First row (or column)."

Pictograms

If you want your staid business charts to be just as eye-catching—or as gaudy—as the charts in USA Today, get with the *pictogram* program. Pictograms are special bar charts in which variously stretched pictures appear instead of, or in addition to, ordinary bars.

AppleWorks's default pictogram—an upward-pointing arrow—won't win any graphic design awards. Fortunately, you can replace it by pasting in your own graphic.

1. **Create a chart of the Pictogram style, as outlined in the preceding section.**

   AppleWorks creates the chart using the default pictogram, the upward-pointing arrow.

2. **Create a graphic in AppleWorks Drawing or Painting module, or find one in a clip art collection (such as AppleWorks's Clippings). Select it and choose Edit→ Copy.**

If the image is very large, shrink it down using the resizing handles until it's an appropriate size for your chart. If you're working from the AppleWorks Clippings, you must begin by dragging the clipping into an AppleWorks document, such as an unused corner of your spreadsheet, before you can shrink it and then copy it. You can then delete it from your spreadsheet.

3. **Choose Edit→Chart Options, or choose Chart Options from the contextual pop-up menu. Then click the Series button in the dialog box.**

   As a shortcut, you can double-click one of the boxes next to the series labels in the chart legend, called A in Figure 5-30.

4. **From the "Edit series" pop-up menu, choose the series you want to appear as a graphic—or All—and then choose Display as Pictogram.**

   AppleWorks displays a sample image of the current pictogram.

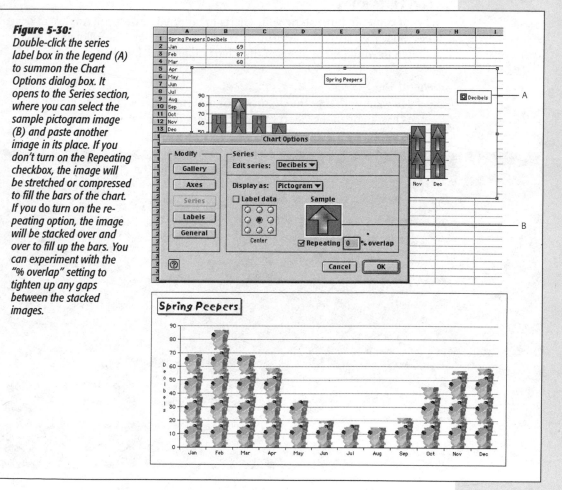

Figure 5-30:
Double-click the series label box in the legend (A) to summon the Chart Options dialog box. It opens to the Series section, where you can select the sample pictogram image (B) and paste another image in its place. If you don't turn on the Repeating checkbox, the image will be stretched or compressed to fill the bars of the chart. If you do turn on the repeating option, the image will be stacked over and over to fill up the bars. You can experiment with the "% overlap" setting to tighten up any gaps between the stacked images.

5. **Click once on the sample image to select it, and then choose Edit→Paste.**

   Your new graphic appears in the sample window (see Figure 5-30). The Label Data checkbox allows you to display the value for each bar right on the chart—usually a distracting element in a pictogram.

6. **Click OK.**

   You return to the spreadsheet, where your finished chart is ready to go.

Tip: For a much cleaner look, you can display pictograms without the bars behind them. Choose Window→Accents to display the Accents window, and click the Line tab. Then click the box next to the label in the legend representing your pictogram series (A in Figure 5-30), and set the Line Width in the Accents window to None.

Chart Formatting

When it comes to burnishing your charts to polished perfection, AppleWorks provides you with an extensive assortment of tricks and tweaks. The following tips correspond to the different sections of the Chart Options dialog box:

General

• If you want to change the chart type or options, double-click any empty space in the chart to open the Chart Options: Gallery dialog box.

UP TO SPEED

Chart Types

As shown in Figure 5-25, AppleWorks offers plenty of different chart types. The key is knowing which one to choose. Here's a crash course in charting:

Bar and Stacked Bar charts are best for showing values or rankings for comparison. For example, bars could represent prices of several different car models.

Area charts can emphasize the relative size of your data over time. For example, area charts would be good at charting the amount of the snowpack in the mountains or the value of a mutual fund. Use the stacked version to show a few funds, or the snowpack at two ski resorts.

Line charts are the best choice for viewing trends over time, such as stock prices or global warming.

Scatter charts are line charts without the lines—just the data points. You can use them to display the same kinds of trends, but emphasizing the data points more than the trend.

Pie Charts display percentages of a whole: the amount of sugar, protein, and fat in a candy bar, or the number of freshmen, sophomores, juniors, and seniors enrolled in high school this year, for example. (Don't use a pie chart if your data contains negative numbers; they'll be converted to *positive* numbers automatically.)

Hi-low charts track pairs of data over time, such as high and low stock prices.

Finally, **Pictograms** are a variation on the bar chart, but with that USA Today twist—you can add a picture or pictures within the bars.

- Click once in the chart to select it, then use the Accents window to add a color, pattern, texture, or gradient to its background—or to change the color or thickness of the chart outline.

Axes

- Click either axis on the chart to select it.

- Change the label font (and the scale numbers on the Y axis) by choosing text attributes from the Format menu.

- Change the axis line width or color, and the gridline color or pattern, using the appropriate tabs in the Accents window.

- If you want to format the division labels along the X axis, you must format the corresponding cells in the spreadsheet.

- Double-click either axis to open the Chart Options: Axis dialog box.

Series

- You can change the color, pattern, texture, or gradient of any series on the chart by clicking its box in the legend, and making a new selection from the Accents window.

- Double-click a series box in the legend to open the Chart Options: Series dialog box.

Labels

- Click the chart title or the legend to modify their text formatting (using the Format menu) and the background color, pattern, texture, gradient, or outline (using the Accents window).

- Double-click the title or legend to open the Chart Options: Labels dialog box.

Further Modifications

Since an AppleWorks chart is actually a special kind of a drawing object, you can continue your customizing efforts using all of the drawing and painting tools and techniques described in Chapters 6 and 7. Combined with the chart-specific customizations described in this chapter, AppleWorks gives you the ability to create a chopped-and-channeled, triple-chrome plated, streamlined, pearlescent show chart that bears little resemblance to the stock unit you began with.

By utilizing these other tools, you can add text to augment or replace the chart title and labels; add arrows, lines, pointers, and callouts to accentuate or elucidate the data; and even resize, rotate, stretch, flip, and slant your chart into USA Today perfection.

Note, however, that when you paste a chart into another document, it loses its link with the spreadsheet that created it, becoming just a drawing object. If you want to retain the ability to modify the chart, paste the chart *and* the spreadsheet into the new document.

Tip: If you paste both the chart and its accompanying spreadsheet into a graphics window, but you don't want the spreadsheet visible, shrink it by dragging one of the corner resizing handles, and then cover it with the chart. See Chapter 12 for more information about using spreadsheet frames in other modules.

Printing the Spreadsheet

When the time comes to print your spreadsheet—which is often much larger than a sheet of paper—AppleWorks provides a few specialized printing options.

Page Breaks

AppleWorks automatically inserts page breaks whenever you've filled up a page full of cells. You can control where those page breaks fall, in order to group information logically on the page. To see how AppleWorks intends to break up your spreadsheet before committing it to paper, choose Window→Page View (see Figure 5-31).

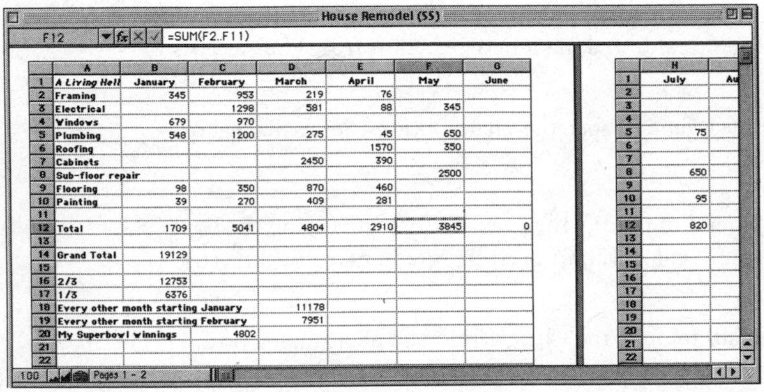

Figure 5-31:
If you don't turn on Page View, you'll see your spreadsheet as a seemingly endless grid of cells. Choose Window→Page View to show where the page breaks will fall in the matrix—then you can insert your own page breaks. For example, select Cell F12 and choose Options→Add Page Break if you want that to be the lower-right cell on page 1.

The page layout you see here is dependent on the margin settings in the Document dialog box (choose Format→Document) and the printer setup (choose File→Page Setup). For example, the Page Setup dialog box lets you change page orientation to "landscape" for a wide spreadsheet, reduce the scale to squeeze a slightly oversized spreadsheet onto one page, and so on.

To insert a page break, select a last cell that you want to appear on the page—what you want to become the lower right-hand corner. Then choose Options→Add Page Break. As long as you're looking at the document in Page View mode, you'll see the results instantly.

To remove an individual page break, select the last cell on the page and choose Options→Remove Page Break. (To remove *all* manually inserted page breaks at once, choose Options→Remove All Breaks.)

Print Range

AppleWorks spreadsheets begin life as relatively huge arrays—40 columns by 500 rows. Unless you trim off the unused portions, they remain that size, even though your data may occupy only a small corner. When you give the command to print, AppleWorks thoughtfully prints only the portion of the spreadsheet that actually contains data.

However, in AppleWorks's view, "contains data" includes formatted cells, even if they're otherwise empty. For example, if you decide to change the font of your entire spreadsheet by using the Select All command, you've just formatted 20,000 cells—even though most are blank.

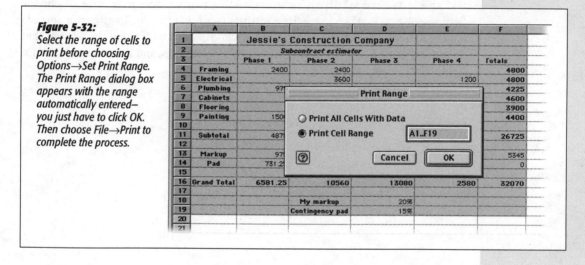

Figure 5-32:
Select the range of cells to print before choosing Options→Set Print Range. The Print Range dialog box appears with the range automatically entered—you just have to click OK. Then choose File→Print to complete the process.

Furthermore, even if you don't apply formatting, your printout will contain all cells *above and to the left of* the lower-rightmost filled-in cell. For example, even if rows A through W are empty (and the first numbers actually appear in row X), they'll still print out—empty.

Figure 5-33:
The Macintosh Print dialog box contains a few extra settings in the AppleWorks 6 section, accessed through the Settings pop-up menu. This is the place to turn off the checkboxes for Print Column Headings, Print Row Headings, and Print Cell Grid to give your printed spreadsheet a more elegant appearance.

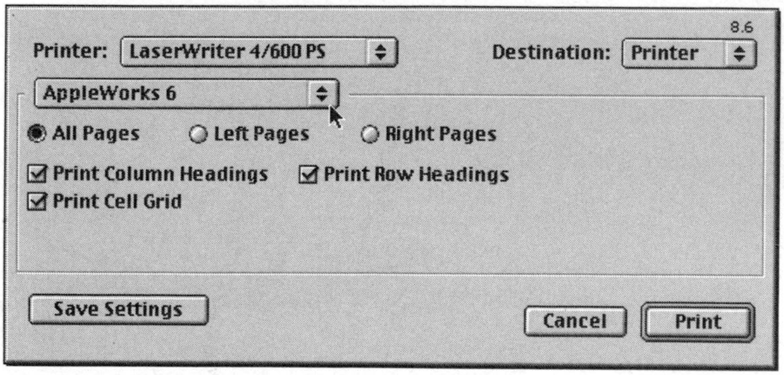

Therefore, before you give AppleWorks the Print command, choose Options→Set Print Range to display the Print Range dialog box. If you'd selected the range of cells you wanted to print before opening this dialog box, the range of the selected cells is listed in the box. If you want to print a different range—or if no cells were selected before opening the dialog box—click the Print Cell Range radio button and type in the range to be printed. Designate the range using the addresses of the top left cell and the bottom right cell, separated by two periods. Figure 5-32 offers an example.

Print Dialog Box

When you arrive at the Print dialog box after choosing File→Print, there are a few AppleWorks-specific choices to be made in addition to the usual "number of copies" and "page range." If you're using a laser printer, you may have to choose Settings→AppleWorks 6 to see these settings (see Figure 5-33). To give your spreadsheet a more finished appearance, you can choose to turn off three checkboxes that are normally on: Print Cell Grid, Print Column Headings, and Print Row Headings.

CHAPTER 6

The Art Department: Drawing

Behind the scenes, computers use two different schemes to reproduce a graphic on the screen, known by the geeks as *drawing* (*vector-based,* or *object-oriented* art) and *painting* (also called *bitmapped* art). AppleWorks can create graphics using both methods, which correspond to its Drawing and Painting modules.

As with tact versus honesty, there are appropriate times to use each. But by combining deft ability with both modes, you can create wonderful graphics in AppleWorks. This chapter covers the Drawing module, which is appropriate for maps, flyers, diagrams, and logos; the next chapter covers the Painting module, which is better suited for touching up photos you've scanned or taken with a digital camera.

Tip: Mastering the drawing tools is vital to success in AppleWorks, even if you never intend to create artwork. That's because the techniques described in this chapter are also required when you design layouts in the Database module, charts in the Spreadsheet module, slides in the Presentation module, and so on.

At the very least, learn the definition of a *drawing object,* how to make its handles appear, and how to move or resize a drawing object.

Intro to Drawing: Shapes, Lines, and Text

Drawing documents are the most versatile of all AppleWorks documents. Drawing documents can hold objects and frames of all kinds, including painting, word processing, table or spreadsheet frames, graphics, and movies.

In a drawing document, every piece of your image is a separate, individually selectable object—hence the term *object-oriented.* The objects in Drawing artwork can include rectangles, circles and ovals, shapes, lines, and frames (which can themselves include text, spreadsheets, paintings, and tables). You can select, resize, and move these objects at any time; it's this ability to manipulate objects over and over again that gives the Drawing module much of its power. Typically, drawing documents are those that need to be edited several times or require precise layouts—such as newsletters, technical drawings, flyers, and the like. If you need to blend, tint, or adjust colors in your work, use the Painting module (Chapter 7) or a Painting *frame* in your Drawing module (Chapter 12).

The Drawing module has one other benefit over the Painting module—the objects you draw are *resolution independent*. That is, you can enlarge them or reduce them as much as you like; when printed and displayed on the screen, their edges always remain perfectly sharp and smooth, something you can't say about enlarged graphics in the Painting module.

Tools, One by One

The Drawing module sports twelve different tools, with which you can create magnificent works of art—they're all in the top half of the Tools window. (The eight dimmed icons just below those tools are available only in the Painting module; the bottom two tools work only in any embedded *tables*, as described in Chapter 12.) Here's a rundown on what each tool does, starting at the top of the Tools window. (See Figure 6-2 for examples of the shapes these various tools create.)

Tip: Most of the time, AppleWorks switches back to the Arrow tool after you've used any other tool, which can become an annoying feature. But if you *double-click* one of the drawing tools, it turns blue and becomes "sticky": that is, AppleWorks won't un-choose that tool, ever, until you click some *other* tool.

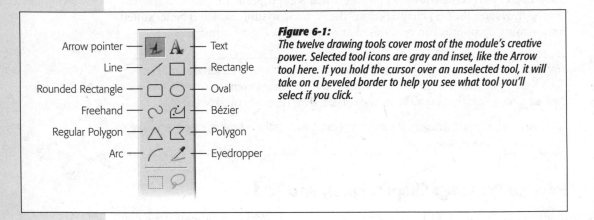

Figure 6-1:
The twelve drawing tools cover most of the module's creative power. Selected tool icons are gray and inset, like the Arrow tool here. If you hold the cursor over an unselected tool, it will take on a beveled border to help you see what tool you'll select if you click.

Arrow pointer — Text
Line — Rectangle
Rounded Rectangle — Oval
Freehand — Bézier
Regular Polygon — Polygon
Arc — Eyedropper

Arrow Pointer

The Arrow pointer is the übertool. With it, you can select and move objects and frames in your drawing document. Without it, you'd be stuck with the pressure of getting every object exactly positioned the moment you created it.

Here are three ways to select the different objects (lines, squares, text blocks, and so on) in a drawing document. All three techniques assume that you've first selected the Arrow tool:

- To select one object, click it; eight small squares—or handles—appear around it. (You can opt for only four handles, if you like; see page 210.)

- If you press and hold the Shift key, you can select more than one object by clicking the second (and third and fourth).

- If you drag in an empty portion of the drawing, a dotted selection rectangle appears; when you release the mouse, all objects that are completely within the rectangle are selected. (This technique is called *drag selecting.*) The Shift key, once again, can be held down while you drag select, which lets you select two or more *groups* of objects by dragging two or more times.

To move an object you've selected, drag it. (If you've selected several objects, drag any *one;* the others go along for the ride.) To delete it (or them), press the Delete or Backspace key.

Text Tool

The Text tool lets you insert a word processing frame into your document, so you can add text of all kinds. There are two ways to go about it:

- After selecting the Text tool, click anywhere in your Drawing document. You get a small text box that expands as you type.

- Drag diagonally in your document to create a text frame of whatever size you want; when you release the mouse, your typing will expand only until it reaches the borders of the box you've drawn.

As with the Rectangle tool (see page 204), you can make your text box a perfect square by holding down the Shift key as you drag.

Tip: Using the Scripts menu (the scroll icon on your menu bar, described in Appendix A), you can create an effect usually found only in $600 illustration software: text that follows a curved line (see page 397).

Create a curved line with the Arc tool, and a text frame containing your words. Using the Arrow tool, Shift-click to select both the text and the arc. Now choose Scripts→Drawing→Text Along Arc. Try to remain calm as your menu bar flashes madly; the script repositions and rotates each letter in your selection. When the smoke clears, your selected text—each letter now a separate text frame—neatly follows the curved line of the arc. (Depending on the font and size you used, you may have to nudge some of the letters into a more ideal position. Choose Options→Turn Autogrid Off, select a letter to move, and press the arrow keys to coax it into more perfect alignment.)

Line Tool

Use the Line tool to draw straight lines. After selecting the Line tool, drag anywhere in your document. To draw lines that are perfectly vertical, horizontal, or on a 45-degree angle, hold down the Shift key while drawing.

Rectangle Tool

The Rectangle tool makes squares and rectangles. After selecting the tool, drag diagonally in your document (from corner to diagonally opposite corner of the shape you want). By holding the Shift key down while drawing, you draw a square.

If, using the Arrow tool, you double-click a rectangle you've created in your document, AppleWorks presents a Corner Info dialog box that lets you round the rectangle's corners. You can even give the rectangle rounded *ends,* creating a capsule-like appearance.

Tip: As described in Appendix A, the Scripts→Drawing→Join Prism Corners command instantly turns two selected rectangles into a three-dimensional box.

Rounded Rectangle Tool

The Rounded Rectangle tool works exactly like the Rectangle tool, but with a difference—the corners are rounded. (Of course, you can turn any existing rectangle *into* this kind of shape using the previous Tip.) Shift-dragging produces a near oxymoron: a rounded square.

Oval Tool

The Oval tool is used to draw ellipses and circles, as you might expect. Once again, click the tool, and then drag across your document window. Drag more vertically if you want a tall, skinny oval; drag more horizontally for a wider one. (Shift-drag for perfect circles.)

Freehand Tool

Use the Freehand tool to draw lines as if you were using a pencil. Don't worry about making the line perfectly smooth—AppleWorks will smooth out the line a bit for you when you release the mouse. (You can turn this auto-smoothing feature off by choosing Edit→Preferences→General and turning off "Automatically Smooth Freehand.")

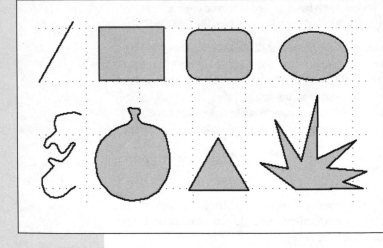

Figure 6-2:
There are ten basic drawing shapes in the AppleWorks Drawing module—plus a Text tool—that you can use as your building blocks. From top left: shapes made by the Line, Rectangle, Rounded Rectangle, Oval, Freehand, Bézier, Regular Polygon, and Polygon tools. From these simple shapes, you can construct a huge variety of artwork styles. Note: you may see shapes made by the Bézier tool referred to as a bezigon *in some of the menus and help documents. Don't worry—Béziers and bezigons are the same thing.*

Holding down the Shift key while drawing *doesn't* make the tool draw straight lines. Fortunately, if a line you've drawn isn't quite up to snuff, you can reshape it after the fact by clicking it (using the Arrow tool) and then choosing Arrange→Reshape (⌘-R). Special handles appear at regular intervals along your shape; drag them to reshape the image without having to redraw it from scratch.

Bézier Tool

Famed in high-end, high-priced graphics applications, the Bézier tool lets you draw smooth, artistic shapes without being a Freehand tool expert. As you drag your cursor in the drawing document, AppleWorks spurts out a series of *control points*—in essence, places where you changed direction—with little handles that let you reshape the curve of the line between the points. Using the Bézier tool is a bit like an extremely complex version of connect-the-dots.

If the Bézier tool sounds tough to understand, you're right. It's one of the most difficult tools to use well, too, requiring a good deal of practice. The payoff is substantial, however: It lets you create shapes and lines with amazing accuracy and grace.

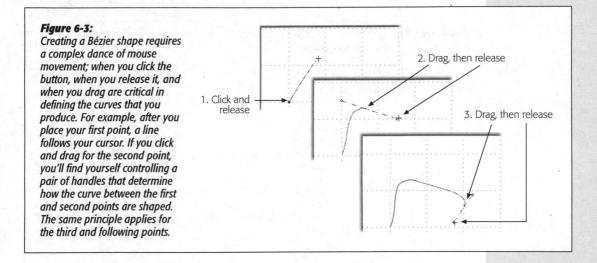

Figure 6-3:
Creating a Bézier shape requires a complex dance of mouse movement; when you click the button, when you release it, and when you drag are critical in defining the curves that you produce. For example, after you place your first point, a line follows your cursor. If you click and drag for the second point, you'll find yourself controlling a pair of handles that determine how the curve between the first and second points are shaped. The same principle applies for the third and following points.

1. Click and release

2. Drag, then release

3. Drag, then release

The dots along a Bézier line

The Bézier tool deals in two currencies: *points* and *handles*. The points act as anchors for line segments, and the handles (which you can move around) define how much the line segment between those points curves.

The basic Bézier technique goes like this: Select the Bézier tool, click to place your first point, and with the mouse button still down, drag to define the curve that spouts from that point. A little handle (which looks like a fat plus sign with a hollow center) appears as you drag, tracing a line back to the point. When you let up on the mouse button, a line flows from the first point to your cursor.

When you click the mouse button again (and again keep the button down), *two* handles appear at the second point; you can drag to adjust the shape of the curve between the first and second points. The third and following points work just the same as the second.

Ending a curve

Once you've started drawing a Bézier shape, there are a few ways to stop. You can select another tool (messy, because AppleWorks draws a long line segment from your last point to near the tool you click); you can double-click your final point, which finishes the shape but leaves a gap between your first point and your last; or you can click the first point you drew, thus enclosing the entire shape. Be careful, though—closing the shape adds the first and last points' curve information together, and you might be surprised at the result.

Drawing good Bézier shapes takes practice, but once you're good at it, you'll be able to do things you thought only possible with the big illustration packages such as Adobe Illustrator or Macromedia FreeHand. Even if you don't get a shape right the first time, you can always use the Reshape menu command, making the various Bézier points and handles spring to life, which you can then tug to change the shape and curve.

Tip: To draw a straight line with the Bézier tool, hold down the Option key while clicking. In fact, you can even make a rectangle with four straight Bézier lines.

Of course, you already have a Rectangle tool, so this notion begs the question, "Why would you want to?" Answer: A Bézier rectangle can be reshaped using Arrange→Reshape (or by pressing ⌘-R).

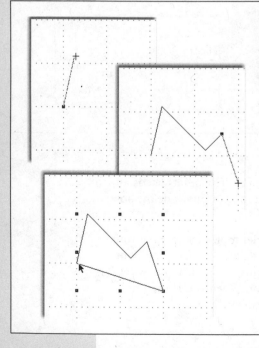

Figure 6-4:
You're just a few clicks away from the perfect polygon with the Polygon tool. Click once to set your first point; a line now follows the cursor. Each click makes another corner, until the final click meets the first point and the polygon is complete. (It's not as though you're using the Bézier tool, where you must drag as part of the shape-creation process.)

Regular Polygon Tool

Click this tool, then drag diagonally in your document window to create polygons with equal sizes and equal angles, from triangles to polygons with up to 40 sides (which look a lot like circles).

To choose a polygon's number of sides, click the Regular Polygon tool (*not* a polygon you've already drawn). Then choose Edit→Polygon Sides to bring up the Number of Sides window, where you can enter the number of sides you want.

Polygon Tool

Now *this* is connect-the-dots. The Polygon tool lets you create irregular polygons—not perfectly symmetrical, in other words—by clicking a few times. AppleWorks draws a line between each click (see Figure 6-4).

In practice, this tool is similar to the Bézier tool, except that the lines between points are always straight. To finish drawing a polygon without creating a fully enclosed shape, double-click when making the last point. To finish drawing a closed polygon, end the shape by clicking the first point that you made.

Arc Tool

The Arc tool lets you draw an arc, starting with the point where your drag begins and ending where you release the mouse button. Shift-drag to create a perfect quarter-circle. To change the Arc tool's settings, select the Arc tool and then choose Edit→Arc Info to bring up the Arc Info window.

Tip: You can also adjust an arc you've already drawn by double-clicking it. The Arc tool dialog box shown in Figure 6-5 appears, allowing you to adjust the arc's angle or outline.

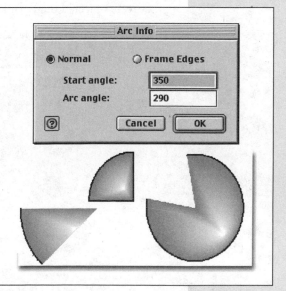

Figure 6-5:
The Arc Info dialog box (top) presents you with three settings. The Normal setting draws a line along only the curve (lower left); Frame Edges adds outlines to the radii that define the arc (lower middle). "Start angle" sets, in degrees, where on the compass the arc begins its clockwise travel. "Arc angle" sets, in degrees, the angle that defines the arc. The arc on the right has a start angle of 350 degrees (just before "noon"), and its arc angle is 290 degrees (described by its dark outline).

Eyedropper

The Eyedropper tool picks up the *line and fill attributes* of any object you click. (More on line and fill attributes on page 213.) The Eyedropper makes reproducing the attributes of a shape you've drawn a breeze—no more guessing or clicking the object to check out its fill, line width, and other parameters.

What to Do with a Selected Object

Once you have an object selected—that is, once you've clicked it with the Arrow tool—you can move it, delete it, change its color, alter its outline, and so on.

Movement and Manipulation

Moving a selected object is easy: with the Arrow tool selected, simply drag the object to its new location.

Tip: If you press Shift just *after* you start to drag an object, AppleWorks confines its movement to perfectly vertical, horizontal, or 45-degree diagonal paths.

If you want to move an object in finer, more precise distances, select it and press one of the arrow keys in the appropriate direction. The result depends on the status of the Autogrid, an underlying alignment grid (see page 408). If Autogrid is turned off, "nudging" an object with the arrow keys moves the object one *pixel* (tiny screen dot) at a time. If Autogrid is turned on, the object moves one grid unit in that direction.

Resizing

Resizing a selected object is also a piece of cake: you just drag the handles that appear around the object's borders to stretch or shrink it. There are a number of ways to resize an object, though, and each has its own strengths and weaknesses.

UP TO SPEED

Understanding handles

When you select an object, it becomes surrounded by handles—small black squares. By dragging a handle, you stretch the graphic object.

The handles on the sides stretch the object in one direction. For example, a handle on the top of an object, between the top left and top right corners, stretches (or crunches) the selected object vertically.

The corner handles are more capable. They can stretch an object *both* vertically and horizontally, giving you more freedom. Holding down the Shift key while dragging a corner handle constrains the stretching (or crunching) to *either* ver-

tical or horizontal stretching, or (if you drag diagonally) to *proportional* stretching (so that the object gets larger or smaller along both axes by the same amount).

So when should you use which handle set? If you want to stretch your image in one direction only, use the middle handles. If you want to resize it by tweaking its size in both directions, use the corner handles.

And if all these handle options strike you as overwhelming or redundant, choose Edit→Preferences→General. In the dialog box that appears, you can set the Object Selection to four corner handles instead of the full set of eight.

For instance, the Object Size palette offers a more precise way to resize than using handles does. To make it appear, choose Options→Object Size (see Figure 6-6).

Here's what the Object Size palette reveals:

Figure 6-6:
The Object Size palette has seven precision settings, plus a Name field, so that you can name the various objects in your drawing—which makes telling the difference between five slightly different circles a breeze. The Object Size palette also lets you precisely (and numerically) position an object, control its size, and rotate it.

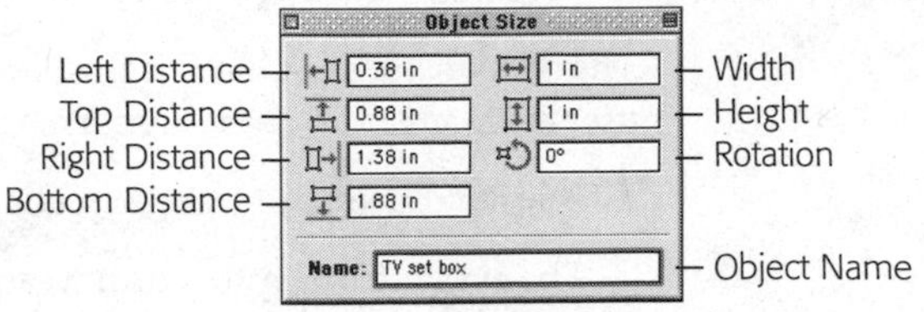

Left Distance — 0.38 in — Width 1 in
Top Distance — 0.88 in — Height 1 in
Right Distance — 1.38 in — Rotation 0°
Bottom Distance — 1.88 in

Name: TV set box — Object Name

- **Left distance.** Displays the distance in inches between an object's left side and the left edge of the page.

- **Top distance.** Displays the distance in inches between an object's top and the top edge of the page.

- **Right distance.** Displays the distance in inches between an object's right side and the right edge of the page.

- **Bottom distance.** Displays the distance in inches between an object's bottom and the bottom edge of the page.

- **Horizontal size.** Displays the selected object's width. If you want to stretch or shrink it horizontally, enter a different number here.

- **Vertical size.** Displays the object's height. If you want to stretch or shrink it vertically, enter a different number here.

- **Rotation.** Displays the object's rotation in degrees. To change it, enter a new number here. If you enter a negative number (such as –45), AppleWorks will convert the number to the proper positive rotation (315).

- **Object name.** Displays the object's name, if you've typed one in.

There's yet a third way to resize an object with some precision, and that's by choosing Arrange→Scale By Percent (or Format→Scale By Percent, depending on the object). This brings up the Scale By Percent window, where you can enter how much you want an object to shrink or grow horizontally, vertically, or both.

Rotating

You can use the Object Size palette to rotate a selected object, as described above, but that's not the only way. In fact, there are three menu items to help you meet your rotating needs. The first is the Rotate 90° command, which rotates the object 90 degrees counterclockwise. Choose Rotate 90° again, and the object rotates *another* 90 degrees counterclockwise.

The second menu command is the Rotate command. By selecting an object and choosing Arrange→Rotate, AppleWorks calls up the Rotate window, in which you can enter the number of degrees that you want the object to rotate counterclockwise. You can get pretty precise with this, choosing rotation amounts down to the thousandths of a degree. If you enter a negative amount in the Rotate window, the object rotates clockwise instead.

The third menu command is the Free Rotate command. As shown in Figure 6-7, you use this fascinating command like this:

1. **Select a drawing object, then choose Arrange→Free Rotate.**

   The cursor turns into a thin X, and a checkmark appears next to the Free Rotate menu item.

   The Free Rotate cursor works like the arrow cursor in most respects; for example, you can use it to select and move drawing objects. But it does something unique, too:

2. **Drag an object's handle diagonally, or in an arc.**

   Instead of resizing the object, dragging the handle rotates the object. (For greater precision, slide your cursor farther away from the object before rotating it.) Shift-drag to rotate the object in 45° increments.

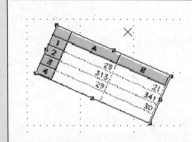

Figure 6-7:
"Rotated spreadsheet with Rotate tool on a drawing field." The title of a still life? No, it's one of AppleWorks' most stalwart object-arrangement tools—the Free Rotate function, which works on any drawing object, including frames (such as spreadsheets).

Tip: The Rotate command works with other objects in a drawing document, including text, painting, table, and spreadsheet frame objects. If you rotate an object and then double-click it to edit it, the object *temporarily* unrotates while you edit it, and then re-rotates once you're done editing.

Reshaping

Although the Bézier tool is one of the most powerful tools out there, it's difficult to get a Bézier shape *just right* the first time—unless you're some sort of Mensa genius with the delicate touch of an eye surgeon. But take heart: after you've drawn a polygon, bezigon, or freehand object, you can reshape it.

To do so, select the object. Then choose Arrange→Reshape, as shown in Figure 6-8. A checkmark appears next to the Reshape menu item, which lets you know that you're in Reshaping mode.

This cursor acts almost the same as the Arrow tool—you can drag and select items with it—but there's one difference. If you click one of the Bézier points, you activate it; now you can drag either it or its curve-shaping handles, which also appear. If you click an object that isn't a Bézier-based object, a polygon, or freehand object, you exit reshaping mode.

If you're reshaping a Bézier-based shape, you have a few options:

- To move a Bézier point, select Arrange→Reshape. Drag the point that you want to move—the object reshapes itself accordingly.

- When you click a Bézier point with the Reshape tool, the point's handles appear. You can drag these handles *independently* to adjust the curves on either side of the point.

- By pressing Option as you click a handle, you remove that handle from the control point. (And if you accidentally remove a handle that you really needed, drag out of the point while pressing Option; it sprouts a new handle.)

For more on Bézier curves, see "Bézier Tool" on page 205.

Tip: You can use the Resize cursor on a regular polygon to make it an irregular polygon. A quick drag can change an equilateral triangle into an isosceles triangle—or even one with no equal sides at all.

Figure 6-8:
In reshaping mode, the object handles disappear, replaced by Bézier points. The cursor is a square with a "+" through it—the Reshape cursor. Drag a point or one of its control handles to reshape the object (right).

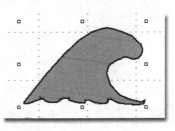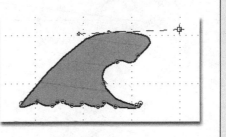

Duplicating

Often, part of designing is repeating a series of elements. AppleWorks offers a simple way to make copies of a selected object—the Duplicate command. To duplicate an object, select it and then choose Edit→Duplicate (⌘-D). AppleWorks pastes the new copy on top of the original object, offset a few pixels down and to the right.

Tip: When you want to make a series of duplicates, duplicate the first one, drag (or nudge by pressing your arrow keys) the copy into its new position, and then duplicate the copy. The second and following copies are placed at the same distance and direction as the first duplicate. This is great if you want to make a series of objects all spaced equidistantly—when making the pickets of a fence, for example.

Another, quicker way to go about duplicating an object is to hold down the Option key as you drag the object you want to duplicate. A dotted outline of the item's frame appears; it may *look* like you're dragging the original object, but what you're actually doing is dragging a copy of it. You can drag this copy anywhere you like; when you release the mouse button, the copy appears, leaving the original untouched.

Note: You can also copy a selected object (by pressing ⌘-C) and then pasting it repeatedly.

Flipping

You can flip a selected object around its vertical or horizontal axis easily enough: choose Arrange→Flip Horizontally or Arrange→Flip Vertically. Flip Horizontally reverses an object about its *vertical* axis. For example, using Flip Horizontally on a text block creates a mirror-readable image. Flip Vertically stands the object on its head.

Deleting

Deleting an object is as easy as selecting it with the Arrow tool and hitting the Delete key. (You can choose Edit→Undo to bring the object back, as long as you haven't done anything else after the inadvertent deletion.)

Changing Color and Line Thicknesses

You can also change the look, color, shading, and line thickness for any object you've selected. To do so, use the Accents palette, described next.

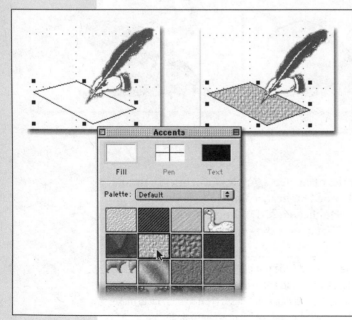

Figure 6-9:
With a couple of clicks, you can go from sedate and classy to thick and sassy by changing an object's Fill and Line (Pen). For example, if you click the blank paper (left), then click a wallpaper pattern in the Accents palette (middle), you fill the paper with the design you selected (right).

The Accents Palette

So what's a drawing if you can't add some customization—fresh colors, thicker lines, and eye-catching gradients? A pencil drawing, that's what, and who needs a computer to do a pencil drawing?

With the Accents window (see Figure 6-9), you can fine-tune the look and color of any selected object—specifically, you can change its *fill* settings (how the inside of the shape looks, including color and pattern), its *line* settings (how the outline looks—its color and thickness), and, if you've selected a block of text, its text color.

Tip: By Control-clicking the Accents window, you bring up a menu that lets you switch between the Accents palette's tabs, and customize the palette's look by hiding or repositioning the tabs. If the Accents window is active, you can use ⌘-right arrow or -left arrow to switch between tabs.

The Five Tabs of Accents

To see the fill, line, and text-color settings for an object in your document, click it with the Arrow tool. You might expect the three large swatches at the top of the Accents palette (Fill, Line, and Text) to change so that they reflect the object you clicked, but—in AppleWorks 6.0—they don't. They indicate only what the settings are for the *next* object you draw.

However, the individual color, pattern, gradient, or line thickness on the Accents palette itself *does* change to indicate the object you've clicked. (If you click an object filled with Goose wallpaper and an eight-point border, you'll see the Goose and "8 pt." icons selected on the wallpaper and line-thickness tabs, respectively.)

To *change* a selected object's characteristics, just click a different color, pattern, gradient, or other setting on the Accents palette.

Tip: If no object is selected when you change the Accents-palette settings, those become the new default settings. Whenever you draw a new object, that is, it will start out life with those fill and line attributes. To change the settings for an individual object, select it *before* you alter its Accents settings.

The bottom portion of the Accents window has five variable aspects, divided into five tabs: Colors, Patterns, Wallpaper, Gradients, and Lines. (These variations are described in the next section.) As you'll soon discover, not all of these settings make sense when applied to fill, lines, and text. In fact, the Fill, Pen, and Text buttons at the top of the Accents palette are sometimes dimmed and unavailable.

- **Fill Color.** Controls the color that fills a selected object.

- **Pen Color.** Controls the color of the line that surrounds a selected object.

- **Text Color.** Controls the color of selected text.

- **Palette Pop-up.** Lets you choose from several color palettes.

- **Color Palette.** In most palettes, there are 256 colors to choose from.

- **Accents Tabs.** Switch between the five Accents modes—color, patterns, wallpaper, gradients, and lines.

- **Fill.** When you're adjusting the colors and patterns that fill the interior of a shape or a text block, you can use the Colors, Patterns, Wallpaper, or Gradients tab.

- **Lines.** When you're tweaking the border that forms the outline of the shape or text block, you're allowed to use the Colors, Patterns, and Lines tabs. (In other words, you can't decorate an object's outline with wallpaper or gradients.)

- **Text.** The Text control at the top of the Accents palette is only active when you select the Colors tab, which you use to adjust the color of the text—it's disabled in all of the other tabs. (Imagine how difficult it would be to read text in a jaunty ice-cream-cone wallpaper pattern.) You can use multiple text colors in the same text frame, by the way—just select a new color on the Accents palette as you type, or highlight some text you've already typed and then choose a new color.

With the understanding that not all five of the following Accents tabs can be applied to Fills, Lines, and Text lettering, here's what the various tabs do:

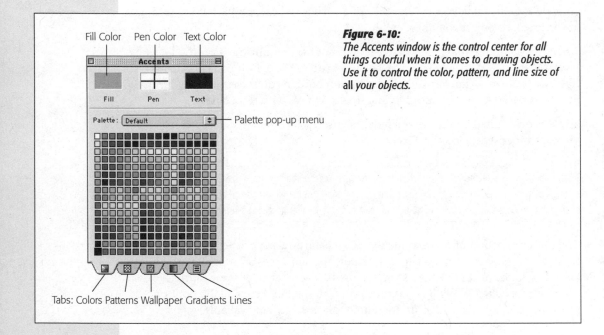

Fill Color   Pen Color   Text Color

Palette pop-up menu

Tabs: Colors Patterns Wallpaper Gradients Lines

Figure 6-10:
The Accents window is the control center for all things colorful when it comes to drawing objects. Use it to control the color, pattern, and line size of all your *objects.*

Colors

Spread throughout a jolly hue-filled palette are the 256 colors available in AppleWorks' default palette—it's the one that's displayed whenever you launch AppleWorks. By clicking one of the small color squares, you change the Fill, Pen, or Text color—depending on which button is selected.

The Default palette is not the only color palette available, however. There are 15 different palettes to choose from, as listed in the pop-up menu above the tiny swatches:

- **Default.** Contains a wide selection of basic colors sampled from the spectrum.

- **16 Colors.** Contains 16 rows of 16 variations in a given color—16 blues, 16 purplish blues, and so on—ranging from light to dark.

- **240 Grays & 16 Colors.** The top row is a selection of 16 colors, and the next 15 rows are filled with shades of gray.

- **256 Grays.** All gray, all the time!

- **Bright Colors.** A selection of dense, bright colors.

- **Cyan to Blue.** Starts with a selection of 16 colors and then moves from cyan to blue.

- **Earth Tones.** Starts with 16 colors and continues through lots of shades of brown.

- **Finder Icon Colors.** The 34 colors from the Finder icons in the Mac OS.

- **Mid-Tones.** Not too bright, not too pale—the mid-tones are, well, the middle ground.

- **Pastel Colors.** Perfect for spring, the Pastel palette includes 16 bright colors and 240 pastels.

- **Presentation.** Similar to the 16 Colors palette, the Presentation palette has a range of 15 variations of 16 colors, plus a row of 16 solid colors on top.

WORKAROUND WORKSHOP

The Limits of Color Palettes

It's a tease—AppleWorks presents you with all of these glorious colors and palettes, and then throws a limitation at you: only two palettes (the Default palette and one other) can be used in a document at one time. This limitation also applies to colors and wallpaper (but not gradients).

There is a way around this limitation: make your own custom palette. Choose one of the palettes that's closest to what you want to work with, and fill it with just the colors (or wallpaper patterns) that you'll want to use in your document. This way, you'll have the colors you need most in your custom palette and can combine this with the Default palette to get the most out of AppleWorks.

To do this, select one of the preset color palettes closest to what you want to create. Double-click a color square to bring up the Color Picker window, which you can use to select a new color. When you close the Color Picker, the color swatch you originally clicked will be changed to reflect the new color.

You can save your new palette for use in any document by selecting Save As from the Palette pop-up menu in the Accents window. Now, your new palette will show up in the Accents window all the time. (If you don't save the modified color palette as a new palette, the changed palette will only apply to the one open *document.*)

Using the same technique, you can create custom Patterns, Wallpaper, and Gradients, too.

CHAPTER 6: THE ART DEPARTMENT: DRAWING

- **Red to Yellow.** If you're into warm colors, this palette of 240 reds, oranges, and yellows below a row of 16 solid colors is made for you.

- **Violet to Magenta.** A range of 240 violet to magenta variations under a row of 16 solid colors.

- **Vivid Colors.** Not quite the same as the Bright Colors palette, the Vivid Colors palette is great for a splash of hue.

- **YellowGreen & GreenBlue.** Great for coloring landscapes filled with grass and trees, this palette presents 240 green variations below 16 solid colors.

Patterns

The Patterns part of the Accents window (see Figure 6-11) lets you apply patterns to your lines and color fills. Select a pattern, and then select a color from the Colors tab. When you create an object with these settings, it's filled with the pattern you selected in the color you selected.

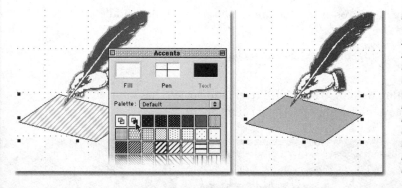

Figure 6-11:
To remove a pattern from a selected object (left), click the second box from the left in the top row of the Accents window, as shown here. The pattern disappears (right), leaving only the color that had already been applied using the first Accents-palette tab. (The first box in the top row gives an object no fill, making it transparent.)

You can make the line around an object invisible by clicking the Pen tool, and then clicking the twin white boxes with black outlines—or by choosing None on the Lines tab. And if you make both the line *and* the fill for an object transparent, the object turns *completely* invisible.

Wallpaper

Instead of filling the inside of, say, a circle or triangle with a color and a pattern, you may prefer to fill it with *wallpaper.* Wallpaper textures are like patterns brought ten years forward. Instead of being 8 x 8-pixel squares of black-and-white dot patterns, wallpaper textures are full-color, 64 x 64-pixel squares, filled with pictures.

To use a wallpaper texture, select an object and then click the wallpaper texture with which you want to fill it, as shown in Figure 6-9. Wallpaper textures only work as fill colors (that is, when the Fill icon is selected in the Accents palette)—you can't use them as Pen or Text attributes.

Each wallpaper palette has 20 selections, and, as with colors, you're not limited to the 20 in the Default palette. There are five other collections to choose from. Here's a sample.

- **Default.** This is the default set of 20 wallpaper patterns collected from the other five texture sets.

- **Gonzo Textures.** The Gonzo textures include a wide variety of colorful and complex patterns.

- **Object Textures.** Roosters, skiers, grapes—these textures are made up of patterns of objects that repeat and might be right at home on some cartoon-kitchen wall.

- **Paper Textures.** Made to mimic textures of actual paper products, this selection will have you fooling the most discerning eyes–well, maybe the first twelve will.

- **Stone Textures.** Make your objects take on the appearance of granite, marble, slate, or concrete—all with one click.

- **Textile Textures.** And where would we be without a selection of cloth patterns from which to choose?

If you want to create your own wallpaper, double-click the square where you'd like the wallpaper texture to appear; the Wallpaper Editor window appears. In it, you can select the size of the texture and edit its colors using the currently selected color palette in the Color tab. You can also save your custom wallpaper textures by choosing Save As from the Palette pop-up menu.

Gradients

A *gradient* is a fancy color blend that shifts hues as it follows a line, a circle, or a square shape, as shown in Figure 6-12. AppleWorks comes with a number of pre-blended gradients to get you started right away. Like the other Accents sections, the Gradients tab has five color palettes: the Default palette and four more specific gradient collections. Here's a look:

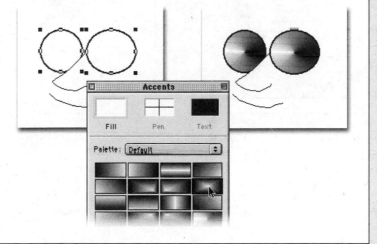

Figure 6-12:
To use a gradient, select an object or two (left) and click one of the gradient squares (middle). Your object takes on the gradient for its fill (right). You can't use gradients for outlines or text–only for fills.

- **Default.** Thirty-two of the best multi-purpose gradients collected in one place for your convenience—all colors, all patterns.

- **Aqua & Blue.** This palette is made up of 16 blue and 16 aqua gradients with a range of gradient patterns.

- **Gray.** These thirty-two killer gray gradients are perfect for giving the illusion of depth.

- **Green & Yellow.** This collection of 16 green and 16 yellow patterns are bright enough to put an eye out.

- **Red & Purple.** Sixteen red and sixteen purple gradient variations should be enough to keep you entertained for days.

WORKAROUND WORKSHOP

The Amazing Non-Rotating Gradient

When you rotate an object with a gradient fill, the object rotates but the gradient doesn't. You have to adjust the gradient separately.

To do so, double-click the gradient square that you used to fill the object. In the Gradient Editor window that appears, you can adjust the gradient's angle, as shown in Figure 6-13.

Wallpaper and Pattern fills don't rotate either, but there you're out of luck—those items can't be easily rotated. Your only hope is to create an entirely new Wallpaper or Pattern that looks as though it's the original one at a new angle.

Figure 6-13:
The Gradient Editor window is chock-full of controls that lead to all kinds of tasty color combinations. You can change the angle either by typing a number of degrees (into the Angle box) or by dragging the black dot in the left-side box.

In AppleWorks, you don't have to use the gradients supplied with the program—you can create your own.

To start, double-click a gradient square in the Accents window. (You can't create a new gradient without wiping out one of the existing ones, in other words.) You'll be presented with the Gradient Editor window (see Figure 6-13). This panel contains three controls and a preview window. By tweaking these—selecting the kind of gradient, the number of colors, and the point from which the gradient radiates—you can create your own thing of beauty.

In the Gradient Editor, you can adjust these controls:

- **Angle.** Lets you set the angle of the color change by typing a number.

- **Angle graphic.** A visual representation of the gradient angle. Drag the black dot to change the angle; drag the white hollow dot to change where the gradient originates from.

- **Sweep.** Lets you pick the type of gradient: *directional, circular,* or *shape burst.* (Only experimentation can show you what these different gradients look like.) The controls will change depending on which type you choose.

- **Colors.** Lets you choose the number of colors in your gradient and—by clicking the color squares—which colors are used.

Lines

Finally, the Lines tab of the Accents window does two things—it lets you control the thickness of the lines surrounding a shape, from no thickness (invisible) to 255 points (about 3.5 inches thick), and whether or not lines have arrows at the ends. To change a line's thickness (or its arrows), select it and then click the line thickness and arrow style you want for the line.

POWER USERS' CLINIC

The Power of Styles

Stylesheets (see page 61) aren't just for text. In AppleWorks, you can create styles that apply to Drawing objects as well.

The easiest way to define a graphic stylesheet is to create an object that has the particular colors, patterns, line thickness, gradients, and text color that you want AppleWorks to memorize. Select that object.

Then choose Format→Show Styles to bring up the Styles window. Click the New button; in the window that pops up, give your object style a name; and turn on "Inherit document selection format." Click OK. Your new style's name appears in the Available Styles portion of the Styles window.

To apply your new style to other objects, select the object you want to transform, select the style's name (in the Styles window), and click the Apply button. Suddenly the new object looks *exactly* like the original one.

Better yet, you can change *all* objects simultaneously just by editing the stylesheet. To do so, click its name in the Styles window. Click Edit. Then, on the Accents palette, change the color, pattern, or line characteristics that need changing; finally, back on the Styles window, click Done. All objects to which you had applied this stylesheet change automatically.

When Objects Collide

The Drawing module is all about creating graphics through making objects of various kinds and colors. But what happens when you get a bunch of objects in your

---

drawing document—how do you manage them? By using three powerful drawing tools: Layers, Groups, and Alignment.

Layers

When you create objects in a drawing document, each is on its own layer, in front or in back of other objects. Sometimes the sequence of objects overlapping other objects isn't quite what you intended, as shown in Figure 6-14.

The trick here is moving the objects you've created to the proper layers, so that the ones you want in front are actually in front, and the ones you want in back are actually in back. To do this, you'll use four menu commands in the Arrange menu:

- **Move Forward** and **Move Backward** moves the selected object or objects forward or backward one layer, closer to the "top" or "bottom," as shown in Figure 6-14.

- **Move To Front** and **Move To Back** moves the selected object or objects *all* the way to the front or back (top or bottom). Use Move to Front if you want something to overlap all other objects; use Move to Back to send, for example, a large background-color rectangle so that it backs up all other objects.

Figure 6-14:
When layers go bad, a simple scene made up of clippings (see page 279) looks as if it were a set of random objects thrown on the canvas (left). By rearranging the front-to-back order of the cat, tree, sun, and cloud clippings—and the rectangle that makes up the ground—the scene takes on a much more orderly appearance.

Groups

When you have several objects that go together (such as a series of squares, ovals, Bézier curves, and lines that make up a drawing of a pencil), it's often useful to group them together using the Group menu command. Grouped objects are like a clique of seventh graders—they do *everything* together. Move one, and they all move. Resize the group, and all the components inside change size proportionally (except *frames,* as described in Chapter 12). Change the fill color of one, and they all change fill colors. Object groups are a real time-saver in complex drawings, especially if you've just spent a lot of time tweaking objects into proper alignment with respect to each other.

To group a set of objects together, select the objects you want to group by Shift-clicking each object (to highlight them) and then choosing Arrange→Group. To ungroup a grouped object, splitting it back up into its original component objects, choose Arrange→Ungroup.

By using the Group command repeatedly, you can even group *groups,* which lets you add individual items to your grouped item as you need to. The grouped object remembers the order in which its pieces were grouped, so you can go back down the same path and undo each grouping by choosing Ungroup.

Note: Even if you've added a grouped object to the Clippings window (see page 279), AppleWorks remembers its grouping sequence and will ungroup accordingly.

Alignment

Suppose you have a set of objects that you want to align precisely, either by centering them, aligning one of the edges, or making equal space between each item. AppleWorks provides a way to align objects with each other—the Align Objects menu command. Figure 6-15 shows how it might be useful.

To use it, select the objects that you want to align (by Shift-clicking or by drag-selecting, for example), and then choose Arrange→Align Objects, which will bring up the Align Objects window. You have ten choices in this window: you can choose one from column A (Top to Bottom alignment) and one from column B (Left to Right alignment). Here's a look at your choices:

Top to Bottom
- **None.** Doesn't change the Top to Bottom alignment.

- **Align top edges.** Aligns the tops of all the selected objects with the top of the highest object.

- **Align centers.** Aligns the centers of all of the selected objects vertically, so that a horizontal line can pass through all of them. The alignment is done at the half-way point between the top of the topmost object and the bottom of the bottommost object.

- **Align bottom edges.** Aligns the bottoms of all the selected objects with the bottom of the lowest object.

- **Distribute space.** Puts an equal amount of vertical space (or overlap) between each object. In other words, this command evenly divides the *total* amount of empty space between the highest and lowest object, and creates evenly spaced objects. This option anchors the topmost object and distributes the space from there, choosing objects with higher edges to move before those with lower edges.

Left to Right
- **None.** Keeps the Left to Right alignment from being altered at all.

- **Align left edges.** Aligns the left edges of all the selected objects with the left edge of the leftmost object.

- **Align centers.** Aligns the centers of all of the selected objects horizontally, so that a vertical line can pass through all of them. The alignment is done at the halfway point between the left of the leftmost object and the right of the rightmost object.

- **Align right edges.** Aligns the right edges of all of the selected objects with the right edge of the rightmost object.

- **Distribute space.** Puts an equal amount of horizontal space between each object. In other words, this command evenly divides the *total* amount of empty space between the leftmost and rightmost objects and creates evenly spaced objects. This option anchors the leftmost object and distributes the space from there, choosing objects further left to move before those to the right.

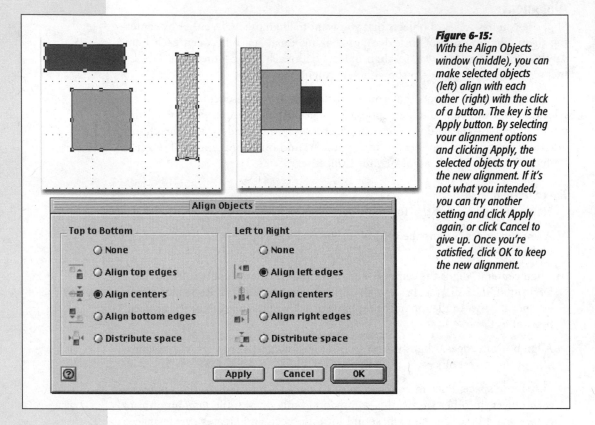

Figure 6-15:
With the Align Objects window (middle), you can make selected objects (left) align with each other (right) with the click of a button. The key is the Apply button. By selecting your alignment options and clicking Apply, the selected objects try out the new alignment. If it's not what you intended, you can try another setting and click Apply again, or click Cancel to give up. Once you're satisfied, click OK to keep the new alignment.

AppleWorks as PageMaker

The versatility of the Drawing module, combined with the beauty of Painting frames and the awesome power of Word Processing frames, lets AppleWorks simulate the program that launched the desktop-publishing industry: PageMaker. By creatively using Drawing documents, you can produce fine page layouts that rival those produced by professional-level programs.

A key to using Drawing documents for good layouts is the Document window. It contains all kinds of useful formatting information, including number of pages, document margins, and page numbering—it's an important stop if your document will be more than one page long.

For example, to add (or remove) pages to your drawing document, choose Format→Document, and change the numbers in the Size portion of the resulting Document window. If you're creating a document more than one page long, you can "lay out" additional pages, either to the right of or below the first one, by typing a new number in the Pages Down and Pages Across fields (see Figure 6-16).

Tip: Keep your document in Page View by selecting Window→Page View. That way, you'll see all of the page borders and any Master Page items (see below) while you're working.

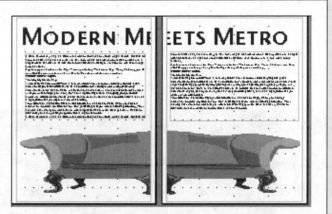

Figure 6-16:
Although these pages will come out of the printer as a single stack of papers, using the Document window to request multiple "pages across" (instead of down) has its uses. For example, you can span pages that will be bound side-by-side with a single piece of art (such as this couch)—a difficult task if all you have to work with is one page above another.

POWER USERS' CLINIC

The Power Grid

AppleWorks has a built-in grid to help you be precise in drawing and positioning your objects. By default, it appears as a series of one-inch squares made up of eight dots per side, but you can change this look and spacing. Choose Format→Rulers→Ruler Settings to open the Ruler Settings window, where you can alter the number of divisions (as well as the ruler's units). This graphics grid doesn't appear in printouts; if you choose Options→Hide Graphics Grid, it doesn't even appear on the screen.

You can activate the grid by choosing Arrange→Turn Autogrid On. (If it's already on, the menu item says Arrange→Turn Autogrid Off instead.) Once the grid is active, you can align objects to it just by dragging them slightly; they jump automatically to the nearest intersection of gridlines, whether they're visible or not. (In fact, even when the grid is turned off, you can make some selected object align with it: choose Arrange→Align To Grid.)

Autogrid is a great way to get items to align properly, but it can be frustrating when you're striving for precise object placement. Autogrid can interfere with almost every part of the drawing process, from rotating to drawing Bézier curves, so it's important to know how to shut it off.

The Master Page

The Master Page in AppleWorks is one way to trim down the work necessary to get a great document layout completed (such as a newsletter or multi-page brochure). All drawing documents have a Master Page, but since it starts out blank, a Master Page doesn't actually *do* anything until you put something on it. Items on the Master Page (such as objects, text, or tables) appear on *all* of the document's pages, so they're handy for stamping repeating items, such as a logo, letterhead, or page number placeholder.

To put items on the Master Page, choose Options→Edit Master Page. When you do so, a checkmark appears next to the menu item, indicating that you're in Master Page territory. Your drawing document now presents you with the Master Page, which starts out blank. Whatever elements you draw, paste, or type onto this page will appear on all pages.

Master Pages are fantastic for creating borders for your documents. To create a border, draw a square on the Master Page that's as big as the page itself; give it a colorful thick line. Alternatively, use the border clippings from the Clippings window (see page 279) along the edges of the Master Page to create a stylish, ornate border. There are some superb borders available in the Clippings window—just do a search for the word *border*.

POWER USERS' CLINIC

Frames Within Frames

It comes up much more often than you might think: a situation where you want to place one text frame on *top* of another one. For example, on the front page of your newsletter, you might want to create a little Table of Contents or In This Issue box. When publishing an article, you might want to feature a *pull quote*, a small box block of larger type that calls the reader's attention to one particular excerpt from the article, and serves as an attention-getting visual accent.

You might well wonder how you're supposed to create a text block inside the text block—you obviously can't do it by dragging the mouse diagonally, the way you created the bigger text block, because doing so simply highlights whatever text is already there.

The secret: With the Textual or Text Frame tool selected, *Option*-drag diagonally on top of your existing text. You create a superimposed text frame. Alternatively, drag the icon of the Text tool or Text Frame itself off of the Tools window and into your document.

Either way, you've now created a superimposed text box; forcing the text of the larger article to *wrap* around the smaller box is up to you. For instructions in using the Text Wrap command, see page 228.

To see the fruits of your labor, choose Options→Edit Master Page again, which puts you back into regular page mode. If you don't see the items that you put on your Master Page, don't panic. You have to select Window→Page View to see them— Master Page items only appear in Page View mode, and when printed.

Text Frames

Text frames are little word processing documents (text boxes) embedded in drawing documents. They're the key to using the Drawing module for page-layout purposes.

Figure 6-17:
A text frame inside a drawing document acts like a word processing document. Almost all of the word processing features described in Chapters 2 and 3 are available, such as drag-and-drop text editing, spell checking, and full text formatting. (The exceptions: Section-related commands, such as columns and changing headers and footers.)

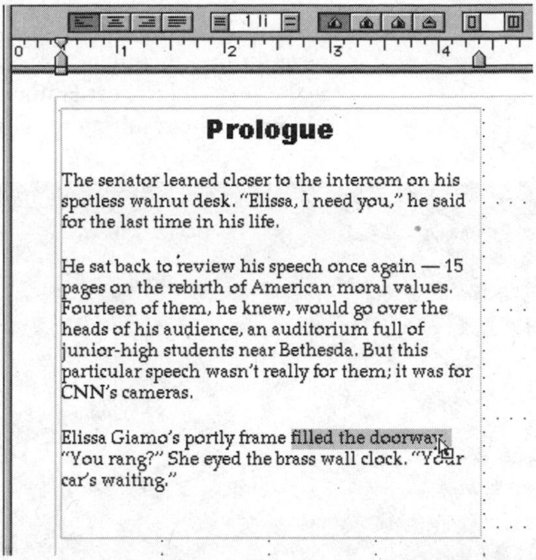

Prologue

The senator leaned closer to the intercom on his spotless walnut desk. "Elissa, I need you," he said for the last time in his life.

He sat back to review his speech once again — 15 pages on the rebirth of American moral values. Fourteen of them, he knew, would go over the heads of his audience, an auditorium full of junior-high students near Bethesda. But this particular speech wasn't really for them; it was for CNN's cameras.

Elissa Giamo's portly frame filled the doorway. "You rang?" She eyed the brass wall clock. "Your car's waiting."

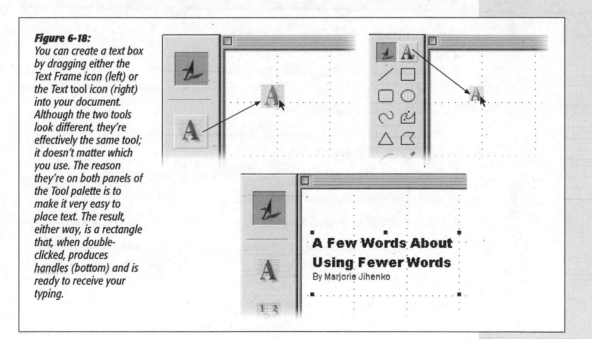

Figure 6-18:
You can create a text box by dragging either the Text Frame icon (left) or the Text tool icon (right) into your document. Although the two tools look different, they're effectively the same tool; it doesn't matter which you use. The reason they're on both panels of the Tool palette is to make it very easy to place text. The result, either way, is a rectangle that, when double-clicked, produces handles (bottom) and is ready to receive your typing.

A Few Words About
Using Fewer Words
By Marjorie Jihenko

A text frame is a rectangle that holds text. It's like a miniature word processing document inside another document (see Figure 6-17). You can move text frames anywhere on a drawing document, which is great when you need headlines, picture captions, and other short, punchy blocks of text.

To make a text frame, select either the Text tool from the Tool palette (or the Text Frame tool from the Frames palette) and click your drawing document. A text frame appears in the document; you can start typing right away. Alternatively, you can *drag* the Text tool or Text Frame icon into your document, as shown in Figure 6-18; double-click the resulting rectangle, and begin typing there.

WORKAROUND WORKSHOP

The Disappearing Text Box

If you drag diagonally to create a text box in your Drawing document, it may be a temporary thing. If you click something else without entering any text in your new frame, the empty text frame disappears—an annoying feature, especially when you're trying to create a series of empty text frames that you intend to *link* to accommodate longer articles. Text boxes need some letters and numbers to anchor them in our reality.

There are two ways around this problem. The first way is to enter text into the frame as soon as you create it to keep it in existence. The second is to drag the Text tool (or Text Frame tool) into the document, as if you were trying to drag the tool button itself off of the Tools window and onto your drawing. AppleWorks creates a modest text frame near where you release the mouse button, but this text frame is different: It doesn't go away when it's empty. (You must double-click this box to begin typing.)

Linked Frames

When your article too long to fit in one text box, *Linked* frames can pass text from one text frame to another, making them ideal for multiple columns of text or for "continued on page 3" situations. Here's how you create a couple of linked text frames:

1. **Click the Text tool (or the Text Frame tool).**

   You can see these tools illustrated in Figure 6-18. They look like three-dimensional versions of the letter *A*.

2. **Drag diagonally in your document window to create a text box.**

   It appears as an empty box with eight handles around it.

3. **Choose Options→Frame Links to turn the text frame into a linked text frame.**

   The text frame changes appearance, becoming a box made of a dotted line with a handle at each corner, an empty box on top, and a box with a black triangle on the bottom (see Figure 6-19). You now have a single linked frame.

   To create a second linked frame:

4. **Click the black triangle at the bottom of the first linked frame.**

Your cursor becomes a text insertion cursor (featuring a short horizontal bar near the top).

5. **Change to a different page, if necessary. Drag diagonally to create a second text frame.**

Text now flows from the bottom of the first frame to the top of the second. It's pretty wild: if you make the first text box smaller, more of the article appears automatically in the second one. And if you delete some text from the first one, text from the second flows backwards to take up the slack.

To create a third linked text frame, just click the black triangle box at the bottom of the *second* text frame, then draw the *third* frame. Repeat until you've created enough text boxes to contain the entire article.

Note: When the *last* text frame in a linked series has more text than fits, a small box with an X through it appears in its lower-right corner. Remember to expand that frame, or link on another one. Otherwise, the end portion of your text won't print out.

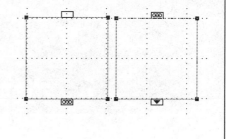

Figure 6-19:
The rectangles on the tops and bottoms of these linked text frames shows how text will flow between them. The empty rectangle marks the start of the linked frames—text will start flowing from here. The linked circles at the bottom of the first frame and the top of the second frame indicate that a link exists between the bottom of the first frame and the top of the second, and text will flow from the bottom of the first to the top of the second. The black triangle at the bottom of the second frame indicates that this is the end of the linked frame series.

Entering and Importing text

Now that you know all about text frames, it's time to start filling them up with glorious text. Click a text frame with the Arrow tool to select it—you can move it about like any other object. Click twice, though, and you enter the editing mode, where you can enter or edit text. Notice that the menu bar has now changed from the Drawing menu set to the Word Processing menu set, and the power of the Word Processing module is now yours to command in this Drawing document.

There are a few ways that you can get text into your freshly minted text frames:

- After double-clicking a text frame, you can enter text the old-fashioned way, by typing away at the keyboard.

- If you want to insert a previously created file, click the text frame twice to bring it into editing mode, and then drag the icon of an AppleWorks word processing file, or a plain-text file, directly off your desktop (behind the AppleWorks window), or out of an open Finder window, and onto the active frame.

A black cursor shows where in the frame the text will be imported, which is an important consideration if there's already some text in the text frame. If there isn't any text in the frame, the new text appears at the top of the first frame and flows through any linked frames until the end of the text—or the frames.

- Alternatively, double-click a text frame, choose File→Insert, and then select an AppleWorks word processing document that you want to import. (You can't import plain-text files this way, alas.)

- You can also open a document, copy whatever text you want to bring into your text frames (using the Edit→Copy command), and paste that text into the frames (Edit→Paste). Use this method to transfer text from a program whose documents AppleWorks can't read, such as Microsoft Word; it preserves such text formatting as bold, italic, and various font styles.

WORKAROUND WORKSHOP

Inserting Text from a File

Although AppleWorks can insert *graphics* in a plethora of file formats into its documents via the File→Insert command, it can insert *only* AppleWorks Word Processing documents—not even documents from other word processors that you've saved in Plain Text format.

To get around this limitation, open the text document using File→Open; choose File→Save, thus saving the file as an AppleWorks Word Processing document. Then, put your text frame into editing mode by clicking twice; choose File→Insert. Select the Word Processing document that you made from the text document, and click Insert. The file will flow into your text frames like magic.

Wrapping

If you'd like to break up the gray of the text on your page in new and interesting ways, it's time to turn to *text wrap*. AppleWorks has surprisingly robust text wrapping abilities, which can make text columns flow around graphics like a river around a boulder (see Figure 6-20).

Here's how to go about it:

1. **Select the text box containing the text that will do the wrapping. Choose Options→Frame Links.**

   For some subtle technological reason, AppleWorks' Text Wrap feature works *only* on text boxes that have been turned into linked frames, even if you have no intention of linking any other frames to this one.

2. **Select the object you want the text to wrap around. Choose Options→Text Wrap.**

   The Text Wrap window appears. You have three wrap-type choices—None, Regular, and Irregular—in this window (see Figure 6-20). **None** prevents text from wrapping, which means that your text may become superimposed on a graphic; **Regular** wraps the text around a rectangular force field surrounding the object;

Irregular wraps text around the object's contour, hugging its sides.

There's one other choice in this window: the Gutter field. The number you enter in this field is the amount of space (in points, of which there are 72 per inch) you want maintained between the text and the object.

3. **After making your choices, click OK.**

You return to your document, where the article text now wraps around the object inside it.

Figure 6-20:
The Text Wrap feature is ideal for pull quotes (the enlarged text boxes that often call the reader's attention to a particular excerpt in the article). Start by creating a box on top of the article (top). By calling up the Text Wrap window and selecting an Irregular wrap (center), you can make text hug the drawing object instead of trampling over it (bottom). (Hint: You can double-click one of the three icons in the Text Wrap window for faster service, instead of having to click OK.)

Printing

At some point, you're probably going to want to print your masterpiece. But before you do, preview the document to eliminate any surprises—and to admire your handiwork, of course.

To see your document as it's going to print, choose Window→Page View. AppleWorks shows your document exactly as it's going to emerge from a printer. It also shows all the master page items, indicates where page edges and margins are, and gives you a sense of how a multi-page item will look when you're done.

If you're printing a multi-page document (such as a newsletter), or one that folds in on itself (such as a three-panel brochure), plan ahead to see how the pages and panels should be arranged. Make a mockup out of some scrap paper, fold it as you want your final product to be folded, label each page, and then unfold it to see how the document should be laid out before printing. (Some pages may even need to be flipped upside-down—an easy feat in the Drawing module, fortunately.) You'll save yourself a lot of time later with some early preparation.

WORKAROUND WORKSHOP

The Perfect Text Wrap

Although AppleWorks can easily wrap text to fit the contours of shapes created with the drawing tools—circles, triangles, and the like—it sees graphics dragged in from the Clippings windows (page 279) as simple rectangles. (Actually, it sees *any* object whose background color isn't transparent as rectangles; most clippings come with a pre-installed white background that you can't change.) The Irregular text-wrap flows around the bounding box of a clipping, in other words, not the graphic inside.

Jeff Honeywell, obituaries editor for the New York Daily Post, looked up from his desk. Nearly his entire field of view was solid, steroid-enhanced, bers was hard to miss.

"I know, I heard," Jeff rehis eyes and let his head loll meled Jeff's shoulder. He was Subtlety was not part of his

"Come on, dude! I thought you of your journalistic career! chat. This is where you make

"If Larry wants to see me in his office, stand conflict. Look at me. I'm breaking out in

Boyd lowered his big chiseled crew-cut head next to Jeff's curly coppery blond one. "Listen, man, ambition and conflict-avoidance don't mix. Pick one or the other, dude."

filled by a pinstriped torso. At 220 pounds of former-football-playing muscle, Boyd Champlied. "I'm delaying the inevitable." He closed over the back of his chair. But Boyd pum-*always* pummelling people's shoulders. genetic makeup.

were dying to get beyond this phase Your editor has *asked* you to come your move. It's a no-brainer."

there's conflict involved. I can't hives."

To get around this limitation, select the Polygon tool. Trace the visible edges of the clipping to make a polygon with roughly the same shape. Once you've finished with the polygon, set its line width to None in the Line portion of the Accents window, and then set its fill to invisible in the Patterns portion of the Accents window. Choose Options→Text Wrap and give the polygon an irregular text wrap. Select both the polygon and the clipping. (You may be tempted to group them, but don't—doing so will make the text wrap once again around the rectangular Clipping.) Drag them, together, on top of a linked text frame to see how your wrap works.

In other words, your text now wraps around the *polygon*—and ignores the clipping completely.

The Art Department: Painting

The AppleWorks Painting module is the yin to the Drawing module's yang, the creative right brain to the orderly left brain. AppleWorks Painting module is where you can let your graphic creativity run amok with paint brushes, pencils, air brushes, and other tools.

The Painting module lets you mix shapes and colors on top of each other—just as you would expect in a canvas on which you're applying paint. Some of the same techniques apply, too. You must begin by laying down the background "paint," and when that's done, you can work on some of the foreground features, saving the detail work for the end.

Once you've created your masterpiece, you'll be able to twist it, bend it, add tints, and do a hundred other things that those Luddite brush-pushers only dream of.

The Painting Module: Photoshop Junior

Although it's not a replacement for the expensive professional retouching program known as Adobe Photoshop, the Painting module has the same basic core—it edits the *pixels* (individual dots) that make up a digital image. You can perform basic artistic efforts (such as brush strokes and blends) as well as import and edit full-fledged digital photos. You can even edit photos you've taken with a digital camera, from taking out the red reflection from somebody's eye to putting someone's head on a dog's body.

The Drawing module, by contrast, can't edit artwork on a dot-by-dot basis like this; it can't add shadowy, foggy, or tinting effects as the Painting tools can. But painting's creative flexibility comes at a price: once *anything* (including spreadsheet frames, text, or tables) is placed in a Painting document, it becomes part of the *bitmap* (see below). So make sure that the item you're placing looks the way you like it before you deselect it. Otherwise, you're stuck with two choices to fix it: editing the object with the paint tools, or choosing Edit→Undo right away to remove the offending item.

UP TO SPEED

Revealing the Bitmap

The Painting module creates and edits what are known as *bitmaps,* which are collections of colored pixels that make up an image. Painting bitmaps is like coloring in the squares in a sheet of graph paper to make a picture, but the squares are very, very small—in fact, on a typical Macintosh monitor, it takes 72 of these squares side by side to fill an inch. Digital photographs taken by your digital camera are high-resolution bitmaps—300 dots per inch, or even more.

Bitmaps can be limiting, however, because their dot-per-inch resolution doesn't change. If you enlarge a bitmap image, it takes on a chunky, jagged appearance, simply because the stretching makes the individual pixels larger. (Artwork in the Drawing module, by contrast, presents no such downside.) The lesson: Avoid enlarging bitmapped images, or you'll face the unspeakable horror known as *pixellation.*

The Tools, One by One

The Painting module uses the same twelve tools as the Drawing module—albeit with a twist—and adds eight more of its own, for a total of 20. The twelve shared tools work largely the same in the Painting module as they do in the Drawing module—but instead of creating individual objects that you can later move or resize, they now create frozen bitmaps in the corresponding shapes. Once you've finished drawing a shape, it becomes part of the painting—there's no moving it, no reshaping it.

The other eight tools are unique to the Painting module, and they form the core of its creative muscle, offering you the ability to either *select* regions of your painting or to paint with specialized, dot-by-dot tools such as a paintbrush or fine-tipped pencil. To select a tool, click it in the Tools window.

Tip: Nine of the 20 Painting tools offer hidden features, which you can reveal by *double-clicking* them. Often, the double-click gets you a dialog box where you can adjust the tool's settings.

The Shared Tools
The following twelve tools are shared by both the Drawing module and the Painting module. (Figure 6-1 in the previous chapter shows these tools.)

Arrow pointer
The Arrow pointer tool in the Painting module isn't quite the big-time power tool that it is in the Drawing module—in fact, if you select it and try to use it by clicking or dragging on a Painting document, it turns into the Pencil tool and makes a pencil mark. (Remember: Edit→Undo is a life saver.) That's because a painting document

doesn't contain any individual, independent shapes or objects to manipulate with the arrow. For the most part, you should avoid this tool when painting.

Text tool

The Text tool lets you put text into your document. You can create a text box in one of three ways:

- **By clicking in your document.** After selecting the Text tool, click in your document window to create a small text box that grows as you type.

- **By dragging diagonally in your document.** Select the Text tool, then drag in your document to create a pre-sized text box, which gets longer if you type beyond its borders.

- **Drag the tool icon itself into the document window.** This technique creates a medium-sized, ready-to-fill text box.

Active text boxes appear with a white background, but don't worry—that's just for your editing benefit. It's easier to see your text against a white background than against a color background.

While the text box is active, you can do anything that you would do in a word processing frame—cut, copy, paste, or even check your spelling. All of the Word Processing module menus are available while a text box is active.

As soon as you switch tools or click outside the currently active text box, however, the text becomes part of the painting, and the white background becomes transparent, letting the painting underneath the text show through. You can't edit the text at this point; if you discover a typo, you must choose Edit→Undo and start again.

Line tool

The Line tool draws straight lines on the painting document. Drag to start a line—one end of the line is anchored to the spot you clicked. The line follows the cursor until you release the mouse button, at which point the finished line appears. Shift-drag to constrain lines to perfectly vertical, horizontal, or 45° diagonal orientations.

Rectangle tool, Rounded Rectangle tool

The Rectangle tools draw rectangles on the painting document, with outlines and interiors decorated according to the settings in the Accents window. (For more information on the Accents window, see page 212.) Shift-drag to draw a perfect square; use the Rounded Rectangle tool to create rectangles whose corners are rounded instead of sharp.

Just as with the other Painting tools, once you've released the mouse button, the rectangle you've drawn becomes part of the painting, and you can't easily change it.

Tip: If you double-click the Rounded Rectangle painting tool, AppleWorks presents you with a Corner Info dialog box that lets you round the rectangle's corners at a certain radius (measured in points) or even give the rectangle rounded *ends*—giving it a capsule-like appearance.

Oval tool

The Oval tool draws ovals and circles with the current Fill and Line attributes selected in the Accents window. Hold down the Shift key as you drag to draw a perfect circle.

Freehand tool

The Freehand tool relies on your mousing skills to draw lines of any shape—the lines inherit the look and thickness selected in the Accents window. When you release the mouse button, AppleWorks fills the space inside the line with the currently selected Fill color or pattern.

Unlike lines you make with the Freehand tool in the Drawing module, AppleWorks doesn't smooth the Painting-mode lines; nor, of course, can you use the Reshape command to adjust the shape after you've drawn it.

Bézier tool

The Bézier tool lets you create curved shapes using points and curve handles. See page 205 for a discussion of this complex line-making tool; for now, note only that, unlike the Bézier tool in the Drawing module, you can't reshape a Bézier shape once you've finished drawing it in the Painting module.

Regular Polygon tool

The Regular Polygon tool lets you draw polygons with equal sides, such as equilateral triangles or squares.

Tip: If you double-click the Regular Polygon tool before you draw, AppleWorks brings up the Number of Sides window, where you can specify the number of sides.

Polygon tool

The Polygon tool offers a game of connect-the-dots; see page 207 for a complete discussion. Hold down the Shift key to constrain your lines to 45° angles.

Arc tool

The Arc tool draws arcs of varying sizes on the Painting document. To draw an arc, select the Arc tool, and then drag in your document window. To draw a perfect quarter-circle, hold down the Shift key while drawing an arc.

Tip: If you double-click the Arc tool, AppleWorks presents the Arc Info window. You can change the Arc tool's starting angle, its drawing angle, and whether or not it makes arcs that are framed on all sides.

Eyedropper tool

The Eyedropper tool works a little differently in the Painting module than it does in the Drawing module. Instead of picking up and memorizing an object's *attributes*, such as its line thickness, it picks up the *color* of the pixel underneath its tip when you click the mouse.

Tip: To make your life easier when clicking the precise colored dot you want using the Eyedropper, zoom in on the document (see page 249) for accurate eyedropper placement.

The Tools, One by One

WORKAROUND WORKSHOP

A Coat of Fewer Colors

Although AppleWorks can *display* images with millions of colors (including digital photos and gradients), the program is limited to the few hundred colors on the Accents palette when it comes to actually *changing* pixels. When you use the Eyedropper, for example, to pick up the color of a pixel, the eyedropper selects the color that's the closest match from the currently selected color palette—it won't mix entirely new colors. To minimize color shifting when you're trying to remove a freckle or red eye in a digital photo, first select the color palette that has the largest number of colors

in the range that you're working with. For example, to remove a freckle, you'll probably want to work with the Earthtones or Red to Yellow palettes—these have the largest number of near-skin colors.

If you *absolutely must* match the color of the pixel that you're trying to edit, you can create your own custom color palette in the Accents window (see Chapter 6 for details) and then mix custom colors in your new palette to match the pixels in the image. This takes some time (and a good eye for color), but it lets you be very accurate in your pixel obsession.

The Painting-Only Tools

Eight tools are unique to the Painting module (see Figure 7-2)—because they affect the artwork on a dot-by-dot basis, a feature unavailable in the Drawing module.

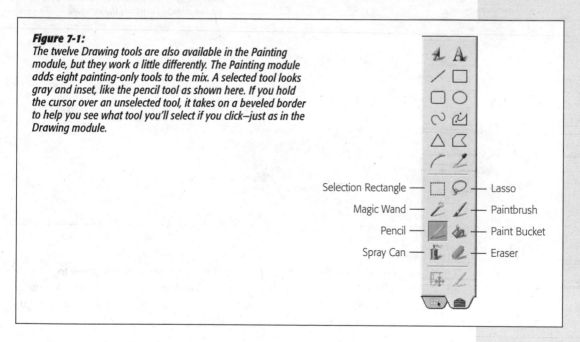

Figure 7-1:
The twelve Drawing tools are also available in the Painting module, but they work a little differently. The Painting module adds eight painting-only tools to the mix. A selected tool looks gray and inset, like the pencil tool as shown here. If you hold the cursor over an unselected tool, it takes on a beveled border to help you see what tool you'll select if you click—just as in the Drawing module.

Selection Rectangle — Lasso
Magic Wand — Paintbrush
Pencil — Paint Bucket
Spray Can — Eraser

Selection Rectangle tool

The Selection Rectangle tool *selects* a rectangular region of the painting, which is a necessary step before moving, deleting, or transforming an area of your painting. Selecting is such an important topic that it gets its own section—see page 239.

Once the "marching ants" (see Figure 7-3) indicate the area you've selected, your cursor turns into the Arrow tool when it's over the selected area. Now you can drag the selection to move it, cut it (Edit→Cut), or copy it (Edit→Copy). If you move it, the space that the selection formerly occupied is empty white.

Tip: Suppose you have an image of jail bars. You want to select it so that you can superimpose it on an image of a master criminal, *without* including the white space between the bars as you select it. The solution: ⌘-click the bars themselves. AppleWorks responds by selecting only the non-white areas of the graphic. (This trick works with both the Selection Rectangle tool and Lasso tools.)

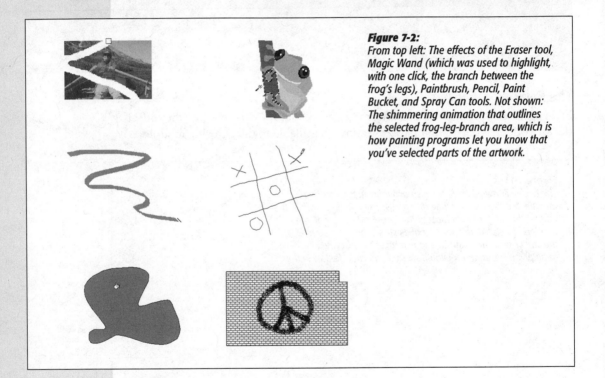

Figure 7-2:
From top left: The effects of the Eraser tool, Magic Wand (which was used to highlight, with one click, the branch between the frog's legs), Paintbrush, Pencil, Paint Bucket, and Spray Can tools. Not shown: The shimmering animation that outlines the selected frog-leg-branch area, which is how painting programs let you know that you've selected parts of the artwork.

Lasso tool

The Lasso tool, like its sibling the Selection Rectangle tool, is designed to let you enclose areas of your painting in readiness for deleting, moving, or transforming. But instead of creating a rectangular selection, the Lasso lets you select an irregularly shaped portion of your painting (see Figure 7-3).

If you're having trouble selecting something small, zoom in to get a better view of the pixels. Hold down the ⌘ key to select the non-white areas inside the item that you're selecting, (just as with the Rectangle Selection tool). The selection has to *cross* a white area for this to work properly.

Tip: Double-click the Lasso tool to select the entire document.

Figure 7-3:
A graphic with irregular edges (left) is a perfect candidate for the Lasso tool. Drag in a loop around the artwork. When you're finished (right), the selection's "marching ants" surround the edges of the artwork. In other words, if you enclose some color pixels on a white background, AppleWorks selects only the color pixels.

Magic Wand tool

The Magic Wand is a potentially useful, but quirky, selection tool. In theory, by selecting it and then clicking a painting document, you select the pixel where you clicked *and* all of the adjacent pixels of the same color. You'd use this feature, for example, when you want to select a shape of a single color either partially or completely inside a field of another color (which prevents the Lasso tool from doing the job).

In practice, this tool can be incredibly stubborn, refusing to select pixels that are *almost* the same color, or pixels that are the same color but touch the selected pixel at a *corner* rather than a side. If you've used a professional editing program like Photoshop, you'll dearly miss the lack of a *tolerance* control that specifies how freely the Magic Wand selects pixels.

Paintbrush tool

The Paintbrush tool lets you release your inner Van Gogh without losing a body part. It lets you paint a line, using the currently selected color, pattern, wallpaper, or gradient fill in the Accents palette (page 212). Hold down the Shift key to constrain painting to vertical, horizontal, or 45-degree angles.

You control the size and shape of the brush tip itself by double-clicking the Paintbrush tool icon. The Brush Shape window appears, in which you can choose from 32 preset brush shapes and sizes; alternatively, you can click the Edit button to edit one of the existing brushes for your own purposes.

Pencil tool

The Pencil tool draws a freeform line that's a single pixel wide, using the color specified in the Accents palette. (If you begin drawing a certain color line against a backdrop that's already that exact color—black on black, for example—you produce a white line instead.) The Pencil is useful for precision pixel editing.

Tip: Double-click the Pencil tool to zoom the document to 800 percent. That way, you can be excruciatingly precise in your pencil edits. Double-click the Pencil again to return to 100 percent magnification.

POWER USERS' CLINIC

Powerful Paintbrush Effects

The Brush Shape window, which appears when you double-click the Paintbrush tool icon, has one power-user feature: the Effects pop-up menu. This item can change the Paintbrush from an ordinary color-applying tool to something that can blend, lighten, darken, or tint the area over which it's used—great for special effects!

Suppose you choose Lighten from this pop-up menu, for example, and then click OK. Now you can retouch a digital photo by "painting" over dark, underexposed areas, marveling as AppleWorks automatically lightens the areas your paintbrush touches.

Paint Bucket tool

The Paint Bucket tool gives you a quick way to fill a completely enclosed area with a color or pattern. This tool fills the area on which it's clicked with the current fill color or pattern, but it leaves pixels of other colors alone—it changes only adjacent pixels that are the *same color* as the pixel you click.

But there's a risk, too; as shown in Figure 7-4, the tiniest gap in the outline of your shape will "leak" paint until it fills the entire *window*. Think of the Paint Bucket tool the same way you might think of spilling paint on a big flat surface—unless the paint hits something that will contain it (such as a raised edge), the paint will spill out and cover surfaces beyond the smaller surface. If you make a mistake and paint floods your image, choose Edit→Undo to get rid of it.

Figure 7-4:
This shot shows a disaster about to happen. If you click with the Paint Bucket right now, the color you hoped would fill the hat will instead fill the entire window, because of the small gaps in the hat outline. You must zoom in to close the gaps before clicking the Paint Bucket to prevent the problem.

Spray Can tool

The Spray Can tool does its best to mimic an aerosol spray-paint can. As you drag across your painting document, the Spray Can spits out a fine mist of colored pixels in a circular area. The longer the mouse button is held down, the more dots are splattered, until the tool's circular area is entirely filled with the new color. If you Shift-drag, as always, the tool is constrained to horizontal or vertical movement.

Tip: Double-click the Spray Can tool to bring up the Edit Spray Can window, where you can change the tool's "nozzle" size (from 1 to 72 dots) and flow rate. You can test your newly edited Spray Can in a special area in the window's left half.

Eraser tool

The Eraser tool is a simple tool. As you drag across your artwork, you erase what you cross, turning it white.

If the Eraser "brush" is too big for the area you're trying to erase, zoom in on that area. While the image will appear to get larger, the eraser stays the same size, in effect shrinking it relative to the drawing. Hold down the Shift key to constrain your erasing activities to horizontal or vertical lines.

Tip 1: If you crave a wider variety of eraser "brush" sizes and shapes, don't use the Eraser at all—instead, use the Paintbrush, whose brush shape you can change, and paint using the color white.

Tip 2: Double-click the Eraser tool to erase *everything* in the painting document. Holy Edit→Undo!

Selections

Making a selection in the Painting module is fairly straightforward—it involves using one of the three selection tools to click or drag in a painting document, as described in the previous section. An animated outline, formed by what graphics pros affectionately call "marching ants," shows you exactly which area of the painting you've enclosed.

But what do you do once you've *made* a selection? Three things—with lots of variations.

- **Move it.** Once a selection is made, you can move it by dragging inside it. You can drag this swatch of painting anywhere in the document, but be aware that you'll be leaving behind a white hole where the selection was. That is, *unless* you press the Option key while dragging. In that case, when you drag the selection, you drag a *copy,* leaving the original behind.

- **Cut, copy, delete, or duplicate it.** Using the topmost Edit menu commands, you can cut, copy, delete, or duplicate your selection. Selecting Edit→Cut cuts the selection out of the painting and places it on the Clipboard (see page 34). Edit→Copy *copies* the selection to the Clipboard, leaving the original in place. Edit→Clear removes the selection from the painting *without* putting a copy on the Clipboard—it's the equivalent of selecting something and hitting the Delete key. Finally, Edit→Duplicate makes a copy of the selection, leaving the original untouched, just as though you Option-dragged the selection.

- **Transform it.** When you've selected a portion of a painting (or the whole thing), you can use menu commands from the Transform menu on the selection, as described next.

Tip: You can Control-click a selection to bring up a contextual menu. It offers a Help command and four transformation effects: Blend, Tint, Lighten, and Darken. These are the same menu commands that you'll find in the Transform menu (explained below) and they blend colors, add a color tint, lighten the selection, or darken the selection, respectively.

Transformations

The key to unlocking the power of AppleWorks' Painting module lies in the Transform menu commands. These commands let you warp your work, rotate it, and otherwise create some truly fabulous effects.

Distorting Images

Three Transform menu commands shift, twist, and distort selections. These transforming commands work by compressing or stretching pixels. (Be aware, though, that distorting a selection too much will pixellate it, producing a jagged or blotchy look.) Here's a look at each of the distortion commands.

Slant

The Slant menu item puts four handles in a rectangle around a selection, whether it's a rectangular selection or an irregular Lasso-type selection. By dragging one of the handles, you can *slant* the selection, distorting it by changing the selection from a rectangle to a parallelogram (see Figure 7-5). By holding down the Shift key while slanting the image, you constrain the slant to one axis.

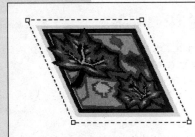

Figure 7-5:
Slanted selections look as though someone pushed one side while the other stayed firmly rooted. The more you drag one of the white handles, the more you slant the image. When you click outside the dotted-line rectangle, you freeze the changes into place.

Stretch

The Painting module's digital equivalent of Silly Putty, the Stretch menu also puts four handles in a rectangle around a selection. These handles move independently, however, letting you stretch the selection in any of four directions for some wild effects (see Figure 7-6). Stretch handles can't be dragged so that the angle formed by the selection lines that come off that handle is greater than 180 degrees.

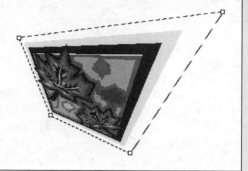

Figure 7-6:
Salvador Dali would have been proud of the Stretch command. It lets you alter selections in ways that are outside the realm of reality, yet look plausible.

Add Perspective

The Add Perspective menu command puts four handles in a square around the selection. By dragging these squares, you can stretch or shrink the distance between two of the points while the other two stay anchored, making your two-dimensional object look as if it were photographed in perspective (see Figure 7-7). If you're *very* accurate with the perspective tool, you can keep on dragging until you've flipped the selection horizontally or vertically, depending on which direction you were dragging.

Figure 7-7:
Proper use of the Add Perspective tool can give the illusion that a two-dimensional object is actually lying down in the third dimension—an effect similar to, and much safer than, standing in the center of railroad tracks and looking down them one direction until the tracks meet. Here, the leaf square has become what looks like a throw rug.

Size and Orientation

The Transform menu has seven menu commands that deal with scaling, rotating, and flipping selections. These items are similar to the ones found in the Drawing module, except, as with everything else in the Painting module, once the item is no longer selected, it becomes a frozen part of the painting.

Scaling

The Transform menu has two menu commands for resizing selections: Resize and Scale by Percent. The *Resize* command puts four handles in a rectangle around the selection, which you can drag to scale the selection horizontally, vertically, or both. If you Shift-drag, you resize the selection without distorting it.

The Scale by Percent command opens the Scale By Percent window, where you can enter the precise percentage amount that the selection should be scaled. To scale a selection proportionally, enter the same number in both resize fields.

WORKAROUND WORKSHOP

Resizing Clippings Smoothly

Here's where the Painting module's resolution limitation rears its ugly head—again. When you bring a clipping (see page 279) into your painting document, it comes in at a pre-determined size and resolution, which may not be big enough for your purposes. If you try to use the Scaling transformations on one of these items to make it larger, it may become coarse and blotchy extremely quickly.

One solution: First bring the clipping into a blank drawing document, resize it , and then copy and paste it from the drawing document into your painting document. You'll get the clipping at the size you want without making it pixellated.

Rotating

The Transform menu has three commands that deal with rotating a selection:

- **Rotate 90°.** This command rotates the selection 90° counterclockwise. (If you want it rotated clockwise instead, you must use this command three times in succession.)

- **Rotate.** This one opens the Rotate window, where you can specify how many degrees the selection should be rotated counterclockwise. Entering a negative number of degrees in this window rotates the selection *clockwise*.

- **Free Rotate.** This command produces four handles around the selection in a rectangle that, when dragged, rotates the object. This method lets you see the rotation in progress as you drag, which gives you a better sense of how the finished selection will fit into its background.

Note: Rotating a selection can introduce some funky "pixel noise" (crumbly-looking edges). If you're affected by this problem, try rotating the item in a drawing document and then copying and pasting it into your painting document.

Flipping

Maybe you have a photograph of someone looking out a window to the right, and you'd really like that person to be looking out to the left. The two Transform menu commands Flip Horizontally and Flip Vertically can solve this problem. *Flip Horizontally* flips the selection around an imaginary vertical line, as if it were viewed through a mirror. *Flip Vertically* flips the selection around an imaginary horizontal line, as if you were standing on your head looking at the object through a mirror.

Special Effects

The seven final menu items in the Transform menu are the real gems of the Painting module. They work their magic by painting over the selected area, moving new pixels in, and so on.

Fill

When you choose Transform→Fill, the selected area gets filled with the current Fill in the Accents window—complete with color, pattern, wallpaper, or gradient. If you're having trouble getting the Paint Bucket to fill an area, as described earlier in this chapter, select the area you want colored in and choose Transform→Fill instead.

Pick Up

The Pick Up menu command "picks up" a copy of the pixels in your document and injects them in the selection. It's almost exactly as confusing as it sounds; Figure 7-8 should make all clear.

Pick Up is great for bringing customized fills into a selection shape or cutting a photo into some shape other than a rectangle.

Figure 7-8:
Drag a selection over another area of the painting–a black circle over a photo of a sunset, for example (top). Then choose Transform→Pick Up. The inside of the selection may seem to disappear, but don't worry–it's just been filled with an exact copy of the pixels underneath it (middle). When you drag the result away from the scene of the Pick Up, you'll see that the selection now contains a perfect copy of what was beneath it. You can now move the selection to its final location–either where it began, or a new location (bottom).

Invert

Invert *inverts* the pixels in a selection to their opposite colors—black becomes white, red becomes blue, and so on. It's the same as looking at a photographic negative.

Note: You can't easily reverse an Invert command by choosing Transform→Invert a second time (unless the original area is still selected). You're likely to lose some of the original blacks, which were turned white in the first inversion and now can't be selected.

Blend

An AppleWorks favorite, the Blend transformation blurs the selection by adding colors between two different colors. Use blends to soften an image, hide minor flaws, or add a photographic, soft-focus effect to a digital shot. You can apply Transform→Blend several times on the same selection; each time, the selection becomes progressively blurrier.

POWER USERS' CLINIC

Making a Convincing Drop Shadow

You can use the Blend command (in conjunction with the Fill command) to create a convincing drop shadow that's blurred around the edges—a nifty, professional trick. Here's how to go about creating a drop shadow for an irregularly shaped clipping.

Start with a blank painting document; bring a clipping into it. Use the Lasso tool to select the clipping. Select a black Fill color in the

Accents window, and then choose Transform→Fill to create a black silhouette of the clipping.

Use the Rectangular Selection tool to select a rectangle *around* the silhouette, making sure that you include a few white pixels on each side. Choose Transform→Blend a few times to soften the silhouette into a shadow— the more times you select Blend, the softer the shadow.

Tint

Choosing Transform→Tint adds a tint of the currently selected Fill color (in the Accents palette) to the selected area. You can apply multiple Tint commands to the same selection, which intensifies the saturation.

Lighten

The Lighten command lightens all of the pixels in the selected area by adding a bit of white to each pixel.

Note: Lighten (and Darken) are both *lossy* operations—that is, they can permanently alter pixels in ways that aren't undoable. If you choose Transform→Lighten five times and then choose Transform→Darken five times to undo the Lighten commands, you'll end up with a muddy gray version of your selection instead of the original.

Darken

The Darken command darkens all of the pixels in a selection by adding a touch of black to each pixel.

Grids, Modes, and Size

A few AppleWorks settings affect the entire Painting module. While you'll probably deal with these items only occasionally, it's good to know where they are and what they do. These items are the grid, the painting *mode*, and the document's size and resolution.

The Grid

Just like the Drawing module, the Painting module has an adjustable, underlying grid that can be used to get precision alignments when you're painting. There are two grid-specific menu commands under the Options menu:

- **Turn Autogrid On** (or **Off**, if it's already on). By choosing Options→Turn Autogrid On, you turn on the Autogrid feature, which constrains most of the tools to specific points on an invisible grid. This can make the shared Drawing/Painting tools, the Rectangle selection tool, and the mouse itself (when you're trying to drag a selection) jerky and difficult to use. It's best to leave Autogrid off for most painting tasks.

- **Grid Size.** If you do decide to use the Autogrid, you can also use this command to summon the Painting Grid Size window. In it, you're given a choice of five grid sizes: 2, 4, 8, 16, and 32 pixels. Smaller grids give more freedom by allowing your cursor movements to "snap to" a broader array of invisible alignment points—but sacrifice accuracy. Larger grids constrain the tools more, but make lines, selections, and so on more likely to align with each other.

Mode Settings

Most of the painting that you'll do in the Painting module is of the splash-on-paint-to-cover-other-paint variety, but the program actually offers *three* painting modes: Opaque, Transparent pattern, and Tint. To change your painting mode, choose Options→Paint Mode, which brings up the Paint Mode window. In it, you can choose:

Figure 7-9:
The difference between the Transparent pattern mode and the usual painting mode (Opaque) is apparent only when you paint a pattern (as selected in the Accents palette) over something you've already painted (left). The Tint mode (right), on the other hand, is especially useful for retouching photos—even colorizing black-and-white photos—because it lets you add a subtle, translucent color tint to what's underneath.

- **Opaque.** This is the aforementioned cover-up painting mode—the mode most people use most of the time. Any shapes or lines drawn in Opaque mode cover up any paint underneath.

- **Transparent pattern.** The Transparent pattern mode (see Figure 7-9) is similar to the Opaque mode, except that the *white* portions of patterns are now transparent, letting the pixels underneath the white areas—whatever you had previously painted—show through.

- **Tint.** The Tint mode (Figure 7-9, right) applies shapes drawn as a tint rather than as opaque paint, blending the pixels together.

Document Settings

Two Format menu commands get into technical terrain, but are essential in understanding bitmaps, digital photos, scanned images, and so on: the Document command and the Resolution & Depth command.

Document dimensions

The Format→Document menu command opens the Document window. In it, you can specify your Painting document's margins, how page numbers are handled, whether or not margins and page guides should appear, and the document's size (in pixels across and pixels down). Remember, 72 pixels equals an inch of the standard Painting document. If your painting is at the default (72 dots per inch) resolution, you can make it span multiple pages by entering large numbers in the document size fields—you're limited to 2,000 pixels in each direction.

Tip: If you're planning to create Web graphics, use the Document command before you start painting. Set the document's size to the dimensions that you'll want for the finished graphic on your Web page—and set the resolution to 72 dpi. That way, AppleWorks shows you exactly how much space you have to work with in the first place.

Document resolution

The Format→Resolution & Depth menu item opens the Resolution and Depth window, where you see three very important settings for the document. The *Resolution* section lets you choose from among five resolution settings: 72, 144, 288, 300, and 360 dots per inch, with 72 as the default.

Resolution may be a difficult concept to grasp, but it's extremely important if you plan to scan, print, or download color photos. Using a resolution that's too low means that your painting prints out with jagged edges and disappointingly blocky text. Using a resolution that's too high may unnecessarily slow the program down, take many times longer to print, take a lot more space on the hard drive, and require that you give AppleWorks more memory.

The rule of thumb is: For graphics you plan to use on a Web page, set your document to 72 dpi. (Higher resolutions gain you nothing.) For graphics you plan to print on an inkjet printer, such as those from Epson, Canon, or HP, work at 150 to

300 dpi, depending on the quality of the printer. (For extremely technical reasons, the dpi potential of the printer *isn't* the same thing as the dpi of your graphic. You don't have to scan at 1,400 dpi to take advantage of a 1,400 dpi printer's high resolution; scanning at 300 dpi is plenty.)

Resolution and your document's dimensions are related. Remember that AppleWorks stores your document's dimensions in *pixels,* not in inches. If you change a 72 dpi painting's resolution to 300, therefore, without changing the document's size, you get a document that's the size of a postage stamp; the smaller the dots that make up the image, the smaller the image. If you enlarge the document's size (in pixels) without bumping up its resolution, on the other hand, you end up with a low-resolution document that spans several pages. Give AppleWorks *plenty* of memory if you increase the document size, resolution, or bit depth, because each such change requires more RAM.

POWER USERS' CLINIC

Zooming

If you're editing a 300 dpi document, you'll get a very high-quality printout—but you'll have a heck of a time trying to edit the fine detail of the artwork, because AppleWorks shows you the painting at *actual size.* At 300 dpi, that's probably pretty small.

Fortunately, you can exercise a great deal of control over your perspective through the zoom controls. The three controls are in the lower-left corner of the document window, as described on page 29.

The first control—the one with the number on it—indicates the current magnification. Click the number to produce a menu with ten options—nine common magnification levels, plus the Other command that lets you enter any magnification you like, from 3.125 percent to 3200 percent.

If you're editing a high-resolution document, in other words, these controls are a godsend. Only by zooming in a great deal can you see and edit the individual, *very* tiny dots that compose your image.

Color depth

The Depth setting lets you control the document's *color depth*—the maximum number of colors your document is capable of displaying at one time. The more colors you make available, the more memory your document consumes.

Figure 7-10:
Color depth becomes most apparent when dealing with gradients, which are composed of fine color gradations. From left to right, these three gradients were made at color depths of 256, Thousands, and Millions. Notice how the first square is dithered (composed of multicolored dots that AppleWorks hopes will fool the eye into perceiving finer shades that aren't really there). The second square looks like a smoother color progression, but you can still see a "banding" effect. The third square looks great. The lesson: higher color depth is better when dealing with gradients and very important photos.

The Thousands of Colors setting works well for photos; 256 colors is fine for non-photo images you intend to use on the Web. If you're looking for the best possible color (important when dealing with digital photos or gradients), bump up the color depth to Millions. (You'll notice that the Memory usage indicator at the bottom of the window goes up accordingly.)

Clippings

You can use clippings (see page 279) in painting documents just as you can in other document types: Simply drag a picture from the Clippings window into your painting document. Unfortunately, as you've come to expect, after you've done so, the clipping becomes part of the painting—a frozen pattern of dots. You can no longer drag it around, resize it by dragging corner handles, and so on.

If you want to resize a clipping, drag it into a drawing document first, resize it to the size you need, and then copy and paste it into your painting document. (The Drawing module can resize clippings without running into resolution problems.) Alternatively, you can *shrink* a clipping when you first bring it into a painting document by choosing Transform→Resize or Transform→Scale By Percent and then shrinking the artwork before you do anything else with it. Shrinking an item in the painting document generally doesn't cause resolution problems; it's *enlarging* that makes painting elements become blocky looking.

You can also put selections from painting documents *into* the Clippings window. Just drag an area of your painting (which you've selected using the Lasso or Rectangular Selection tool) onto the appropriate tab of the Clippings window; AppleWorks inserts a copy there.

Caution: When you use a clipping that began its life as a painting selection, it comes into your document (a word processing, database, or drawing document, for example) as a painting frame, with all of the limitations that come along with the Painting module. For example, if you try to enlarge a clipping made from a painting, it becomes jagged, blotchy, and pixellated. (*Shrinking* such a clipping works fine.)

Understanding Graphics Formats

When you have finished your graphics masterpiece, you're going to want to use it *somewhere*. That's where choosing the correct *graphics format* comes in handy—a choice that presents itself whenever you choose File→Save As and examine the pop-up menu at the bottom of the Save dialog box.

Aside from the AppleWorks or ClarisWorks document formats, you can save a Painting or Drawing document in any of ten other formats:

- **BMP.** The Windows bitmap format, BMP, is useful if you plan to give the graphic (by email, for example) to a Windows user who doesn't have AppleWorks. The BMP format produces the largest files of all the AppleWorks graphics formats.

- **JPEG.** JPEG documents are ideal for photos and other complex graphics destined for a Web page. It's the most popular photo format on the Internet because the files are small (fast to download) and look great.

- **MacPaint.** A holdover from the early Macintosh days, MacPaint 1.0 is an ancient Mac graphics file format. It doesn't have much use these days, but its file sizes are extremely small. There's a reason for those small file sizes—graphics saved as MacPaint documents are converted to black-and-white images. That may make an interesting special effect, but it's not very useful.

- **PICT.** PICT, which stands for Picture, is the format used by the Mac Clipboard. It's rarely useful, however, and the lines in your drawing documents may even shift when saved into this low-precision format.

- **PNG.** A next-generation successor to the GIF file format (described in the sidebar box below), PNG files are great for simple, Web-destined graphics (such as logos, buttons, and the like—everything but photos, for which JPEG is the better choice). Older Web browsers may not be able to show PNG graphics files.

- **Photoshop.** AppleWorks can open and save Photoshop-format documents. Use this format when exchanging files with that high-end image processing software.

- **QuickTime.** QuickTime is Apple's Mac/Windows movie software. Unbeknownst to most Mac fans, there's such a thing as a QuickTime *graphic,* a still image; this choice creates such a file.

- **SGI.** You'll need to save your graphic in the SGI file format only if you're moving it to a Silicon Graphics computer.

FREQUENTLY ASKED QUESTION

What Happened to GIF?

GIF is the single most popular file format of the Web! Am I crazy, or is AppleWorks 6 unable to save my graphics in GIF format?

This file format is ubiquitous on Web pages because it's well suited to making graphics with just a few colors, such as banners, ads, logos, buttons, and so on. The explanation: Corporate politics. The company that has long held the patent on the GIF compression algorithm has recently begun to enforce its patent ownership, asking for payment from companies (like Apple) who want to include the GIF-making software in their products. As a result, companies who make graphics software are moving away from GIF.

One solution: save your Web-bound graphics as PNG files. PNG graphics are ideal for exactly the same kinds of Web images as GIFs—but without the usage fees and attendant litigation. Unfortunately, PNGs may not show up in all Web browsers, so you run the risk of your graphics looking funny to some comers to your Web site—or not showing up at all.

Another approach: Save your images as PNG files, which you then open in another graphics application and convert to GIFs. That's a big pain, but using another program to complete the conversion of AppleWorks graphics to GIF format is the only complete option. You'll have great success, for example, using the shareware program GraphicConverter for this purpose; it's available at *www.missingmanual.com,* among other places.

CHAPTER 7: THE ART DEPARTMENT: PAINTING

- **TGA.** The Targa File Format stores very high-quality photo files. It's rarely used today, however, except in certain video and high-end animation applications.

- **TIFF.** The standard in professional printing, TIFF files are ideal for graphics that are meant to be printed. (All of the graphics in this book, for example, were saved as TIFF files.) TIFF file sizes can be large, so be warned if disk space is limited.

Note: Although AppleWorks is limited to these ten file formats when *saving* a graphic, it can *read* many more—more than 35 different file formats covering graphics, video, and audio. Technically speaking, it can read anything QuickTime can understand, and each new version of QuickTime can translate even more audio and visual formats.

Presentations and Slide Shows

R emember the good old days—when teachers showed class presentations on an old overhead projector with a noisy fan, shuffling through the transparencies to find the ones they wanted, while letting papers with their lecture notes flutter to the floor? Or Aunt Sophie's endless slide shows of her latest vacation pictures? Or the time you snorted yourself awake in the middle of a board meeting as your boss showed graph after graph, accompanied by his hypnotic commentary?

The one thing these shows all have in common is that they *present* graphic accompaniment to a discussion, story, or lecture. With AppleWorks 6, you don't have to use an overhead or slide projector—you can use your computer screen or, thanks to the *video mirroring* feature offered by many Mac models (notably PowerBook laptops), a computer projection system.

Of course, that doesn't mean that you can't print out your presentation onto transparencies or slides if you wish. Even overhead-projector presentations can benefit from the slide-show design features built into AppleWorks.

Presentation Module Basics

Presentation documents are like specialized Drawing documents. You can use any of the drawing tools described in Chapter 6, but the page dimensions are fixed at a size that can be scaled to fit almost any computer monitor: 640 x 480 pixels (screen dots). You might notice that these dimensions have the same ratio, 4:3, as your TV, digital cameras, and video software like iMovie. In other words, you can use pictures from your digital camera, or movies you've made with iMovie, in your AppleWorks presentations. You may have to adjust their size, but you won't have to crop or distort them to get them to fit.

But presentation documents differ from drawing documents in other ways, too. For example, presentation documents offer a selection of visual *transitions,* such as crossfades, from one slide to the next, which you can specify independently for each slide. Additionally, where a drawing document limits you to one Master page, a presentation document can contain multiple Master slides upon which you can base your slides. Throw in the organizational tools and a Notes features (described later), and you'll find that the Presentation module can handle the majority of your presentation needs.

When to Draw and When to Present

In earlier versions of AppleWorks, you used a drawing document, with its Master page, and the Slide Show dialog box (Window→Slide Show) to create presentations. In AppleWorks 6, these features are still available, in part so that presentations created in previous versions of AppleWorks/ClarisWorks will still work.

But the ability to create the older, drawing-based slide shows may still be useful—especially when you want to create a slide show that *isn't* exactly 640 x 480. For more on Drawing-module slide shows and the Slide Show dialog box, see the end of this chapter.

Using a Presentation Template

As described in the next section, it's easy enough to create and design a presentation from scratch. But when you have more desperation than time, use a presentation *template.* (See Chapter 9 for more on templates.) For example, your work routine might go like this, whether the presentation concerns next quarter's sales forecasts or changes to the PTA meeting schedule:

1. **At the Starting Points window (choose File→Show Starting Points), click the Templates tab.**

   AppleWorks shows you all of its templates. Scroll or make the window big enough so that you can see the handful of templates whose names contain the word "Presentation."

2. **Click the presentation template you want.**

   The presentation design you selected appears on the screen, filled with dummy text like "My Presentation" or "Title." (See Figure 8-1.)

   In this example, suppose you choose the Geometric Presentation template.

3. **Double-click the text ("Title," for example) to activate the text box. Delete the dummy text and replace it with the words you actually want to appear in your slide show.**

   If the background of the slide is colored, you may find it difficult to tell when the text has been highlighted. You can always see the cursor, however; to delete the text, in other words, you may have to backspace over it (instead of highlighting it first). In any case, the result is shown in Figure 8-1.

   Repeat this process for any other text boxes on the first slide.

4. **Advance to the next slide by clicking its icon in the Controls palette (Figure 8-1, right). Repeat step 3.**

The second slide in a template is generally a *bulleted list*—a standard element of corporate presentations. You can think of this bulleted list as an outline to help both you and your audience focus on the points you intended to make here.

Figure 8-1:
The quickest way to a slide show is by using a template (left). Replace the dummy text with the text you want (middle); with the Arrow tool selected, double-click the text to edit it. Then advance to the next slide by clicking its icon in the Controls palette (right). Each template comes with at least two Master pages—one appropriate for title slides, another for creating bullet-point lists, and sometimes a third designed to hold a picture or movie.

5. **Replace these bullets just the way you replaced the title.**

In other words, double-click to activate the text box, delete the dummy text (such as "Bullet 1"), and replace it with your own text.

6. **Click the Master Slides tab in the Controls palette (see Figure 8-2), and then click the Master slide whose design you want for the next slide.**

Most slide show templates include two or three different underlying Master slides—design templates that contain pre-designed text boxes and graphic elements. Usually there's one that presents the title only, another style for bullet lists, and a third that's designed to accommodate a picture, chart, or movie.

You can read more on Master slides in the next section. For now, it's enough to note that when you add a new slide in a template file, you must first select the master-slide style on which you want to base it.

7. **Click the Slides tab in the Controls palette (Figure 8-4) and click the + button.**

   AppleWorks creates another slide, represented by another miniature icon in this Controls palette. Edit the dummy text just as you did in step 3.

Continue this way—creating new slides, and editing the text on them—until your slide show is complete. Along the way, you can paste in, or draw, other AppleWorks elements onto any slide: clippings, spreadsheet frames, text frames, tables, lines, arrows, and anything else you need to make your point.

Designing a Presentation from Scratch

True enough, AppleWorks doesn't offer much of a selection when it comes to presentation *templates*. More often, you may want to come up with your own designs.

You create a new slide show the same way you'd create any new AppleWorks document, such as by clicking Presentation on the Starting Points window or choosing File→New→Presentation. Either way, a big empty document window now appears. What tells you that you're in a presentation document is the presence of the Controls palette at the right side of the screen (Figure 8-2).

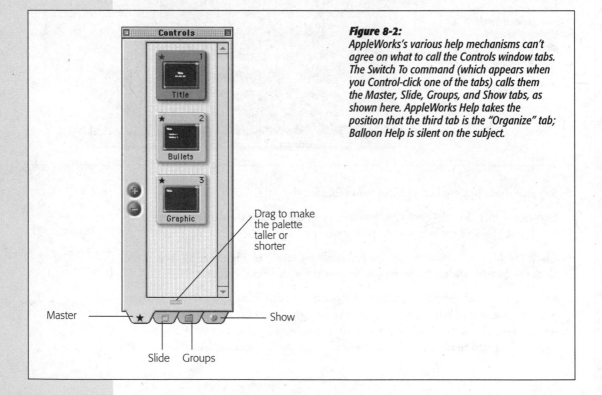

Figure 8-2:
AppleWorks's various help mechanisms can't agree on what to call the Controls window tabs. The Switch To command (which appears when you Control-click one of the tabs) calls them the Master, Slide, Groups, and Show tabs, as shown here. AppleWorks Help takes the position that the third tab is the "Organize" tab; Balloon Help is silent on the subject.

Drag to make the palette taller or shorter

Master

Show

Slide   Groups

The Controls Palette

The Controls window and its four tabs provide a master control center for your presentation. (If it isn't showing, choose Window→Show Presentation Controls to make it appear.) Like the Accents window, the Controls window displays graphics on its tabs rather than words. Unfortunately, the pictures aren't quite so suggestive of function as the color, pattern, and other tab icons on the Accents window. See Figure 8-2 for a rundown.

Creating Master Slides

Most modern presentations include some *static* elements—that is, consistent graphics that appear on every slide, such as a solid-colored background or a company logo. You create your repeated elements on a special background slide called the *Master slide*. As you build your slide show, you can always add new text box and graphic items on top of the Master slide. But the master-slide elements lie behind everything you do. See Figure 8-3 for some examples.

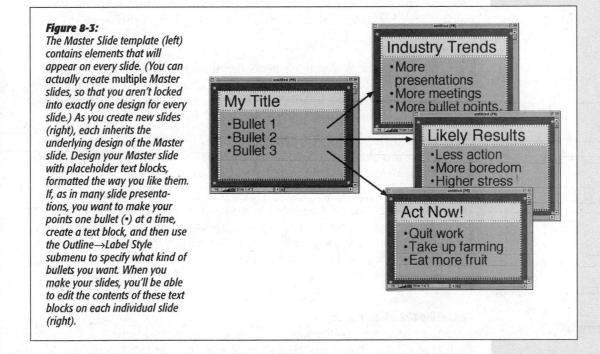

Figure 8-3:
The Master Slide template (left) contains elements that will appear on every slide. (You can actually create multiple Master slides, so that you aren't locked into exactly one design for every slide.) As you create new slides (right), each inherits the underlying design of the Master slide. Design your Master slide with placeholder text blocks, formatted the way you like them. If, as in many slide presentations, you want to make your points one bullet (•) at a time, create a text block, and then use the Outline→Label Style submenu to specify what kind of bullets you want. When you make your slides, you'll be able to edit the contents of these text blocks on each individual slide (right).

To view the list of Master slides available for your presentation, click the Master tab (marked with a star) of the Controls palette (Figure 8-2). In a New presentation, you've only got one Master slide (and one slide based on it). Of course, if all you're going to create is old-fashioned transparency-style slides without any backgrounds or other recurring elements, you can ignore this tab; however, if you want to put such master-page items as a logo or a consistent background on your slides, use the Master tab to do so.

Changing the background color

Unless you're going for that retro, overhead-projector look, change the background color to anything other than white. Click the Master slide to edit it. (The blue slide outline tells you which Master slide is currently selected in the palette.)

Now click the Rectangle tool on the Tools window. (If it isn't showing, click the red toolbox icon at the bottom of the Tools window first.) Then, using the Accents palette, specify a fill color, and then draw a rectangle that fills the entire empty window. (You may find this easier to do if you first zoom out by clicking the smaller of the two "mountain buttons" at the lower-left corner of the window, making the entire document window fit on your screen.)

You'll probably want to set the line thickness for the pen—the outline of the colored box—to None on the Accent window's Lines tab, so that no outline appears around the rectangle.

If you don't mind driving your audience crazy, you can even fill this background rectangle with patterns, wallpaper, or gradients, using the other tabs of the Accents palette. (See Chapter 6 for more information on using the Accents window.)

Adding text blocks

When most people think of static elements, they think of corporate logos, slide dates, confidentiality notices, and so on. But the Master slide is also where you put *placeholder text blocks,* complete with the type style, size, and indented bullets you want. Figure 8-3 shows one example.

When you begin to build your presentation, AppleWorks will automatically create a copy of these text blocks on each slide. You'll be free later to edit the dummy text you put inside them and tailor it for each particular slide.

Tip: If you're used to working in AppleWorks 5 to create your presentations, you're probably used to having to cover up, with a solid-color square, any master-page elements you don't want to show up on a particular slide. In AppleWorks 6, Master slides are more flexible; they behave like templates. When you create a new slide, you get a *copy* of the static elements on the Master page, which you can individually select, move, modify, or delete.

Renaming the Master slide

AppleWorks isn't very creative when it comes to naming your Master slides; it names them Untitled. To rename one, click where it says Untitled to highlight the name, and then type the new name. Only about the first eight characters appear here (except when you're editing it).

Building the Slides

After you've selected a Master slide, click the Slide tab of the Controls palette (Figure 8-4). Click the + button to create a new slide that's based on the Master slide that was most recently selected.

Now a copy of your Master slide appears in the document window, ready for you to modify—by changing the placeholder text in the text blocks, for example, or by adding new text blocks, pictures, QuickTime movies, or other visual elements. You can use the entire arsenal of tools described in Chapter 6—the only difference is that you'll probably want to make everything bigger and bolder than you would when creating, for example, a brochure.

As noted above, you're not obligated to use any of the master-page elements that appear on the slide itself; if your corporate logo is upstaging the photo you want to display, feel free to shrink the logo, move it, or even delete it from the slide. The Master slide won't mind.

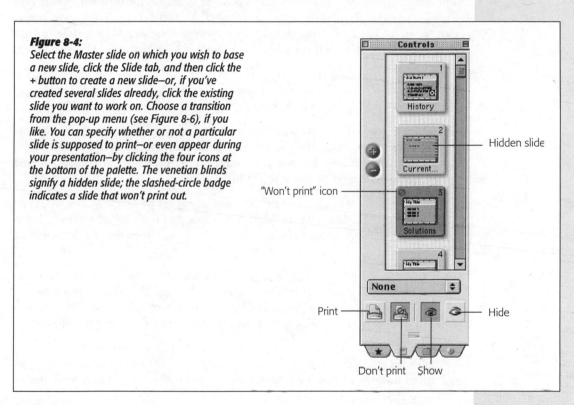

Figure 8-4:
Select the Master slide on which you wish to base a new slide, click the Slide tab, and then click the + button to create a new slide—or, if you've created several slides already, click the existing slide you want to work on. Choose a transition from the pop-up menu (see Figure 8-6), if you like. You can specify whether or not a particular slide is supposed to print—or even appear during your presentation—by clicking the four icons at the bottom of the palette. The venetian blinds signify a hidden slide; the slashed-circle badge indicates a slide that won't print out.

Hidden slide

"Won't print" icon

Print

Hide

Don't print   Show

Working with multiple slides

Each time you click the + symbol, you create another slide in your slide show, represented by another icon in the Slide tab of the Controls palette. To help you keep them straight, consider giving each one a descriptive, but short, name. (Click its existing name—"Untitled"—and then type a replacement name. Press Enter when you're done.)

You can rearrange the slides just by dragging them up or down in the Controls palette; AppleWorks automatically re-numbers them, so that they always appear in numerical order.

Tip: Once you've created a few slides, you may find that the Controls palette is too short to show more than about three slides. You'll have better luck rearranging the slides in your show if you make the Controls palette bigger.

You can't make it any wider, but you can make it taller. To do so, start by dragging the title bar (identified in Figure 8-2) as high as you can—until it bumps into the Button bar. Then stretch the window downward by dragging the tiny set of parallel lines at the bottom of the palette, just above the tabs.

One powerful AppleWorks presentation feature is the ability to *hide* a slide. By temporarily omitting a slide from the "running order," you can re-use the presentation you've already created. You'll be ready when, for example, the boss tells you to give the visiting executive a 10-minute summary of the two-hour talk you gave yesterday. Similarly, you have individual control over whether or not each slide in your presentation prints out when you use the File→Print command (to create handouts of your talk, for example).

The key to all of this slide-by-slide control is the row of four icons at the bottom of the Slide tab (see Figure 8-4). Here they are, presented from right to left:

- **The Hide icon.** When you click this icon, you see gray stripes appear across the selected slide or slides, and the closed-eye icon darkens (see Figure 8-5). You've just told AppleWorks that you don't want the selected slide or slides to appear when you give the slide show. You've just *hidden* the slides.

- **The Show icon.** You can make hidden slides reappear by first selecting them and then clicking this icon, which darkens to show that the selected slides will now appear in the slide show. (The gray stripes disappear from the slide's thumbnail image, too.)

- **The "Don't Print" icon.** The third icon from the right is actually meant to represent a printer with a piece of paper coming out—and the piece of paper bears a red slashed circle. If you select a slide and then click this icon (which then darkens), you prevent that slide from printing out when you choose the File→Print command.

- **The Print icon.** The leftmost icon at the bottom of the palette turns printing on again for the selected slide or slides. In other words, when it's darkened, the selected slide will print out.

Deleting a slide

If you hide a slide *and* choose "Don't Print," it's as good as gone from your presentation—but you can recover it later. However, if you're certain you won't be needing a particular slide any more, delete it by clicking the slide and then clicking the – button at the left side of the palette. (AppleWorks doesn't let you remove the last slide, however; AppleWorks insists that there be at least one slide in the list.)

Tip: You can also remove a slide by dragging its icon clear out of the Controls palette and onto the desktop Trash can, if it's visible.

Adding notes

Fortunately for anyone who's ever tried to display a slide show while reading notes from index cards, AppleWorks can generate speaker notes for you, which look like the ones shown in Figure 8-5. You can type notes pertaining to the slide and use the drawing tools to add arrows or other embellishments. Nothing that you add in the Notes View appears in normal view or in the presentation.

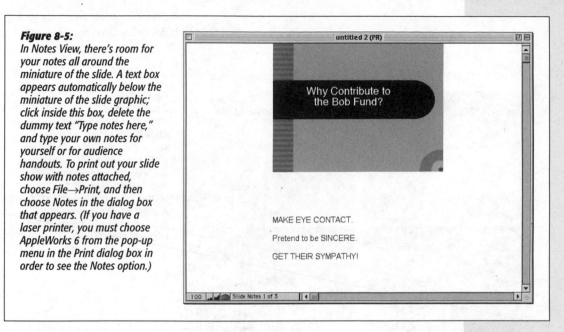

Figure 8-5:
In Notes View, there's room for your notes all around the miniature of the slide. A text box appears automatically below the miniature of the slide graphic; click inside this box, delete the dummy text "Type notes here," and type your own notes for yourself or for audience handouts. To print out your slide show with notes attached, choose File→Print, and then choose Notes in the dialog box that appears. (If you have a laser printer, you must choose AppleWorks 6 from the pop-up menu in the Print dialog box in order to see the Notes option.)

Why Contribute to the Bob Fund?

MAKE EYE CONTACT.

Pretend to be SINCERE.

GET THEIR SYMPATHY!

Tip: Besides using this feature for speaker or handout notes, you can also use it to write notes to yourself as you create the presentation, for example, "Can we say this? Ask legal dept."

To add such notes, enter Notes View by choosing Window→Notes View. When you do so, you'll see the slide reduced to half of its original size. See Figure 8-5 for instructions on adding your own notes. (To exit Notes View so that you can continue editing your slides, choose Window→Notes View again.)

Adding transitions

In a mostly futile attempt to help corporate presenters add excitement and energy to deadly-dull presentations, presentation-software companies have designed animated *transitions,* such as crossfades, to smooth the appearance of each new slide.

In general, these transitions have been wildly overused—a good presentation should be able to stand on its own without any such software dazzle. But if you promise to use the transition effects tastefully and consistently within each slide show, here's the trick: After selecting a slide in the Controls palette, choose one of the 26 effects from the pop-up menu at the bottom of the palette (where it probably says None). The final pages of this chapter offer a visual catalog of these effects.

Groups

The Groups feature lets you file away your slides into electronic folders. Organizing your slides in this way offers two advantages: first, you can delete an entire folder full (group) at once. Second, you can rearrange segments of your slide show by dragging individual slides into Group folders, which you can then drag up or down in the list; all the slides inside go along for the ride.

To make a group, click the Groups tab (Figure 8-7). You'll notice that one group folder already appears here, called Untitled Folder. It contains all of the slides you've created so far.

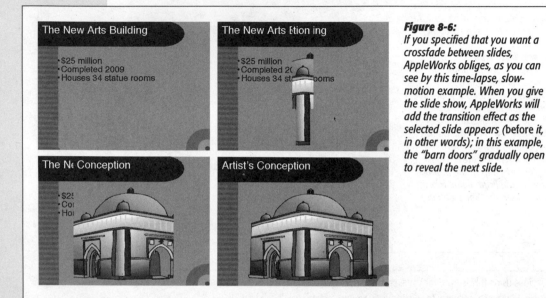

Figure 8-6:
If you specified that you want a crossfade between slides, AppleWorks obliges, as you can see by this time-lapse, slow-motion example. When you give the slide show, AppleWorks will add the transition effect as the selected slide appears (before it, in other words); in this example, the "barn doors" gradually open to reveal the next slide.

POWER USERS' CLINIC

Making Animated Bullets

One of the most popular slide show effects of all time is the *bullet build*, in which several bullet points (like those shown in Figure 8-4) appear one at a time, thus preventing your audience from "reading ahead" while you're talking.

AppleWorks makes it fairly easy to create such blow-by-blow effects—just make as many slides as there are bullets. Add another bullet point on each of these successive slides. When it comes time to play your slide show, another bullet appears in the list each time you advance the slide (by clicking

the mouse button, for example). You can even incorporate transition effects into the appearance of these bullets; the Wipe Horizontal transition is especially effective in revealing bullet items, because it makes the bullet "unwrap" from left to right.

In general, you'll want to create your bulleted lists by placing a special text box, formatted with the bullet outline style you prefer, on a Master slide. Base the bullet slides on this Master slide.

Create a new group folder by clicking the + button. (Delete one by clicking its icon and then clicking the – button.) To reassign some of your slides to other group folders, click the "flippy triangle" to expand the first folder (see Figure 8-8). Then drag the icons of the appropriate slides, one by one, into the other folders you've created. (You can't Shift-click or drag-enclose folders on this tab to select more than one at a time, alas.)

When you return to the Slides tab, you'll see that your individual slides have been reordered according to the larger sequence you've established on the Groups tab.

To delete a group folder—and all of the slides inside it—highlight it and then click the - button. And to rename one of these group folders, click its name and then re-type, exactly as though you're renaming a standard folder. Press Enter or click anywhere else when you're done. (You can rename slides here, too, in exactly the same way.)

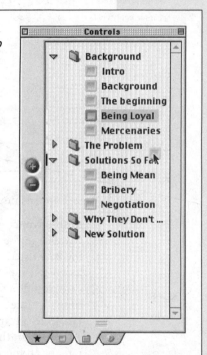

Figure 8-7:
Organize your slides into groups on this tab. Move the slides from one group to another and then, if you wish, reorder the groups. As you drag the slide, its ghosted image appears beneath your cursor tip; as you drag the cursor onto a different folder, a black vertical indicator line appears to the left of the folder's name, as shown here. All of these changes will have the corresponding effect on the order in which they appear on the Slides tab.

The Show Tab

The first several tabs on the Controls palette let you design your *slides;* the Show tab lets you design your *show.* Here's where you specify, for example, how you want to advance from one slide to the next—by clicking the mouse, by waiting a pre-determined interval, and so on.

Slide show options

When it comes time to show people your handiwork, AppleWorks goes into a special trance. All the familiar landmarks of the screen—menu bar, windows, icons, and so on—disappear, and the screen is flooded with the magnified image of your first slide.

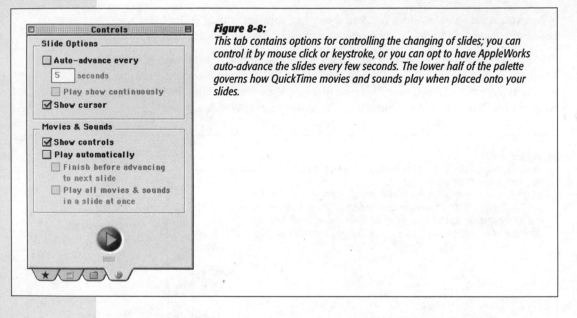

Figure 8-8:
This tab contains options for controlling the changing of slides; you can control it by mouse click or keystroke, or you can opt to have AppleWorks auto-advance the slides every few seconds. The lower half of the palette governs how QuickTime movies and sounds play when placed onto your slides.

What happens next is determined by the options at the top of this tab.

- **Auto-advance every __ seconds.** In many situations, you'll want AppleWorks to advance to the next slide whenever you click the mouse button or press any of the keys listed below. But occasionally you may want to create a slide show that loops continuously, unattended, at a show or meeting, in "kiosk" mode. In that case, you don't want to have to babysit the computer, clicking the mouse every time it's time to change the slide. By turning on this checkbox, you tell Apple-Works to advance automatically at a specified interval—every five seconds, for example. (In the little box, type the number of seconds you want each slide to remain on the screen.)

- **Play show continuously.** Turn on this checkbox if you want AppleWorks to play the show continuously, looping from beginning to end and then back to the beginning, until you interrupt it by clicking the mouse.

- **Show cursor.** This option lets you specify whether or not you want the arrow cursor to appear on the screen during the slide show. If you'll be giving your slide show right on the screen, you may want the arrow cursor visible, so that you can point out important parts of your diagrams or pictures while you talk.

On the other hand, if your slide show consists of nothing but photos or QuickTime movies, you may want to turn the cursor off so that it doesn't distract. Similarly, if you prefer to be in front of your audience, indicating the key points of your slides by pointing a laser pointer at the projection screen while someone else advances the slides, you'll want to turn the cursor off.

QuickTime movie controls

As shown in Figure 8-9, it's easy to place QuickTime movies and sounds onto your slides—a sure way to make any presentation livelier, and a terrific way to play movies you've created using, for example, iMovie. A QuickTime movie you've placed on a slide behaves exactly like a rectangle you've drawn using the drawing tools: you can resize it, drag it around, move it in front of or behind other objects, and so on.

These options pertain to movie and sound files you've inserted onto your slides.

- **Show controls.** This checkbox determines whether or not the QuickTime controls appear during a slide show, as shown in Figure 8-8. Hiding the controls makes your slide show look better, because it removes the computery trappings of the QuickTime scroll bar.

  At first glance, however, hiding the controls may also make it difficult for you to start the movie playing (if you've chosen not to have it begin automatic playback). After all, if the scroll bar and its play button aren't visible, how are you supposed to start the movie or sound?

  The sneaky answer: Double-click inside the first frame of the movie as it appears on the slide. Double-click again to interrupt the playback, if you want. (When you click outside the movie frame, you advance to the next slide—when you click inside the movie frame, you play the movie.)

Figure 8-9:
It's easy enough to place a movie or sound into a slide (left)—while building a slide show, just choose File→ Insert, navigate to the movie or sound file you want, and then double-click it. During the slide show, the movie or sound plays automatically when its slide appears— unless you've changed the options on the Show tab of the Controls palette (Figure 8-8).

All right then, but what if you've chosen to have your cursor *hidden?* How are you supposed to start playback if you can't see your arrow? There's a solution here, too: Option-click anywhere on the screen. AppleWorks dutifully begins playback.

- **Finish before advancing to next slide.** Suppose you've told AppleWorks that you want your slides to advance automatically, once every five seconds. That's fine, but what if one of the slides contains a 20-second movie clip? Turn on this checkbox if you want AppleWorks to continue playing the movie to its end, and only then to advance to the next slide.

- **Play all movies & sounds in a slide at once.** This option handles situations where you put more than one movie or sound file on a single slide. If you're not careful, asking AppleWorks to play them all simultaneously could lead to a cacophony of confusion—but if handled tastefully, it could let you add a music soundtrack that plays behind the piece of movie footage.

Tip: Be careful about putting a movie or sound file on your Master slide. If you do that, and the Play Automatically checkbox is turned on, that movie or sound will play from the beginning each time you change slides. And if you've also turned on "Finish before advancing to next slide," you'll *really* be in trouble.

Once the movie is playing, you can stop it by clicking directly on the movie picture—or by clicking the Pause button beneath it, if you've elected to display the movie controls.

Troubleshooting QuickTime movies and sounds

Multimedia files like movies and sounds gobble up lots of memory. Adding even a few to your slide show makes AppleWorks likely to crash, freeze, and otherwise make your life miserable. If you plan to put these kinds of files into your presentations, don't even think about proceeding without increasing the program's memory allotment (see Appendix B).

Another caution: When you place a QuickTime movie or sound file on your slide as an *inline object* (see page 333), the control *badge*—the tiny film icon at the lower-left corner of the movie frame, which you can ordinarily click to summon the scroll bar and other controls—has no effect. You can't play the movie at all, in other words, unless you either set it to play automatically or, during the slide show, double-click it.

Caution: AppleWorks doesn't store QuickTime sounds and movies as part of the AppleWorks document file—instead, it saves *links* to those files on your hard drive. If you transfer the AppleWorks file to another computer without also transferring the multimedia files, the program won't be able to display your sounds or movies. You'll get nothing but a dialog box asking if you'd like to search for the missing files.

If you need such file portability, create a folder for your presentation; into it, place copies of your multimedia files *and* your AppleWorks document. Then you can copy that whole folder and be assured you'll have all the pieces required for your multimedia *tour de force.*

Playing the Slide Show

When you're ready to give your presentation, click the big Play button on the Show tab, or the Play button on the Button bar, or choose Window→Slide Show. AppleWorks immediately changes the resolution (magnification level) of your screen to 640 x 480 pixels, enlarging everything on your slides, and displays the first slide.

Tip: If you *Option*-click the Play button, AppleWorks doesn't change your screen's resolution setting.

If you've specified that you want mouse control over your slide show, you can advance to the next slide by clicking the mouse, or by pressing these keys:

- **Next slide.** Press the right arrow key, down arrow key, Page Down, Return, Tab, or Space bar.

- **Previous slide.** Press the left-arrow key, up-arrow key, Page Up, Shift-Return, Shift-Tab, or Shift-Space bar.

- **Last slide.** Press the End key.

- **First slide.** Press the Home key.

- **Stop the slide show.** Press the letter Q key, Esc, or ⌘-period.

When the slide show is complete, AppleWorks leaves the last slide on the screen and ignores any of the "Next Slide" commands, giving you the opportunity to gracefully turn off the monitor, switch off the video projector, or just put your computer to sleep. This courtesy saves you the humiliation of blasting your audience with the image of your disorganized desktop, the computer equivalent of the blinding white screen at the end of a photo slide show.

To quit the presentation mode and return to your desktop, you have to press the letter Q, Esc, or ⌘-period.

Note: When the slide show stops, AppleWorks restores your screen to its original resolution settings (800 x 600 pixels on an iMac, for example). Unfortunately, the damage is done: When the screen was resized, all of your desktop icons and application tool palettes, including AppleWorks' own palettes, got shoved inward onto the newly shrunken screen area. Moving them back outward is, unfortunately, left to you.

Drawing-Module Presentations

As noted earlier in this chapter, older versions of AppleWorks offered a different scheme for creating slide shows, one that's still available in AppleWorks 6: you create a drawing document that's as many pages long as you want slides in your show. As you'll read in the following discussion, Drawing-based presentations are far less flexible and more frustrating to create than slide shows you create using the Presentations module. You can have only one Master slide, you can't edit the items on it when making the slides themselves, and so on.

If they're so limited, therefore, you might wonder why on earth AppleWorks 6 still offers this feature. As it turns out, there are two very good reasons:

- Thanks to this vestigial feature, AppleWorks 6 can still open presentations created with earlier versions of AppleWorks or ClarisWorks.

- Drawing-document slides can have sizes and shapes other than the 640-by-480-pixel format of presentation documents. Because drawing document slides' shapes are determined by the size of the page, you can create slides that are taller than they are wide, very large, or very small—flexibility the Presentation module doesn't give you.

Creating the Master Page

In a drawing-document slide show, you can create only one Master page. Choose Options→Edit Master Page to view the "Master slide." Place your background elements on this page, exactly as you would when creating an AppleWorks presentation document. For example, you might want to begin by placing a full-page colored square to serve as the background. In this case, however, *don't* create text boxes to serve as placeholders for the text that will appear on your slides; when you create slide shows out of drawing documents, you won't be able to edit these text boxes. Instead, you must place a new text box manually on each slide you create.

When you have the Master page the way you want it, again choose Options→Edit Master Page; you're back at your document, ready to start adding the slide-specific text and graphics. Immediately, however, you may notice that your master-page elements have disappeared. That's because they appear only in Page View, which you can open by choosing Window→Page View.

At last the master-page elements appear. Now you're ready to start designing your first slide, adding text and graphics as necessary. Of course, you don't have placeholder text boxes inherited from the Master slide, so you'll have to create and format a new text block on each slide—if you're smart, you'll copy and paste the first text block to your other slides, which saves you time in formatting and placement.

Managing Multiple Slides

It isn't as easy to add single slides in a drawing document as it is in a presentation document. To do so, you must choose Format→Document, and increase the number of slides (pages) by changing the number in the Pages Across or Pages Down box. (For best results, increase the number in only *one* of these two boxes, so that your slides, when scrolled in Page View, form *either* one horizontal row or one vertical column.)

Tip: Consider adding a lot of slides simultaneously—increasing the number in the Document Options dialog box to a very large number—so that you won't have to keep returning to this dialog box to add each new slide. In other words, add more than you think you'll need; then, when you're finished creating slides, choose Format→Document again and set the Page count to the actual number of slides you want. AppleWorks deletes the empty ones that were left over.

To switch from one slide to another, you must use the scroll bars; the Drawing module offers no Controls palette to give you an easy way to navigate your slide collection.

Hiding Master Page Items

In a drawing document-based presentation, you can create only a single Master page. Slides you base on it contain all of the elements from that Master page—and you can't delete or edit them, as you can when using the official Presentation module. Therefore, you may have to play some tricks when it's necessary to hide certain elements from certain slides. To do so, place an opaque rectangle, the same color as the background, on top of the element you want to hide (such as the page number on a Title slide). Of course, this restricts your choices in backgrounds; you'll find it extremely difficult to seamlessly position opaque objects over gradients or some wallpaper textures.

Hiding and Configuring Slides

Choosing Window→Slide Show gets you to the Slide Show dialog box (Figure 8-10), your slide-show control center. This is where you can make slides transparent, or hide them, and set up your slide and QuickTime options. This is also where you start your slide show playing.

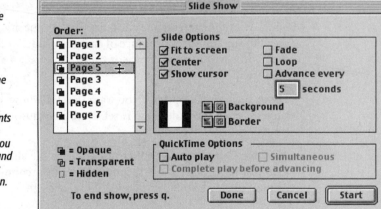

Figure 8-10:
In this dialog box, you set the options for a Drawing document-based slide show. You can hide slides or make them transparent, as well as change the order in which the pages appear in your slide show. Most of the rest of the options have direct equivalents in Presentation documents, discussed above; however, you can also set border, frame, and background options here for slides that don't fill the screen.

The three sections (other than the buttons) in this dialog box are Order and visibility, Slide Options, and QuickTime Options:

Order and visibility

At the left side of the screen, you see a list of Pages; they represent the slides in your slide show. You can drag the names of these pages up and down to reorder their appearance in the show.

Each time you click the tiny icon to the left of a page's name, the icon changes to one of three conditions: opaque, transparent, or hidden. (The legend below the list shows you which icon to switch.) *Opaque* means normal. Make the slide *hidden* if it contains notes that you'll want to print out, but not have appear on the screen during your slide show.

A *transparent* slide gets superimposed on top of the preceding one; you can create as many transparent slides as you like. The previous opaque slide shines through all of them. Use transparent slides to build a layered slide—for example, to create bullets that appear one at a time in a list, add each successive bullet to another transparent slide.

Slide Options

The eight options in this section control how your slide show runs.

- **Fit to Screen:** This checkbox magnifies or reduces the page size to fit your screen. Of course, if the size of your screen doesn't match the proportions of your slide show, your slides may become distorted during the slide show.

- **Center:** Turn on this checkbox if you want each slide centered on your screen during the show—a feature that's primarily useful if the slide shape is smaller than your actual screen.

- **Show Cursor.** This option determines whether or not the cursor is visible while the slide show is running, as described on page 262.

- **Fade.** As in the Presentation module, you can specify that you want a transition effect to smooth the appearance of each new slide. In the Drawing module, however, you have only one choice of transition effect—a crossfade—and it applies to *every* slide in your show.

- **Loop:** Turn on this option if you want the slide show to play over and over again, such as when the slide show is set up to play automatically in a kiosk or store display.

- **Advance Every.** If you'd rather not advance the slides by clicking your mouse, turn this checkbox on and specify how many seconds you want between slides. AppleWorks will conduct the slide show by itself.

- **Background:** Here's an alternative to the master-page method for providing a colored background behind all your slides. Choose from the upper-left pop-up menu here to choose a color, and from the upper-right pop-up menu to choose a wallpaper pattern.

- **Border.** These two pop-up menus create the border around each slide. (If Fit to Screen is turned on, you won't see any border, however.) This color or wallpaper texture will fill all parts of the screen that your page doesn't fill—a useful option when the slide dimensions are smaller than the dimensions of your screen.

QuickTime Options

As with the Presentation-type slides, Drawing-type slides can incorporate QuickTime movies and sounds. The options here correspond to those on the Show tab of the Controls palette, described on page 264.

- **Auto play.** Turn on this option to make each QuickTime movie begin playing as soon as its slide appears. If you don't turn this on, the next won't be available.

- **Simultaneous.** This option makes all movies and sounds on a slide play at once— which may be a useful option when combining the music track with a video clip.

- **Complete play before advancing:** This checkbox prevents AppleWorks from advancing the slide in mid-movie or mid-sound. (This option works only if you've also turned on the "advance every __ seconds" option.)

When you're finished setting up the show, click Done to return to working on your slides, or click Start to watch your slide show.

Playing the Slide Show

As noted above, you can play the slide show by choosing Window→Slide Show, and then clicking the Start button.

Tip: Another way to begin a Drawing-based slide show is to press Option while choosing Window→Slide Show.

When the slide show is over, you return to the Slide Show dialog box. Click Done to maintain any changes you've made in this dialog box, or Cancel to return to your slide show without preserving the settings you changed.

AppleWorks Transitions: A Catalog

As noted earlier in this chapter, AppleWorks offers 26 different animations that dissolve one slide into the next during your slide show. For best results, use them sparingly and with good taste. (For example, consider using only *one* transition style for your entire show, to provide consistency.) Here's a representative rundown.

Barn Door Open

The center of Slide A splits open; the halves slide apart, revealing Slide B.

Blinds Horizontal, Blinds Vertical

This one's eye-catching—too much, almost: the venetian-blind effect. You can opt for either horizontal or vertical blossoming stripes.

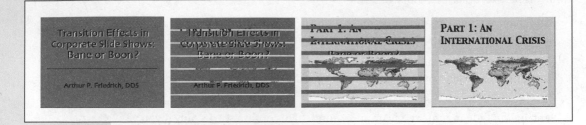

Box, Circle, Diamond, Heart, Star, Keyhole

Your shape appears in the middle of Slide A, growing to reveal Slide B beneath.

Checkerboard

Use this one when you're getting ready to appear on "Hollywood Squares."

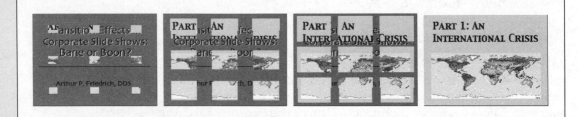

Expanding Triangle

A wedge pierces slide A, and zooms to the right, revealing Slide B.

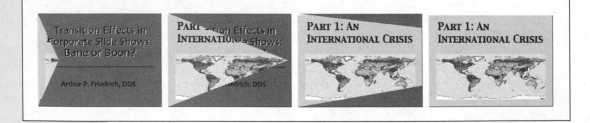

Fade

Here's your basic cross-dissolve—one of the least annoying effects of all.

Pinwheel, Radial

These effects are variations on the same theme: spinning from Slide A into Slide B.

Jaws, Zigzag

If you work for a manufacturer of pinking shears, these related effects are for you.

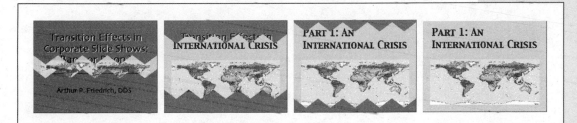

2

Part Two: AppleWorks Power

Templates, Clippings, and Assistants

L et's face it—there are plenty of obstacles to doing some of the projects that we'd *really* like to get done using our computers. Sometimes our muses (or the little voices in our heads) desert us when it's time to roll up our sleeves and get creative. If it's not that, the large dinner and all-too-comfy couch keep us from getting started on those things that we really ought to accomplish.

AppleWorks addresses a lack of creativity and sheer laziness with three time-saving shortcut tools: templates, clippings, and assistants. Whether it's preparing a school report complete with graphs and footnotes, figuring out if you really can afford that house down the block, or creating some business stationery for your new dot-com startup, AppleWorks has a way to help you start—and finish—important projects.

Templates: A Leg Up

AppleWorks *templates* can serve as the starting point for a long list of projects. Each template opens in its own window, with a complete set of starter text and graphics, making your job one of finishing up what the template started, rather than starting from scratch. Templates work like pads of printed stationery—each sheet torn off the pad has certain common elements (such as a company logo), but the rest of the content is yours to create. Templates save you time on the stuff that repeats from document to document.

AppleWorks ships with its own set of templates; you'll find them on the Templates tab of the Starting Points window (see page 10). When you click that tab, you're presented with a plethora of taste-tempting templates—36 in the basic set. The templates cover the gamut, from making a greeting card to creating a to-do list. Even better, AppleWorks has a built-in connection to a repository of templates housed on a remote Internet server—170 templates at AppleWorks' release, and growing. (The next chapter covers these Internet connections.)

Here's how you open a template (see Figure 9-1):

- Click the Templates tab in the Starting Points window (if Starting Points isn't open, you can get to it by pressing ⌘-1).

- Look for a template in the window that matches most closely what you want to do. Click its icon once to open it.

- The template opens up as a new, untitled document, complete with placeholder text, graphics, and formatting.

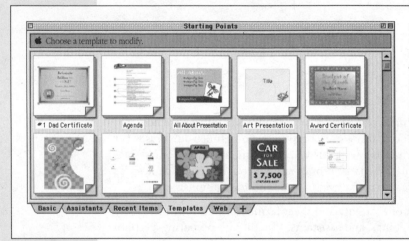

Figure 9-1:
The 36 templates here are made up of four kinds of AppleWorks documents— word processing, drawing, database, and presentation documents. It's useful to view the templates in gargantuan-icon mode. (To do that, Control-click the Templates window, choose Starting Point Settings from the contextual menu, and then choose Thumbnail Size→ Large in the resulting dialog box.)

Make Your Own Templates

With just a few simple actions, you can add your own templates to the Templates window, which can save you time if you crank out the same kind of report, newsletter, or other publication week after week. Here's how you go about it.

First, create the document that you want to turn into a template, and then choose File→Save. Click the Template button at the bottom of the dialog box that appears, and save the template (with whatever name you give it) into the AppleWorks 6→Starting Points→Templates folder. Now, when you open the Templates portion of the Starting Points window, you'll see your newly added template.

You can also *remove* templates that you'll never use by pulling them *out* of the AppleWorks 6→Starting Points→Templates folder. (Doing so is an excellent idea. The fewer files in the Starting Points folders, the faster AppleWorks starts up.)

You can either throw those files away—a bold move, since you'll be without those templates forever, or until you reinstall AppleWorks—or you can move them to another folder. That way, you can just move them back into the Templates folder if you decide you need them.

The 36 Starter Templates

AppleWorks ships with 36 templates—ready-to-use Drawing, Word Processing, Presentation, and Database documents:

- **Drawing documents.** #1 Dad Certificate, Award Certificate, Banner, Brochure, Calendar, Car for Sale, Caterer Business Cards, Caterer Envelope, Caterer Letterhead, Flash Cards, Greeting Card, Homework sheet, Messages, Postcard, Poster, Salon Business Cards, Salon Envelope, Salon Letterhead, Teacher Business Cards, Teacher Envelope, Teacher Fax Cover Page, Teacher Letterhead.

- **Word-processing documents.** Agenda, Grocery List, School Report, To-Do List.

- **Presentation documents.** All About Presentation, Art Presentation, Elegant Presentation, Geometric Presentation, Family Slide Show, Hip Presentation.

- **Database documents.** Caterer Addresses and Labels, Event Tracker, Salon Addresses and Labels, Teacher Addresses and Labels.

Here's how you go about using them:

Replacing the dummy text and graphics

Once you've opened one of the AppleWorks templates, your first task is to replace the dummy data inside it with information of your own (unless, of course, you actually *do* run a salon). You can leave the graphics alone, but remember that you can edit these, too.

To edit text in a template, select the Arrow tool and double-click the text that you want to edit. The first click selects the frame that contains the text, and the second puts the frame in editing mode, where you can use all of the word processing editing functions described in Chapters 2 and 3. (In Word Processing templates, one click suffices.)

Making changes to a template for next time

You can modify one of these templates to suit your future needs by opening it in AppleWorks, making the changes you want (say, changing the background in the Geometric Presentation template), and then saving the template in the Templates folder with the same name, making sure that the Templates radio button is selected. When asked if you want to replace the existing file, click OK. Your modified template will work like the original, but now it contains your own hand-tailored text and graphics. (To leave a copy of the *original* template for safekeeping, give your edited template a different name.)

Default Templates: Real Time Savers

One special kind of template is incredibly useful for day-to-day AppleWorks use: the *default* template. Default templates apply certain formatting options to *every* new document opened in an AppleWorks module, saving you the time of doing it yourself. For example, suppose you write a *lot* of letters to the editor, and you'd like every word processing document you open to be formatted using the Palatino font, with your return address and today's date already in place. Yet you don't want to go through the hassle of setting up, opening, and modifying a Template, as described in the previous section.

To create a default template for the Word Processing module, do the following:

1. **Create your template.**

   In other words, create a new word processing document. Fill it with all the text and formatting that you'll want to have appear in *every* new word processing document.

2. **Choose Save As from the File menu.**

   The Save dialog box appears.

3. **Select the Templates radio button (in the lower right portion of the window). Name the document:** *AppleWorks WP Options.*

   The name is crucial. Even one extra space will throw AppleWorks off.

4. **Navigate to the AppleWorks 6→Starting Points→Templates folder. Click Save.**

   Now, every time you open a word processing document, it'll have the formatting, graphics, and text that you put into the template. The default template will also appear in the Templates portion of the Starting Points window.

Tip: To disable a default template, open the Templates folder. Either rename the default template or remove it from the Templates folder altogether.

You can create a different default template for *each* module. Use the same steps provided above, but change the name of the saved template as shown here:

Default Template File Names

Template type	File name
Word processing	AppleWorks WP Options
Spreadsheet	AppleWorks SS Options
Database	AppleWorks DB Options
Drawing	AppleWorks DR Options
Painting	AppleWorks PT Options
Presentation	AppleWorks PR Options

If you save the default template using the wrong two-letter abbreviation (say you create a database template and save it as *AppleWorks PR Options),* the default template won't work for *either* module type. It will, however, appear in the Templates portion of the Starting Points window.

Tip: It's probably no surprise that you can put a Macintosh alias of the AppleWorks program in your Menu for speedy access. But you can also put a template there—or a collection of them; choosing a template's name opens AppleWorks automatically and creates an untitled document based on that template.

Clippings: Artist in a Box

For those who don't have a whit of artistic talent but do have an urge to create graphically great documents, AppleWorks provides a solution: Clippings. *Clipping* is just another word for clip art—pre-made, professionally designed artwork that's ready to be dropped into your documents, without your having to attend art school or even know how to draw a straight line. The Clippings window organizes artwork so that you can quickly find the art you need.

AppleWorks comes with over 200 different pieces of clip art in fifteen categories: Animals, Food, Household, Landscapes, Occasions, Other, Photos, Plants, School, Seasons, Space, Sports, and Transportation. (Note to the techies: They're stored as individual files in the AppleWorks 6→Clippings folder.)

The key to using clippings is the Clippings window (see Figure 9-2). You open it by choosing File→Show Clippings. (If the command reads Hide Clippings, the Clippings window is already open.)

Tip: When you open the Clippings window, it appears blank—that's because you start out on the Search page, where you can type what you're looking for—*snowman* or *Halloween,* for example, as described later in this chapter. Click one of the other tabs below the window to see some of the actual graphics awaiting you.

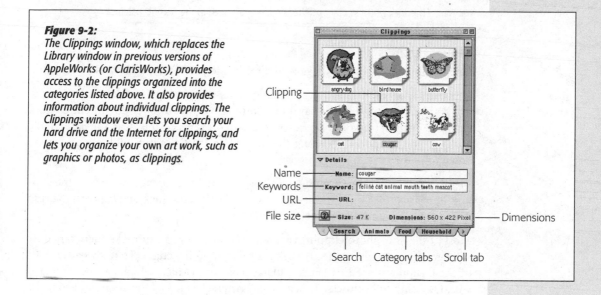

Figure 9-2:
The Clippings window, which replaces the Library window in previous versions of AppleWorks (or ClarisWorks), provides access to the clippings organized into the categories listed above. It also provides information about individual clippings. The Clippings window even lets you search your hard drive and the Internet for clippings, and lets you organize your own art work, such as graphics or photos, as clippings.

These are the elements of the Clippings window (see Figure 9-2, which shows its "flippy triangle" open:

- **Selected clipping.** When you click a clipping's icon, you see its name and vital statistics displayed below.

CHAPTER 9: TEMPLATES, CLIPPINGS, AND ASSISTANTS   **279**

- **Clipping name.** The clipping's name is shown here, where you can change it.

- **Keyword.** Any keywords associated with the clipping are shown here. (*Keywords* are what the Clipping window's Search command looks for. You can use them to file a single clipping, in effect, under more than one name.)

- **URL.** If the clipping is from the Internet, its URL (Web address, or *uniform resource locator*) appears here.

- **Size.** The selected clipping's size (in kilobytes) appears here.

- **Search.** Click the Search tab to search for specific clippings. If the "Search Web Content" checkbox is turned on, and if you're already connected to the Internet, AppleWorks now searches the much larger library of clip art there. See Chapter 10 for the specifics of Internet searches (as well as everything Internet in AppleWorks).

- **Category tabs.** These tabs list the various clipping categories. Actually, there are more tabs than you can see at once; click the right- or left-arrow tab to *scroll* through the additional, hidden tabs.

- **Dimensions.** The size of the clipping (in pixels) is shown here.

Tip: You can operate the Clippings window's tabs completely by keyboard. To do so, press Option-Tab to highlight the Clippings window, and then press ⌘-left arrow or -right arrow to highlight the particular tab you want. (This trick works in other palette windows, too, such as the Accents palette.)

Using Clippings

Using a clipping is as easy as dragging it directly into your open AppleWorks document.

Suppose, for example, that you're making a flyer advertising a kayak that you're selling, and you want to use the kayaking clipping. With your flyer document open (a Drawing document would be best—you could even use the "Car for Sale" Template), click the Sports tab along the bottom of the Clippings window and scroll down until the kayaking item is visible.

Then, drag it out of the Clippings window and into your document, where the clipping appears automatically. You can also double-click the kayaking clipping to bring it into your document—you get the same result.

Most of the non-photo clippings are *scalable:* that is, you can make them larger or smaller without making the artwork jagged around the edges. That's because most of these clippings are *EPS* (Encapsulated PostScript) files, which can be stretched without losing smoothness. To scale a clipping, select it in your document to make its handles appear, then drag the handles (see page 208).

Photos, unfortunately, are stuck at one resolution. You can shrink them without ill effect, but enlarging them beyond their original size usually produces a *pixellated* (jagged) image.

Note: Since clippings can require a lot of memory, you may need to give AppleWorks more memory if you run into trouble while importing a clipping. If AppleWorks fills up its memory partition, you'll either get an error message telling you that AppleWorks is running low on memory, or the program might even crash. Furthermore, the more clippings (and other EPS files) are in your document, the longer it takes to open and save.

Finding the right clipping

But what if you're selling a surfboard? Alas, there's no surfboard in the clippings installed with AppleWorks. The solution is the Search tab.

To search the clippings that came with AppleWorks, type what you're looking for (such as *surfboard)* in the Search field. Make sure that the Search Web Content checkbox is unchecked.

When you click the Search button, AppleWorks cruises through the clippings on your hard drive, looking to see if your search term matches any of the *keywords* or clippings titles. If it does, those matches appear in the window below the search field.

Note: The AppleWorks search engine isn't terribly smart; it just does its best to match the word you've entered with a keyword or title. That means that the search word *cat* can turn up a satellite dish, because the first three letters of the word "satellite" are reasonably close to "cat."

Although most of the clippings that come with AppleWorks (including those searchable via the Internet) are drawings, don't be fooled: AppleWorks is quite capable of handling any file type that QuickTime can handle. This includes photographs (saved as JPEG or TIFF graphics), GIF files, Photoshop documents, MP3 files, and even QuickTime movies.

Customizing the Clippings Window

While having access to tons of searchable clip art would be a great thing by itself, AppleWorks doesn't stop there. You can add your *own* clippings and categories to the Clippings window, complete with searchable keywords.

Adding your own clippings and categories

Adding your own clipping to the Clippings window is simple: just drag the item you want out of your document and onto the appropriate tab of the Clippings window. AppleWorks places a *thumbnail* (miniature picture) of the item (with its name) in the Clippings category tab.

Tip: When you add a clipping from an AppleWorks document, AppleWorks remembers the clipping's size and shape. As a result, you can create several different sizes and shapes of the same clipping and put each in the Clippings window. Later, you can choose from small, medium, and large motorcycles (or whatever clipping you chose) without having to resize the clipping.

To aid in searching through clippings, you can add keywords to each clipping. The clippings that came with AppleWorks already have a few associated keywords, but you can add more if you like. On the other hand, clippings that you add won't have *any* key-words, so you should type in a few to aid with your searches. It wouldn't hurt, while you're at it, to rename the clipping to something more descriptive than *clipping 1*.

Caution: Be careful when dragging your own art to the Clippings window from *outside* of AppleWorks. Clippings created this way are often *links* (like aliases) to the artwork that you dragged into the Clipping window—that is, the artwork itself may not get embedded into your Clippings palette. The problem: If you move or delete the original file, your Clipping won't work any more.

One way to tell if the Clippings window has stored a link or the actual graphic is to select its icon in the Clippings palette and then look at its size at the bottom of the window. If the Size field in the Clippings window reads <1K, then you're probably dealing with a link (or a *very* tiny file).

POWER USERS' CLINIC

Making Sure Clippings are Clippings

AppleWorks stores all of its clippings as individual graphics files in a special folder. If you're clever, you might consider adding your own items to the Clippings window by moving files directly into this special folder. (Among other advantages: Doing so eliminates any confusion as to whether the Clippings window stores a particular graphic as a *link* or as a complete embedded file.)

Inside the AppleWorks folder is the Clippings folder. In this folder you'll see a series of folders with very familiar names: the names of all of the categories in the Clippings window. To add a clipping to a category, just drag a graphics or movie file into the appropriate category folder.

You can add your own categories to the Clippings window, too, by making and naming a new folder in the AppleWorks 6→Clippings folder. New folders show up in the Clippings window tab row the next time you open it.

You may also notice two folders in the Clippings folder that *don't* show up in the Clippings tabs: Cache and Disabled Items. The Cache folder is a place for temporary files created by AppleWorks when it looks for Internet-based clippings. The Disabled Items folder is where AppleWorks stores disabled tabs (tabs removed from the Clippings window). The way this is structured gives you a way to disable a tab without launching AppleWorks: just drag the corresponding category folder into the Disabled Items folder. To re-enable such a tab, just move its folder out of the Disabled Items folder and back into the Clippings folder.

Removing a clipping from the Clippings window

Removing a clipping is easy; there are three ways to go about it. You can Control-click the clipping and select Delete Clipping from the contextual menu, which deletes the clipping, or you can select the clipping and press ⌘-delete. And, of course, you can open the AppleWorks 6→Clippings folder to delete the actual graphics file manually.

Organizing your Clipping categories

The Clippings window is great for organizing large amounts of art, but it takes some work to get things straight. If you want to move a clipping to another panel, drag it to a different tab. If the tab you want isn't visible, drag the clipping onto the right or left *arrow* tab, which scrolls the tabs until your target is in view. If you want to copy the clipping to another tab rather than move it, hold down the Option key while dragging.

To create your own category tab (where you can organize your clippings), click the + tab at the right end of the tab row (or choose Add Tab from the contextual menu that appears when you Control-click). The Add Tab window appears, where you can name your tab and choose what kind of tab it is from a pop-up menu (labeled Location). You have two choices here: My Computer and Internet Based. (There is a third tab called Disabled Items, which is used to re-enable disabled tabs—more on this feature later.)

FREQUENTLY ASKED QUESTION

AppleWorks 5 Libraries

How do I use the AppleWorks 5 or ClarisWorks 5 clip art library with AppleWorks 6?

The Clippings function in AppleWorks 6 replaces the Library function in older versions of the program. Fortunately, it's possible to bring these libraries into AppleWorks 6.

To do so, drag the individual libraries into the AppleWorks

6→Clippings folder. One important point—the libraries *must* be in the Clippings folder itself, not inside one of the category subfolders. Nor should you put the entire Libraries folder into the Clippings folder; put the individual *files* (each containing many clip art images) from inside it there.

Once you've installed them properly, each library shows up as a locked tab in the Clippings window.

The My Computer menu item creates an empty tab—and an empty folder inside the AppleWorks 6→Clippings folder. You can add any clipping you like to the new tab.

The Internet Based tab is different. When you select Internet Based in the Location pop-up menu, the Add Tab window expands to contain a new item: the URL field. By entering a URL (Web address) in this spot, AppleWorks downloads the graphics from the URL in the field and embeds them in the new clippings tab.

Tip: The Internet Based graphic-downloading feature is, of course, designed primarily for you to download new clippings from AppleWorks-related Web sites. But you can grab all of the graphics from *any* Web page on earth using this feature! This feature is great for stripping the graphics from some unsuspecting Web site, downloading all the photos of your favorite star, and so on.

To disable a tab—make it disappear from the Clippings window—Control-click it and choose Delete Tab from the contextual menu. You'll be presented with a dialog box containing three choices: Cancel, Disable Tab, or Move to Trash. Choose Disable Tab to temporarily remove the tab from the tabs row. If you choose Move to Trash, AppleWorks deletes the tab (along with all of its contents) from the Clippings window. If you change your mind, you still have a chance—the tab's contents are still in the Trash until you empty it. To re-enable a disabled tab, click the + tab and choose Disabled Tabs from the Location submenu in the Add Tab window that appears. You'll get a list of disabled tabs; you can then re-enable the ones you select. Clearly, you're better off disabling a tab rather than deleting it.

Changing the Clippings window's behavior

By Control-clicking the Clippings window, you can call up the Clippings Settings window, where you can exercise some control over how the Clippings window looks and acts. In the Clippings Settings window, you can control three settings: partial matches, Cache size, and Thumbnail size.

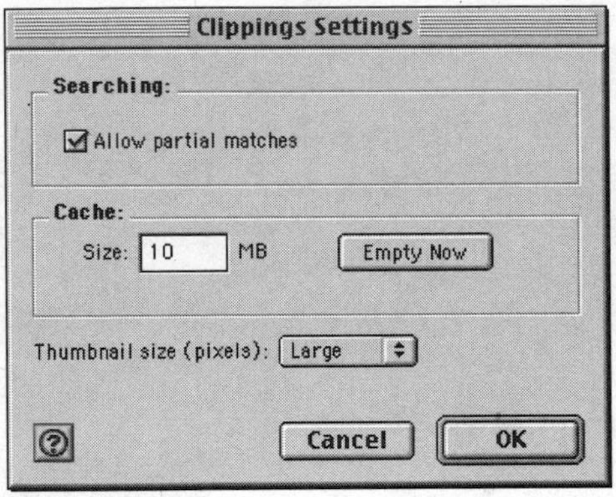

Figure 9-3:
"Allow partial matches" lets the Clippings Search function show you clippings whose names only partly match what you typed. The second, Cache, lets you set the size of the Clippings Cache—a temporary storage center for Web graphics you download—and empty it if you want. The pop-up menu lets you set the size of the thumbnail images: small, medium, or large.

Tip: The contextual menu that appears when you Control-click the Clippings window also offers Show/Hide Tabs, Reposition Tabs, and Sort commands. Show/Hide Tabs shows the tabs if they're hidden and hides them if they're visible. You might want to hide tabs if you want to simplify the Clippings window interface. You can always switch between Clippings areas by Control-clicking on the Clippings menu and selecting the area you'd like to switch to in the Switch To submenu.

Reposition Tabs lets you choose where you want the tabs—on the left, right, or bottom edge of the Clippings window. Finally, the Sort menu lets you sort the Clippings window's contents by their names, the dates on which they were created, their sizes (from smallest to largest), and their kinds.

Assistants: Better than a Butler

Similar to what Microsoft calls a Wizard, an AppleWorks assistant walks you, step by step, through a complicated process, such as the creation of an elaborate document.

You click buttons, such as Back and Next, to control your walk through the various questions the Assistant asks you. For example, on successive screens, the Business Card calculator Assistant asks you for your name, job title, and so on; when you click the final Create button, fully formed, nicely designed business cards appear on the screen, ready to print.

Six AppleWorks assistants have a permanent home in the Assistants tab of the Starting Points window. Here's a look at each:

• **Address List.** This assistant walks you through the creation of a database document to hold names and addresses.

- **Business Cards.** The Business Cards Assistant helps you build your own business cards by creating a well-formatted database document.

- **Calendar.** Based on the start date you provide, the Calendar Assistant automates creating a single-month calendar in two steps.

- **Certificate.** Use the Certificate Assistant to create your own certificates of appreciation, merit, or achievement, or even your own diploma.

- **Envelope.** The Envelope Assistant creates a business envelope complete with delivery address and return address, and it sets the document size so that it prints properly.

- **Home Finance.** By walking through the Home Finance Assistant, you can answer some basic questions, such as, How much home can I afford? What's my net worth? and How much will my investments be worth in the future?

Two other assistants are only available from specific places in AppleWorks:

- The **Create Labels** Assistant makes mailing labels from an AppleWorks database document. Page 151 has full details.

- The **Footnote Assistant** enters footnotes into word processing documents. (You can also insert footnotes manually, of course, by choosing Edit→Insert Blank Footnote. But the Assistant formats the footnote automatically, using *citation* formatting. You know: "Cooper, Danny: *An Analysis of Vocal Stress Quantifiers in Marital Combat,* 1994," and so on.)

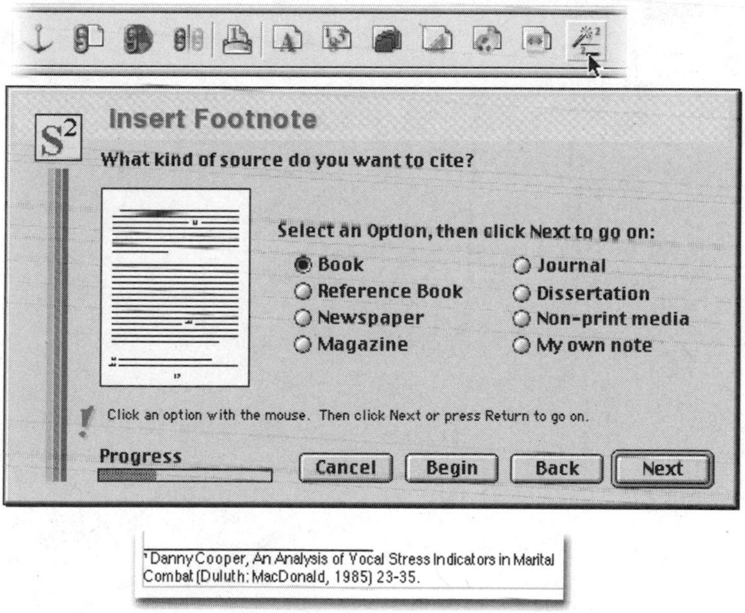

Figure 9-4:
To insert a footnote, put the cursor where you want the citation number to be, and then click the Insert Citation icon on the button bar (top). The Footnote Assistant appears (middle); as shown here, you're asked what kind of citation (and what kind of footnote) you want to create. You'll be asked to provide the author's name, publisher name, and other citation elements. When you're finished, the completed footnote appears at the bottom of the page (right).

To use it, the Insert Citation button must be available in the button bar. If it's not, choose Preferences→Edit→Button Bar. In the Customize Button Bar window that comes up, double-click the Insert Citation button in the Word Processing section of the button bar—or drag the button up to the button bar (see Figure 9-4, top). Click Done.

When you're ready to insert a footnote, proceed as shown in Figure 9-4.

CHAPTER 10

AppleWorks on the Internet

While the most visible new feature of AppleWorks 6 is its new look, the overhaul is only skin-deep, and its novelty wears off quickly. But there *are* some truly meaty and worthwhile new AppleWorks features, and its Internet integration tops the list.

For several years, we've been deluged by programs marketed as "Internet-enabled," which often meant as little as offering a company Web address on the software box. AppleWorks, however, goes far beyond. It can directly download new templates, grab a regularly updated AppleWorks newsletter, and even search a database of hundreds of clippings for just the right piece of art.

TROUBLESHOOTING MOMENT

Problems with Internet Connections

Although Apple's done a great job bringing the Internet to AppleWorks, it doesn't always work correctly. If you're having trouble using AppleWorks' Web features, try these troubleshooting steps:

First, make a connection to the Internet with your modem *before* using AppleWorks' Internet features. Some AppleWorks features, such as the clippings downloads, don't dial the Internet automatically, as does, say, your Web browser. (If you're using a cable modem or DSL, this doesn't apply to you.)

If you're still having no luck, try visiting a Web page or checking your email. Sometimes initiating Internet activity in another application can clear things up for AppleWorks.

Sometimes the AppleWorks server gets swamped and it won't let you in until the traffic lightens up. Sometimes waiting until later is a good troubleshooting technique, too.

Finally, make sure that your QuickTime extensions are installed and working properly. Several users have reported that if QuickTime stops working, so does AppleWorks.

Starting Points

Apple considers the Internet integration in AppleWorks so important that it put a Web tab in the Starting Points window (page 10). There are two icons in this tab: Newsletter and Templates; they give you access to updated AppleWorks information and a plethora of Web-based clippings.

Be warned, though, that when you click this tab, you're asking AppleWorks to make a connection to the Internet and *download* the latest newsletter and templates documents, which can take some time: the newsletter weighs in at over 150K, and the Templates master document is more than twice that size. Once AppleWorks has downloaded these documents, however, they're ready to be used right away (see Figure 10-1).

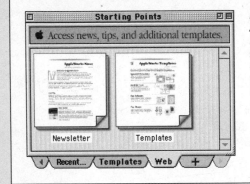

Figure 10-1:
A click on the Web tab in the Starting Points window brings up the Newsletter and Templates icons (left)—after they're downloaded from the Web. Just click the Newsletter or Templates icon to bring up that document: You don't have to wait for another download (as you do when, for example, using a downloaded clipping), because the template document has already been downloaded.

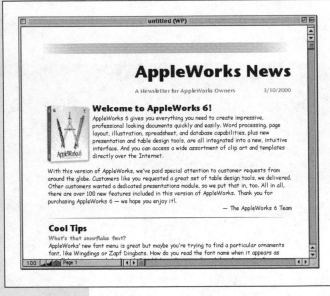

Figure 10-2:
Exclusively for AppleWorks owners, the AppleWorks News comes directly to you via AppleWorks itself as a word processing document. If you really like a particular issue, you can always save it on your hard drive by choosing File→Save. The newsletter arrives in the form of an untitled Word Processing document with a dateline in the upper-right corner, letting you know how old the latest newsletter is.

Newsletter

Published regularly, the AppleWorks News is delivered to you via AppleWorks' Web tab—and it beats hunting for soggy papers on your front doorstep on a rainy morning. In it, you'll find news, tips, special offers, and messages from the AppleWorks team (Figure 10-2).

Templates

Although AppleWorks comes with lots of templates, those are just a smattering compared to the gamut of templates that you can access via the Web tab's Templates icon. When you click this icon, AppleWorks opens the Templates category index, which lists six categories of templates. (There are over 100 Web-based templates in these categories at this writing, and the list is growing.) Here's a quick look at the categories:

- **Special Occasions.** Party invitations, greeting cards, holiday wish lists—everything you need for a great party (except food, drinks, music, guests, and a location).

- **Just for Kids.** There's no age requirement to view these templates, which include sharp-looking maps, graphs, find-the-objects games, math flash cards, nursery rhymes, and lots more. This is the largest Templates category, and there's *lots* of good material here.

Tip: The Hidden Pictures documents, which capitalize on AppleWorks' ability to layer one painting frame over another, are especially clever. Rub with the Eraser tool to reveal, hidden in the landscape, elegant dinosaurs, animals, and so on.

- **For Schools.** These templates help you produce newsletters, flyers, student databases, and more.

- **For Home.** A smallish category, the For Home category helps you get your house in order with templates such as a family medical record tracker, a home budget, and a set of canning labels.

- **For Business.** This category includes an emergency contact list, a job search database, and some sample résumés.

- **For Everyone.** Included in this catch-all category are club agendas, flyers, a music database, and a weekly planner.

Here's how you go about downloading a new template:

1. **On the Starting Points window's Web tab, click Templates.**

   AppleWorks connects to the Internet. Eventually, it offers the latest main templates document shown in Figure 10-3.

2. **In a category description, click the blue underlined link.**

   AppleWorks again opens an Internet connection and downloads the *index* document for that section. The index appears in an untitled word processing window;

it offers descriptions of individual templates with links to download those templates. (You have a choice of paper sizes: either US Letter or A4.)

3. **Click a link to download that template.**

   It opens into an untitled window.

4. **Save the document (File→Save), giving it a new name of your own.**

   In practice, this whole process feels a lot like using a Web browser.

Remember that each time you click one of these links, AppleWorks has to download a document, which can be large; for example, the Just for Kids index document is over 1MB, which can take a while to download by modem. Fortunately, the download times for individual templates are typically much shorter than they are for the section index documents.

Note: Some of the downloadable templates require fonts that aren't installed by default by AppleWorks. Never fear: You can find these fonts in the AppleWorks Extras folder of the AppleWorks CD.

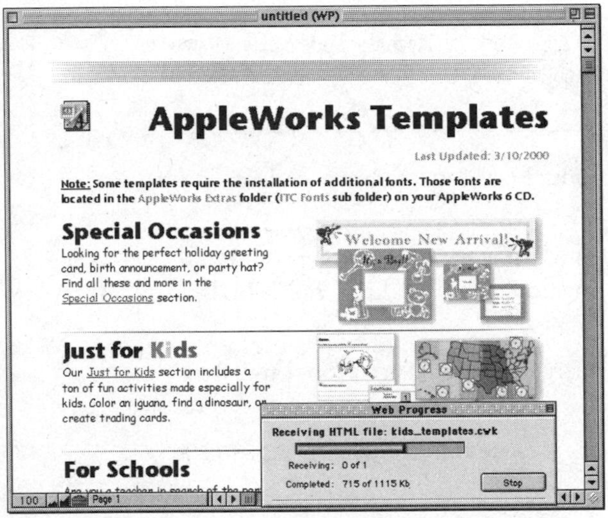

Figure 10-3:
The templates document in the Web tab is nothing more than a cleverly formatted AppleWorks document with links to various template categories on it. Click one, and AppleWorks downloads the index page (another word processing document) for that category, where you'll get a list of individual templates that you can download.

Web-Based Clippings

As with the templates, you're not limited to the clippings that shipped with AppleWorks. There are thousands of pieces of clip art available on the Internet, waiting to dress up your documents—and these aren't lame line-art drawings, either. Apple has included some solid, colorful, eminently usable artwork with AppleWorks, both with the program and on the Internet.

Downloading Clippings from Apple

To access the Web-based clippings, you use the Search window to search a vast repository of clippings on the Internet. To do this, click the Search tab along the bottom of the Clippings window (it's the leftmost tab) to bring up the Search function. Make sure that the Search Web Content checkbox is checked; enter a search term in the Search field; and then click Search.

After making an Internet connection (and downloading *thumbnails*—miniature, icon versions—of the appropriate files), AppleWorks displays any matches in the window. Once the search results show up, you're free to drag a clipping into your documents. When you drag the thumbnail image in, AppleWorks downloads the real thing and places it into your document.

Figure 10-4:
A search for the word "surf" turned up over 40 matches, which AppleWorks downloaded into the Clippings window— the surfing Santa is especially cool. The full-size images remain on the Internet, to be downloaded when you actually drag a thumbnail into a document. The banner/ starburst across the top left corner reminds you that this graphic is Internet-based, and that it's either new or has been modified since the last time you accessed it. (The banner and starburst don't appear in the actual clipping.)

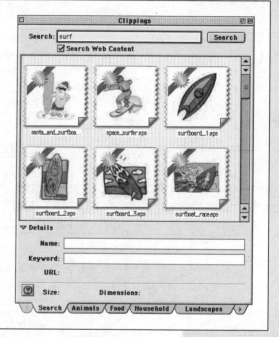

Caution: Modem users beware! The files downloaded during the search process are not small. AppleWorks first downloads a special search document (containing the results of the keyword search), which is often over 650K. After determining what matches are made, the program downloads thumbnails of each clipping, which only take a couple of seconds each, but there may be 100 or more of these. Finally, when you drag one of the Web-based clippings into your document, AppleWorks *then* downloads the full-size clipping before it inserts it into your document.

All told, a successful search for clippings can require nearly a megabyte of downloaded data, which can seem slow even to schools with high-speed connections, for whom Apple obviously intended this feature. Be warned before you use this feature—or be equipped with this book to read while you wait.

Downloading Graphics from Web Pages

Clippings searches aren't the only way to get Web-based graphics into the Clippings window. As mentioned in Chapter 9, you can also use the Clippings window to download the graphics from *any* Web page.

To do this, create a new tab in the Clippings window by clicking the + button. (Alternatively, you can Control-click the Clippings window and choose Add Tab from the contextual menu that pops up.) When the Add Tab window pops up, name the tab and select Internet Based from the pop-up menu, which makes the window display the URL field.

In the URL field, type the full Web address of the page whose graphics you want to steal (such as *http://www.apple.com),* and click OK. AppleWorks then contacts that Web site, downloads the HTML file that makes up that Web page, and looks through it for references to graphics files. The program then downloads those graphics into the tab.

Once you've downloaded graphics into a Web tab, they're available for use in the same way as any other graphic—just drag one into a document window. If you open an Internet Based tab, AppleWorks may not have the graphics in its cache and may have to download them again.

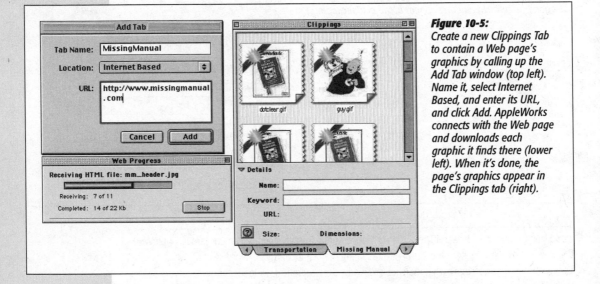

Figure 10-5:
Create a new Clippings Tab to contain a Web page's graphics by calling up the Add Tab window (top left). Name it, select Internet Based, and enter its URL, and click Add. AppleWorks connects with the Web page and downloads each graphic it finds there (lower left). When it's done, the page's graphics appear in the Clippings tab (right).

Note: The graphics that you download from someone else's Web page were created or paid for by someone else. You'll be OK if you use them in your own documents. But using swiped graphics in documents that you *distribute* (or post on your own Web page) is just asking for calls from delighted law firms.

Creating Web Pages

AppleWorks isn't just on the receiving end of Web-based content—you can use it to *create* Web pages as well. You don't have to know the HTML Web-programming language to do it, either. Instead, creating a Web page in AppleWorks is as simple as creating an AppleWorks document and saving it in a special format.

FREQUENTLY ASKED QUESTION

Multi-Page Web Pages

What happens if the word processing page destined to be a Web page is more than one page long?

If the word processing document page spills over into multiple pages, don't fret. When you save the page, AppleWorks combines all of those word processing pages into one long single HTML file. Your Web-page visitors will simply have to scroll down to see the additional material.

Page breaks and section breaks (Chapter 3), by the way, don't work when your word-processing document is converted to Web pages. Instead of turning your Web document into multiple pages, such breaks simply create horizontal lines on the finished Web page.

Figure 10-6:
When it comes to Web pages, what you see isn't necessarily *what you get, but it's close. The text in the Word Processing document (top) gets converted into a close approximation when opened in a Web browser, such as Internet Explorer 5 (bottom).*

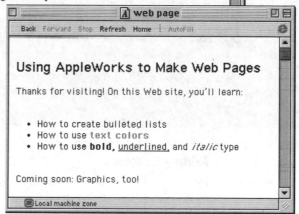

The basis for Web pages in AppleWorks is the word processing document. By putting text and graphics into a word processing document and saving it as an HTML file, you make AppleWorks convert the text formatting into the proper HTML codes, so that the text displays properly in a Web browser. AppleWorks can't do *everything* that a high-end Web page creation program can, but it *can* make decent Web pages with very little effort on your part.

Adding Text

Text is at the heart of almost every Web page, and it's going to be at the heart of your AppleWorks Web pages.

As you create your word-processing document, feel free to use basic text appearance commands (such as Bold and Italic), text formatting commands (left, right, and center alignment), and text colors. Note, however, that AppleWorks does not preserve columns or fully justified text when it converts your document to a Web page; you get only a single column and flush-left text.

Tip: Don't use underlined text or blue text in your Web-bound documents. Your Internet visitors are likely to think that words you've formatted that way are links, and they'll click in frustration.

As you work on your word processing document, remember to use the styles in the Outline menu—bullet, checklist, diamond, Harvard, or Number styles—where appropriate; they wind up looking great on the finished Web page (see Figure 10-6). When you want a horizontal line to cross your page—a frequent Web-design trick—use the Format→Insert Page Break or Format→Insert Section Break command in AppleWorks.

POWER USERS' CLINIC

Precision Text Placement

When you use tabs in your word processing document, AppleWorks converts them to a bunch of individual presses of the Space bar. (Web pages don't understand what tabs are.) As a result, you must use other means to get your text placed exactly where you want it.

That's where tables (see Chapter 12) come in very handy. By placing a table in your document, entering text in the cells, customizing the table and table cell sizes, and then making the lines of the table itself invisible, you can put text virtually anywhere on your Web page with great precision.

In fact, invisible tables is exactly the mechanism used by many expensive Web-page design programs; invisible tables underlie a huge percentage of the world's Web pages.

Adding Graphics

Just as in other word processing documents, you can add graphics to your Web-bound documents either as *floating graphics* or as *inline graphics*. Floating graphics float above text as though in a separate layer. Inline graphics behave as though they're words you've typed in the line of text: delete some text, and the graphic slides over as a result. (More on these distinctions on page 333.)

To add a floating graphic, select the Arrow tool in the Tools window. Either drag a graphic in from the Clippings window (or the desktop), or paste a graphic you've copied to the Clipboard. To add an *inline* graphic, do the same thing—after first clicking in the text where you'll want the image to appear.

Although you can position floating graphics anywhere in a word processing document, that placement doesn't survive the conversion to a Web page. Instead, floating graphics wind up pushed against the left or right side of the page. You can control the left-to-right positioning of inline graphics, on the other hand, using the alignment controls on the ruler—left, right, or center.

Caution: Because of limitations in the HTML language, text wrapping (see page 228) doesn't get converted predictably from AppleWorks into Web-page format. If you must convert AppleWorks documents that contain text wrapped around graphics, test the results in as many Web browsers as possible (such as Netscape Communicator and Internet Explorer, which come with every Mac).

After adding graphics to your Web page, you may want to add a faint, tinted background or graphic to your Web page, as is common on many Web pages. To do this, choose Edit→Preferences→HTML Import/Export to open the Configure HTML preferences window (which is shown in Figure 10-7 and covered in greater detail in Chapter 11).

In the Document Background portion of this window, you can either select a background color (from one of nine choices, including None), or you can click the Set Background Image button to choose a graphics file for your Web page's background. Navigate to, and double-click, the image file that you want to use—an image saved in JPEG, GIF, or PNG format, for example.

Figure 10-7:
When you save a document that contains graphics, AppleWorks automatically splits them out as individual files, stored together in a new folder on your hard drive. The button at the bottom of this window lets you specify the graphics file format of those images: JPEG or PNG. (Use JPEG to assure broadest compatibility for the world's Web browsers.)

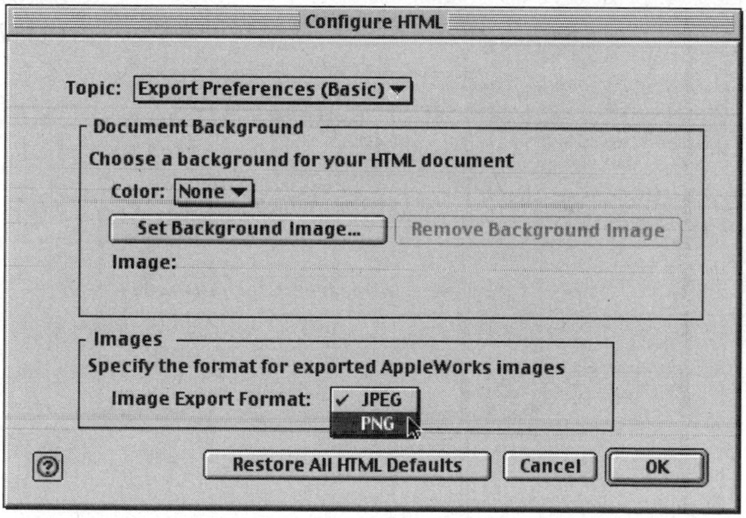

Configure HTML

Topic: Export Preferences (Basic) ▼

Document Background
Choose a background for your HTML document
Color: None ▼
Set Background Image...   Remove Background Image
Image:

Images
Specify the format for exported AppleWorks images
Image Export Format: ✓ JPEG
PNG

Restore All HTML Defaults   Cancel   OK

Adding Links

Adding links—like the blue underlined links on a Web page—to your documents is relatively easy, thanks to AppleWorks' built-in *links* feature. You can create links that, when clicked, take you to a Web page, your email program, or even another file on your hard drive.

Creating a link to a Web page

To create a blue underlined link that, when clicked, lets your Web-site visitor open a different page, use the Create Link→Internet command, which works as shown in Figure 10-8.

The link doesn't have to be text, such as "Click here." It can also be a drawing object, such as an inline frame—a table, spreadsheet, or a painting frame. But be warned—*floating* frames won't work for links. (See page 333 for a discussion of inline and floating frames.) The procedure is the same in either case: select the item that's to become a link and then use the Create Link→Internet command.

To link to other documents on your own Web site, you must still enter the *entire* URL of that page in the URL box, as shown in Figure 10-8.

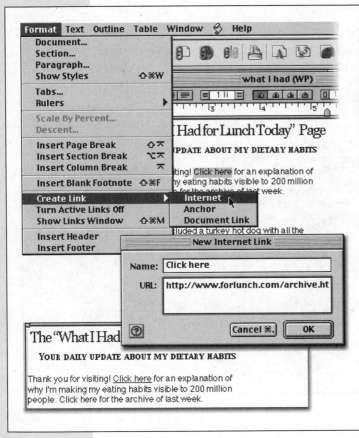

Figure 10-8:
Highlight some text in your document (such as "Click Here," as shown at top). Choose Format→Create Link→Internet to summon the Create Link dialog box (middle). In the URL box, type the URL of the Web page to which you want to link. Click OK. The result (bottom): a blue, underlined link that, when you save the document as HTML, becomes a working hyperlink.

Creating a link to an email address

To add an email link, select the text that you want to turn into an email link (such as "Click here to email me"). Choose Format→Create Link→Internet Link, which opens the New Internet Link dialog box. This time, however, in the URL box, type *mailto: yourname@isp.com* (put the actual email address in place of *yourname@isp.com*, of course). Now, when somebody clicks that link on your Web page, her email program opens automatically with a new blank message, pre-addressed to the email address you specified.

POWER USERS' CLINIC

The Links Window

A more powerful way of making links—especially if you're going to be making more than one—is the Links window. Choose Format→Show Links Window to bring up this window, which shows a list of links you've created. It offers five buttons, as shown here; they let you create a new link, edit an existing link's text (or the URL to which it "points"), remove a link, create a "folder" to organize links, and go to the selected link, respectively. The three tabs along the bottom—Anchor, Document,

and Internet—correspond to the various kinds of links you can create.

To create a Web link when this window is open, make sure that the Internet tab is selected, and then, in your document window, select some text or a graphic. Click New to bring up the Create Link dialog box. Name the link, enter the URL to which the link should connect, and click OK. Your new link appears in the Links window's left side.

Tip: To edit the text of a link, choose Format→Turn Active Links Off, which disables links so that you can select and edit them as though they were regular text. If you don't, you'll find it spectacularly difficult to edit the text of a link—after all, clicking it launches that link!

Creating a link to another AppleWorks document

Besides creating links to other Web sites, AppleWorks can create links to other documents on your hard drive. These links look just like Internet links—they're blue and underlined—but instead of opening a Web page on an Internet server, these links open a document on your hard drive instead. Using this feature, you could, for example, create your own "home page" that lists all the chapters of a book you're working on.

To create a document link, select the text or graphic that you want to turn into a link, and then choose Format→Create Link→Document Link. The New Document Link window appears, where you can name the link and specify the document to be opened. See Chapter 12 for more on document links.

Note: While document links (links to other documents that can be embedded in AppleWorks) look like everyday links when converted to HTML, they don't work—they've just turned into blue text with an underline.

Editing and deleting links

Once you have links embedded in your documents, you may want to change the URL to which they point—or remove the links (without removing the text or graphics to which they are attached). The Links window is your key to doing these things.

Start by choosing Format→Show Links Window (see the previous sidebar for an illustration); ensure that the Internet tab is selected. To edit a link, click its name in the Links window and then click Edit, which summons the Edit Internet Link window. Here you can change the link's name and URL; click OK to save the changes.

Deleting a link is even easier. Select the link's name in the Links window and click Remove. The text or graphic to which that link was attached gets changed back into regular text or graphics.

Tip: You can use the New folder button (the one with the word New and a miniature folder) to create a "folder" in the Links window. Use these folders to organize the links in documents with lots of links.

Saving the Page

When you've created an Internet-worthy document, you can save the page as an HTML document. But before you do, save the document as an *AppleWorks document first.* This way, you can go back and edit the original—remember that many aspects of an AppleWorks document get lost in the transition to HTML documents. Furthermore, AppleWorks won't *import* all of the HTML formatting that it exports to begin with—tables, for example.

A typical Web page is composed of a single text file (which contains the text of the page, plus a lot of code written in the HTML language), plus the graphics that appear on that page. The HTML document and each graphic have to exist as individual files, unlike AppleWorks documents, where text and graphics are stored in the same file.

To get ready, therefore, create a new folder to hold your Web page and its associated graphics. Although not strictly necessary, a dedicated folder for Web pages and graphics helps keep things organized.

To save your document as a Web page, choose File→Save As. In the Save As dialog box, choose File Format→HTML. Add the file extension *.htm* to the end of your Web page's name, for the benefit of some browsers on Windows computers that won't see your page otherwise.

Navigate to the folder you just created, and then click Save. AppleWorks translates the document into HTML. In the process, it converts any graphics in the document into individual JPEG or PNG-format graphics files (see Figure 10-7). Those graphic files are saved in the same folder as the HTML document you're saving—which is important in order for the Web pages to work correctly.

To preview your newly saved ".htm" page, open it using a Web browser's File→Open command. If you want to make changes, open the *AppleWorks* version of your Web page, edit it, and save it again as both an AppleWorks document and an HTML document.

UP TO SPEED

HTML Heads-up

HTML, which stands for HyperText Markup Language, is a computer language that describes, to other computers, how Web pages should look. HTML documents are merely text documents made up of what are known as *tags*. These tags describe how elements are aligned on the page, how text is formatted, what links in the page link to, and so on. Although it may look highly technical at first glance, it's not really so complicated once you start delving into it. The Web is filled with excellent references and beginners' tutorials in good HTML (search for *HTML basics* at your favorite Web search page); you might start with, for example, *www.html goodies.com/primers/basics.html* or *www.builder.com/ Authoring/Basics*.

Bookstores and libraries are also creaking with basic HTML guides, too.

Uploading Your Pages

Now that you have a shiny new Web page, you must upload it if you expect anyone on the Internet to see it. This part, unfortunately, is beyond the powers of AppleWorks; it just *makes* the pages.

To post them on the Web, you must transfer them to a Web *file server*—a computer that's always connected to the Internet. If you're an America Online member, you get 2MB of Web-page space per screen name. Use the keyword: *MyPlace* for instructions on uploading your Web pages. If you're a member of an Internet service provider (ISP) like EarthLink, you, too, get free file-server space for storing your Web pages. (Visit your ISP's Web page for specific instructions. You'll find that it generally requires an uploading program like the free Fetch application, which is available at *www.missingmanual.com,* among other places.)

Tip: AppleWorks 6 offers one useful Internet feature that Apple barely even mentions: direct access to your *iDisk,* the free, 20-MB, Internet-based hard drive that Apple gives to everyone with Mac OS 9 and an Internet account. (For details on setting up your iDisk, visit *www.apple.com.)*

Bringing the icon of your iDisk onto the screen is generally a several-step task—but the AppleWorks Scripts menu (the scroll icon) makes doing so simple. Connect to the Internet (by, for example, choosing →Remote Access Status and clicking Connect).

Now choose Scripts→Mount iDisk. You'll be asked for the password and account name you established when you signed up for the iDisk. Then, after a long pause, your iDisk icon appears at the right side of your screen, ready to accept your backup files or whatever else you care to store there.

Preferences, Customization, and Macros

T hanks to some clever programming by Apple engineers, AppleWorks is one of the most customizable applications on earth. You don't *have* to tweak it to your tastes, but by spending a little bit of time adjusting its settings, you can mold AppleWorks to a form that lets you work faster and more efficiently.

This chapter is designed to appeal to the power-hungry and the control freaks. It shows you how to create your own custom buttons, add (or remove) buttons from Button bars, control how your documents are translated into HTML Web-page documents, and make sure that your palettes look and act the way you want them to. You can have the leanest, meanest AppleWorks interface imaginable—or you can fill your screen with colorful clutter.

The AppleWorks Preferences

The primary tool for molding AppleWorks is the application's preferences. There are three main sets of preferences:

- **General Preferences.** These cover AppleWorks' behavior at startup, its auto-save feature, and more.

- **Button Bar Preferences.** These controls govern buttons, the Button bar, and which of the former go on the latter.

- **HTML Import/Export Preferences.** Adjust these options if you become a fan of AppleWorks' Web-page (HTML) importing and exporting features.

In general, you can adjust each AppleWorks option so that it affects *either* the entire AppleWorks application *or* just the currently open document. If no document is open, the Preferences window title bar says simply "Preferences." Changes made to preferences while no documents are open affect AppleWorks as a whole.

If you *do* have a document open (called "Mondo Drawing," for example), the Preferences window's title bar says "Preferences for Mondo Drawing," and many of the changes affect *only* the Mondo Drawing document, leaving AppleWorks' general preferences alone. When you save a document with such custom preferences, those preferences are memorized along with the document.

If you have more than one window open, the Preferences window sets preferences for the frontmost document.

Tip: To make preferences apply to AppleWorks as a whole even when a document is open, click the Make Default button at the bottom of the Preferences window (shown in Figure 11-1). (This button is dimmed if no document is open.)

General Preferences

By choosing Edit→Preferences→General, you open the General Preferences dialog box. This window has five different panels—General, Files, Text, Graphics, and Spreadsheet; each part governs a different aspect of AppleWorks. To switch between the various panels of the General Preferences window, use the Topic pop-up menu at the top of the Preferences window (Figure 11-1).

Topic: General

The General Preferences panel covers the most basic AppleWorks operations—what's shown at startup, how the Font menu behaves, and what the default document type is. The General Preferences panel has three sections:

At Startup, Show

This section controls what happens first when AppleWorks is launched—that is, when you double-click its icon on your computer desktop. It has three options:

- **Nothing.** After you launch AppleWorks, no Starting Points window appears. Instead, the only clue you have that AppleWorks is even running is the appearance of the AppleWorks menu bar (and Button bar, if you want it). The next move is yours: you must open a new document (File→New) or open one you've already created (File→Open).

- **Open Dialog Box.** AppleWorks, when launched, displays the standard Open File dialog box, so that you can immediately select an existing document to open.

- **Starting Points.** This is the option you're probably used to: it makes AppleWorks open the Starting Points floating window, ready for you to create a new document (see page 10).

Tip: Regardless of your "At Startup" setting, you can summon the Open File box by pressing the ⌘ key just after starting the AppleWorks application.

On ⌘-N, Create

This option governs what kind of document is created when you press ⌘-N. It lists the six types of documents that AppleWorks creates: Word Processing, Spreadsheet, Database, Drawing, Painting or Presentation. The factory setting is Word Processing; change it to whichever kind of document you create most often.

Font Menu in Actual Fonts

This checkbox controls how the Font menu works. If checked, the Font menu shows the font names in the actual typefaces, so you can *see* what a font looks like before you select it. If you have a very slow Mac, and the Font menu makes you wait too long before it opens, turn this option off.

Tip: You may be tempted to turn off "Font Menu in Actual Fonts" for the sake of *symbol* fonts, such as Symbol and Wingdings, whose names you can't read when they appear in their own font (because each character is a symbol, not a letter). But there's a much easier way to read their actual names: Press Option as you open the Font menu. Doing so makes every font appear in the standard menu typeface—for this visit to the Font menu only—so that you can read the names of your wackier fonts.

Figure 11-1:
The General Preferences panel governs some of AppleWorks' most basic functions—what happens when the program starts, how the Fonts submenu looks, and what the default document type is. Click Reset Defaults to restore these options to their factory settings.

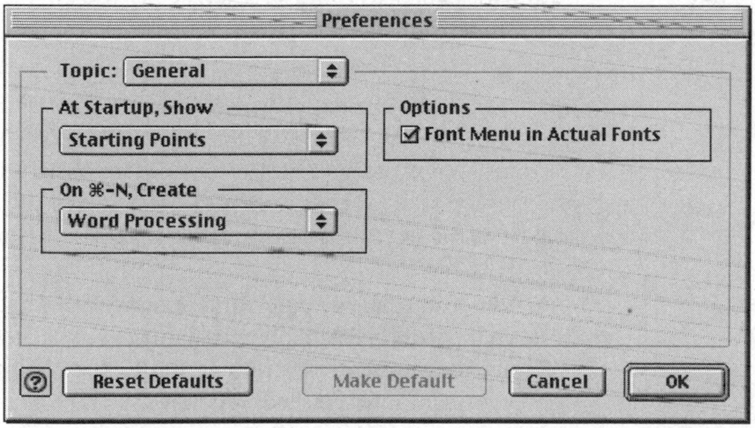

Topic: Files

The Files Preferences panel (choose Topic→Files in the Preferences dialog box) controls how AppleWorks deals with its documents. Here's what each does (see Figure 11-2):

Saved Document

This section contains three checkboxes:

- **Remember Translator** affects what happens when you open a document that *isn't* an AppleWorks document—for example, a text file you've downloaded from the Internet—and then re-save the document. If this checkbox is turned on, then instead of converting the file to an AppleWorks document, the program re-exports it in its original (text) file format. (This feature doesn't, alas, apply to *graphics* file formats. In fact, it applies only to text files and HTML documents.)

- **Create Custom Icon.** When you save a painting or drawing document from AppleWorks, it usually appears on your desktop with the standard AppleWorks file icon. But if you turn on Create Custom Icon, you should get, as the file's icon, a miniature version of the image that's in the actual document.

  Unfortunately, in the original 6.0 AppleWorks release, this feature worked only rarely; it was fixed in the free 6.0.3 upgrade.

- **[v6.0] Suffix.** This option makes AppleWorks add "[v6.0]" to the end of new documents' names, so that you can tell them apart from documents created with earlier versions of the program.

Auto-Save

When checked, this option is supposed to make AppleWorks save your documents automatically according to the time interval you specify here. In theory, it's a great feature for people who've ever lost data because of a system freeze or crash (because they forgot to use the File→Save command every few minutes).

Tip: In fact, the Auto-Save feature doesn't save your document for you. It saves a *copy* of your document, under a cryptic name like A485034637EDD6B15FA34BEF96CBD2, in the AppleWorks 6→Auto-Save folder. That explains why it's possible to use the File→Revert command to undo all the changes you've made to your document since *you* last saved it–even if Auto-Save has kicked in in the meantime. It's because AutoSave was working on an independent clone of your actual document.

Auto-Save also enables AppleWorks' *auto-recover* feature. If your computer crashes while you're working, AppleWorks launches automatically when you start the computer again. It presents you with an untitled copy of the document that was open when your computer crashed. You may even be offered a choice: You can open the last version of the document that *you* saved, or you can open the one AppleWorks' AutoSave feature saved. In any case, if luck is with you, the document is in the same shape it was in when the crash occurred.

In the original 6.0 release of AppleWorks, the Auto-Save feature is certifiably flaky, contributing to many freezes and crashes. The feature became stable and useful only in the 6.0.3 AppleWorks update version.

Note: Behind the Macintosh scenes, the AppleWorks auto-recover feature works by placing aliases of
your open documents into the System Folder→Startup Items folder. If, following a crash, you don't want
AppleWorks to launch automatically, press the Shift key just *after* the startup extensions have loaded
during the startup process. Doing so prevents anything in the Startup Items folder from opening automatically. Now you can open the System Folder→Startup Items folder and manually remove the alias(es)
AppleWorks put there, if you decide you want control over what files you open, and when.

Recent Items

This option turns on a special command in the File menu called Open Recent. The
submenu here lists the documents you've opened most recently. By choosing their
names from the File→Open Recent submenu, you save yourself a good deal of hunting around through the folders of your hard drive trying to find something you had
opened only yesterday.

Using the Preferences dialog box options here, you can specify how many documents AppleWorks tracks (ten, for example).

Opened Documents

When you open a document that was created using an older version of AppleWorks
or ClarisWorks, AppleWorks generally displays a warning message: "This document
was created by a previous version of AppleWorks. A copy will be opened and '[v6.0]'
will be added to the filename." When you click OK, AppleWorks 6 converts the older

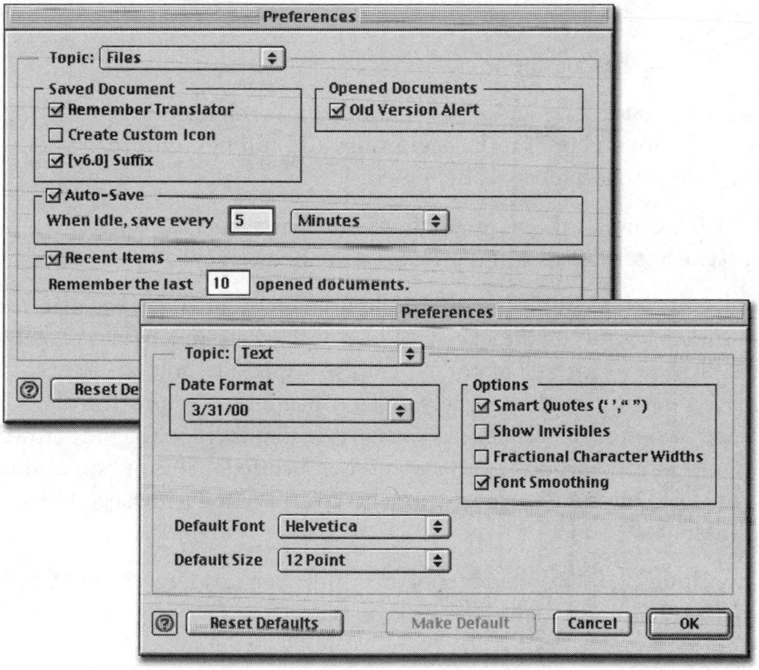

Figure 11-2:
*The Files Preferences panel
(top left) governs how
AppleWorks handles the
documents it creates.
Especially important here is
the Auto-Save feature,
which can help you out in
times of trouble–or crashes.
At lower right: the Text
panel, which actually
doesn't have much to do
with text. Instead, it offers
several font-related options.
Use the Smart Quotes
feature when word
processing, but turn it off
when creating a document
you'll be saving as a Web
page; curly quotes turn into
garbage characters when
sent over the Internet.*

document into an AppleWorks 6 format, leaving the original document untouched on the hard drive.

Note: Even though the new document bears the name of the original (plus "[v6.0]"), don't be deceived. It hasn't actually yet been saved, and behaves as though it's a new, untitled document.

If you turn off this checkbox, all of the above is still true—you just won't see a message to that effect.

Topic: Text

The Text Preferences panel (choose Topic→Text in the Preferences dialog box) deals with how text is treated in AppleWorks documents (see Figure 11-2).

- **Date Format.** This pop-up menu lets you choose between five date formats, such as "4/1/00" and "Saturday, April 1, 2000." This setting most noticeably affects the way the date is formatted when you use the Edit→Insert Date command (see page 83).

- **Default Font.** This pop-up menu lets you select a *default* (starting) font for text—the type style that appears when you for start typing in a new Word Processing document, for example.

- **Default Size.** Select the default point size for your text from this pop-up menu. It lists nine common font sizes: 9, 10, 12, 14, 18, 24, 36, 48, and—if you spend most of your time designing movie posters—72 points.

Options

This checkbox group has four options.

- **Smart Quotes** replaces straight computer quotes (") with the more professional-looking curly quotes (" or ") at the beginnings and endings of words. It does the same things for single quotes (from ' to ' or ').

- **Show Invisibles** reveals the normally invisible characters that control text formatting (such as tabs, spaces, and presses of the Return key).

- **Fractional Character Widths** is a technical parameter that affects the placement of individual characters on the screen. Most printers have much finer resolution than your screen; as a result, some typefaces—especially boldface type—look oddly spaced when printed (especially on laser printers). Turning this checkbox on shifts the placement of all letters in your text so that they look slightly crowded on the screen—but they look spectacular when printed. (This option also prevents *rotated* text in your drawing documents from printed with jagged edges on inkjet printers.)

- **Font Smoothing** smoothes the edges of any on-screen text larger than 12 points by *antialiasing* (adding a slight blurry outline).

Note: Of course, on the Macintosh, the →Control Panels→Appearance→Fonts tab offers exactly the same font-smoothing options, which affect *all* applications, including AppleWorks. The choice here in the AppleWorks Preferences dialog box *overrides* the Mac OS setting.

Topic: Graphics

This panel of the Preferences dialog box (Figure 11-3) affects three tools in the Painting and Drawing modules:

Polygon Closing

This section governs what happens when you draw polygons using the Polygon tool.

- **Manual** means you have to re-click the first point in a polygon to finish it, thus forming a fully enclosed shape. (If you double-click as you place the last point of your polygon, you end the shape *without* closing it.)

- **Automatic** does the closing job *for* you—when you double-click the last point of a new polygon, AppleWorks draws a line from your double-click back to the first point, thus enclosing the shape.

Object Selection

This two-option setting determines what happens when you click an object in the Drawing module—whether eight handles appear or only four (at the corners). Use the simpler option when you're working with very complex drawings with many overlapping shapes, where additional handles might be confusing. Use the standard eight-handle arrangement if you think you might have a need to stretch the selected graphic object in one dimension only—horizontally, for example.

Options

Although the two items in the Options section *look* like they depend on each other, they actually operate independently:

- **Automatically Smooth Freehand** refers to lines drawn with the Freehand tool. Ordinarily, AppleWorks smoothes the lines you've drawn with this tool to get rid of caffeine jitters. If you happen to have drawing skills of steel, or you like the unsteady look of hand-drawn lines, turn off this checkbox.

- **Mouse Shift Constraint** governs what angles are allowed when the Shift button is held down while drawing. (Chapter 6 describes how the Shift key makes it easy to draw perfectly straight or diagonal lines.) Normally set to 45°, you can set it to any angle you like between 1° and 45°; smaller numbers here allow more freedom of movement when you Shift-drag.

Topic: Spreadsheet

Batting last in the General Preferences lineup is the Spreadsheet Preferences panel (Figure 11-3). Here's what each item does:

Pressing arrow keys

This item has two options that govern what happens when you press the arrow keys on your keyboard while editing a spreadsheet.

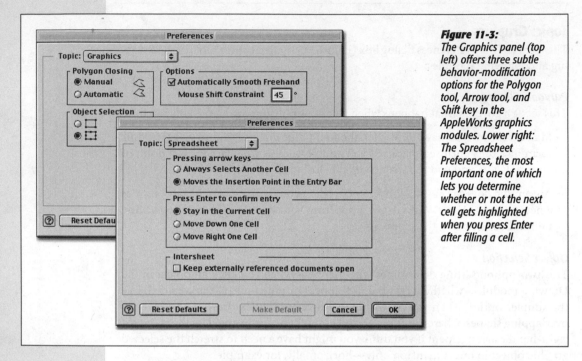

Figure 11-3:
The Graphics panel (top left) offers three subtle behavior-modification options for the Polygon tool, Arrow tool, and Shift key in the AppleWorks graphics modules. Lower right: The Spreadsheet Preferences, the most important one of which lets you determine whether or not the next cell gets highlighted when you press Enter after filling a cell.

- **Always Selects Another Cell.** If you're editing text in the Entry bar, pressing the arrow keys generally walks the blinking insertion point through the formula you're building. If you turn on this option instead, however, pressing an arrow key automatically accepts the entry and highlights the next cell in the spreadsheet (in the direction of the arrow key you press). Use this option if you don't often include formulas in your spreadsheets.

- **Moves the Insertion Point in the Entry Bar** is the usual option: When you're editing a formula in the Entry bar, your arrow keys move the cursor among the characters in the Entry bar instead.

Press Enter to confirm entry

This set of buttons determines what happens in your spreadsheet when you press the Enter key:

- **Stay in the Current Cell** confirms the entry you've just typed, but leaves the cell you've just edited highlighted.

- **Move Down One Cell** or **Move Right One Cell.** When these options are selected, pressing the Enter key confirms the entry you've just typed and selects the next cell in the spreadsheet.

Intersheet

Believe it or not, this item doesn't refer to a dot-com startup company specializing in linens. Instead, **Keep externally referenced documents open** determines what happens if cells in the current spreadsheet refer to cells or frames in other documents (see page 174). If this checkbox is turned on, AppleWorks opens those other documents automatically.

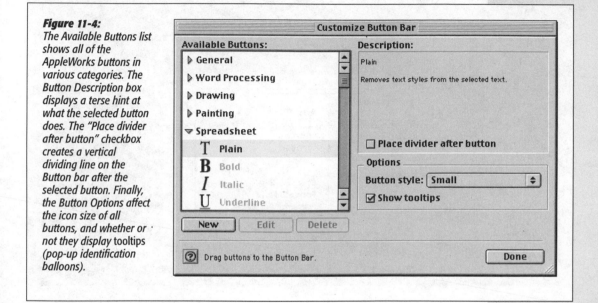

Figure 11-4:
The Available Buttons list shows all of the AppleWorks buttons in various categories. The Button Description box displays a terse hint at what the selected button does. The "Place divider after button" checkbox creates a vertical dividing line on the Button bar after the selected button. Finally, the Button Options affect the icon size of all buttons, and whether or not they display tooltips *(pop-up identification balloons).*

Editing the Button Bar

The window that appears when you choose Edit→Preferences→Button Bar contains the keys to unfathomable power within AppleWorks (Figure 11-4). It lets you customize AppleWorks' Button bar—even to the extent of designing new buttons, complete with icons that you draw yourself, that can perform impressive computer-wide tasks like opening documents, launching programs, opening certain documents, leaping to a specified Web site, triggering an AppleScript (see Appendix A), or running *macros* (software robots, as described at the end of this chapter).

Tip: You can also use the Button bar's contextual menu to open the Button Bar Preferences dialog box. To do so, Control-click the button bar itself, and choose Customize Button Bar from the pop-up menu.

There are hundreds of buttons in the Available Buttons list—and that doesn't count the buttons that you create yourself. This button list contains shortcuts to many AppleWorks features, which can save you time and effort. Fortunately, they're divided into categories, saving you from having to scroll through an endless list of options to find the buttons you want. Here's a brief look at the categories:

• **General.** This category contains buttons that work in any AppleWorks module. Some examples include font-related buttons, standard editing buttons (Cut, Copy, Paste, and Clear), printing buttons, linking buttons, Macro buttons, buttons to launch Assistants, and control-window buttons. There's even a button that, with one click, sends an email to AppleWorks Support (Apple's help desk).

WORKAROUND WORKSHOP

Replacing the Font Menu

It was one of the loudest complaints heard on the Internet when AppleWorks 6 first appeared: Font, Size, and Style menus don't appear on the menu bar, as they did in previous versions of the program. Instead, AppleWorks 6 offers only a single Text menu, whose commands—Font, Size, and Style—force you to choose from submenus when you want to change your type specs.

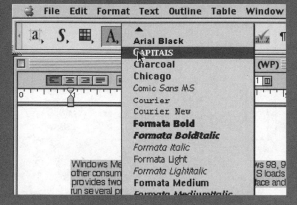

Fortunately, there's a workaround: Add the Font, Font Size, and Font Style buttons to the Button bar, as described in this section. These buttons work exactly like the Font, Font Size, and Font Style menus of previous AppleWorks versions, as shown here. (You'll find these buttons in the General category of the dialog box shown in Figure 11-5.)

• **Word Processing.** As you would expect, this category contains buttons specific to the Word Processing module; most duplicate existing menu commands. There's a huge selection in this category, including alignment buttons, superscript and subscript buttons, ruler buttons, citation and footnote buttons, and table-control buttons. (See Chapter 12 for more on tables.)

• **Drawing.** Here's another category with lots of choices, all of which apply to the Drawing module: text-wrap buttons, every conceivable object-alignment button, resizing and manipulation buttons, grouping buttons, layer-control buttons, and line-size buttons.

• **Painting.** This smaller, focused category contains Painting module-specific buttons for things like transformation (lighter, darker, tint, blend, and so on), flip and rotate, line-control, and paint mode.

• **Spreadsheet.** As a reflection of the Spreadsheet module's depth, the Spreadsheet button list is very long. Some highlights: cell and text formatting buttons, cell-control buttons, and chart buttons.

• **Database.** The Database button list offers buttons specific to the Database module, including text formatting, mode, adding and deleting records, and sorting.

- **Presentation.** The Presentation list sports a mere five buttons: Controller, Start Show, Next Slide, Previous Slide, and Show/Hide Notes.

- **User Buttons.** This category houses any custom buttons that *you* create. (If you haven't created any, this category doesn't even appear.)

Buttons in the General category can appear when any kind of AppleWorks document is open; however, buttons in a module category (such as Spreadsheet) can appear only when documents of that kind are open. (Buttons that you create appear in whichever modules you specify, as described in the next section.)

It's worth noting, too, that buttons may appear and disappear from your Button bar as you open and close documents. For example, the button that opens the Accents palette may show up on the bar even if no documents are open; but the Font pop-up "button" disappears when there's no text on the screen to format.

Note: Some buttons appear in more than one category. That's because these buttons—text controls, for example—are usable in more than one mode. When selecting buttons for your Button bar, remember that the ones in the General category are not the only ones that may have global, or near-global, uses in AppleWorks.

Customizing Your Button Bar

You can add any—or all—of the buttons in the list described above to your Button bar. But moderation is a virtue—once the on-screen portion of the Button bar is filled up, you have to *scroll* the Button bar, by clicking the tiny arrows at each end, to see the buttons that are off the screen. At that point, it may actually be easier to choose a menu command than to scroll through your Button bar on a hunt for the equivalent button.

Note: When you open the Customize Button Bar window, you'll notice that some of the buttons are grayed out. They represent buttons that are already on your Button bar.

Adding a button to the bar

You can add a button to the Button bar in either of two ways: You can drag the button you want from the button list to the Button bar, or you can double-click the button in the list. Dragging the button has the advantage of letting you determine where the button falls on the Button bar. Double-clicking, while faster, puts the new button at the left end of the Button bar, pushing all of the other buttons to the right.

Note: If you add a button from a specific module's category (such as Spreadsheet) while no document of that kind is open, AppleWorks still adds the button to the Button bar—but you won't be able to see it until you open a document of that type, and it may not show up where you expected it to.

Rearranging the buttons on the bar

Once buttons are on the Button bar, you may want to rearrange them. To do so, just drag the buttons around on the Button bar. You can do this at any time while working in AppleWorks—not just when you're in the Customize Button bar dialog box. As you drag, the button floats around with your cursor; a solid black vertical line appears where the button is to be placed when you release the mouse button.

Adding a vertical divider

To put a vertical "category divider" line after a button that's already on the button bar, Control-click the button. From the pop-up menu, choose "Place divider after button." A short vertical line appears to the right of the button you clicked. (You can also add one as you're customizing the buttons, as shown in Figure 11-4.)

To remove the line, choose "Place divider after button" from the same pop-up menu.

Removing a button from the bar

Removing a button from the Button bar is also easy: Control-click the button, and then choose Remove Button from the pop-up menu. You can also drag the button to the Trash on your desktop.

Both of these removal methods delete the button from your Button bar, not from the Customize Button bar dialog box list.

Tip: The best way to identify the buttons on your Button bar is to point the cursor at one and wait. After a second or two, a *tooltip* appears—a Balloon Help-like balloon that names and describes the button's function.

On the other hand, if this feature is driving you crazy, turn it off by choosing Edit→Preferences→Button Bar, turning off "Show Tooltips," and clicking OK.

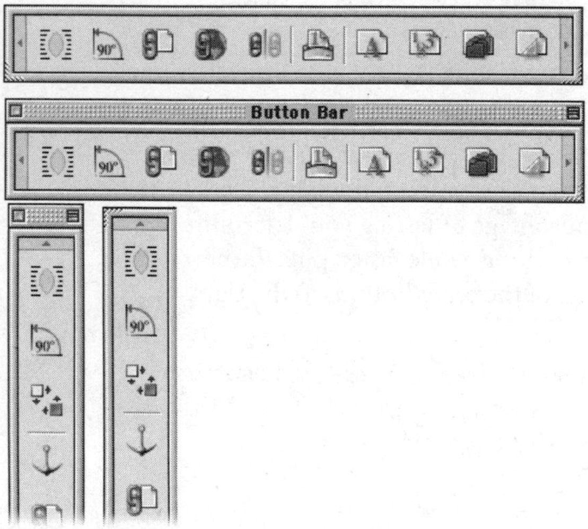

Figure 11-5:
The Button bar can assume one of four shapes—a horizontal anchored bar (top), horizontal floating palette (second from top, complete with a tiny close box in the upper-left and "collapse box" in the upper-right), a vertical floating palette (lower left), or a vertical anchored bar. Choose the one that best matches your screen. (Hint: Most monitors are wider than they are tall, so a vertical button bar makes better use of your screen space, and lets you see more of your document without scrolling).

Reshaping the Button Bar

AppleWorks' Button bar comes installed as a horizontal strip attached at the top of the screen. You're welcome to place the Button bar anywhere you like, however—just drag the bar's puffy gray border. If you drag the bar near any edge of the screen, it attaches itself there. If you drag the bar *away* from the edge of the screen, it turns into a floating horizontal palette. (Unfortunately, you can't reshape the Button bar into a square palette, as you could in previous AppleWorks versions.)

Tip: You can make the Button bar longer or shorter by dragging the diagonal stripes at the corners.

Creating New Buttons

If the hundreds of canned buttons aren't enough for you, you can always create your own buttons. Buttons that you create can do one of five things: play a macro (see the end of this chapter), open a document, launch another application, open a particular Web page, or play an AppleScript.

To create a new button, open the Customize Button Bar window (choose Edit→Preferences→Button Bar); click the New button. You'll be presented with the New Button window (Figure 11-6), where you create your new button and define its powers.

The New Button window's three parts let you specify the button's name and description, its function, and where the button works. Whatever you type as its name and description will appear as the "tooltip" balloon that appears when you let the cursor hover over the button for a few seconds: Choose wording that you'll understand later.

Note: As you type your button name, description, and (when applicable) Internet address into the New Button or Edit Button dialog box, you may find it frustrating that your text doesn't wrap within the boxes where you can type. Even though the Description box is tall enough to accommodate several lines of text, whatever you type simply scrolls off to the left as your typing continues.

There's really no tip here—just a sympathetic back-pat. It's a bug in AppleWorks 6.0.

Determining your button's function

The second section of the New Button Window is where you specify what your button does. The Action pop-up menu lets you make one of five choices:

- **Play Macro.** When you choose this action, the second pop-up menu lists any macros you've created. From this pop-up menu, choose the macro you want to run when your button is clicked. (See the end of this chapter for instructions on creating macros.)

- **Open Document.** If you select this action, a Choose button appears. Click Choose to select, from wherever it may be on your hard drive, a particular document that you want AppleWorks 6 to open when your new button is clicked.

- **Launch Application.** This button is very similar to the Open Document button, but instead of opening a document, it lets you open another software program, which you can select by clicking the Choose button below the Action pop-up menu.

- **Open URL.** When you choose this option, a URL blank appears, in which you can type an Internet address, such as a standard Web page URL, FTP address, or email address (which you must precede with the phrase *mailto:*). When your completed button appears on the Button bar, you'll be able to open the specified Web page in your browser, or create a pre-addressed email message, with a single click.

- **Execute Script.** The button you create using this Macintosh-only option plays an *AppleScript*—a pre-recorded series of steps, created by an advanced Mac user, that can do anything from backing up your hard drive to emptying the Trash. Click Choose to select an AppleScript; see *Mac OS 9: The Missing Manual* for a crash course in writing AppleScript programs.

Editing or deleting a homemade button

After you're finished creating, describing, and programming your button, click OK. You return to the Customize Button Bar dialog box, where you'll see your new button at the bottom of the list (in the User Buttons category).

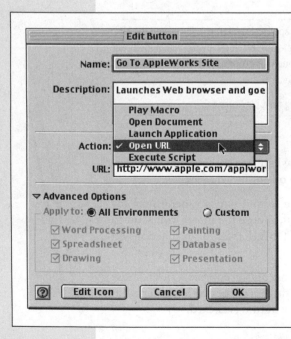

Figure 11-6:
Click the Advanced Options triangle to reveal the extra panel of options shown here. Click Custom if you want your hand-designed button to show up only when certain kinds of AppleWorks documents are open (which you select by turning on the checkboxes). Click "Apply button only to active document" when you don't want your button to appear in every AppleWorks document, but only in the one that's open. You can also click Edit Icon to change the look of the button, as described on the next page.

Provided you haven't added this button to your Button bar already, you can re-open the Edit Button dialog box (Figure 11-6) by clicking the name of one of your buttons (once) and then clicking Edit. (You can edit and delete only buttons that you've created yourself—AppleWorks' buttons are immune to your machinations.)

You can delete one of your buttons from the bar by clicking its name once and then clicking Delete. (AppleWorks doesn't let you delete it if it's currently installed on your Button bar, however.)

Caution: When you click Delete, the selected button is gone—there's no opportunity to say "Wait—I didn't mean *that* button." Nor does the Edit→Undo command function in this context. The lesson: be *sure* that you want to delete the selected button before you click Delete.

POWER USERS' CLINIC

Changing a Button's Appearance

By clicking the Edit Icon button in the New Button or Edit Button dialog box (Figure 11-6), you bring up the icon editor, shown here, where you can give your custom button its very own look.

The icon editor is a stripped-down version of the Painting module described in Chapter 7. The ten tools on the left let you select, add, and remove pixels of various colors. (The two squares below the first eight familiar tools represent

a filled rectangle and a hollow rectangle tool, respectively.) The bottom-left rectangles represent pop-up menus that let you choose line and fill colors for the rectangles, line, pencil, and paint-bucket tools.

When you're finished painting, click the Save button in the Edit Button Icon Window, and then click OK in the New Button or Edit Button window. Your new button icon joins the other buttons in the Available Buttons list.

Exporting Buttons

Your homemade buttons don't have to stay locked forever in your copy of Apple-Works. You can share these custom buttons with anyone who has AppleWorks 6. Here's how:

1. **Open a new document.**

   As it turns out, you can give a custom-made button to others only by giving them a *document* in which the button is embedded.

2. **Choose Edit→Preferences→Button Bar.**

   The Customize Button Bar window opens.

---

3. **Click New. Define a new button.**

See "Creating New Buttons" in the previous section for instructions.

4. **Click the triangle next to Advanced Options. Turn on the appropriate module checkboxes. Turn on "Apply button only to active document."**

This checkbox embeds the button in the document.

5. **Click OK in the New Button window, and then click Done in the Customize Button Bar window. Save the document on your hard drive, and then distribute it as you see fit (the document, not the hard drive).**

When you give this document to another AppleWorks 6 user, he can choose Edit→Preferences→Button Bar to open the Customize Button Bar window. Your custom button appears in the User Buttons category at the bottom of the list. He can drag this button to his own Button bar or edit it like any other button.

Two cautions: First, buttons based on macros don't work unless you *also* embed the macro itself into the same document. For instructions, see "Exporting Macros" near the end of this chapter.

Second, some buttons, when clicked, open specific documents, AppleScript scripts, or programs on your hard drive. Obviously, if your recipients don't have the same files in precisely the same folder locations on *their* hard drives, your buttons won't work.

They can solve the problem by selecting such a button (in the Customize Button Bar window), clicking Edit, and clicking the Choose button to re-assign the button to a different file (or different location).

HTML Import/Export

The last of the three Edit→Preferences commands, called HTML Import/Export, governs how AppleWorks deals with Web-page documents (HTML files) in all its forms. Most of these settings are primarily useful if you're experienced in creating Web pages, and you know something about the HTML programming language.

Choose Edit→Preferences→HTML Import/Export to open the Configure HTML dialog box, shown in Figure 11-7. Like the General Preferences window, the Configure HTML window has several panels, each of which is listed in the Topic pop-up menu:

Topic: Export Preferences (Basic)

The Export Preferences window controls how AppleWorks saves Web pages—that is, what happens when you choose File→Save As and choose, from the File Format pop-up menu, HTML.

- **Document Background.** This area of the basic HTML preferences governs the background of the Web pages you create. To specify this background, you can either choose a solid color among the nine listed in the Color pop-up menu, or you can select a graphics files to serve as the backdrop (click Set Background

Image, and then navigate to, and double-click, any JPEG or GIF graphics file on your Mac). The name of the graphics file you selected appears next to the Image label.

If your page already has a background image, you can remove it by clicking Remove Background Image.

• **Images.** This pop-up menu offers two choices—JPEG and PNG. It lets you specify an exported graphics format for the individual graphics embedded in your Web pages. For a discussion of these graphics formats and their usefulness, see page 294.

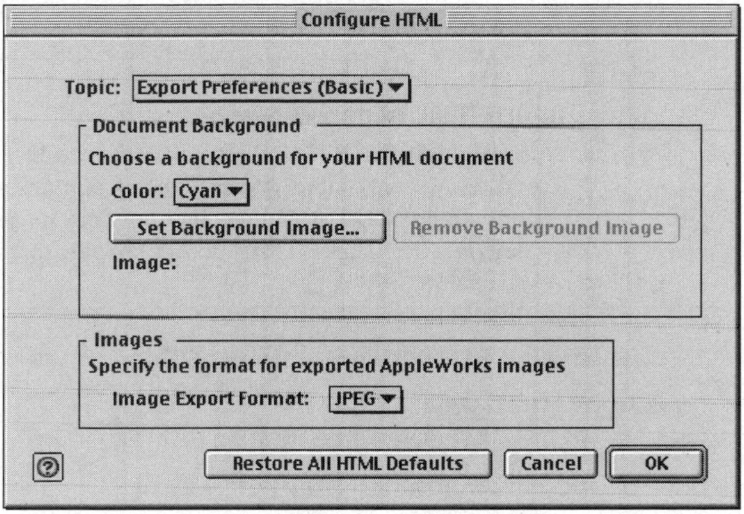

Figure 11-7:
A request from the 200 million citizens of the World Wide Web: If you must use a background color in your Web page (which you choose here), please use one that contrasts with the color of your text. And if you must use a background picture, please choose a graphic with very low contrast in very little "activity," so that we can read the text of your Web page on top of it.

> **Configure HTML**
>
> Topic: [Export Preferences (Basic) ▼]
>
> ┌─ **Document Background** ─────────────
> │ **Choose a background for your HTML document**
> │ Color: [Cyan ▼]
> │ [Set Background Image...] [Remove Background Image]
> │ Image:
> └──────────────────────────────────
>
> ┌─ **Images** ──────────────────────────
> │ **Specify the format for exported AppleWorks images**
> │ Image Export Format: [JPEG ▼]
> └──────────────────────────────────
>
> ⑦   [Restore All HTML Defaults] [Cancel] [OK]

Topic: HTML Export (Advanced)

There are two ways to create Web pages: you can type out HTML codes in a word processor, much the way programmers do, or you can design the page graphically in a program like AppleWorks and use its automatic conversion routines to turn your work into an HTML document.

Unfortunately, every Web browser is different—there's Internet Explorer, Netscape Communicator, iCab, and America Online, and various Unix-based browsers. A particular Web page may look slightly different in each browser, and can even look different in the Mac and Windows versions of the *same* browser. Professional Web-page designers, therefore, often object to the automatic conversion routines offered by programs like AppleWorks. They desire flexibility and control enough to view, edit, and adjust the actual HTML commands that describe a Web page in order to ensure better compatibility for the kinds of browsers that might be viewing the page.

If you fall into that category, this special preferences panel (Figure 11-8) is for you. The controls in this window let you choose an AppleWorks formatting attribute (such as underlined text) and link it to an HTML start and end tag (such as <U> and </U>, the commands for *start underline* and *end underline*). The description, at the lower-right side of the dialog box, identifies the selected formatting item, so that HTML experts can better understand how to customize the program's tags.

Note: Many Web-page design programs generate illegal or browser-specific HTML code, much to the irritation of HTML programmers. AppleWorks generates better code—but it still sometimes produce *unoptimized* HTML—codes that will take longer to download and consume more space than necessary.

If you're an HTML purist, therefore, use AppleWorks only to generate the initial HTML document. Then open it up in a dedicated HTML editor, such as BBEdit, GoLive, or even the Web-page designer that's included with Netscape Communicator.

Topic: HTML Import (Advanced)

This section of the HTML Preferences (Figure 11-8) is the mirror to the HTML Export (Advanced) topic. It relates the tags in an imported HTML document to various AppleWorks attributes. By adjusting its settings, you can control how AppleWorks translates HTML into AppleWorks formatting.

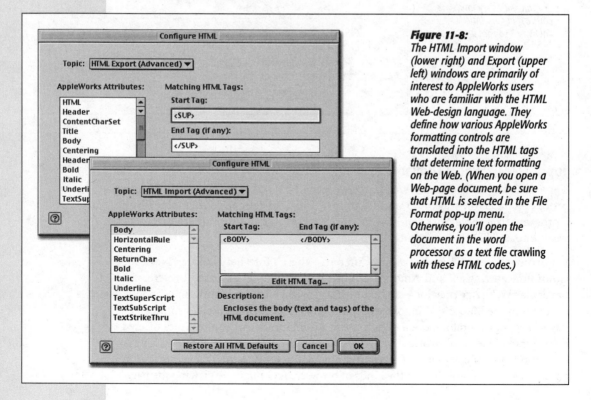

Figure 11-8:
The HTML Import window (lower right) and Export (upper left) windows are primarily of interest to AppleWorks users who are familiar with the HTML Web-design language. They define how various AppleWorks formatting controls are translated into the HTML tags that determine text formatting on the Web. (When you open a Web-page document, be sure that HTML is selected in the File Format pop-up menu. Otherwise, you'll open the document in the word processor as a text file crawling with these HTML codes.)

Note: Upon inspection, you'll discover that the Import list is a subset of the Export list. In other words, AppleWorks can interpret more HTML formatting than it can create.

That's a good reason to *preserve* the original AppleWorks document from which you generate your HTML pages. For example, if you were to save a document containing a table as HTML and re-import it, the table would be gone.

To set how a tag is interpreted by AppleWorks, select an AppleWorks attribute on the left; the associated HTML tags are displayed on the right. If you want to change a tag that's translated into a given attribute, click Edit HTML Tag to type in a new set of tags. You can assign as many tags as you like to each attribute (see Figure 11-8). For instance, you may want both the <U> and <I> tags translated into italics in AppleWorks. (You can't add to the list of tags, however.)

Escape Codes (Advanced)

The last HTML preference panel deals with how AppleWorks handles *escape codes*. Escape codes are specialized text codes that let HTML handle special characters—such as curly quotes, ampersands (&), and accented letters (such as ü and ñ symbols). Web-page designers need escape codes because these special typographical characters are often parts of the HTML coding itself; if you were to type a & symbol into your HTML programming (instead of using a special code, "&", to represent it), your Web page could become garbled.

Most people leave this set of preferences alone unless their escape codes aren't working properly.

Tip: The Restore All HTML Defaults button changes all of the HTML settings back to their original settings. Use it if you've hopelessly loused up your HTML preferences.

Customizing Your Palettes

AppleWorks is rife with *palettes*—the floating windows that give you access to special features such as Accents and Clippings. You can't create your own palettes, but you can customize the ones AppleWorks gives you, including Tools, Accents, Clippings, Starting Points, Controls (for presentations), and Links.

Moving or Hiding the Tabs

These palettes all have tabs along their bottom edges. If that lower-palette location bothers you, you can move those tabs to the right or left side of the palette instead. You can also hide these tabs entirely. Figure 11-9 shows the procedure.

Settings for Starting Points and Clippings

Two of these windows—Starting Points and Clippings—offer additional, special-ized settings. Once again, the trick is to Control-click inside these windows. Then choose, from the pop-up menu, Starting Points Settings or Clippings Settings (see Figure 11-9).

Starting Points Settings

This window has three pop-up menus:

- **Banner.** If you examine the Starting Points window, as shown in Figure 11-10, you'll discover that each of its panels offers an instructional banner at the very top of the window that might say, for example, "Starting new document from scratch."

  But what happens when you create a new Starting Points tab of your own, by clicking the + button as described on page 12? What banner should AppleWorks display at the top of your own customized tab? Unless you intervene, you'll get nothing but an empty banner—the Default Banner—with an Apple logo at the far left side. Use this pop-up to place, above your own Starting Points panel, a banner inherited from one of the other Starting Points panels.

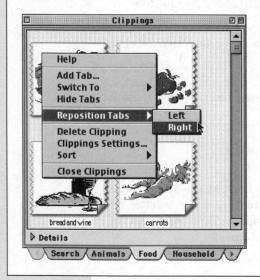

Figure 11-9:
The key to modifying the palette is the contextual menu that appears when you Control-click the palette. To move the tabs off the bottom of the palette, choose Reposition Tabs→Left or→Right, as shown here. To hide tabs, choose Hide Tabs from the same contextual menu. To make the hidden tabs reappear, choose Show Tabs from the contextual menu.

Note: This pop-up menu, and the Background pop-up menu described next, are available only when you're editing Starting Points panels you've added yourself—not when you're editing the Basics, Assistants, Templates, or other factory-installed tabs.

- **Background.** The finely striped background image upon which your Starting Points icons sit—an echo of the ribbed plastic of the iMac and Power Mac models—is also a graphic that you can replace. Using the Background pop-up menu, you can, in theory, tailor your own customized Starting Points panel with any of the six choices: Default Background, Assistants, Basic, Recent Items, Templates, and Web. You may not want to waste your time, however: all six backgrounds are identical. (Fortunately, you can replace them with your own graphics, if you're sly; see the sidebar box on the next page.)

- **Thumbnail Size.** The *thumbnails* are the icons that represent the various assistants, templates, and other files listed in the Starting Points windows. Use this pop-up menu to choose the size of these icons—small, medium, or large. (The large icons are by far the clearest and easiest to understand, but they also take up the most screen space.)

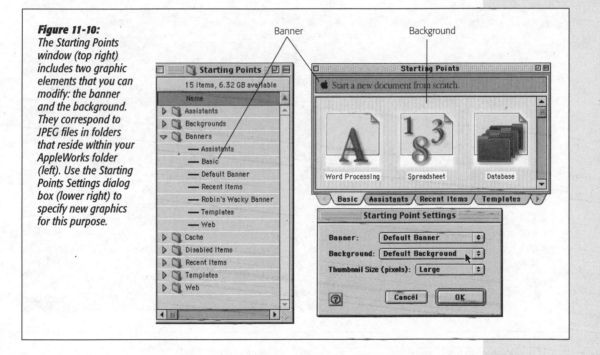

Figure 11-10:
The Starting Points window (top right) includes two graphic elements that you can modify: the banner and the background. They correspond to JPEG files in folders that reside within your AppleWorks folder (left). Use the Starting Points Settings dialog box (lower right) to specify new graphics for this purpose.

- **Sort.** Use this command (available on all Starting Points tabs except Basic) to rearrange the icons alphabetically ("by Name"), chronologically ("by Date"), by the space each takes up on your hard drive ("by Size"), or by AppleWorks document type ("by Kind").

Clippings Settings

As discussed in Chapter 9, the Clippings Settings dialog box lets you specify whether or not the Clippings Search command finds clippings whose names only partially match what you've typed. It also lets you determine the size of the clippings *cache* (or empty it, if you choose) and clipping-icons sizes, too. For details on the Clippings Settings dialog box, see page 284.

Making Your Own Banners and Backgrounds

There's no particular reason you should be satisfied with the choice of banners and backgrounds that appear in the Banners and Backgrounds pop-up menus shown in Figure 11-10. Behind the scenes, the images that form the top strip and background of each Starting Points panel are actually independent graphics files—ordinary JPEG files, in fact, created by Adobe Photoshop!

You'll find them in your AppleWorks→Starting Points→Banners and AppleWorks→Starting Points→Backgrounds folders, as shown in Figure 11-10. By opening this folder and duplicating, editing, or deleting the graphics files you find here, you can touch up the AppleWorks banners and backgrounds, or even substitute entirely new ones of your own design, as shown here.

Banner graphics are 1200 pixels wide by 36 tall; backgrounds are tiny squares, 48 pixels square, that AppleWorks *tiles* (repeats over and over to fill the window). But if your goal is to dress up your Starting Points window with some graphics of your own, you can save yourself the headache of calculating these dimensions by simply modifying graphics already in the Starting Points folder.

To modify one of the canned AppleWorks banners or backgrounds—for the Basics or Templates tab, for example—choose File→Open from within AppleWorks. Navigate to the AppleWorks 6→ Starting Points→Banners or→Backgrounds folder. Open one of the existing graphics. It opens into a Painting document, as described in Chapter 7. Use the painting tools to touch it up or mangle it, according to your tastes. Then choose File→Save As, choose the JPEG file format, navigate (if necessary) to precisely the same folder, give the document precisely the same name, and click Save.

To edit the banner (for example) for a tab you've created yourself, do exactly the same thing—but in the final step, give the file a different name. Finally, use the steps in this chapter to assign the new banner to the Starting Points tab you created yourself.

Use exactly the same procedure to change the background for one of your tabs, except navigate to the AppleWorks 6→Starting Points→Backgrounds folder instead.

Figure 11-11:
Few AppleWorks users suspect that they can move the Tools window around the screen or change its orientation, even to a horizontal one, as shown here. To switch between the horizontal and vertical versions of the Tools window, click the tiny zoom box in the right corner—the second square from the right. The upper-right square collapses the Tools window into nothing but a floating "grip strip."

Moving or Reshaping the Tools Window

There's one final window that you can tailor to your tastes: the Tools window. It acts a lot like the Button bar (see Figure 11-11). For example, you can attach it to any side of the screen—top, bottom, left, or right—and you can also detach it to be a free-floating window, exactly as described in "Reshaping the Button Bar," earlier in this chapter.

Macros

Macros automate things that you do in AppleWorks, turning lengthy or repetitive tasks into effortless single-click operations. For example, a macro might perform, at blinding speed, three successive search-and-replace operations on articles turned in to you by your newsletter writers: changing all double hyphens to long dashes (*em dashes*), two spaces after a period to a single space, and every occurrence of "price point" to "price."

In general, a macro feature is found only in the most expensive and sophisticated computer software. Programming ability is usually required to create macros. But AppleWorks is different; it can actually record the steps you take manually, watching you like a hawk, and—behind the scenes—writing down every mouse click, menu command, and so on. Almost any action in AppleWorks can be recorded into a macro, from drawing Bézier curves to searching for and replacing text.

Once a macro is recorded, you can play it back like a tape by clicking a button on your Button bar. As you lean back in your chair, AppleWorks takes exactly the same steps you took originally, automatically, as though a ghost is driving AppleWorks. True, some effort is required up front to understand macros and to record the ones that will help you get your work done. But once you've created a stable of macros, your work in AppleWorks can be much more efficient.

Recording a Macro

Here's how you go about recording a macro.

1. **Choose File→Macros→Record Macro (or press ⌘-shift-J).**

The Record Macro window appears (Figure 11-12).

2. **Type a name for the macro.**

The name for the macro can be 31 letters long, even if the Name box isn't wide enough to show it all at once. For best results, make the name descriptive.

3. **Specify a keystroke to trigger this macro, if you like.**

If you click Function Key, the small keystroke box becomes highlighted and filled with the name of a function key, such as F5. (Function keys are the F-keys at the top row of your keyboard.) If you click the lower box, you'll trigger this macro only when you press a three-key combination—⌘-Option plus a key you specify (by pressing it while this dialog box is open).

4. **Turn on Play Pauses, if appropriate.**

This checkbox makes AppleWorks record the timing of the steps you're about to show it, complete with hesitations and pauses, not just the steps themselves. (When this box isn't checked, AppleWorks will reproduce your macro by flying through the steps at high speed.)

If a document was on the screen at the moment you began step 1, you're also offered the Document Specific checkbox, which means that this macro will operate only when this particular document is open.

5. **Specify which AppleWorks modules you want this macro to work in.**

You'll find the corresponding checkboxes on the right side of the dialog box. By selectively turning off these checkboxes, you can make your macros context-specific—that is, F3 can perform one function in the Drawing module, and a different one in the Spreadsheet module.

6. **Click Record. Perform the steps you'll want the macro to do for you.**

AppleWorks now watches everything you do, memorizing your every move. A blinking cassette icon on your menu lets you know that the software's watching. Sort your database, create the chart, type some text, and so on.

If you make a mistake and decide to abort the recording, choose File→Macros→ Cancel Recording.

7. **When you're finished showing the macro its assignment, choose File→Macros→ Stop Recording.**

Your Macro is now recorded and ready to be played.

Playing a Macro

To play a previously recorded macro, you have several options:

- Press the key combination you specified in step 3.

- Choose File→Macros→Play Macro to bring up the Play Macro window, where you see a list of the macros you've recorded (Figure 11-12). Those that aren't available in the active document or module are dimmed and unavailable. Double-click the name of the macro you want to play (or click it once and then click Play).

- Trigger the macro by clicking its button on the Button bar, if you put one there as described on page 311.

In any case, AppleWorks now springs into action, re-creating every step you took with great speed and authority.

Tip: You can interrupt a macro's playback by pressing the Esc key or ⌘-period.

After some experimentation, you'll discover that AppleWorks' ability to impersonate your presence at the helm isn't perfect. It faithfully re-creates keystrokes, most mouse clicks, and commands—but doesn't fare as well when it comes to mouse dragging or scrolling. It can't reproduce dragging a clipping into a document, for example, or drawing using the Freehand tool. Nor can you count on a macro reproducing clicks on the Button bar; if the buttons shift position (as they do when you edit the Button bar or open a different kind of document), the macro clicks futilely in the wrong spot.

Still, how often do you need a macro to reproduce a drawing? The macro feature works particularly well in the Word Processing, Spreadsheet, and Database modules, where it's really needed. For example, some AppleWorks users produce the same kind of report, sorted the same way and using the same layout, incorporating the same kind of graph from the same spreadsheet, week after week. In such situations, macros save time and tedium.

Editing a Macro

Once you've created a Macro, you can't edit the steps it incorporates; if you want to change some aspect of the steps you took, you must re-record the macro under a different name, or delete the macro and then re-record it.

Figure 11-12:
The Record Macro window (top) lets you name a macro, assign it a keystroke, indicate where it should work, and set its options—all before you record it. (A similar window opens when you edit a macro.) Bottom: the Play Macro box, which serves as a cheat sheet for the keystrokes you've assigned to your various macros. Macros that appear in gray don't apply to the module or document you're using.

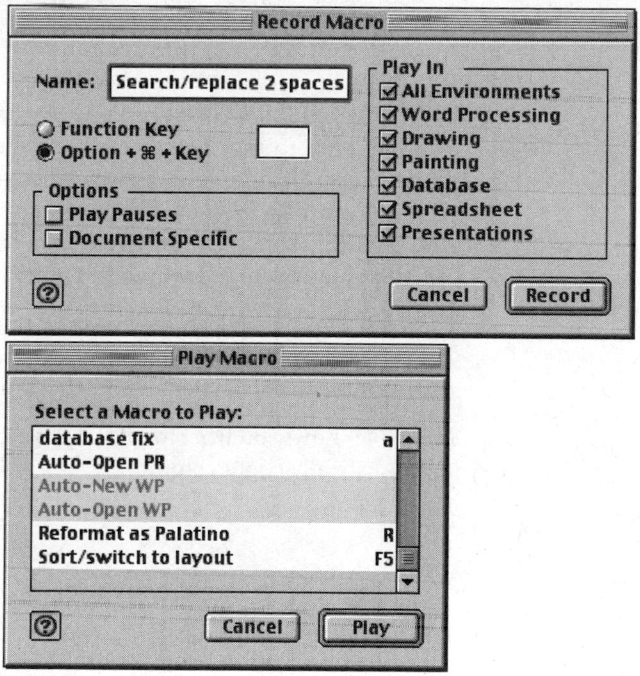

You can, however, change several administrative aspects of the macro. Choose File→Macros→Edit Macros to open the Edit Macros window. Click the name of the macro you want to edit, and click the Modify button. (You can also delete the selected macro by clicking the Delete button.)

This opens the Edit Macro window, which looks (and works) the same as the Record Macro window (except for the OK button in place of the Record button). Here you can change the name of the macro, the keystroke that triggers it, the set of modules in which it's active, and so on, as described on page 323.

FREQUENTLY ASKED QUESTION

Exporting Macros

After about 100 attempts, I finally got this incredible macro to work perfectly. Can I transfer this somehow to my laptop or my boss?

Sharing macros is a great way to win friends and influence people. You can only transfer a macro, however, when it's attached to a document.

To share a macro you've created, therefore, choose File→Macros→Edit Macros, select the macro you want, and make sure that the Document Specific checkbox is selected. Click OK.

Now, save the document. Email it or transfer it to the lucky recipient. On her end, she should open the document, choose File→Macros→Edit Macros, click the macro's name, click Modify, and then—if she wants the macro to work in any document instead of just the one you sent her—she should turn off the Document Specific checkbox.

Self-Triggering Macros

By giving a macro a special name, you can designate it as self-running, so that Apple-Works triggers it automatically whenever you create a new document, open Apple-Works, or open an existing document. For example, you could create a macro that sorts your database every time you open it; or saves a certain spreadsheet as a new file with today's date every time you open it; and so on.

These self-running macros are powerful things, so create them with caution—and if you treasure your relationships with your coworkers, be careful about embedding self-running macros in documents that you distribute.

This table shows you what to call each macro (left column), and what event triggers it automatically (right column).

Macros named this:	Run automatically when you:
Auto-Startup	launch AppleWorks
Auto-New WP	create a Word Processing document
Auto-New SS	create a Spreadsheet document
Auto-New DB	create a Database document
Auto-New DR	create a Drawing document
Auto-New PT	create a Painting document
Auto-New PR	create a Presentation document
Auto-Open WP	open a Word Processing document
Auto-Open SS	open a Spreadsheet document
Auto-Open DB	open a Database document
Auto-Open DR	open a Drawing document
Auto-Open PT	open a Painting document
Auto-Open PR	open a Presentation document

Tip: For best results, designate "open document" self-running macros as Document Specific—in other words, attach them to particular AppleWorks documents. Otherwise, you'll find these macros running every time you open any presentation document, spreadsheet document, and so on, which may not always produce the results you want.

Part Three: Integration

3

Combining the Modules: Frames, Tables, and Other Mixtures

The first eight chapters of this book described the *pieces* of AppleWorks—the individual facets of its personality. But if AppleWorks were little more than six well-designed applications on the same CD, it wouldn't be nearly as much fun. This chapter documents the payoff of having six programs under a single software roof: It shows you how to *combine* the tools of the different modules.

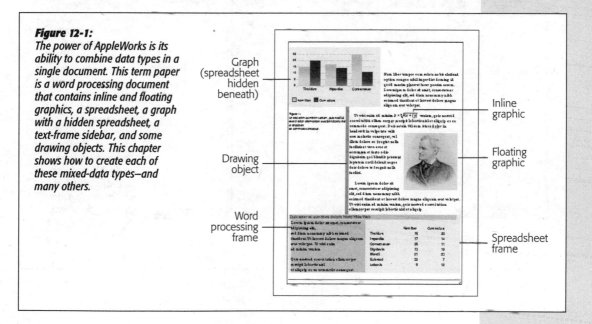

Figure 12-1:
The power of AppleWorks is its ability to combine data types in a single document. This term paper is a word processing document that contains inline and floating graphics, a spreadsheet, a graph with a hidden spreadsheet, a text-frame sidebar, and some drawing objects. This chapter shows how to create each of these mixed-data types—and many others.

Graph (spreadsheet hidden beneath)

Drawing object

Word processing frame

Inline graphic

Floating graphic

Spreadsheet frame

The integration of AppleWorks modules ranges from the simple, such as drawing a line in a word processing document, to the complex, such as creating drawings that *contain* word processing boxes that *contain* spreadsheets, all of which are filled with movies and sounds and links to Web pages. (Figure 12-1 shows an example.)

AppleWorks provides three basic mechanisms for mixing data from different modules: *drawing tools, mail merge,* and *frames.* This chapter covers each in turn.

AppleWorks also offers a few bonus mini-modules that don't appear in the Starting Points window, but that are available for use in almost any kind of document: the Equation Editor, tables, movies and sounds, and links.

Drawing Tools

You don't have to use the AppleWorks drawing tools (see Chapter 6) only in a drawing document; you can use them in *any* AppleWorks module. When you want to draw a vertical line down the side of a spreadsheet page, or a shaded rectangle behind a paragraph of text in the word processor, or a five-pointed star in a slide show, no problem—just click the appropriate tool on the Tools window and begin drawing. (Figure 12-2 shows the procedure for summoning the drawing tools if they're not already staring you in the face.)

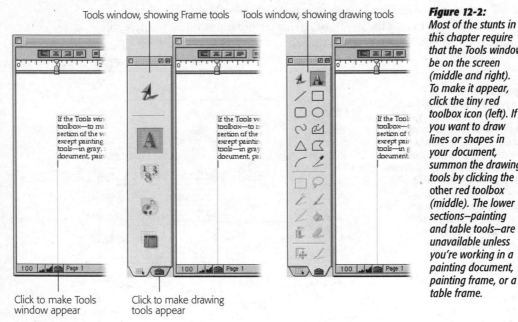

Tools window, showing Frame tools   Tools window, showing drawing tools

Click to make Tools window appear

Click to make drawing tools appear

Figure 12-2:
Most of the stunts in this chapter require that the Tools window be on the screen (middle and right). To make it appear, click the tiny red toolbox icon (left). If you want to draw lines or shapes in your document, summon the drawing tools by clicking the other red toolbox (middle). The lower sections–painting and table tools–are unavailable unless you're working in a painting document, painting frame, or a table frame.

Graphics in the Word Processor: Inline vs. Floating

The simplest kind of integration is just adding a graphic—a drawing object created with the drawing tools, clippings, photos, sounds, movies, or frames, for example—to a word processing document. In AppleWorks, you can choose whether or not you want such images anchored to one spot on the word-processor page; to use the technical lingo, you can choose whether you want graphic elements to appear as *inline* objects or as *floating* objects.

Inline graphics: They go with the text flow

Inline objects flow with the surrounding text, as if they were typed characters (see Figure 12-3). If you add more text above an inline object, the object moves down the page along with the surrounding text. Because an inline object is part of the line of text, the spacing for that line of text expands to accommodate the height of the object, just as it would if you increased the font size of one word. And because it's a part of that line of text, text can't wrap around an inline graphic.

If you place an inline image into your word processor document as a paragraph unto itself—that is, if you press Return both above it and below it—then you can use the text-alignment buttons in the ruler to center the selected object, move it to the left or right margin, and so on. You can also use the margin indents and the tabs to further adjust the horizontal position. You can also nudge the graphic upward or downward from the bottom edge of the surrounding text (Figure 12-3 again).

Tip: When you paste or drag a graphic into your document as an inline object, it almost always ruins the paragraph's line spacing (because it's much taller than a line of text). The only way to prevent this problem is to place your graphic into a paragraph of its own by pressing the Return key before you paste or drag, and again afterward.

Figure 12-3:
The Format→Descent command slides a graphic up or down relative to the text. If the graphic is a drawing object, dragging the handle resizes it. But if it's a painting object, adjusting its size crops the graphic or adds white space around it. To resize a painting image, copy it into a painting document or frame, make your adjustments, and then copy it back again.

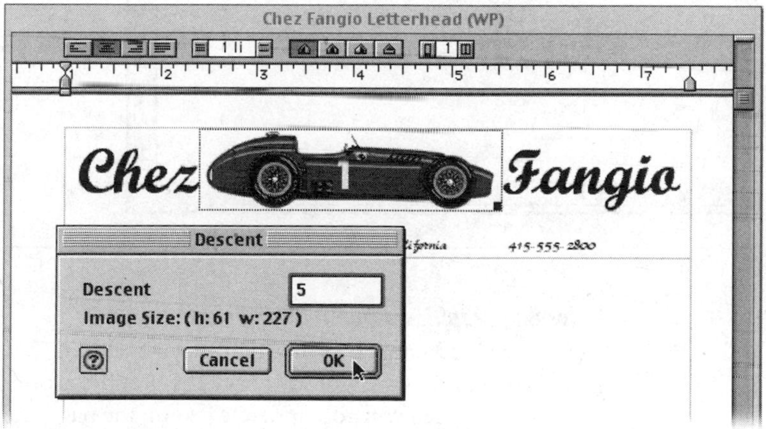

In older versions of AppleWorks, you'd have used inline graphics when creating documents where a graphic and its text description are supposed to line up—a classroom roster where each line contains the student's name and photograph, for example. If you later add or remove students from the top of the list, the images and text for the others will remain together. In AppleWorks 6, *tables* (described later in this chapter) serve this purpose much more elegantly; inline graphics are still sometimes handy, however, such as when you want to place a not-very-tall image (such as an equation) right into your text.

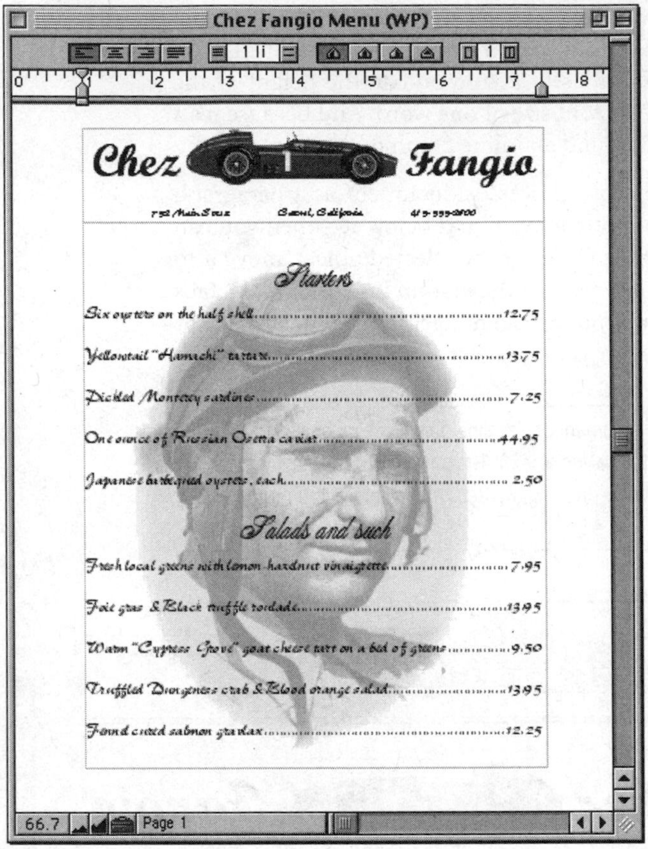

Figure 12-4:
In this example, you've pasted a graphic as a floating object (the large, faint portrait), dragged it into position, and used the Arrange→Move To Back command. Now the typing appears on top of the picture instead of being covered by it. In other words, you've created a word processing document with an inline graphic (the car) in the header and a floating graphic under the text as background.

Floating graphics: Rooted to one spot

Floating objects, on the other hand, are anchored to a place on the *page* instead of being tied to the *text*. You can drag the graphic around to plop it anywhere on the page—and when you add or delete text on the page, the object doesn't budge. Floating objects can float on top of the text, blocking out the words, or behind the text, like a watermark. Much more useful, however is AppleWorks' ability to *wrap* text around a floating object (see Figure 12-3, and also refer to page 228).

You'd insert images as floating objects when you want to add an illustration to a page in a certain spot or when you have more than one image to arrange on the page—perhaps touching or overlapping.

Inline vs. floating: How to choose

Determining whether a graphic is an inline object or a floating one is up to you: If you paste or drag into a *word processing* document or frame (when the blinking insertion point is visible), you get an inline object.

But if you click the Arrow (or anything but the Text tool) on the Tools window before pasting or dragging the graphic, you're in drawing mode, and you get a floating object. As Figure 12-4 shows, knowing how (and when) to create each kind of graphic is a very useful skill.

Movies, Sounds, and Equations

Not every object that you drag or paste into an AppleWorks module must be a piece of visual artwork. You can also add QuickTime movies, sound files, and typographically correct equations to almost any kind of AppleWorks document.

Inserting Movies and Sounds

You can insert a movie file or sound file into an AppleWorks document exactly the way you would a graphic—by pasting, dragging, or using the Insert command. What happens next, however, is very different.

QuickTime—Apple's multimedia software—handles the presentation of audio and video files in AppleWorks. Therefore, the kinds of files AppleWorks can display depend on the version of QuickTime you're using. When you install AppleWorks 6.0, the installer also places QuickTime 4.0.1 on your hard drive if you don't already have it. Each time Apple updates QuickTime, more file formats join its repertoire.

For example, as of QuickTime 4.1.2 (current at this writing), QuickTime—and therefore AppleWorks—can understand, open, or insert these document types:

- **Video files.** AVI (the standard movie file type on Windows), MPEG-1 (the movie file format used on Video CDs, which isn't the same as DVDs), QuickTime movies, DV clips (the kind captured by iMovie and File Cut Pro), OpenDML (another Windows standard), and QuickTime VR (panoramic "virtual reality" photos).

- **Audio files.** MP3, AIFF (a popular Mac and Windows exchange format), tracks from a music CD, System 7 sounds (the double-clickable kind found in your System file), Sound Designer II files, DV sound files, uLaw (popular on Unix computers), and WAV (the Windows standard format).

- **MIDI files.** Karaoke MIDI, Standard MIDI, General MIDI. (And if you don't know what MIDI is, then you probably aren't a musician who has connected a music synthesizer to the Mac for the purposes of recording and editing it using special software—and then exported the resulting music as a MIDI file that can be shared with other musicians.)

- **Still images.** BMP, GIF, JPEG (and JIFF), MacPaint, PICT, TIFF, QuickTime Image Format, PNG, RGB Planar, SGI, Targa. (For descriptions of these formats, see page 248.)

- **Animation formats.** 3DMF, animated GIF, FLC, PICS, Flashpix, Flash.

Note: Displaying multimedia files is a demanding task for AppleWorks. Before creating any of these documents, increase AppleWorks' RAM allocation if you haven't already done so. Quit AppleWorks, highlight the AppleWorks application icon (which is inside the AppleWorks 6 folder), and choose File→Get info→Memory. In the box for Preferred Size, increase the memory allocation to 12,000 K or so—if your Mac has that much memory to spare—and then close the window. The next time you open AppleWorks, the program will have that much more memory at its disposal, and will be less likely to give you "out of memory" problems .

Tutorial: Inserting a movie

Suppose that you're planning to open a new motor-racing theme restaurant. You've got your theme, you've just prepared a fabulous menu—all you're missing is money. But you'll need more than a menu to pitch your investors. In addition to printed materials, you'll want to prepare some multimedia documents for your laptop so that you can wow your loan officer and potential business partners.

1. **Create a new word processing document. Paste or type a summary of your restaurant plans.**

   Make sure that the Tools window is visible, and that the drawing tools are available, as shown in Figure 12-2.

2. **Click the Arrow tool.**

   AppleWorks switches into what it thinks of as drawing mode; at this point, any multimedia file you insert will become a floating object.

3. **Drag the icon of a movie file from your hard drive to the document window.**

   Alternatively, choose File→Insert, locate the movie file you want to import, and then click Insert.

   After a moment, an image appears: the movie's first frame, complete with resizing handles and a filmstrip icon—the QuickTime control button—in the lower-left corner (Figure 12-5).

   The image is probably sitting on top of some of your text. In the next step, you'll turn on text wrap to make the text flow around the image.

4. **Drag the movie frame to reposition it, if you like, and then choose Options→Text Wrap.**

   The Text Wrap dialog box appears. (If you remember from Chapter 6 that the Text Wrap command works only when you turn on Options→Frame Links, you've got excellent retention. However, that rule applies only in the *other* modules—not the Word Processing module.)

The movie frame is rectangular, so choose Regular and leave the gutter at 5 points.

5. **Click OK.**

   AppleWorks flows the text around the movie frame. If you move the movie frame, or add or remove some text, AppleWorks will readjust the text wrap automatically.

6. **Double-click the filmstrip control button (shown in Figure 12-5).**

   The QuickTime movie controls—including a horizontal scroll bar—appear beneath the frame. Click the Play button (the triangle) to view the movie. (Or, if you simply double-click the movie frame, the movie plays without making its scroll bar appear.) Step through the movie one frame at a time by pressing the left or right arrow keys, or by clicking the step-forward or step-reverse buttons at the right end of the scroll bar. If the movie contains sound, click the loudspeaker button on the left to access the volume control.

Figure 12-5:
Any movie file, regardless of format (QuickTime, AVI, and so on) appears the same way in an AppleWorks document. To make the controller scroll bar appear, click the filmstrip icon in the movie's corner (left). When the scroll bar appears (right), click the Play (triangle) button to view the clip. Press ⌘-period to interrupt playback.

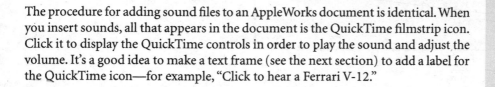

The procedure for adding sound files to an AppleWorks document is identical. When you insert sounds, all that appears in the document is the QuickTime filmstrip icon. Click it to display the QuickTime controls in order to play the sound and adjust the volume. It's a good idea to make a text frame (see the next section) to add a label for the QuickTime icon—for example, "Click to hear a Ferrari V-12."

Tip: If no scroll bar appears below the movie or sound when you click the filmstrip button, it's because you imported your movie or sound, accidentally or not, as an *inline object.* (You skipped step 2 of the preceding steps, in other words.) Only floating movie and sound objects sprout QuickTime scroll bars.

To transform your inline object into a floating one, click the movie frame or sound filmstrip icon, choose Edit→Cut, click the Arrow tool, and then choose Edit→Paste.

Movie options

If you click the movie frame and choose Edit→Movie Info, the Movie Info dialog box appears (Figure 12-6), providing a variety of playback options for your clip.

- **Use Movie Bounds.** If you've adjusted the size of the movie window since inserting it in your document, you can check this box to return it to its original size. (This checkbox is available only if you *have* resized the movie.)

- **Selection Only.** Suppose you've imported a 30-second movie clip, but only 10 seconds of it are relevant to the document you're working on. As shown in Figure 12-6, you can highlight only a certain portion of the footage. Then you can turn on this checkbox; henceforth, the movie will always play only the portion that you've highlighted on its scroll bar. Even if you try to drag the scroll bar manually, AppleWorks refuses to play any other portion of the movie.

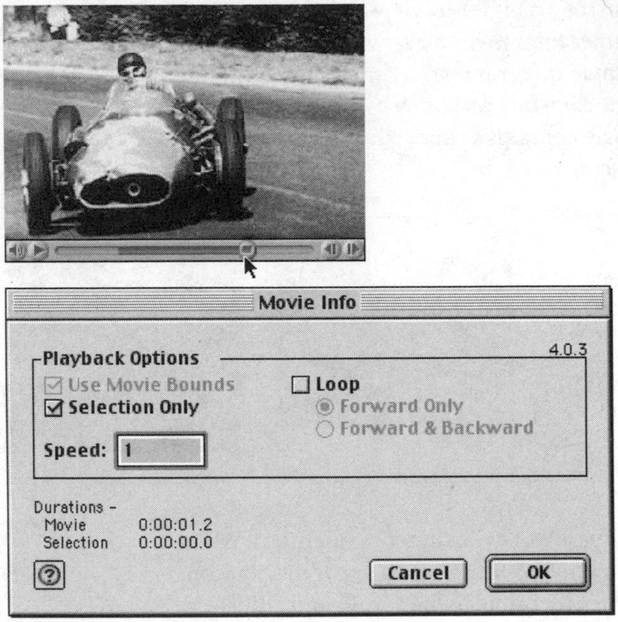

Figure 12-6:
Shift-drag the slider to designate the beginning and end of a footage selection; QuickTime darkens the scroll bar to show where it's been selected (top). Now, if you choose Selection Only in the Movie Info dialog box (bottom), AppleWorks will play back only your selected portion. You can also copy or cut the selection and paste it into another movie or into a different position in the same movie file. For example, you can rearrange a scene by highlighting the selection, choosing Edit→Copy, moving the slider elsewhere in the movie, and then choosing Edit→Paste.

- **Loop.** This checkbox makes the movie auto-repeat forever once you've started playing—or at least until you stop the playback with a single click on the movie frame. The two radio buttons determine whether the loop starts at the beginning each time or plays to the end, and then plays *backward* to the beginning, before repeating the entire cycle.

- **Speed.** If you're more interested in freaking out your spectators than entertaining them, you can make your movie play at double or triple speed, in slow motion, or even backward *and* too fast or too slow—just by changing the number in this box. The number 1 represents normal playback speed. Higher numbers designate a faster speed, and decimals less than one represent a slower speed—for example, .5 makes the movie play at half speed. Enter a negative number to play the movie backwards.

Creating Equations

Do you fret over the possibility that $s_x^2 = \frac{1}{n}\left(\sum_{i=1}^{n} x_i^2 - n\overline{X}^a\right)$, or do you just want to be able to write "⅔ cup of flour" in a recipe? In either case, AppleWorks lets you create such typographically impressive equations, from a simple fraction to the most obtuse differential equation.

Most people, including Apple, describe AppleWorks as six programs rolled into one. But actually there's a secret *seventh* program: the Equation Editor, a complete application designed to do nothing but help you make mathematical and scientific equations that are typographically refined. It's an independent application that generates graphic objects, which you can insert as inline graphics or floating objects.

Tip: The Equation Editor may look familiar; exactly the same program comes with Microsoft Word, WordPerfect, and many other programs.

As a matter of fact, you can use Equation Editor with just about any application on your computer. To open it directly, look inside the AppleWorks 6→AppleWorks Essentials→Equation Editor folder. Double-click Equation Editor, build the equations you want as described here, choose Edit→Copy, and then paste the result into any program that can accept graphics.

Before you create an equation, decide whether you want it to be inline or floating.

- To insert an inline equation, click inside your text at the point where you want the equation to appear.

- To insert an equation as a floating object, click the Arrow tool to switch AppleWorks into drawing mode (see Figure 12-2).

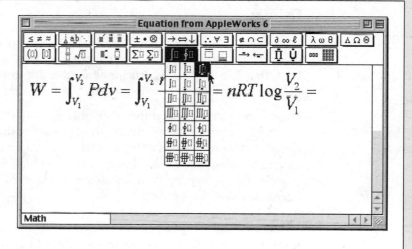

Figure 12-7:
Create an equation using the number and letter keys on your keyboard, and the 19 pop-up menus for operators, radicals, Greek letters, and other doodads. The upper row of pop-up menus contains symbols and operators, while the lower row provides templates to properly layout fractions, square roots, sums, functions, and so on. Closing the window when the equation is complete transports your equation back to AppleWorks.

Then proceed like this:

1. **Choose Edit→Insert Equation.**

   The Equation Editor splash screen appears briefly, followed by the "Equation From AppleWorks 6" window.

2. **Create an equation, as shown in Figure 12-7.**

   You can further format your equation using the commands in the Format, Style, and Size menus.

3. **When the equation is complete, close the Equation Editor window.**

   AppleWorks inserts the equation in your document as either an inline object or a floating object. You can resize it using the resizing handles, just as you would any other graphic.

To edit an equation you've created in this way, double-click it. AppleWorks automatically opens the Equation Editor program and pastes in your equation, ready to edit.

Equation Editor includes its own online help, available under the Help menu while you're editing an equation. You'll find its help screens to be of very little help if you snoozed through algebra class. But if you do know your trinomials from your quadratics, the help system can help you present your equations as easily as possible.

Tip: If you exhaust the capabilities of the Equation Editor, consider upgrading to its more capable, grown-up sibling, MathType. You'll find information on its expanded capabilities at *www.mathtype.com*—as well as a section on how to get the most out of Equation Editor.

Frames

You can paste a picture, graphic, or table into the body of the text in any old word processor. But AppleWorks' "through the looking glass" approach is a different story. It lets you place one kind of data inside another document as a *frame,* a rectangular window into a different world—a different AppleWorks module.

Frames give you all the features of another module without having to leave your original document. For example, in a word processing document, you could create a spreadsheet frame to illustrate your numerical point. In a database layout, you could create a painting frame to hold your scanned-in logo. In a spreadsheet, you could create a word processing frame to hold a couple of paragraphs that explain your interpretation of the numbers.

The Four Frame Types

It might be comforting to assume that *any* AppleWorks data type (word processing, database, spreadsheet, presentation, drawing, painting) can be conveniently inserted into *any* module; unfortunately, it's not that simple. There aren't six frame types—in fact, there are only four, and not the ones you might expect. Here's a rundown of the rules:

- AppleWorks offers four kinds of frames: word processing, spreadsheet, painting, and *table,* described later in this chapter.

- There's no such thing as a drawing frame; the drawing tools are always available, in every module. They create lines, geometric shapes, and freeform lines *on top of* whatever you've got in your document. No confining rectangular frame is necessary.

- There's no such thing as a database frame, either. You can, however, incorporate your database information into word processing, spreadsheet, or table frames using the mail merge feature described later in this chapter.

- Nor do presentation frames exist; you can't slap a slide show into your word processing document, handy though that might be. (On the other hand, you *can* present your word processing document *as* a slide show, oddly enough; the Window→Slide Show command turns each page of the document into a separate "slide.")

You create a frame by clicking one of the four frame tools on the Tools window, as shown at center in Figure 12-2—Word Processing, Spreadsheet, Painting, or Table. Then drag diagonally in your document to show AppleWorks how big you want the frame to be.

No matter what kind of frame you have in your document, it's treated as an *object*—like a rectangle you've drawn in the Drawing module. Click an object *once* to select it—to make its corner handles appear—in order to reposition, resize, or delete it. Click it *again* to enter the frame and edit its contents.

When you double-click a frame to edit it, AppleWorks behaves exactly as if you were working in the corresponding full-blown module; the menus and Button bar change to reflect the features of that module. When you click a spreadsheet frame, the Calculate menu appears; when you click a word processing frame, the Text, Outline, and Table menus appear; and so on.

Understanding Frames, Module by Module

Now that you know about the four kinds of frames, here's a cheat sheet that indicates which frames you can make in which AppleWorks document types:

- **Word Processing, Spreadsheet, Drawing, Presentation.** All four frame types are at your disposal: text frames (even in a text document), spreadsheet frames (even in a spreadsheet), painting frames, and tables.

- **Database.** Once again, you can create text frames, spreadsheet frames, painting frames, and tables—but only in *Layout mode* (choose Layout→Layout). (If you can think of a reason *why* it might be useful to create a spreadsheet or table in Layout mode—which you'll be able to see, but not edit, in Browse mode—you're a very creative soul.)

- **Painting module.** This time, you can create only three kinds of frames: text, spreadsheet, and table. (Nothing happens if you click the Painting frame icon on the

Tools window.) But beware—the instant you click outside of any newly created frame, it becomes frozen into a *picture* of that text, spreadsheet, or table. It's now part of the painting; you can't edit the numbers or text you typed into it.

The Frames Tutorial

If you're in business, or hope to be, you can't exist for long without adding a spreadsheet or graph to a word processing document. If you're creating, for example, a business proposal to show potential investors, you can include a graph showing sales, expenses, and profit forecasts. By including a "live" graph, if your sales or expense estimates change, you can enter the new numbers; AppleWorks will update the graph for you.

Drawing the spreadsheet frame

Start with a word processing document that contains the text of your proposal.

1. **On the Tools window, click the Frames tab.**

   The Frames panel is shown at center in Figure 12-2.

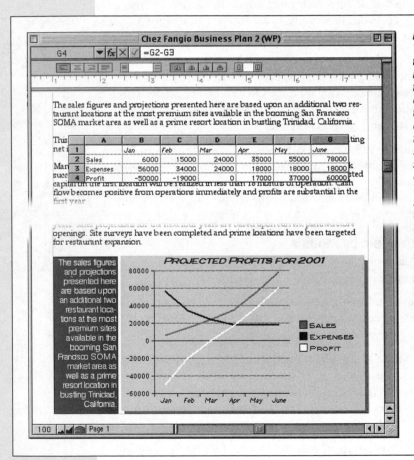

Figure 12-8:
You can include a graph in a text document in two ways. First, you can copy a graph from a spreadsheet document and paste it into the word processing document. The result is a frozen, uneditable graph. Second, you can insert a spreadsheet frame containing the graph data (top). If you don't want the spreadsheet numbers themselves to appear in the document, then later, you can hide them under the graph (bottom). If you need to change the numbers at some point, you can pull the spreadsheet out from under the graph and open its frame to edit the numbers.

2. **Click the Spreadsheet tool icon. Drag diagonally inside the document, creating a rectangle large enough for your spreadsheet.**

   Alternatively, drag the *tool icon itself* into your document window. AppleWorks creates a frame of a pre-programmed size, already selected so that you can drag one of the handles to adjust its size.

   Either way, AppleWorks now creates a new spreadsheet frame, ready for you to start entering data.

3. **Enter the data for the graph in the spreadsheet, beginning with the title and the X-axis labels in row 1, and the data-series labels in column A.**

   If you've previously created an AppleWorks spreadsheet that already contains the information you need, you can skip this step. Instead, copy the data from that document and paste it in cell A1 of the newly created spreadsheet frame.

   When you're finished, the spreadsheet should look something like Figure 12-8. (Refer to Chapter 5 for details of spreadsheet and graph creation.) Working in a spreadsheet *frame* is no different than working in a spreadsheet document—all the menus, Button-bar buttons, and other features of the Spreadsheet module magically appear when you're editing in a spreadsheet frame.

Creating a chart

If you'd wanted to include a spreadsheet instead of a graph in your document, your work would be complete—except perhaps for tweaking the formatting of the spreadsheet. Instead, continue on toward a chart.

1. **Choose Options→Make Chart.**

   The Chart Options dialog box appears, as shown back in Figure 5-25. For the restaurant data—forecasted profits—a line chart would be a good choice.

2. **Double-click the Line chart icon in the gallery.**

   AppleWorks closes the dialog box. You return to your document, where a standard-issue line chart now appears.

   Make any changes you desire to make the chart more attractive and readable. For example, you might click the colored box for each data series in the legend, and use the Accents window to change the line thickness or color. (See Chapter 5 for details on customizing charts.)

3. **Click once outside the chart to switch back into drawing mode.**

   The selection handles reappear around the chart. Drag it into position on your page, ignoring for the moment the spreadsheet and the text on the page.

4. **With the graph still selected, choose Options→Text Wrap.**

   The Text Wrap dialog box appears. Since this graph is rectangular in shape, you'll choose Regular and leave the Gutter setting at 5 points.

5. **Click Regular. Click OK.**

   AppleWorks wraps the text neatly around the graph. To finish the page cleanup, you have to next hide the spreadsheet behind the graph.

6. **Click the spreadsheet to select it. Drag one of the corner handles diagonally toward the center of the spreadsheet, shrinking it until it's smaller than the chart.**

   If you were to delete the spreadsheet frame from the document, the chart would become an uneditable image, frozen in time—a shadow of its former "living" self. But by hiding the spreadsheet behind the chart, you'll always have the source numbers handy. When you change the numbers, the chart changes to match. (You might consider *grouping* the spreadsheet frame and its chart—click one, Shift-click the other, and then choose Arrange→Group—so that you can't accidentally move or delete one without the other.)

7. **Drag the spreadsheet on top of the chart.**

   The spreadsheet disappears behind the chart—with only the Cheshire-cat grin of its black handles still visible. Since you created the chart *after* the spreadsheet, it's "in front" of the spreadsheet, on a higher drawing layer. (If, by some fluke, you can still see the spreadsheet, choose Arrange→Move Backward.)

Adding text frames in text documents

You can add a caption or a new title to the graph using a text frame. Now, ordinarily, you create a new text box (text frame) by clicking the Text tool on the Tools palette and then dragging diagonally in, say, your drawing document.

That won't work when you're working in the word processing document, however; after all, dragging diagonally in the word processing document just highlights the text that's there. No, you have to be sneakier when you want to create a text frame within the text document. You must either drag the Text tool itself out of the Tools window and into the document, creating a text frame of a pre-determined size—or use the multitalented Option key, as described in this example.

1. **Click the Text tool, and release the mouse. Position the cursor over your text document—and then *Option-drag* diagonally until the resulting rectangle is the desired size.**

   The insertion point is now blinking inside the new text frame.

2. **Enter a title for the chart—*Projected Profits for 2001*, for example.**

   Use the commands in the Format menu to style the title in a manner befitting your hopeful forecast. Then click the Arrow tool in the Tools window, and drag your newly created text frame into position above the chart.

   You can also use a text frame to insert a *sidebar*—an inset text box like the Power Users' Clinics boxes in this book—in a text document. For example, you can add a sidebar containing a brief biography of your restaurant's namesake.

3. Repeat step 1, making a narrow rectangle to hold your sidebar text. In the Accents window, select a light fill color.

This color is going to form the background for your sidebar.

4. Enter or paste in your sidebar text.

At any time, you can click the Arrow tool on the Tools window to adjust the size, shape, or position of your sidebar box.

5. Choose Options→Text Wrap to force the underlying text to step aside.

Now you've got a sidebar element that looks as good as a sidebars in any professional document—including this one.

Tables

Tables, a new AppleWorks 6 feature, represent a special kind of frame that you can create in any AppleWorks module. Tables let you present information in a grid or matrix. In less-accomplished word processors, formatting and creating such a display is frequently a cause of panic (see Figure 12-9).

Note: Tables are a new feature in AppleWorks 6—unless you've been using the *Japanese* version of AppleWorks/ClarisWorks, in which case you've been enjoying the Tables feature since version *4!*

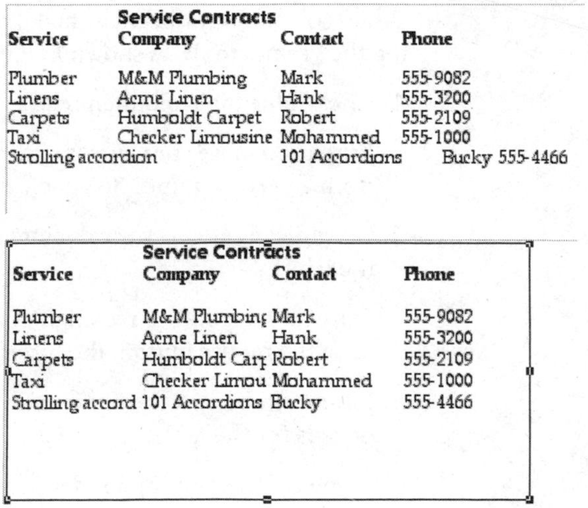

Figure 12-9:
In the dark days before AppleWorks 6, you might have had to create tables painstakingly, by pressing the Tab key between columns, and making an appointment with your therapist every time a particular column item was too wide (top). In AppleWorks 5 and earlier versions, life was only slightly better—you had to insert a spreadsheet frame into your document, which had its own problems (such as chopped-off text, as shown at bottom).

Service Contracts

Service	Company	Contact	Phone
Plumber	M&M Plumbing	Mark	555-9082
Linens	Acme Linen	Hank	555-3200
Carpets	Humboldt Carpet	Robert	555-2109
Taxi	Checker Limousine	Mohammed	555-1000
Strolling accordion		101 Accordions	Bucky 555-4466

Service Contracts

Service	Company	Contact	Phone
Plumber	M&M Plumbing	Mark	555-9082
Linens	Acme Linen	Hank	555-3200
Carpets	Humboldt Carp	Robert	555-2109
Taxi	Checker Limou	Mohammed	555-1000
Strolling accord	101 Accordions	Bucky	555-4466

Unlike the two alternate methods shown in Figure 12-9, AppleWorks tables feature automatically stretching cells—as you type more information into one of the cells, its entire row grows vertically to accommodate the new text. This self-alignment feature is by far the most important aspect of tables. But they're filled with other useful features, such as the ability to place pictures, sounds, movies, and even other frames inside a table cell. (See Figure 12-10.)

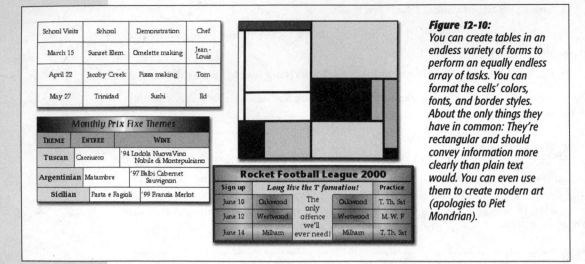

School Visits	School	Demonstration	Chef
March 15	Sunset Elem.	Omelette making	Jean-Louis
April 22	Jacoby Creek	Pizza making	Tom
May 27	Trinidad	Sushi	Ed

Monthly Prix Fixe Themes

THEME	ENTREE	WINE
Tuscan	Cacciucco	'94 Lodola Nuova Vino Nobile di Montepulciano
Argentinian	Matambre	'97 Balbi Cabernet Sauvignon
Sicilian	Pasta e Fagioli	'99 Franzia Merlot

Rocket Football League 2000

Sign up	Long live the T formation!		Practice
June 10	Oakwood	The only offence we'll ever need!	Oakwood	T, Th, Sat
June 12	Westwood		Westwood	M, W, F
June 14	Milham		Milham	T, Th, Sat

Figure 12-10:
You can create tables in an endless variety of forms to perform an equally endless array of tasks. You can format the cells' colors, fonts, and border styles. About the only things they have in common: They're rectangular and should convey information more clearly than plain text would. You can even use them to create modern art (apologies to Piet Mondrian).

Adding a Table

In a word processing document, you can add a table as an *inline* object by choosing Table→Insert Table; in any module, you can add a table as a frame by using the Table tool. As always, begin by making sure that the Tools window is open and showing the Frames tools, as shown in Figure 12-2.

1. **Click Table tool, and then release the mouse.**

   When you move your cursor back over the document window, the cursor changes from an arrow pointer to a table icon.

2. **Drag diagonally in your document window, creating a rectangular outline for the new table.**

   For example, draw a rectangle that's about three by four inches. When you release the mouse button, the Insert Table dialog box appears (Figure 12-11).

3. **Enter numbers in the Rows and Columns boxes to determine the initial layout of cells for the table.**

   If you try to cram in too many rows and columns to fit the box you've drawn—the limit is six rows or columns per inch—AppleWorks beeps and lets you know the maximum number allowed.

4. **Click OK.**

   AppleWorks creates the new table with the insertion point blinking in the first cell.

5. To enter text into the upper-left cell of the table, just start typing—otherwise, click another cell and then type.

You can jump into any neighboring cell by pressing ⌘-arrow key (up, down, left, or right).

If your typing reaches the bottom of a cell, the row of cells automatically expands to accommodate the text. This, of course, is one of the primary benefits of the table feature; but if you need each row to be exactly the same height, you can turn this feature off by choosing Table→Auto Resize.

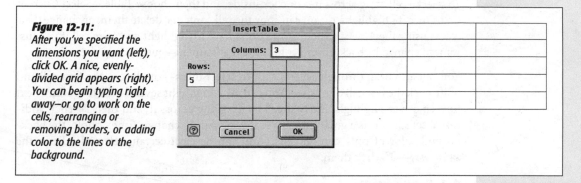

Figure 12-11:
After you've specified the dimensions you want (left), click OK. A nice, evenly-divided grid appears (right). You can begin typing right away—or go to work on the cells, rearranging or removing borders, or adding color to the lines or the background.

Adding and Deleting Rows and Columns

Just as your table rows are infinitely stretchy to accommodate text that overflows a cell, so the table itself can accommodate almost anything anyone can do to it:

- **To add another row:** Drag across an entire existing row. Choose Table→Insert Cells. AppleWorks creates a duplicate of the row just above the one you selected, complete with any extra or missing divider lines, blocked-out diagonal line cells, adjusted row heights, and so on.

  As a matter of fact, if you begin this step by highlighting *more* than one row, AppleWorks duplicates the entire set of them, giving you an easy way to create, for example, five more rows.

- **To remove a row:** Highlight the entire row (or more than one row). Then choose Table→Delete Cells. (If you deleted the wrong cells, choose Edit→Undo and try again.)

- **To adjust column widths:** Move the I-beam cursor over a cell dividing line. When it changes to the line-adjusting cursor shape, drag the line horizontally.

Tip: Usually, dragging a line in a table moves the *entire* line, from top to bottom (or side to side) of the entire table. If you turn on Table→Line Segment Selection, however, dragging a line moves only *that cell border,* thus throwing the line out of alignment with the rest of its row or column. (Turn off Table→Line Segment Selection to restore the original behavior.)

As a shortcut, you can Option-drag to adjust only a single cell border, not the entire table line.

Selecting a Table

When you click a table frame to select it, AppleWorks summons the Arrange menu that's usually found in the Drawing module. Now you can move, delete, cut, or clear the table, change its outline or overall color scheme using the Accents palette, and so on.

With a *second* click on a selected table frame (or a double-click an unselected table), you enter the table-editing mode, where you can enter and edit text in cells, manipulate cell borders, and access the commands in the Table menu.

Selecting Cells

To select a cell, drag across it—or click inside, and then choose Table→Select Current Cell. Once it's highlighted, you can copy the cell contents, delete them, or change their colors using the Accents palette. (You don't have to highlight an entire cell if you just want to change its background color or text alignment—just click in the cell.)

You can also drag through several cells to select them—or click in the first cell and Shift-click the last cell of a range. You can even highlight several cells that aren't next to each other: Highlight the first cell by dragging across it, and then ⌘-click additional cells. (This is a great time-saver if you want to change, for example, the background color of only certain cells.) You can deselect certain selected cells in the same way—⌘-click them.

Subdividing Cells

You can divide table cells into smaller cells in two ways. You can use the Table Cutting tool, as shown in Figure 12-12.

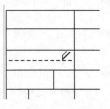

Figure 12-12:
In Table editing mode, click the Table Cutting tool (left), which is supposed to look like an Xact-O knife. Then drag across cells to slice and dice them into smaller and smaller fragments (right). When you're finished chopping up cells, click the icon to the left of the Table Cutting tool, which puts you back into regular table-editing mode.

You can also divide cells in a more orderly fashion by selecting a cell or a rectangular group of cells, and choosing Table→Subdivide Cells. AppleWorks displays the Subdivide Cells dialog box—which looks just like the Insert Table dialog box—in which you can specify how you want to subdivide the selection. This is the secret to adding a table within a cell within a cell within a cell.

Caution: Unfortunately, tables with subdivided cells don't come out well when you export your AppleWorks document as an HTML document (Web page), which is one of the occasions when this feature would be most useful.

If your desire is to create *fewer* cells instead of more, Option-click a cell border and press Delete to remove one border at a time. Alternatively, highlight two or more cells that form a rectangular shape; then choose Table→Merge Cells. AppleWorks combines the selected cells into one megacell. If you'd typed anything into the cells, it's all still there—but now each piece of text is separated by a Tab instead of a cell dividing line.

Borders and Background Shading

AppleWorks lets you change the border style of individual cells, blocks of cells, or the entire table. A border you apply to a range of cells affects only the outside border of the range, not the intra-range borders.

You can change cell and table borders in any of these ways:

- **To change individual cell outlines:** Select a cell or range of cells. Then choose Table→Line Styles; from the pop-up menu, choose a solid, dashed, dotted, or double line style.

  Then, on the Accents palette, click Pen. The Line, Colors, and Patterns tabs are now available; anything you click on these panels changes the border styles of the highlighted cells. Choose the other line features you desire.

- **To change cell background colors:** Once again, start by dragging through the cells you want to change. Now click the Fill button at the top of the Accents palette; the Color and Pattern panels are now available to you for changing the background of the selected cells.

- **To change the overall table border:** It's worth noting that the very outside table border—the frame border, in other words—is considered a *separate* outline, a box that's just *outside* the cell borders; you can change its color and line characteristics independently of the cell borders. To do so, click the Arrow tool on the Tools window; click the table once, if it's not already selected. Then, on the Accents palette, click Pen; use the Line, Colors, and Patterns tabs to change the table outline.

GEM IN THE ROUGH

Creating the T-Cell

AppleWorks requires cells to be rectangular—but if you need a T-shaped or L-shaped cell, you can hide cell borders so that a random grouping of cells can appear to be one entity (as shown in Figure 12-10 at lower right).

To do so, turn on Table→Line Segment Selection. Click the cell wall that you'd like to make invisible. In the Accents palette, click Pen, then click the Line tab; choose None. Repeat with other cell walls as necessary.

By the way: This procedure hides the *lines,* but preserves the "cellness" of your table. The contents of the cells, in other words, remain in their individual cells, even though you've hidden the borders. Remember that you can also remove cell borders *completely,* allowing cell contents to merge, by Option-clicking individual line segments and then pressing Delete. (Unfortunately, AppleWorks lets you remove cell borders in this way only if doing so *won't* create a T- or L-shaped cell.)

Tip: Because the table outline and cell outlines are independent, you can create an attractive two-toned, 3D look to the outline of your table. Start by formatting the overall table border with one color and line thickness; then drag through the table cells from upper-left to lower-right, highlighting all of them, and use the Accents palette again to choose a *different* line style or color.

- **To change the overall table background color:** Make sure that the table itself (and not any cells inside it) is selected. Now, on the Accents palette, click Fill; the Color, Pattern, *and* Wallpaper and Gradient tabs are now available to you, making it possible to create vivid (or overwhelming) tables like the one shown at lower-right Figure 12-10. (This whole-table formatting doesn't override individual cell formatting, however; if you've made one cell blue, giving the overall table a different color or pattern doesn't disturb the cell you formatted individually.)

Table Text Formatting

You can format text in a table cell using all the tools available for word processing—the ruler, the commands in the Text menu, and so on. You can also choose Table→Vertical Alignment to make text attach itself to the top, the bottom, or the vertical center of its cell.

AppleWorks also gives you the ability to use *style sheets* (see page 61) with tables; Figure 12-13 shows an example.

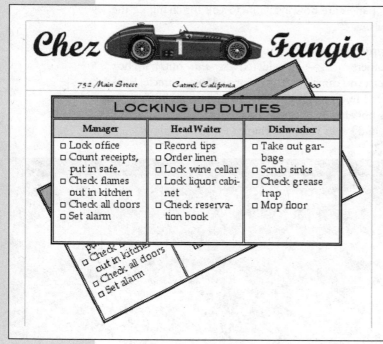

Figure 12-13:
You can format individual cells using table style sheets. You can, for example, format a cell using Outline style, so that each paragraph is preceded by a bullet, number, or checkbox. To do so, drag through the text to highlight it; then choose Format→Show Styles to make the Styles window appear. Double-click a style's name to apply it. And speaking of formatting: Because tables are objects, you can layer, rotate, or group them, just like other objects.

Table Styles

In addition to using word processing style sheets to format *text* in your cells, you can also use *table* style sheets to format the cells themselves. Using table styles offers the usual benefits of style sheets:

- It's very easy to apply complex formatting (yellow interior, bright red top row with a thick double underline beneath it, diagonal slash through the upper-left cell) to a table with a single click.

- When you change the definition of the style (making that light blue a darker blue, for example), all of the affected tables in your document are instantly updated.

Applying a table style

AppleWorks comes with four prefab table styles, and you can make more of your own. To use a table style, see Figure 12-14.

Figure 12-14:
Choose Format→Show Styles to open the Styles window (right); double-click one of the table styles you see there (such as "Blue & Purple Table"). If you'd selected the entire table, Apple-Works reformats the entire table (bottom left); if you'd highlighted only a few cells within it, AppleWorks treats the selection as a miniature table unto itself.

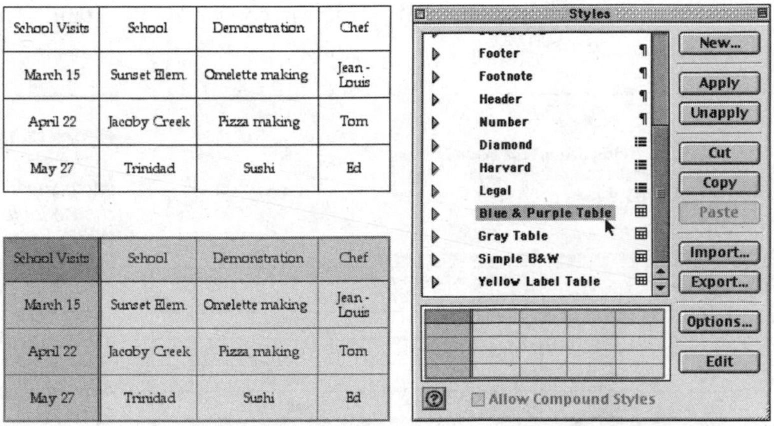

Defining a table style

To create a new table style, format a table exactly the way you want it, complete with fonts, borders, backgrounds, diagonal lines, and so on. Cell sizes aren't included in the style.

1. **Choose Format→Show Styles.**

   The Styles window appears.

2. **Click New.**

   AppleWorks displays the New Style dialog box.

3. **Name the new style, choose the Table radio button, and turn on the checkbox for "Inherit document selection format." Click OK.**

   The dialog box closes; you return to the Edit Styles window. You're still in the style-editing mode, however; if you need to make any additional formatting changes, you can do so with the "S" editing cursor. When you're finished, click Done.

Your new style is now included in the list of available styles.

Note: If you apply a table style to a table whose design doesn't match the one you used as a model, your results may vary. Table styles track the configuration of the outermost rows and columns, and of the "interior" cells. If a certain table is two by three cells, it doesn't *have* any interior cells, so the "outer cells" definition of your table style won't kick in.

Converting Table to Text (or Text to Table)

All of this table formatting is well and good, but most of the world's tables aren't, alas, in AppleWorks format. Résumés you created in AppleWorks 5, tabular data exported from databases, and other kinds of columnar data fill the earth.

Fortunately, if these old-style tables were created using tab stops between columns (as most are), AppleWorks can convert it into a table frame. Figure 12-15 shows the procedure.

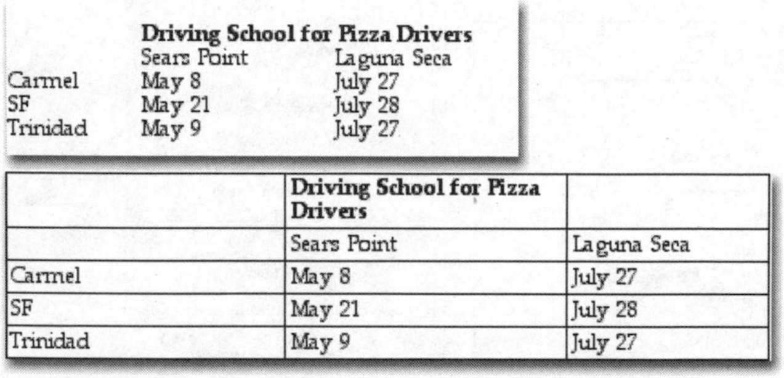

Driving School for Pizza Drivers

	Sears Point	Laguna Seca
Carmel	May 8	July 27
SF	May 21	July 28
Trinidad	May 9	July 27

	Driving School for Pizza Drivers	
	Sears Point	Laguna Seca
Carmel	May 8	July 27
SF	May 21	July 28
Trinidad	May 9	July 27

Figure 12-15:
To convert a humble tab-built table (top) into a SuperTable, highlight it. Then choose Table→Convert To Table. Apple-Works transforms the text table into an inline table frame (bottom). You can convert an inline table to a drawing object table—in order to wrap text around it, for example—by selecting it and then choosing Edit→Cut. Finally, click the Arrow tool in the Tools window; choose Edit→Paste.

You can also convert a table *back* into tab-separated text, for the purposes of pasting into another word processor, for example. Doing so requires that you convert the table into an *inline* table (one that's in a word processing document), if it isn't already, like this:

1. **On the Tools window, click the Arrow tool. Click the table to select it.**

   The usual selection handles appear around its perimeter.

2. **Choose Edit→Cut.**

   The table disappears from the document.

3. **Create a new word processing document (or open an existing one). Click where you want the table to appear, and then choose Edit→Paste.**

   The table appears.

---

4. Click the Arrow (on the Tools window), select the table, and then choose Table→ Convert To Text.

AppleWorks turns your table into a series of tab-separated text columns. Any formatting you've done to your original table's borders and fancy cell-merging tricks disappear in the process.

The Tables Tutorial

AppleWorks creates every new table with a nice, even matrix of cells—but that's just the starting point for table design. You can move cell dividing lines, add new dividers, remove dividers that you don't want, add background color or patterns, and format the text.

Here's an example: Suppose that you want to make the title stretch across all three columns, as shown in Figure 12-16. Your first objective is to remove the cell dividing lines from the first row.

1. **Drag through the three columns in the top row. Choose Table→Merge Cells.**

   You wind up with one giant cell stretching across the top of the table.

2. **Enter a title for the table in the top row, such as *Monthly Prix Fixe Themes.* Click the Center text alignment button in the ruler.**

   You might also want to format the title using the commands in the Text menu; a larger, more interesting font would definitely be in order.

3. **Choose Table→Vertical Alignment; from the submenu, choose the middle icon.**

   AppleWorks shifts the text downward, so that it's nicely centered in the cell. For the next step, you'll need the Accents palette; if you don't see it on the screen, choose Window→Show Accents.

4. **In the Accents palette, click the Colors tab, click Fill, and choose a color for the cell background.**

   Next, you'll fill in the first cell in the second row. Remember that you can navigate your table cells by pressing ⌘-arrow keys, like this:

Figure 12-16:
AppleWorks automatically adjusts row height to accommodate the contents of a table cell, but you can override its decisions by manually adjusting the table lines. In a table, you can format individual text characters in a cell; you can even use Tab and Return characters within a cell. You definitely can't do any of that in a spreadsheet.

Monthly Prix Fixe Themes		
THEME	**ENTREE**	**WINE**
Tuscan	Cacciucco	'94 Lodola Nuova Vino Nobile di Montepulciano
Argentinian	Matambre	'97 Balbi Cabernet Sauvignon
Sicilian	Pasta e Fagioli	'99 Franzia Merlot

5. Press ⌘-right arrow to make the insertion point jump into the first cell in the second row. Type *Theme*; press ⌘-right arrow; type *Entree*; press ⌘-right arrow; type *Wines*. Continue filling out the table until it looks something like Figure 12-16.

6. To indicate a cell intentionally left empty (or a food that's off-limits to your wheat-free, low-glycemic diet), click a cell or drag through several cells, and choose Table→Diagonal Line.

The Diagonal Line dialog box appears, where you can choose the type of line to cross out the cell with, its width, color, and pattern.

7. Use the pop-up menus to specify a diagonal line style, and then click OK.

AppleWorks applies the mark to each cell in the selection.

Mail Merge

When the time comes to send out invitations to the high-school reunion, letters for your latest fund-raiser, thank-you letters to your legion of hard-working campaign workers, or liability releases for the parents of every player on the soccer team, AppleWorks is standing by to aid you with a *mail merge,* better known as "personalized form letters."

In the preceding pages, you may have noticed that the Database module was conspicuously absent from the fun of frames. There's no such thing as a Database frame, but you *can* use database data in other modules using a mail merge. A merge, or mail merge, combines data from selected fields of a database with a word processing document (or frame), spreadsheet document (or frame), or table.

Tip: You might assume that you can't merge database information with a drawing document, but you can—if you first insert a word processing frame, spreadsheet frame, or table.

Using a mail merge, you write a letter as you normally would in the Word Processing module; then you insert *merge fields* that are linked to a database file. The difference in impact is huge; instead of this:

> Dear Sir or Madam: Please consider donating even more this year
> than you did last year.

—your letter will say:

> Dear Mr. Jackson: Thanks to your generous donation last year of
> $50, we have been better able to serve all your neighbors on Baxter
> Road. We hope that this year, you'll consider a donation of $75.

AppleWorks performs this trick by inserting *placeholders,* which are linked to the database, into the word processing document. Then when the time comes to print the letter, AppleWorks plugs in the information from the database and prints one letter for each record in the database—each personally tailored for the recipient.

The basic steps for creating a mail merge are:

1. Create a database.

2. Create a form letter with merge fields linked to the database.

3. Perform the merge.

The usual result of a merge is printed documents, but AppleWorks can also combine all the merged documents into one new document, or save each merged document as a new file.

The Merge Form

You create the form letter (which Apple calls a *merge form*) just as you would any other word processing document. You can insert your database-field placeholders either as you type the letter, or after it's complete.

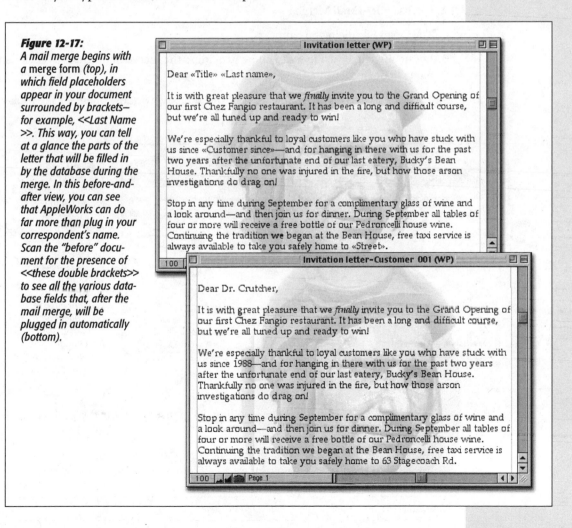

Figure 12-17:
A mail merge begins with a merge form (top), in which field placeholders appear in your document surrounded by brackets— for example, <<Last Name >>. This way, you can tell at a glance the parts of the letter that will be filled in by the database during the merge. In this before-and-after view, you can see that AppleWorks can do far more than plug in your correspondent's name. Scan the "before" document for the presence of <<these double brackets>> to see all the various database fields that, after the mail merge, will be plugged in automatically (bottom).

Invitation letter (WP)

Dear «Title» «Last name»,

It is with great pleasure that we *finally* invite you to the Grand Opening of our first Chez Fangio restaurant. It has been a long and difficult course, but we're all tuned up and ready to win!

We're especially thankful to loyal customers like you who have stuck with us since «Customer since»—and for hanging in there with us for the past two years after the unfortunate end of our last eatery, Bucky's Bean House. Thankfully no one was injured in the fire, but how those arson investigations do drag on!

Stop in any time during September for a complimentary glass of wine and a look around—and then join us for dinner. During September all tables of four or more will receive a free bottle of our Pedroncelli house wine. Continuing the tradition we began at the Bean House, free taxi service is always available to take you safely home to «Street».

Invitation letter~Customer 001 (WP)

Dear Dr. Crutcher,

It is with great pleasure that we *finally* invite you to the Grand Opening of our first Chez Fangio restaurant. It has been a long and difficult course, but we're all tuned up and ready to win!

We're especially thankful to loyal customers like you who have stuck with us since 1988—and for hanging in there with us for the past two years after the unfortunate end of our last eatery, Bucky's Bean House. Thankfully no one was injured in the fire, but how those arson investigations do drag on!

Stop in any time during September for a complimentary glass of wine and a look around—and then join us for dinner. During September all tables of four or more will receive a free bottle of our Pedroncelli house wine. Continuing the tradition we began at the Bean House, free taxi service is always available to take you safely home to 63 Stagecoach Rd.

Merge fields inherit the font formatting (fonts, styles, and so on) of the form letter; after the merge is complete, you can't tell which words were in the form letter and which words came from the database. If you *do* want the merge fields to stand out, you can use any of the usual font formatting techniques to change their appearance (such as bold or italic). Each field is a single inline object as far as the word processor is concerned, however; so although a field may contain several words, they all must share the same font formatting.

Before you set up a form letter, you'll need to create the database to merge with, if you don't already have one. Then proceed like this:

1. **Create a new word processing document, or open an existing document.**

   If you're adding merge fields to an existing document, place the insertion point where you want the first field (just after "Dear Mr. and Mrs.," for example).

2. **Choose File→Mail Merge.**

   The Open File dialog box appears.

3. **Locate the database file that will be providing the merge data. Double-click its name to open it.**

   The Mail Merge window appears, and the database window opens in the background (see Figure 12-18).

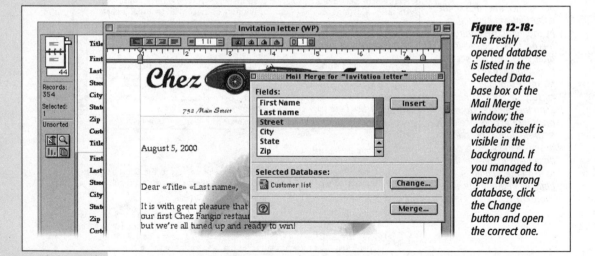

Figure 12-18:
The freshly opened database is listed in the Selected Database box of the Mail Merge window; the database itself is visible in the background. If you managed to open the wrong database, click the Change button and open the correct one.

4. **Double-click a field name in the scrolling list to insert it in the merge document at the insertion point.**

   All the fields in the selected database—not just those of the current *layout*—are listed in the scrolling list. You can use a field more than once, if you desire.

Note: You can't insert summary fields into your form letter.

---

5. **Position the insertion point where you want the next field inserted; repeat step 4.**

   The Mail Merge window remains open, so you can click back and forth between it and the document window. Continue this way until you've inserted all of the field placeholders you need.

Tip: In order to see your entire document window and the Mail Merge window on a small Mac screen, drag the Mail Merge window off the right edge of the screen so you see just the field names. As long as you double-click the fields to insert them, you don't need to use the Insert button. You don't need the scroll bar, either; you can scroll the list by dragging inside it.

---

6. **Choose File→Save.**

   AppleWorks saves the form letter along with its links to the database file. From now on, whenever you open this document and choose File→Mail Merge, you'll see the appropriate database listed in the Mail Merge window Database box.

Note: You can't incorporate data from more than one database into a single form letter. (You can, however, incorporate *one* database into *more than one* form letter.)

Making the Merge

Before executing the merge, determine whether you want to merge with *all* the database records or just a part of the database. For example, you might want to send your birthday-party invitations only to people who live in your town. You'll have to perform a Find to extract the desired recipients. You can also sort the database before merging so that the documents are printed in your preferred order.

Here's the procedure for all of this:

1. **Open the form letter document, if it's not already open.**

   AppleWorks opens the form letter document, but not the database file.

2. **Open the database to be used for the merge.**

   AppleWorks will merge the data from the *visible records* only. (If you need to review your database basics, see page 87.)

   For example, if you want to use all of the records in the database, choose Organize→Show All Records. To use only a subset of the records, use the Find Mode or Match Records to filter out a subset of the database (page 140).

   You can even choose Organize→Sort Records if you want the merged documents to print in a certain order.

3. **Return to the merge form document by clicking its window. Choose File→Mail Merge.**

   The Mail Merge window appears, as shown in Figure 12-18.

---

4. Click Merge.

AppleWorks displays the Mail Merge Destination dialog box. This is where you tell the program what you want to do with the merged documents.

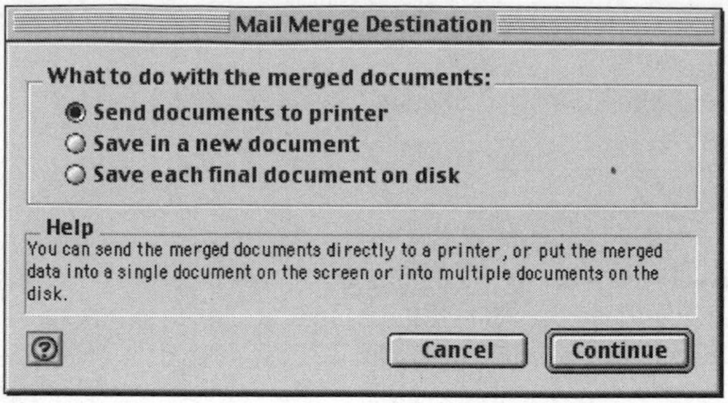

Figure 12-19:
After you tell AppleWorks which database to merge with in the Mail Merge window, you have to tell it what to do with the merged documents. The default choice is "Send documents to printer," but that option doesn't give you the chance to look over the letters before they print.

The Mail Merge Destination dialog box offers you three choices:

- **Send documents to printer.** This option prints each form letter as though it's a separate document, even though no new files are created from the merge. When you click Continue, the Print dialog box appears. Enter the number of copies you want of each merged document, and then click Print; in a moment, the merged documents begin to flow from your printer.

- **Save in a new document.** This option creates a massive new word processing document that contains all of the completed form letters, one after the other. (A page break precedes each letter, so that each begins at the top of a fresh page.) This option gives you the advantage of being able to inspect the result before committing it to paper. It also lets you send the merged file by email, paste it into another word processor, and so on.

- **Save each final document on disk.** Use this choice to create a new file for each merged document—if you have 97 records in your merge database, you'll end up with 97 new AppleWorks documents. You'd use this choice when, for example, you wanted to email these individual documents to their recipients.

When you click Continue, the Save dialog box appears. AppleWorks will create a new folder with the name of the form letter document and the name of the merge database, separated by a hyphen—for example, *Bday letter-Addresses*.

When you click Save, AppleWorks begins creating the new documents and saving them into the new folder. Each document is titled with the name of the folder with a number added, for example, *Bday letter-Addresses 001, Bday letter-Addresses 002,* and so on. A progress bar appears as AppleWorks churns through the merge-and-save process.

Tip: *Before you execute a big merge, it's a good idea to preview a few records to make sure the fields came out the way you intended. Unfortunately, AppleWorks doesn't provide an easy preview function. Instead, choose "Save in a new document" from the Mail Merge Destination window and click Continue. AppleWorks displays a progress bar that tells how many records have been merged. After five or ten records, click Stop. The new file appears in an Untitled document window. Scroll through the pages to make sure the fields appear properly. If they don't, you can go back to your form letter and modify it. If all appears OK, close the window without saving it, choose File→Mail Merge, and go ahead with the full-blown merge.*

Links

If you create a lengthy, complex document—an employee training manual or a recipe book, for example—navigating it to find the information you're looking for can become a challenge. And if your prose refers readers to other documents or Web pages, you can be certain that many of them won't go to the trouble to look up those references—and some of those that do won't find what they're looking for.

AppleWorks provides three kinds of *document links* to solve these problems. Once you've set up the links, they work just like Web-page links: When you click a word, phrase, button, or picture, you're transported to another part of the same document, to a different document, to your email program, or to a page on the Web.

- *Internal* document links provide an easy way to jump to another spot in the same document. For example, clicking the phrase, "His favorite dish was Pasta Fazool," would move you to the end of the document, where you'd find a recipe for that dish.

- *External* document links open other AppleWorks documents on your hard drive. For example, when you click the link, "See Chapter 89 for details," that document would open on cue. Links can also jump to a certain *spot* in another document; for example, clicking "See Number 25 in *101 Full-Moon Metaphors*" can open the appropriate document *and* jump to the correct paragraph.

- *Internet* links open a Web page in your Web browser. For example, if you click the underlined portion of "The Rat Pack homepage is the definitive resource," your browser opens and visits *www.theratpack.com.* Or if you click "Click here to email your Senator," your email program launches and opens a new, pre-addressed outgoing message.

Anchors

To create a link to another part of your document, or to a specific part of another document, you must first insert an *anchor* to mark the destination.

1. **Select the text or object for your anchor.**

   Bits of text, drawing objects, spreadsheet cells, inline frames (but not floating ones), or painted images can all be anchors.

2. Choose Format→Show Links Window.

The Links window appears (Figure 12-20). Click the Anchor tab to display a list of any previously defined anchors.

3. Click New, enter a name for the anchor, and click OK.

AppleWorks adds the anchor name to the list. If you need to edit or remove an anchor, highlight it in the list and click the appropriate button.

Anchors are invisible in the document until you jump to one—either by clicking a document link or by double-clicking the anchor in the Links window. At that point, AppleWorks highlights it.

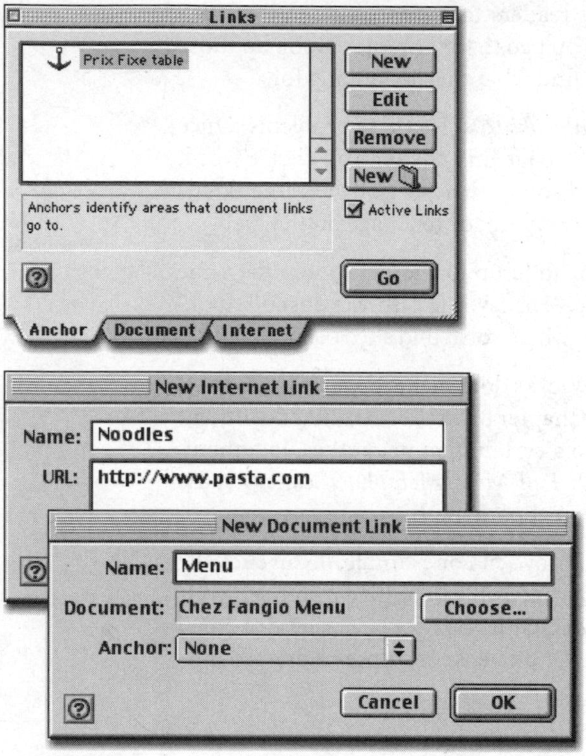

Figure 12-20:
The Show Links Window offers five buttons, as shown here; they let you create a new link, edit an existing link's text (or the URL to which it "points"), remove a link, create a "folder" to organize links, and take you to the selected link, respectively. The three tabs along the bottom—Anchor, Document, and Internet—correspond to the various kinds of links you can create.
Bottom: The New Internet Link and New Document Link windows, which appear when you click New or choose one of the Format→ Create Link commands.

Document Links

If you've defined an anchor, you can create document links that lead to it. Like anchors, document links can be text, objects, spreadsheets cells, frames, or painted images.

1. Select a word, phrase, or other linkable object. Choose Format→Create Link→Document Link.

(You can use the Button bar instead, if you like, as shown in Figure 12-21.) The New Document Link window appears (Figure 12-20).

2. **Enter a name for the link. Using the Anchor pop-up menu, choose the name of an anchor you've already created in your document.**

   All the anchors you've defined for this document appear in the list.

   To create a link that jumps to a *different* AppleWorks document, click Choose, navigate to the file on your hard drive, and click Open.

   To link to an *anchor* in another document, follow up by choosing an anchor name from the newly updated Anchor pop-up menu. (If you leave the pop-up menu set to None, the document will open at the beginning.)

3. **Click OK.**

   Click the new link to test it.

Text that you've defined as a link appears blue and underlined in the document, just like links on a Web page. Images or frames, however, don't give you any such visual clues that they're links. You do get one hint, however: when you move the cursor over any kind of link—text, image, or frame—the arrow pointer changes shape: a pointing-hand icon with a document on top.

Note: Attention, Web-page creators: While document links (links to other documents) look like everyday links when converted to HTML, they don't work—they've just turned into blue underlined text.

Internet Links

Instead of pointing to a document on your hard drive or an anchor in a document, Internet links point to a Web-page address. As long as your computer is hooked up to the Internet, clicking an Internet link opens your default Web browser, connects to the Internet, and displays the linked Web page.

1. **Select an object or some text for your link.**

   As always, text, pictures, frames, and other objects can serve as link material.

2. **Choose Format→Create Link→Internet.**

   The New Internet Link window appears (Figure 12-20).

3. **Type a name for the link; enter the complete Web address (such as *http:// www.apple.com/appleworks)* or email address in the URL box. Click OK.**

   To test the new link, click it; your Web browser opens, memory permitting, and you visit the specified Web page. Or, if you entered an email address, your email program opens automatically with a new blank message, pre-addressed to the address you specified.

Tip: Internet links appear as blue, underlined text. When you move your cursor over an Internet link, the arrow pointer changes to a pointing-hand icon with a globe on top.

Internet links don't just have to launch your Web browser or email program; you can also use Internet links to download a file using the FTP protocol or display a list of messages in an Internet newsgroup. When you enter the address in the URL window, just use the appropriate prefix, as shown here:

Prefix	Effect	Example
http://	Open a web page in your default browser.	*http://www.missingmanual.com*
ftp://	Download a file from an ftp server.	*ftp://ftp.apple.com/lists/*
mailto:	Launch your default email program and address a message.	*mailto:prez@whitehouse.gov*
news:	Open your default newsreader and display a list of messages in a newsgroup.	*news:comp.sys.palmtops.pilot*

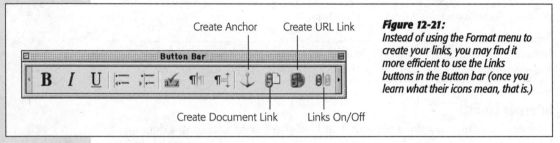

Create Anchor   Create URL Link

Create Document Link   Links On/Off

Figure 12-21:
Instead of using the Format menu to create your links, you may find it more efficient to use the Links buttons in the Button bar (once you learn what their icons mean, that is.)

Editing and Deleting Links

You can edit links in two different ways: by editing the text or graphic *trigger* in your document, or by changing the underlying *target* (the Web address, anchor, or document that opens, for example).

Editing the link triggers

If you try to edit the text or object you've designated as a link, you may find yourself frustrated: When you click in an effort to select it, AppleWorks dutifully *opens* the linked document, Web page, or section. Fortunately, choosing Format→Turn Active Links Off turns the links into mere mortal text that you can edit. You can also turn off the Active Links checkbox in the Links window, or use the Links On/ Off button in the Button bar (Figure 12-21).

Editing the link's target, or deleting a link

Once you have links embedded in your documents, you may want to change the URL to which they point—or remove the links (without removing the text or graphics to which they are attached). The Links window is your key to doing these things.

Start by choosing Format→Show Links Window; click the appropriate tab. To edit a link, click its name in the Links window and then click Edit, which summons the Edit Internet Link window. Here you can change the link's name and URL; click OK to save the changes.

Deleting a link is even easier. Select the link's name in the Links window and click Remove. The text or graphic to which that link was attached gets changed back into regular text or graphics.

Tip: You can use the New Folder button (the one with the word New and a miniature folder) to create a "folder" in the Links window. Use these folders to organize the links in documents with lots of links.

Creating a "Live" Table of Contents

By using document links and Internet links, you can easily make a "live" table of contents. It might list the contents of:

- **Your daily Web rounds.** It's a list of your favorite Web sites, each with a live link.

- **Your Mac's applications.** AppleWorks document links aren't limited to opening AppleWorks documents; they can open *anything* on your hard drive. You might create a tidy application launcher document that contains links to the programs you use most frequently.

- **Your project chapters.** Maybe it's a *literal* table of contents, listing the chapters of a book you're writing; each link opens a different chapter.

- **A long document that needs navigation help.** Such a directory can be a great help for navigating a large document—for example, a restaurant proposal.

In any case, here's how you might proceed:

1. **Create a new document, using the restaurant header, and make a table of contents listing the various sections of your document (Figure 12-22).**

   By creating a table of contents in a separate document, you'll be able to keep both the table of contents and the proposal open on screen at the same time, making it much easier to navigate.

2. **Open the proposal document. Create an** *anchor* **for each section you've listed in the table of contents.**

   See page 359 for details on creating anchors.

3. **Select the first heading in the table of contents. Choose Format→Create Link→Document link.**

   The New Document Link window appears, with the selected text as the link name.

4. **Click Choose.**

   The Open File dialog box appears.

5. **Navigate to the proposal document and click open.**

   The new document link window now shows the document name.

6. **From the Anchor pop-up menu, choose the first anchor. Click OK.**

   You've created the first document link for the table of contents.

7. **Repeat steps 3 through 6 for each heading in the table of contents.**

The table of contents is complete. You're now ready to take your show on the road, whether it's a senior thesis or a meeting with the loan officer for the big presentation of your Car Racing Theme Restaurant proposal. If you've done your homework, she'll soon be waving the green flag.

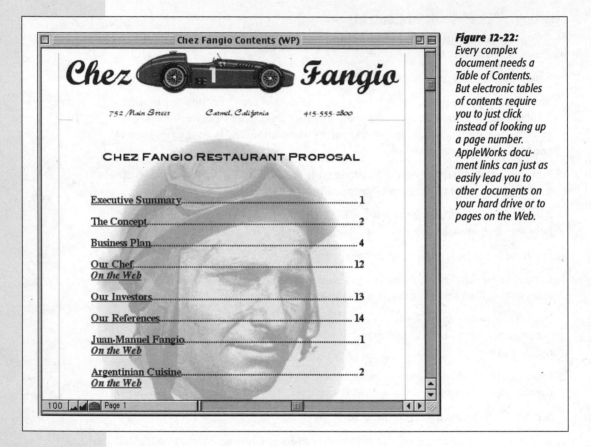

Figure 12-22:
Every complex document needs a Table of Contents. But electronic tables of contents require you to just click instead of looking up a page number. AppleWorks document links can just as easily lead you to other documents on your hard drive or to pages on the Web.

CHAPTER

13

Sharing Documents

N o one is an island, not even AppleWorks—especially in the Internet Age, when it's so easy to send files via email. Sooner or later, you'll probably want to open a file that someone created on another computer, or you'll want to distribute something *you* created in AppleWorks.

Although it may require a little research and good luck, transferring your AppleWorks work is possible, whether from machine to machine, Mac to Windows, Windows to Mac, or from one AppleWorks version to another. This chapter covers all of these situations and more.

AppleWorks 6: The Missing Translators

In days gone by, you could save your AppleWorks documents in any of dozens of different file formats, so that your friends, owners of other word processors, database, and spreadsheet programs, could open your AppleWorks work. Do you enjoy the simplicity and elegance of AppleWorks, but your office requires Microsoft Word documents? No problem—you could just save your AppleWorks file, choose (for example) Word from the File Format pop-up menu, and click Save. When your colleagues opened the resulting Word document, they'd have no idea that you actually created it in AppleWorks.

Previous versions of AppleWorks could *open* documents from dozens of different word processing, database, and spreadsheet programs, too. All this was made possible by a commercial program called MacLinkPlus, which was thoughtfully licensed by Apple and included with every copy of AppleWorks and ClarisWorks.

In its current, financially conservative condition, however, the new Apple decided that it didn't want to pay the licensing fees for MacLinkPlus. To the astonishment of longtime ClarisWorks and AppleWorks users, AppleWorks 6 doesn't come with MacLinkPlus.

As a result, AppleWorks 6 by itself can save its word processing and spreadsheet documents only in a handful of file formats: the AppleWorks format itself (including previous AppleWorks versions), plain text files with no formatting, HTML (Webpage format), and—in version 6.0.3 and later—an intermediary format called RTF (Rich Text Format). Microsoft Word and most page-layout programs can open (and export) RTF files; most formatting comes through intact, including bold, italic, text colors, font sizes, and even embedded graphics. But tables, frames, and other elements get lost in the translation.

The Missing Manuals Discount

Even RTF won't help you when somebody sends you, for example, an actual Microsoft Word document that hasn't first been converted to RFT format. If it's important to you to be able to open (or create) such documents, whether on Macs or Windows, MacLinkPlus is still the answer.

MacLinkPlus is now an additional expense, however. Fortunately, thanks to the tireless negotiations of this book's publisher, the offer in the back of this book entitles you to an instant Internet download of MacLinkPlus at 60% off the street price.

Tip: If you own a copy of AppleWorks 5, you can use its file translation capabilities in AppleWorks 6. Install *just the translators* from the AppleWorks 5 CD. These older translators can't handle some of the newer AppleWorks data types, such as tables—but they're fine for converting everyday word processing and spreadsheet documents.

The Built-in Format Translators

If you want to give an AppleWorks 6 document to somebody else who has AppleWorks 6, either the Mac or Windows version, you'll have no problems whatsoever. Just save the file normally (add *.cwk* to the end of its name for use on Windows), and then drag its icon onto the disk, onto the networked hard drive icon, or into an email, that goes to your intended recipient. (See the end of this chapter for specifics on these transfer methods.) AppleWorks 6 documents require no translation or conversion from Mac and Windows; an AppleWorks 6 document is an AppleWorks 6 document, regardless of the kind of computer it's on.

When you want to send your documents to people who use programs *other* than AppleWorks 6, the situation changes dramatically. Now you come face to face with one of AppleWorks 6's greatest shortcomings: its lack of file translation. Without MacLinkPlus, as described in the previous section, your options for saving your work in the file format that other people can open are extremely limited.

The key to converting your work is the File→Save As menu command, which opens a Save dialog box and offers all of AppleWorks' file translation capabilities (see Figure 13-1). In the following sections, you'll read about the Save As file-format pop-up menu options that appear when you try to save each kind of AppleWorks document: word processing, spreadsheet, database, drawing, painting, and presentation.

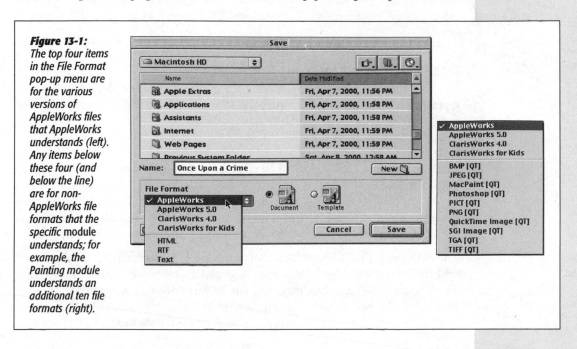

Figure 13-1:
The top four items in the File Format pop-up menu are for the various versions of AppleWorks files that AppleWorks understands (left). Any items below these four (and below the line) are for non-AppleWorks file formats that the specific module understands; for example, the Painting module understands an additional ten file formats (right).

Exchanging with Older AppleWorks Versions

AppleWorks 6 can open documents made by any earlier version of AppleWorks or ClarisWorks. Or rather, it creates an *untitled duplicate* of that older file, leaving the original untouched on your hard drive. That behavior is a safety mechanism that prevents you from making a change to an older document, and in the process updating it to AppleWorks 6.0 format—which can never again be opened in the older version.

It can also *export* special versions of your documents that can be opened by those older applications. When you choose File→Save As, for example, the first four translation options in the File Format pop-up menu (Figure 13-1) are AppleWorks *version translators*. They let you save your AppleWorks 6 document into one of these formats:

- **AppleWorks.** This option refers to the standard AppleWorks 6 file format.

- **AppleWorks 5.** Choose this format if you intend to distribute your work to somebody who uses the previous version of AppleWorks, including AppleWorks 5.0.3, ClarisWorks 5.0, and so on.

- **ClarisWorks 4.** Use this option when exporting your documents to people who use the even older AppleWorks predecessor, ClarisWorks 4.

- **ClarisWorks for Kids** is a special, now discontinued version of ClarisWorks that was designed with a simplified interface for use by kids.

Caution: When you save your document into file formats that older versions of AppleWorks can read, AppleWorks 6 *tables* are translated into pictures that you can't edit after translation. (That's because tables were a new feature introduced in AppleWorks 6.) If you'd rather send your recipients tables that they can edit, create the tables the way you did in previous AppleWorks versions—by using a *spreadsheet frame,* as described in Chapter 12.

Exchanging Word Processing Documents

When saving a word processing document that you'll want to open into other programs, AppleWorks offers only three file-format options: plain text, HTML (Web page) documents, and RTF (Rich Text Format) exports.

Plain text

When you choose File→Save As and choose the Text option from the File Format pop-up menu, the result is what's known as a *plain text* file. The good news is that any word processor on earth, regardless of the computer it's running on, can open plain text files and reveal the words inside. You can even paste the contents of a text file into an email message for added certainty that your recipient will get every word.

The bad news is that plain text files don't contain *any* formatting. Bold, italic, colors, font choices, centered text, tables, graphs, graphics, embedded frames, and virtually all other kinds of formatting that make AppleWorks documents so attractive disappear in the translation. For most purposes, the loss of even rudimentary text formatting makes it worthless for creating documents that you'll exchange with co-workers.

HTML

The other file-format option available to you when saving word processing documents is HTML, or Web-page documents (see Chapter 10).

In times gone by, you might have scoffed at this solution; you might have assumed that the documents you distribute in this format would have to be opened in your recipients' *Web browsers,* not their word processors. Until recently, opening such exported documents in a word processor produced nothing but a screen full of programming codes. But modern word processors, especially Microsoft Word, do a reasonable job of converting HTML documents into traditional word processing documents, *formatting intact* (Figure 13-2).

If you've embedded graphics in your AppleWorks word processing document, begin the exporting process by creating a folder on the hard drive. This folder will contain both the text (HTML) file as well as the graphics files, which AppleWorks will save separately as individual files (see page 295). Then it's up to you to transfer the entire folder to your recipients. When they open the HTML document, they'll see a document that looks *mostly* like the original (see Figure 13-2).

RTF

As noted on page 366, by far the most useful text-export option is RTF, which Apple restored to AppleWorks in version 6.0.3. Microsoft invented this intermediary file format to help move documents among rival word processors and page-layout programs with formatting (even graphics) intact.

Being able to import and export RTF files isn't as convenient as creating and opening Word documents directly, but it's a lot less hassle than HTML exports.

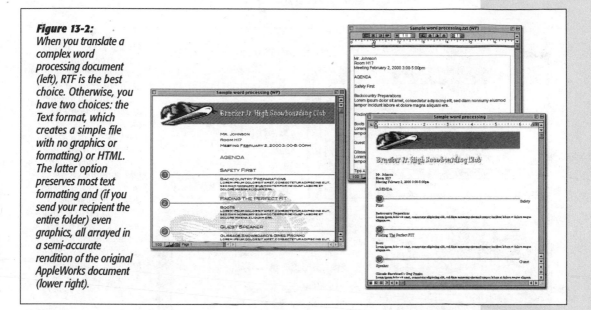

Figure 13-2:
When you translate a complex word processing document (left), RTF is the best choice. Otherwise, you have two choices: the Text format, which creates a simple file with no graphics or formatting) or HTML. The latter option preserves most text formatting and (if you send your recipient the entire folder) even graphics, all arrayed in a semi-accurate rendition of the original AppleWorks document (lower right).

Saving your AppleWorks file as HTML, RTF, or Text

To export your AppleWorks word processing document as one of these three kinds of files, choose File→Save As. In the resulting dialog box, use the File Format popup menu to specify Text, RTF, or HTML. To help you differentiate the exported file from your original AppleWorks document, and to assist Windows computers in opening the file you're sending, add the suffix *.htm* (if it's HTML), *.txt* (if it's text), or *.rtf* (if it's Rich Text Format) to the end of the file's name.

Click Save to complete the translation. The result is a new icon on your hard drive, independent of the original AppleWorks document icon.

Exchanging Spreadsheet Documents

When saving an AppleWorks spreadsheet document, you have exactly one file-format choice: ASCII ("ASK-ee") text. This option saves the data in the spreadsheet's cells as a plain text file, like the one described in the previous section, in which a press of the Tab key separates one cell's contenthis from the next.

These *tab-delimited* text files can be smoothly imported into a variety of spreadsheet and database programs (including Microsoft Excel), but, as usual, there's a catch. First, remember that a plain text file contains no formatting or graphics whatsoever. Any colors, fonts, borders, or graphs you created in AppleWorks are lost in the translation.

Worse—much worse—no AppleWorks *formulas* are included when a file is saved as ASCII text. The resulting file contains only the *results* of your formulas, current as of the moment you saved the file.

If transferring spreadsheets to Excel is important to you, in other words, the additional purchase of MacLinkPlus may be worthwhile.

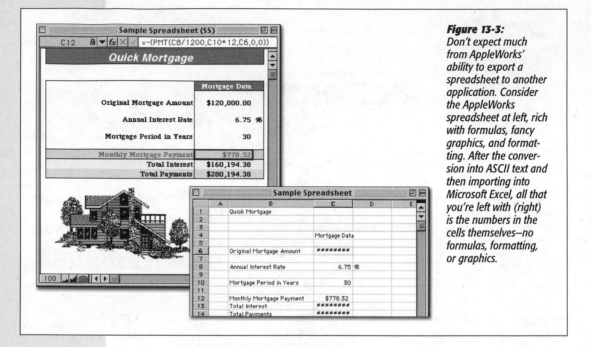

Figure 13-3:
Don't expect much from AppleWorks' ability to export a spreadsheet to another application. Consider the AppleWorks spreadsheet at left, rich with formulas, fancy graphics, and formatting. After the conversion into ASCII text and then importing into Microsoft Excel, all that you're left with (right) is the numbers in the cells themselves—no formulas, formatting, or graphics.

Exporting Database Documents

Just as with spreadsheet documents, AppleWorks offers only a single intermediary export format for transferring database files. Again, it's ASCII text.

Here again, your database information gets converted into a tab-delimited text file, meaning that each database record becomes a single line of typing in a text file, with the contents of each field separated by a tab. Every database program for Mac and Windows, including Microsoft Access and FileMaker Pro, can easily import tab-delimited text files. Once again, however, your exported text file doesn't include any formulas, formatting, layouts, or graphics from your original AppleWorks file. All that's left are the database field names and field contents.

If you're the *recipient* of such a file, importing the tab-delimited text file from AppleWorks isn't quite as easy as just double-clicking its icon. Instead, open your database program (say, Access or FileMaker Pro) and choose File→Import. You encounter an impressive-looking dialog box in which you're supposed to indicate what fields go where in the target database.

For example, to import your AppleWorks data into FileMaker Pro, first set up a database file to receive the data, complete with fields and layouts. Then, when you choose File→Import, FileMaker Pro asks you to match the fields in the incoming text file with the fields you've created in FileMaker. After you've done so, FileMaker Pro fills its fields with the information from the text file.

Tip: Tab-delimited text files are also readable by Microsoft Excel. In other words, you can translate your AppleWorks database files into Excel spreadsheet files by using the tab-delimited text file as an intermediary.

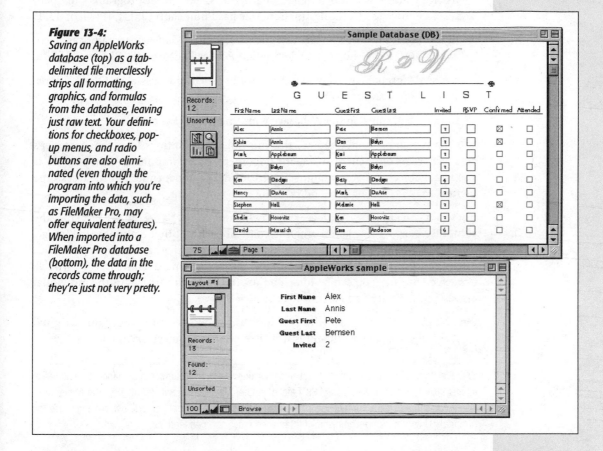

Figure 13-4:
Saving an AppleWorks database (top) as a tab-delimited file mercilessly strips all formatting, graphics, and formulas from the database, leaving just raw text. Your definitions for checkboxes, pop-up menus, and radio buttons are also eliminated (even though the program into which you're importing the data, such as FileMaker Pro, may offer equivalent features). When imported into a FileMaker Pro database (bottom), the data in the records come through; they're just not very pretty.

Exchanging Drawing Documents

If you read this far in the chapter, you're probably far from ecstatic about AppleWorks' ability to export your work into file formats that other computers and other programs can open. But one corner of AppleWorks suffers no such limitation. The program can save *graphics* files—your drawing and painting documents—in a *huge* range of popular Mac and Windows file formats.

This generosity isn't a feature of AppleWorks per se; rather, AppleWorks relies on the QuickTime graphics software built into your Mac to do the dirty work of translating graphics files. That's why, when you save drawing and painting documents, you're offered so many file-format options.

When choosing File→Save As to save a drawing document for export, you have ten graphics formats from which to choose—BMP, JPEG, MacPaint, Photoshop, PICT, PNG, QuickTime Image, SGI Image, TGA, and TIFF. See Chapter 7 for descriptions of these formats, or use this list as a guideline:

- To save your drawing document as a graphics file that *Mac* programs can open, save as Photoshop (if the destination Mac has Photoshop), PICT, JPEG, or TIFF.

- To save your drawing document as a graphics file that *Windows* programs can open, save as BMP, Photoshop (if the destination PC has Photoshop), JPEG, or TIFF.

- To use the graphic in print layout programs (such as PageMaker, QuarkXPress, or InDesign), save as TIFF.

- To use the graphic on the Web, save your image as JPEG or PNG.

You may remember from Chapter 7 that drawings and paintings, from the computer's perspective, are different. In a drawing document, each component of the artwork is a separate object that you can move, resize, or delete, independent of the rest of the picture, making editing easy and printing sharp and clear.

But when you *export* an AppleWorks drawing document, it becomes a *bitmap*—the computer stores it by memorizing the color of each dot that composes the image, forgetting all about the objects that compose the image. In other words, AppleWorks, in essence, turns your drawing document into a painting document. After you've exported your file, you can no longer adjust the positions or sizes of the individual circles, lines, squares, and text inside it.

On the other hand, that's why you used the Save As command: your original AppleWorks drawing document is still alive, well, and object-oriented.

Tip: Only one of the export formats prevents your drawing from becoming a bitmapped, painting-like image: PICT. If you open an exported PICT file in another Macintosh drawing program, or in AppleWorks again, you'll find that the components of the image are still independent objects (which, if you use the Arrange→Ungroup Picture command, you can even move independently).

Exchanging Painting Documents

You can save painting documents in the same ten graphics file formats described in the previous section. Fortunately, because painting documents begin life as bitmaps, they're no less editable after they've been exported as they were in the original AppleWorks document.

Exchanging Presentation Documents

You can't save an AppleWorks 6 presentation document in *any* other file formats, with or without MacLinkPlus. No previous version of AppleWorks offers the presentation feature, so you can't export to them; and there is no common presentation-program-exchange file format, so there's no intermediary file format you could use to export your show to, for example, Microsoft PowerPoint.

If you're truly desperate to get your slide images out of AppleWorks 6, you can create a drawing document with as many pages as there are slides in your presentation file (as described at the end of Chapter 8). Then you can copy the elements of each presentation slide onto the corresponding drawing-document page like this:

1. **View the Master page for the first slide.**

   See Chapter 8 for details on Master slides.

2. **Choose Edit→Select All, then Edit→Copy.**

   You've just copied all of the graphics and text boxes from the Master slide.

3. **Switch to the drawing document. Choose Edit→Paste.**

   The slide elements you copied appear on the drawing document.

4. **Return to the presentation. On the Controls palette, click the Slides tab. Click the first slide. Repeat steps 2 and 3.**

   You've just transferred the *foreground* elements (that is, what's *not* on the Master slide) to the drawing page.

5. **Scroll to the second page of the drawing document. Repeat steps 1 through 4 for the second and subsequent slides.**

   It's not elegant, and it's a lot of work, but it's one way out.

Finally, export the drawing document pages as described in "Exchanging Drawing Documents," earlier in this chapter. The result is a series of graphics files, such as JPEG or BMP files, which you could, in a pinch, import into (for example) Microsoft PowerPoint. (If you hope to be able to edit the individual text boxes or graphics on the exported images once in PowerPoint, use the PICT format when you export from AppleWorks.)

Opening Files From Other Programs

The other side of the compatibility coin is *opening* files created by other programs. As with exporting files, AppleWorks excels at opening *graphics* files, thanks to its connection to the QuickTime extensions. When it comes to opening other kinds of documents, however, AppleWorks is much more limited. Without the assistance of MacLinkPlus, AppleWorks can open only four kinds of non-graphics documents: ASCII Text, HTML, Text, and (in version 6.0.3 and later) RTF.

If buying MacLinkPlus isn't on your agenda, reading documents from your co-workers and friends requires that they do the conversion work on *their* end. You must ask the people sending you files to save them in formats that AppleWorks can read. Here are a few common applications and the file formats in which others should save files so that you can read them.

Microsoft Word

To bring Word files into AppleWorks, ask your friends to save them as *Rich Text Format* (RTF) files; the words, their font formatting, and even embedded graphics will come through alive. (This extremely useful feature isn't available if you're using AppleWorks 6.0, the original release. Visit *www.missingmanual.com* to download the free updater to AppleWorks 6.0.4, or whatever's current as you read this.)

Once the document arrives on your machine, choose File→Open, choose File Formats→RTF, and double-click the RTF document to be opened. AppleWorks imports the file as a word processing document, doing its best to format the text as it looked originally.

FileMaker Pro

Ask your friends to export their records from FileMaker as *tab-separated text* (which is FileMaker's term for tab-delimited text).

Once you've received this transfer file, create an AppleWorks document with fields that match those in the original file. (A phone call to your colleague may be in order here.)

When your empty AppleWorks database is ready to be filled, choose File→Insert. Select the tab-separated text file that FileMaker created and click Insert. You'll be asked to match fields in the text file with the fields in your AppleWorks database. Make your connections, as shown in Figure 13-5, and then click OK.

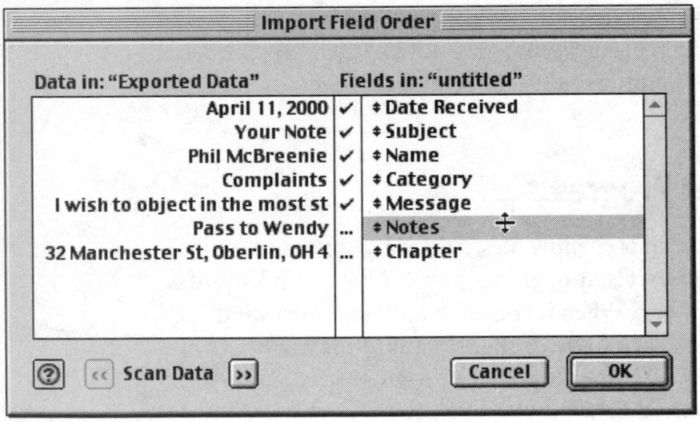

Figure 13-5:
The FileMaker data (one record at a time) appear at left. Drag the AppleWorks fields (on the right) up and down until they match the correct bits of data coming in from the external file (indicated by the double-headed arrow). You can also click the central column to specify which AppleWorks fields will get incoming data. Finally, click the Scan buttons to scroll through the various records in the incoming file, making sure that you've lined up the fields correctly. Click OK to complete the import.

AppleWorks handles the rest, importing the FileMaker data into your new Apple-Works database. As usual, you won't be able to take advantage of such data-entry niceties as checkboxes, pop-up menus, and radio buttons that were in the FileMaker database—you'll have to re-create these special fields in AppleWorks. Nor will any formatting, graphics, or formulas survive the translation.

Tip: If you drag a tab-separated text file's icon onto the AppleWorks 6 application icon, AppleWorks opens it as a spreadsheet–not necessarily a bad thing, but not a database, as you might hope.

Microsoft Excel

Ask your friends to save their Excel spreadsheet files as tab-delimited text files (or what AppleWorks calls ASCII text)—precisely the same exchange format as for transferring database information, described in the previous section.

In AppleWorks 6, choose File→Open, choose File Format→ASCII Text in the dialog box, and finally, navigate to and open the text file. (If you *don't* choose File Format→ASCII Text, AppleWorks will open the tab-delimited file as a word processing document, filled with jumbled numbers and tabs). As always, the usual warning applies: tab-delimited files can't contain graphics, formatting, or formulas.

Tip: As noted in the previous tip, you can also convert a tab-delimited text file into an AppleWorks spreadsheet just by dragging its icon onto the AppleWorks application icon.

Graphics programs

Because AppleWorks can read a broad array of graphics-files formats, receiving graphics files from the Web or from somebody who doesn't use AppleWorks is generally extremely easy. Request that the files submitted to you are in any standard graphics format, such as BMP, EPS, TIFF, JPEG, Photoshop, PICT, or GIF. (Although you may recall from Chapter 7 that AppleWorks can't *create* GIF files, it can indeed *open* them.)

Then, to open the graphic you've received, choose File→Open, navigate to the file, and double-click it. (If it doesn't show up in your Open File dialog box, then it probably wasn't saved in one of the standard graphics file formats.)

Mac to Windows and Back

Tough as it may seem to get AppleWorks data to and from other applications, getting them from one computer platform to another involves even more complications. There are solutions, however.

Transferring Files by Disk

Even in the day of new Macs without floppy drives, floppies still abound on both Macs and Windows. Furthermore, Macs can read floppy disks from Windows PCs—a treat for those who need to do Mac-to-PC (or vice versa) file trades. (The same benefits to apply to Zip disks, too—a Mac can read a PC-formatted Zip disk without even batting an eye.)

Transferring AppleWorks files between Macs and PCs, therefore, is a relative breeze. To do a transfer, copy the file to a PC-formatted floppy (whether you're using a Mac or a PC), and then drag the icon *from* the floppy to the hard drive of the destination computer.

Tip: To create a PC floppy disk on your Mac, insert the floppy disk, choose Special→Erase Disk, and then select DOS from the Format pop-up menu. (Converting a disk to PC format erases anything on it.)

It's also possible to use the Macintosh-formatted disk on a Windows PC, but the necessary software is an added expense. The most comprehensive utility program for this purpose is MacDrive 2000, which works with Windows 95, Windows 98, Windows NT, and Windows 2000 (about $60). For more information, visit *www.media4.com*.

Safe File Names

On Windows, every document's name ends with a three-letter suffix, such as *.txt* for text files or *.cwk* for AppleWorks documents, that helps Windows identify what kind of file it is. If you plan to send a Macintosh AppleWorks file to a Windows machine, you must include this three-letter suffix in the file's name, or you'll shortly be receiving a bewildered phone call or email from your recipient.

Meanwhile, Windows documents can theoretically have much longer names than Macintosh documents. If somebody emails you an AppleWorks document with a very long name from a Windows machine, be prepared to see it show up on your Mac with an oddly truncated name; the longest Mac filename can have only 31 letters.

For an enormous, free reference library of good information regarding Macs, Windows, and persuading the two to get along, visit the MacWindows Web site *(www.mac windows.com)*. Another handy resource is *Crossing Platforms* (O'Reilly & Associates), a two-way translation dictionary for Mac people moving to Windows or vice versa.

Transferring Files by Email

Another great way to get AppleWorks documents from one computer to another, including Mac and Windows machines, is email. As anyone who's tried to send email attachments of this kind can tell you, however, you can't be casual about the way you send such files—make one mistake, and the document emerges at the other end of the transmission as garbage characters.

Four problems complicate the matter of sending documents by email from Mac to PC or PC to Mac:

- The document needs to be in the file format that the other computer can open. For example, you can't send an AppleWorks document to a Windows user who doesn't actually *have* AppleWorks. You can, that is, but your poor recipient won't be able to open the file.

Fortunately, this often confounding principle becomes irrelevant if both you and your correspondent own AppleWorks 6.

- The name of the document, if you're sending the file from a Macintosh to a Windows machine, must end with the letters *.cwk.*

- The *encoding method* used by your email program must result in a file that your recipient's email program can open.

This technical hurdle confuses many beginners, who aren't even aware that email cannot, technically speaking, transmit file attachments—it can only *convert* them into streams of text (the only data the Internet can actually understand), which get reconstituted at the other end. Unfortunately, your email program and your recipient's may use different forms of encoding. The result: your recipient may not be able to open the document you emailed.

Mac email programs, for example, usually convert file attachments using something called *BinHex* encoding; PC programs expect *Base64* or *MIME* encoding.

Fortunately, most Mac email programs let you specify which method you're using; Outlook Express for the Mac *automatically* uses a Mac-and-Windows-compatible encoding method—called AppleDouble. If you have a choice when sending the file attachments to a PC, specify AppleDouble, MIME, or Base 64 encoding, because PCs don't understand BinHex.

If you're sending a file from a PC to a Mac, to the other hand, you don't even have to think about the encoding method; every Mac email program understands the Base 64 or MIME encoding formats automatically.

- Finally, many email programs automatically *compress* file attachments, making them smaller, so they take less time to transmit. Most Macintosh email programs compress files using a software module called *StuffIt;* on the PC, the equivalent is called *ZIP* compression. The lesson here is to send ZIP-compressed files to PC users, and StuffIt archives to Mac users.

Both Macs and Windows machines can open either kind of compressed file—as long as they have the free program called StuffIt Expander. This program comes pre-installed on every Macintosh; Windows users must download it from *www.aladdinsys.com.* Put another way, it's more of an effort for a PC user to open a StuffIt file than for the Mac user to open a ZIP file.

Therefore, if you're a Mac user, consider *not* compressing the files you send to Windows colleagues; most email programs offer this on/off switch. Not compressing files usually means that you can't attach more than one file per email message—especially if you're using America Online, which *automatically* uses StuffIt to compress files if there's more than one attached to an email message.

Transferring Files by Network

Moving AppleWorks documents between Macs and PCs via a network can be a fast and reliable way to make the transfer, particularly if you make such transfers frequently. Just as with almost any other aspect of using Macs and PCs together, however, there are stumbling blocks, caveats, and workarounds. The trick is to get Macs and PCs talking to each other on a network in the first place, because, of course, they don't speak the same networking language.

Setting up the Network

The cheapest and most reliable way to physically connect Macs and PCs is with Ethernet cables. Every recent Macintosh has a built-in Ethernet connector, and adding an Ethernet connector to a PC (if it doesn't already have one) involves installing a circuit board (a *network interface card*) for as little as $10.

To connect the two, all you need is an Ethernet cable for each computer and an Ethernet *hub,* a very inexpensive central box that can accommodate 4, 8, 12, or more Ethernet cables that snake out to different computers. Then you need only appropriate software, as described in this section, to let Macs and Windows connect.

Ways to Make the Connection

Here are a couple of ways to transfer AppleWorks files between Macs and PCs via a network.

- **Make a server.** Recent versions of both Windows and the Mac OS both have small *Web servers* built in—software that turns the computer into a tiny Web site that's accessible by any other Macs or Windows PCs. They can connect your machine either via the Internet or over a local network, like the Ethernet system described above. Usually, as in the Mac's Web Sharing control panel, you can specify a single folder on your hard drive that you want to make available to others on the network.

  By putting the AppleWorks documents you want to share into that special folder, Mac and Windows users on the network can transfer the file to their machines after connecting to yours from within their Web browsers. (The Mac's Personal Web Sharing feature requires that your Mac have a full-time Internet connection, however; regular dial-up modems won't let other people connect to your machine.)

- **Set up a proper network.** If you're willing to buy some utility software and devote a weekend or two to the task, and if you have a technical guru on hand to help you when the setup gets tricky, you create a network of *file servers.* That is, you can make the contents of your hard drive (or a folder on it) available to other computers on the network, whether Macs or Windows PCs.

  To make this cross-platform file sharing work, you can either make your Mac speak the *Windows* networking language, or make Windows PCs speak the *Mac's* networking language. Doing so requires a product like DAVE *(www.thursby.com)* or PC MacLAN *(www.miramarsys.com).* Both programs allow Macs and PCs to bridge the digital divide and converse over a network.

Tip: If you drag an AppleWorks document from a Windows PC onto your Mac, it may lose its invisible *type and creator* codes—invisible four-letter codes that tell the Macintosh which application "belongs to" that document.

If this problem bites you, drag the document's icon onto the AppleWorks application icon to show the Mac which program the document belongs to. Alternatively, open AppleWorks, and then choose File→Open to open the orphaned document.

Either way, after you make some subtle change to the document and then use the File→Save command, AppleWorks reassigns the invisible type and creator codes, so that the problem won't recur with that document.

APPLEWORKS 6: THE MISSING MANUAL

Troubleshooting

I f you use a computer long enough, problems will arise. If you use AppleWorks—especially the original 6.0 release—you may feel like you're having more than your share; odds are, you're right. AppleWorks 6 is based on new technology, designed in part with the migration to Mac OS X in mind; as a result, the program —especially the original, 6.0 release—can sometimes feel slow, or may even crash.

But don't bloody your head against a wall just yet. You can take certain steps to mitigate these annoyances and make AppleWorks faster and more reliable.

Tip: If you're in a hurry, here are the best two troubleshooting tactics in this entire chapter. First, *admit that AppleWorks 6.0 was buggy.* Upgrade to the latest bug-repaired version, 6.0.4 or later (which includes a debugged CarbonLib extension) as soon as possible (from, for example, *www.apple.com/AppleWorks*). Second, *give AppleWorks more memory.* You'll find instructions on page 384.

Understanding AppleWorks

If you understand how AppleWorks works, you'll be better able to handle problems that crop up. Of course, you may not be able to *solve* a few of them (that's why bug-fix releases like AppleWorks 6.0.4 and CarbonLib 1.0.4 exist), but at least you'll be able to work around them.

What AppleWorks Needs to Run

AppleWorks doesn't stand alone as a single icon on your hard drive. Instead, it relies on several pieces of support software, which get installed when AppleWorks is installed. If you have trouble with AppleWorks, you can sometimes solve the problem by replacing or updating the component that controls that area—the QuickTime extensions when you're having trouble importing graphics files, for example.

CarbonLib

CarbonLib ("Carbon lybe"), an icon in your System Folder→Extensions folder, is a chunk of programming code that AppleWorks requires to run on any operating system *before* Mac OS X. Nor does *any* version of CarbonLib work—AppleWorks 6 requires CarbonLib 1.0.2 or later to launch at all.

Unfortunately, CarbonLib 1.0.2 (provided with the original AppleWorks 6) was finicky, to say the least. Many, if not most, of AppleWorks 6.0's crashes and other odd behaviors stem from this piece of software. As Apple continues to refine CarbonLib, these crashes are becoming less and less common; the 1.0.3 version, for example, immediately cleared up dozens of crashing problems. To be sure that Apple-Works is performing at its peak, make sure that you have the latest version of CarbonLib available (see Figure 14-1). (Updates to CarbonLib, as with all Apple system-software updates, are available at *http://asu.info.apple.com.*)

You'll be seeing a lot more of CarbonLib as time goes on. CarbonLib is Apple's way of easing the transition from the classic versions of the Mac OS (including Mac OS 9.x) to the brand new Mac OS X; it lets programs written for Mac OS X run on earlier versions of the Mac OS. Since Mac OS X and earlier Mac OS versions are fundamentally different, CarbonLib's job is a complex and difficult one.

QuickTime

AppleWorks can translate almost every graphics file format in existence thanks to QuickTime, another important icon (set of icons, actually) in your System Folder→Extensions folder. If you're having difficulties with images in AppleWorks (such as not being able to open or save a graphic that you *know* should work), check to make sure that QuickTime—the latest version—is correctly installed on your Mac.

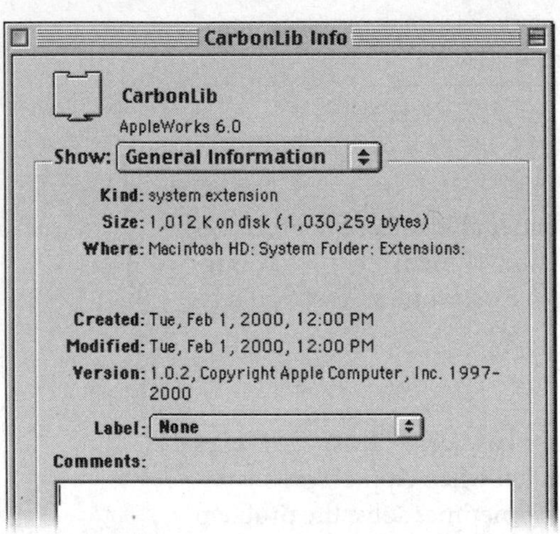

Figure 14-1:
What version of CarbonLib do you have? You can find out by highlighting its icon (which is in System Folder→ Extensions) and then choosing File→Get Info→General Information (or pressing ⌘-I). The CarbonLib Info box pops up; you can discover the version number about halfway down the window (where it says, of course, Version). Get CarbonLib 1.0.3 or later if you value your productivity.

Tip: AppleWorks installs QuickTime 4.0.1 into your System Folder *even* if you have a newer version already installed, such as QuickTime 4.1.2. After installing AppleWorks, therefore, don't forget to re-install your updated QuickTime version.

Internet Config

The Internet Control Panel keeps track of your Internet preferences—such as your email address and preferred home page. AppleWorks 6 requires that both this control panel and its accompanying extension, Internet Config, be installed correctly if you want to use the AppleWorks Internet features. (The Internet control panel should be in the →Control Panels folder; the Internet Config extension should be in your System Folder→Extensions folder.)

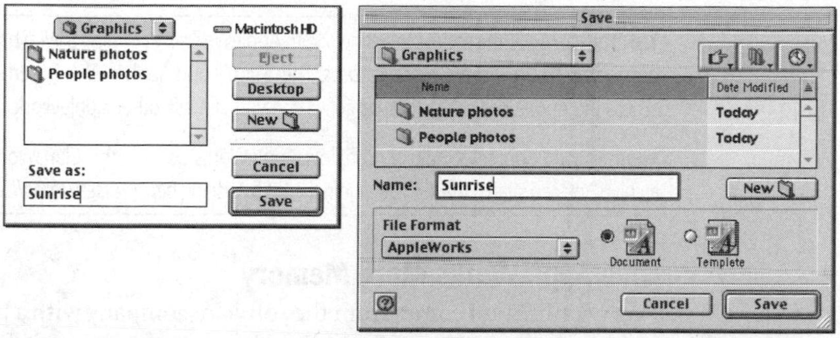

Figure 14-2:
The old look (left) for the standard Save File dialog box and the new one (right). The three "pop-up icons" at the upper right give you access to recently used documents, to your disks and desktop, and to items you've identified as Favorites.

POWER USERS' CLINIC

Self-Repair

Like recent Microsoft applications, AppleWorks can repair itself if some of its required software components get moved, renamed, or deleted. But unlike Microsoft applications, AppleWorks doesn't replace these components automatically; you must *tell* it to do so by running the program called AppleWorks First Run, which is in the AppleWorks 6→AppleWorks Essentials folder.

If you run up against an error message saying that AppleWorks can't launch because, for example, QuickTime or CarbonLib is missing, then double-click the AppleWorks First Run program to launch it. This program cheerfully re-installs the missing components and, if necessary, restarts your computer.

Navigation Services

In an effort to modernize the Mac's Open File and Save File dialog boxes, Apple introduced Navigation Services—a new design for these dialog boxes (see Figure 14-2 for an example of the new features.)

Navigation Services, a software kit built into Mac OS 8.5 and later, accounts for the delays you may experience when using the File→Open, File→Save (on a new document), or File→Save As commands. This delay is, unfortunately, a fact of the software included with the original AppleWorks release.

Fortunately, Apple has been working on fixing this problem, too; the AppleWorks 6.0.3 updater gives you much speedier Navigation Services software. (Saving a document—by pressing ⌘-S, for example—that's *already* been saved isn't slow. It's only the appearance of the Open File or Save File dialog boxes that causes the slowdown.)

Basic Troubleshooting Techniques

A few general Macintosh troubleshooting techniques may help solve your AppleWorks woes. These techniques include giving AppleWorks more memory, calming any extension conflicts, making sure your software is up-to-date, and getting rid of problem preferences.

Tip: You can go to the source to get help with AppleWorks by pointing a Web browser to *www.info.apple.com/support/pages.taf?product=appleworks*. There you'll find Apple's Web-based help area, and you'll be able to access the AppleWorks Tech Exchange, where you can ask other AppleWorks users for help.

Another good source of help from fellow AppleWorks users is the ClarisWorks mailing list and mailing list archive. You can search the archive or join the list by visiting *http://listserv.temple.edu/archives/claris-works.html*.

Give AppleWorks More Memory

Every application comes from the software company with a predetermined memory appetite—an amount of RAM that the program claims for itself when you double-click its icon.

Unfortunately, marketing departments of modern software companies often pressure their programmers to set a low memory requirement. After all, memory is expensive, and software that's RAM-greedy decreases sales. By increasing the memory requirement, you may, in fact, be restoring your software to the memory setting it was *really* intended to have.

AppleWorks is a great example. If you give it more memory, you'll find that almost every feature works more smoothly, the program crashes less often, and everything seems faster and more responsive.

Step 1: Highlight the AppleWorks icon

This step frequently throws beginners, because they may not realize that:

- **You can't adjust the memory appetite for a program that's running.** Check your Application menu (at the far right end of your menu bar). Do you see AppleWorks listed there? If so, choose its name, and then choose File→Quit.

- **You can't adjust the memory appetite for a folder.** The AppleWorks icon sits inside an AppleWorks 6 *folder*. Be sure you've opened that folder and highlighted the *application* icon inside it.

Step 2: Open the Get Info→Memory panel

You can do so by choosing File→Get Info→Memory, by Control-clicking the AppleWorks icon (as shown in Figure 14-3), or by pressing ⌘-I, and then choosing Memory from the pop-up menu in the middle of the resulting dialog box.

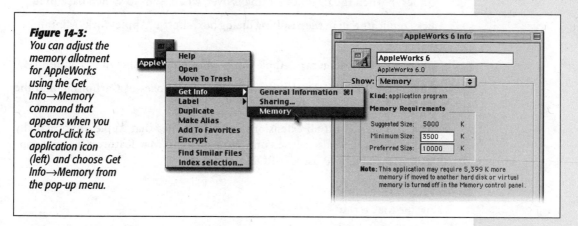

Figure 14-3:
You can adjust the memory allotment for AppleWorks using the Get Info→Memory command that appears when you Control-click its application icon (left) and choose Get Info→Memory from the pop-up menu.

Edit the number in the bottom box—the Preferred Size. If you've been having trouble with the program or getting memory error messages, increase this number by 10 or 20 percent. (If the problems persist, increase it another 10 percent.) After changing the Preferred Size number, close the Get Info window. The job is done.

Tip: You're most likely—almost certain, in fact—to encounter out-of-memory messages when using the AppleWorks Graphics and Presentation modules, especially when you're working with photos or QuickTime movies. You've been warned. Increase AppleWorks memory allotment *a lot,* if you have the memory to spare, before working on a digital photo, movie, or a slide show that contains them.

Extension Conflicts

Extension conflicts are the *number one* source of freezes and crashes on the Mac. If you're experiencing more than your share of such problems while using AppleWorks, you may have an extension problem on your hands.

Extensions are small software packages that affect various aspects of your Mac's behavior. Each extension is represented by one of the icons that appear at the bottom of the screen during the Mac's startup process. Since they act upon the Mac OS at a basic level, they may interfere with other programs that expect the Mac OS to be *unchanged* at that basic level. The result can be just general flakiness or more serious malfunctions such as freezes and crashes.

To resolve an extension conflict, use the Extensions Manager—a program whose sole purpose in life is to determine which extensions, control panels, and startup items are on or off.

One way to go about troubleshooting an extension conflict goes like this:

1. **Choose →Control Panels→Extensions Manager.**

   The Extensions Manager program opens. Note the name of the Set (such as "My Settings"); when the troubleshooting is over, you'll want to switch back to it.

2. **Click Duplicate Set; in the resulting dialog box, choose "AppleWorks Minimum," and click OK.**

   Now the pop-up menu says "AppleWorks Minimum," as shown in Figure 14-4.

3. **Choose Edit→All Off. Click to turn on the checkboxes of CarbonLib and the QuickTime extensions.**

   You've just turned off all extensions except the ones that AppleWorks actually needs to run. You've also turned off lots of standard Mac features: Internet connections, the ability to use CD-ROMs, and so on.

4. **Click Restart.**

   Now the Mac restarts.

5. **Open AppleWorks. Check to see if the problem persists.**

If the AppleWorks-related crashes seem to be gone after restarting, you've successfully determined that one of your extensions or control panels is the source of your headache.

To figure out *which* extension is the troublemaker, you're in for a multi-step procedure called a *conflict test*. This routine involves restarting your Mac repeatedly, each time with a different set of extensions and control panels, until, by trial and error, you narrow your possibilities down to the single one that's causing the problem.

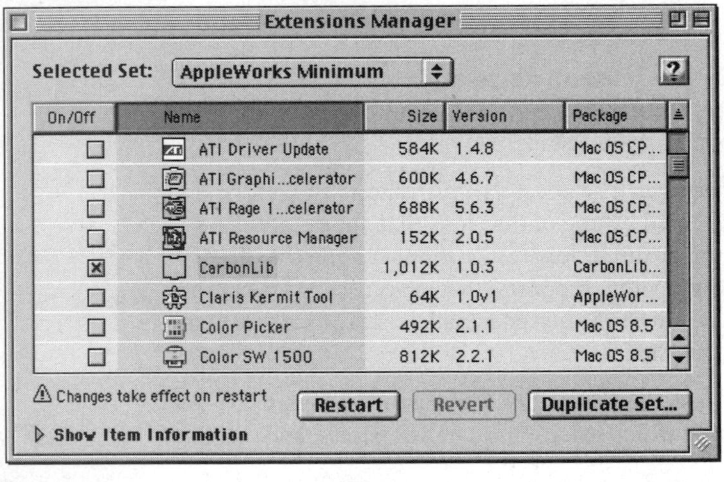

Figure 14-4:
The Extensions Manager can be your best friend when solving an extension conflict. Saved sets of extensions appear in the pop-up menu at top; the lower section lists the control panels and extensions installed on your Mac. CarbonLib and the QuickTime files are the ones AppleWorks requires to run. (Scroll all the way down to see Startup Items, where you can turn off the Auto-Save aliases that AppleWorks puts there.)

For more information, check the Mac OS's built-in help under "Resolving system extension conflicts." For less tedium, buy Conflict Catcher, a program that automates all of this testing. (You can also download, from *www.casadyg.com,* a free three-week trial version.) And for your own sanity, remember that all of this is helpful only if you're experiencing a *repeatable* problem, one that happens every time you perform some AppleWorks step. Intermittent problems are much more troublesome to troubleshoot, and a conflict test won't help you.

Out-Of-Date Software

Sometimes, problems can stem from out-of-date software, particularly when that software is a *device driver* (the software for your printer, scanner, Zip drive, and so on). This is especially true for AppleWorks—if you hear that a free AppleWorks updater is available from Apple's Web site, get it immediately—and its supporting extension, CarbonLib.

Another certainty: AppleWorks 6 is incompatible with older versions of the software for USB-equipped Hewlett-Packard printers in the 600 and 800 series; you'll know you have the problem if the Print dialog boxes don't come up properly when you print an AppleWorks document. Epson printers, likewise, suffer printer problems related to out-of-date drivers—word processing documents may have letters or words truncated.

To solve these problems, install the latest versions of these printers' software drivers. You can find them at the manufacturers' Web sites, or at the VersionTracker Web site *(www.versiontracker.com),* which maintains a *huge* database of the latest Macintosh software updates.

Corrupted Preference Files

Occasionally, a program's preference file becomes scrambled, causing all manner of strange application behavior. To see if this syndrome is causing your AppleWorks problems, open the System Folder→Preferences folder. Move the AppleWorks folder out of the Preferences folder (onto the Desktop, for example).

Now open AppleWorks, which now creates a fresh, untroubled set of preference files. (This process makes the program take longer than usual to launch. That's because AppleWorks is busily re-creating its preference files, including cache files for Assistants, fonts, and translators. The fonts cache can take an especially long time to re-create.)

If the problem goes away, throw out the old AppleWorks preferences folder on your desktop—it probably has corrupted files in it. If the problem persists, on the other hand, then you can assume that corrupt preferences aren't the problem. If you like, move the newly created preferences folder to the Trash, and move the *old* AppleWorks preferences folder back to the Preferences folder where you found it. After all, there's nothing wrong with it.

Note: The corrupted-preference-file syndrome can also affect the Finder. Because the Finder acts as a liaison between all running programs and the Mac OS, corrupted Finder preferences can affect other programs as well—particularly when you're saving or opening a document. Throwing away the Finder Preferences file (in the System Folder→Preferences folder) and then restarting the Mac is a useful trouble-shooting step, too.

Famous AppleWorks Problems

Whatever problems you're having with AppleWorks, look at the bright side: You're probably not alone. The Internet's discussion boards teem with messages about bugs and glitches in AppleWorks 6—the original 6.0 release, that is.

Problem: It's Slow

Some have complained about AppleWorks 6.0 being sluggish, even on the zippiest of Macs. As noted earlier in this chapter, the new CarbonLib and Navigation Services technologies are largely responsible. Fortunately, Apple continues to revise and improve these important software components; CarbonLib 1.0.3, for example, made AppleWorks dramatically faster; the AppleWorks 6.0.4 update made things faster still (it came with an even better CarbonLib).

You can take some steps to make AppleWorks faster, however. Try these tips:

- Give AppleWorks more memory, as described earlier in this chapter.

- Limit the number of items in the AppleWorks 6→Starting Points folder and the number of fonts installed on your Mac. AppleWorks loads those things as it launches; the more items it has to load, the slower it opens.

- Choose Apple Menu→Control Panels→Apple Menu Options; set the three Re-member Recently Used Items values to zero. Your menu will no longer list the most recently opened documents, programs, and network disks, but you may gain a slight speed boost (in all your programs, not only AppleWorks).

- Along the same lines, open AppleWorks and choose Edit→Preferences→General →Files. Set the number of remembered items to 1, then open the AppleWorks 6→Starting Points→Recent Items folder and drag the contents to the Trash.

Internet Problems

As mentioned in Chapter 10, the Internet portion of AppleWorks (the Web tab in the Starting Points window and the Search portion of the Clippings window) doesn't always take the initiative to open an Internet connection. The workarounds:

- Connect to your Internet Service Provider with your modem (using the →Remote Access Status program, for example) *before* you launch AppleWorks.

- Load a Web page in a browser or check your email; sometimes some unrelated Internet activity coaxes AppleWorks into action.

- Try again later—sometimes Apple's servers get swamped.

- Make sure that QuickTime extensions and the Internet control panel are both installed.

The Problems Apple Knew About

Sit down and prepare to be shocked—Apple knew very well about a few problems with AppleWorks. You can read more about some of them in the Late-Breaking News document on the installation CD, but here are some highlights:

- **AppleShare IP 6.3.1.** The Mac OS Server Admin Agent extension, part of AppleShare IP 6.3.1, prevents AppleWorks from launching. You can turn this extension off using Extensions Manager. Keep your eyes open for an update to this extension.

- **AOL Instant Messenger.** If you're using Mac OS 8.5 or 8.5.1 and you have the America Online Instant Messenger extension installed, AppleWorks 6 won't launch. Here, you have two choices: disable AOL Instant Messenger in Extensions Manager, or upgrade your Mac to Mac OS 8.6. (The Mac OS 8.6 updater is included on the AppleWorks 6 CD, if you choose to take the latter route.)

- **GlobalFax 2.5.6.** If your faxed AppleWorks 6 documents are being sent with AppleWorks 6 window names (such as Button bar) instead of the documents' own names, upgrade to GlobalFax 2.6.8 or later.

- **QuicKeys 4.0.** According to Apple's documentation, QuicKeys 4.0 isn't compatible with AppleWorks 6; upgrade to 4.1 or 5.0.

- **ViaVoice 1.0, 1.0.2.** The "Transfer to AppleWorks" 1.0 doesn't work unless you rename your AppleWorks 6 icon (in the AppleWorks folder) to just *AppleWorks*. This fakeout restores function to the "Transfer to AppleWorks" command.

Freezes when switching applications

Sometimes AppleWorks freezes when you switch to it from another program (such as Netscape Communicator 4.72). Try launching AppleWorks before any other applications.

Printer problems

If text that you've rotated looks jagged when printed, smooth the text with Fractional Character Widths. Choose Edit→Preferences→General and select Text in the pop-up menu. Make sure the Fractional Character Widths checkbox is checked. Click OK.

Weird color shifts

When you use one of the AppleWorks color palettes other than the basic, factory-installed one, some of your Mac's items (such as menu bars and window edges) may change to new and interesting colors. This happens when your Mac's →Control Panels→Monitors control panel (or Monitors & Sound control panel) is set to 256 colors. To correct the problem, set your Mac's monitor depth to Thousands or Millions, using the same control panel.

The magical reappearing document

AppleWorks 6's new auto-save feature tracks changes to your AppleWorks documents while you work. If the Mac crashes, AppleWorks launches, unbidden, after you restart, and opens the automatically saved document. Recovered documents are usually in great shape, even if you haven't saved them before.

On the other hand, this automatic-opening routine can also be annoying. To turn it off, choose Edit→Preferences→General; choose Files from the pop-up menu at top. Uncheck the Auto-Save checkbox. Alas, doing so turns off the useful Auto-Save feature completely.

If you like the way AppleWorks can automatically save your documents periodically, but don't like the way AppleWorks launches itself following a Mac crash or freeze, read on. AppleWorks 6 saves aliases to those automatically saved items in the System Folder→Startup Items folder; the original auto-saved items, meanwhile, reside in the AppleWorks 6→AutoSave folder. If, after a crash, you press the Shift key *after* all of your extension icons have appeared on the screen, but *before* the Trash can appears, you prevent whatever's in the System Folder→Startup Items folder from opening—including automatically saved AppleWorks documents.

Part Four:
Appendixes

4

AppleWorks, Menu by Menu

ppleWorks 6 is six programs rolled up into one tight package; it contains a *lot* of menus—one set for each module. As you've probably discovered, to your annoyance or delight, AppleWorks menus *change* depending on the kind of document or frame you're working on.

For example, suppose you've put some text and a spreadsheet frame (such as an at-a-glance financial report for a club meeting) into a drawing document. When you're working with the text, the menus become word-processing menus; when you click a spreadsheet frame, the menus change to the spreadsheet set.

This Appendix covers the menus module by module.

Common Menus

A few menus are the same no matter what kind of AppleWorks document is open.

File Menu

Many of the File-menu commands (including New, Open, Close, Save, and so on) form complete sentences if you add the words, "an AppleWorks document"—for example, "Open (an AppleWorks document)," "Print (an AppleWorks document)," and so on.

- **New.** Creates a new AppleWorks document. The submenu lets you choose the kind of document you want to create: Word Processing, Spreadsheet, Database, Drawing, Painting, or Presentation. Keyboard equivalent: ⌘-N.

Tip: Which kind of document the ⌘-N keystroke produces is up to you; out of the box, AppleWorks is set to give you a word-processing document. Choose Edit→Preferences→General and then click the General tab to view the pop-up menu that controls this behavior.

- **Open.** Opens the standard Macintosh Open File dialog box so that you can choose an existing AppleWorks document to open. The pop-up menus at the bottom of the dialog box can be set to show all the files (of whichever format) that AppleWorks can read, or it can be set to show only a specific kind of AppleWorks document, such as Spreadsheet documents. Use the File Format pop-up menu to screen out all documents except those of a specific type, such as GIF and JPEG. Keyboard equivalent: ⌘-O.

- **Show/Hide Starting Points.** Opens the Starting Points floating window, even if there are AppleWorks documents already open. (See page 10 for details on Starting Points.) If the Starting Points window is open, Show Starting Points becomes Hide Starting Points. Keyboard equivalent: ⌘-1.

- **Close.** Closes the frontmost document window. You'll first be asked if you want to save any unsaved changes. Keyboard equivalent: ⌘-W (for *Window*).

- **Save.** Saves the changes you've made to the frontmost document. This command is dimmed when you've already saved the file and haven't made any changes since. Keyboard equivalent: ⌘-S.

- **Save As.** Makes a copy of the active document (and prompts you for a name and location); closes the original document and leaves the copy open on the screen. Keyboard equivalent: ⌘-Shift-S.

- **Revert.** Throws out any changes you've made to the frontmost document since you last saved it.

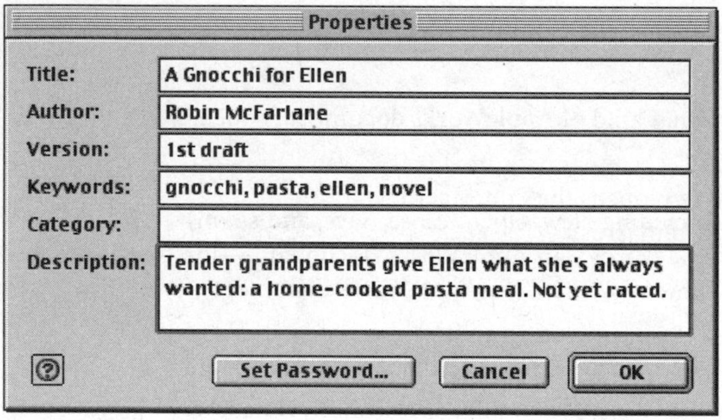

Properties
Title: A Gnocchi for Ellen
Author: Robin McFarlane
Version: 1st draft
Keywords: gnocchi, pasta, ellen, novel
Category:
Description: Tender grandparents give Ellen what she's always wanted: a home-cooked pasta meal. Not yet rated.
⦿ Set Password… Cancel OK

Figure A-1:
The Properties dialog box is a compact filing card that lets you record various details about the document and its creation. Sorry, refugees from Microsoft Word: there's no way to search for these keywords. Still, this box provides a handy place to store textual notes about a document (especially in graphics, spreadsheet, database, and presentation documents where there's no other good place to note why you created a document and when).

- **Properties.** Opens the Properties window (Figure A-1), where you can enter some information about the document, such as its title, author, and a brief description. This information doesn't appear in the document itself, but it is saved with the document. You can also set a password for the document from the Properties window.

UP TO SPEED

Password-Protecting Your Documents

To keep prying eyes from reading a confidential document, you can attach a password to it. Once that's done, Apple-Works won't open the document until that password is correctly typed.

To assign a password to a document, choose File→ Properties to bring up the Properties window; click the Set Password button. You'll be asked to enter a password for the document; after you click OK, you'll be asked to enter it again, to rule out the possibility of typos. Finally, click OK in the Properties window, and then save your document.

The next time anyone tries to open the document, they'll be asked for a password, and they won't be allowed to proceed without it.

(Note: The AppleWorks password feature is by no means government-level security. Determined evildoers can scrape the *text* out of your protected documents using shareware programs or even Microsoft Word, password or no. Other kinds of AppleWorks data, such as graphics and even spreadsheet data, are far more secure.)

- **Insert.** Lets you insert another file (such as a graphic or text file) into the frontmost document. You could use this command when, for example, collecting numerous chapter documents into a single master book-manuscript file.

- **Show/Hide Clippings.** Opens the Clippings floating window (see Chapter 9). If it's already open, then the menu says Hide Clippings instead. Keyboard equivalent: ⌘-2.

- **Macros.** The Macros submenu has three commands, all pertaining to the software robots known as *macros* (see Chapter 11). **Record Macro** opens the Record Macro window, in which you can record your own Macros. (If you're recording a macro, this menu item says Stop Recording, which ends the macro-recording process). **Play Macro** opens the Play Macro window, in which you can choose a prerecorded macro to play. **Edit Macro** opens the Edit Macro window, in which you can modify or delete prerecorded macros.

- **Mail Merge.** Lets you choose a database to merge into a word processing or spreadsheet document, and then opens the Mail Merge floating window. Use this command for creating form letters, as described in detail on page 354.

- **Page Setup.** Opens the Page Setup dialog box, where you can control how AppleWorks prints your pages by choosing paper type, page orientation, and so on. The options in the Page Setup window depend on the printer icon you've clicked in the ⌘→Chooser program.

- **Print.** Prints the frontmost document. The Print dialog box appears first, in which you can specify how many copies you want printed, which pages you want, and so on. Keyboard equivalent: ⌘-P.

- **Open Recent.** AppleWorks lists the documents you've been working on most recently in this easy-access submenu. To open a recent document, just choose its name from this list; you don't have to remember where you'd filed it.

- **Quit.** Exits AppleWorks, after first offering you the chance to save any unsaved changes to the open documents.

Window Menu

The Window menu controls how AppleWorks manages its open windows—including the Button bar, the Tool palette, and the Accents window.

- **New View.** Opens a new window—a new view—of the *same* document. This isn't a copy of the document; it's just a copy of the *window,* which you can scroll, resize, or zoom independently. Changes you make to one view appear in all views.

- **Open Frame.** As you can read in Chapter 12, you can edit a frame (an embedded spreadsheet or text box, for example) right in the document window that contains it. For easier editing, however, you can use this command to open the frame into its own document window, which you can enlarge to capitalize on the full size of your screen—a necessary step when, for example, you want to add or delete a spreadsheet frame's rows or columns.

- **Page View.** Shows a preview of your document as it will look when printed— arranged on pages. This view gives you an idea of where pages will break, how the margins will look, and so on. Keyboard equivalent: ⌘-Shift-P.

Note: Word processing documents are *always* in Page View. Page View isn't available for presentation documents; instead, the command now says Notes View, where you can read notes you've written to yourself (see page 259).

- **Slide Show.** Opens the Slide Show window (page 265). If you've created a presentation document, the Slide Show command immediately begins to "play" the slide show on the screen; if it's a drawing document-based show (as described at the end of Chapter 8), a dialog box appears letting you arrange slides, specify a background color, and so on.

- **Show/Hide Button Bar.** Shows or hides the Button bar (see page 15). Keyboard equivalent: ⌘-Shift-X.

- **Show/Hide Tools.** Shows or hides the Tools window (see page 15). Keyboard equivalent: ⌘-Shift-T.

- **Show/Hide Accents.** Shows or hides the Accents palette (page 213). Keyboard equivalent: ⌘-K.

- **Show Presentation Controls.** Shows or hides the Presentation Controls window (page 255). This command is available only when the frontmost window is a presentation document.

- **Tile Windows.** Shrinks all open windows, changes their dimensions, and arranges them on the screen so that all of them are visible at once. (If more than a few documents are open, the resulting windows are extremely small.)

- **Stack Windows.** Arranges all open windows in a stack, as shown in Figure A-2. Both of these window-arrangement commands are available only when more than one document window is, in fact, open.

- **[Document names].** The names of all open documents appear at the bottom of the Window menu, so that you can jump from one to another by choosing its name. Documents you haven't yet saved and named are called Untitled 1, Untitled 2, and so on—a two-letter abbreviation identifies the kind of document each is, such as "untitled 3 (WP)."

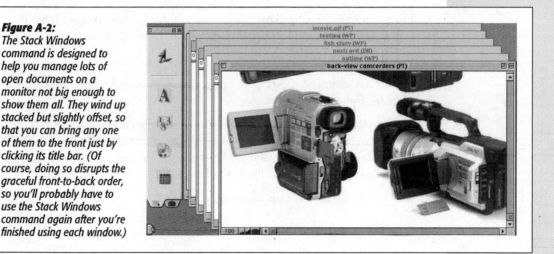

Figure A-2:
The Stack Windows command is designed to help you manage lots of open documents on a monitor not big enough to show them all. They wind up stacked but slightly offset, so that you can bring any one of them to the front just by clicking its title bar. (Of course, doing so disrupts the graceful front-to-back order, so you'll probably have to use the Stack Windows command again after you're finished using each window.)

Script Menu

The Script menu isn't actually identified by name on your menu bar; instead, it shows up as a tiny scroll icon to the right of the Window menu. This menu lists scripts that you (or someone else) have created using AppleScript, the built-in, Macintosh-wide programming language that automates tedious sets of steps. (The Web is filled with excellent introductions to the AppleScript language.)

This menu lists the name of every script in your AppleWorks 6→AppleWorks Essentials→Scripts folder. In other words, to install a new AppleScript in this menu, just drop it into the Scripts folder—and to eliminate a command from the Script menu, remove the corresponding icon from the Scripts folder.

Several such scripts come with AppleWorks 6. To run one of these canned software systems, just choose its name from the Script menu. Note, however, that several of the scripts work only in one module, such as the Word Processing module. They're listed in the Scripts menu, in fact, as module-named *submenus* to make this distinction clearer. (Scripts in the Universal submenu, however, work in any module.)

- **Open Scripts Folder.** Switches out of AppleWorks, jumps to the Finder, and opens the AppleWorks 6→AppleWorks Essentials→Scripts folder so that you can add or remove items from it.

- **About AppleWorks Scripts.** Displays a dialog box containing general information about the AppleWorks scripts.

- **Mount iDisk.** *iDisk* is an Internet-based, 20-MB hard drive on which you can store and back up files. It requires an Internet account, Mac OS 9 or later, and either a very fast Internet connection or great patience. (For instructions on signing up for the this free Apple Web-page service, visit *http://www.itools.mac.com/itoolsmain.html.*)

Once you've set up your iDisk, this script mounts the icon of your iDisk on your desktop. It requires an Internet connection and Mac OS 9 to work.

Database submenu

The Database submenu offers only one script, which works only in the Database module (or frame):

- The **Duplicate Record Multiple** script duplicates the currently selected record the number of times you specify. You might use this command when working on your address book, for example, and you're about to enter ten people who all work for the same company that has the same address and central phone number.

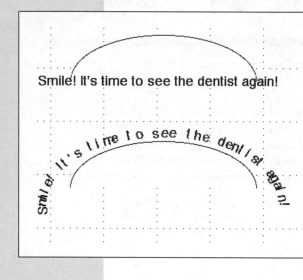

Figure A-3:
Start by drawing an arc and typing a text block in the Drawing frame or document, and then highlighting both at once. Using the Text Along Arc AppleScript command, you force AppleWorks to split each letter of the text into its own text block and rotate it as necessary to fit the arc.

After the conversion, individual letters may need nudging into alignment. Turn off the Autogrid (Options menu). Then select the misplaced letter and press the arrow keys to nudge it into place.

Drawing submenu

- **Join Prism Corners.** Begin by creating and selecting two rectangles using the drawing tools, and then choose this command—AppleWorks draws lines that join the corners of the two rectangles, producing a line drawing of a three-dimensional box.

- **Text Along Arc** script creates a dramatic typographical effect of text proceeding along a curve, as shown in Figure A-3.

Linear Regression

- This script for mathematics fans, misfiled, is actually a Spreadsheet-only command. It works on a set of rows *and* columns in a spreadsheet, performing a *linear regression* on those numbers. It produces a dialog box that identifies the slope, intercept, and correlation of the numbers you had highlighted.

Spreadsheet submenu

- **Draw Cell Borders.** This script draws borders around all the sides of the selected cells—something you could certainly do manually, but not nearly as easily.

- **Negative Cells Red.** This script changes the text color of cells with negative numbers to red, as is common (and useful) in spreadsheet software.

Universal submenu

These unusual commands let AppleWorks communicate with the Finder. For example:

- **Copy File's Path** copies to the Clipboard the *path* of the current document (assuming that you have, in fact, already saved the document). The path is a string of text that identifies where the file has been stored on your hard drive—in which folder: for example, *Macintosh HD:Documents: New Chapter Files*. In a pinch, you could even paste this path into an AppleWorks document to help you figure out where you'd saved it.

- The **Reveal in Finder** command, on the other hand, switches out of AppleWorks and jumps to the desktop, opening the folder that contains whatever document you have open and highlighting its icon. (Works only on documents that you've already saved.)

Word processing submenu

For use in word-processing frames and documents only:

- **Extract Containing.** This script is a relative of the Find command, but can be much more useful. It asks you to specify a piece of text to search for. Then it searches the frontmost document for paragraphs that contain the text you entered. It then makes a new word processing document and pastes those paragraphs into it—a good way to round up only the relevant paragraphs from a long article you copied from the Web, for example.

- **Find Repeated Words.** Searches a block of text you've highlighted, on the quest for words you may have repeated (such as "to to") by accident. Offers you the chance to delete the repeated word, case-by-case.

- **Small Caps.** Turns the selected text into *small caps,* an elegant typographical style that Looks like This.

- **Title Caps.** Capitalizes the first letter of every word in the selected text except for small words like articles and prepositions (*in, the, of,* and so on)—the style of capitalization normally found in newspaper headlines and the like.

- **Word Caps.** This command is exactly like Title Caps, except that it capitalizes the first letter of each word, *including* articles and prepositions.

Help Menu

The AppleWorks Help menu offers three help-related items:

- **About Balloon Help.** Brings up a window that tells you how the Balloon Help command, described in the next paragraph, works.

- **Show Balloons.** Turns on the Mac's Balloon Help function, which makes a small text-filled balloon caption identify each button, window, and control you point to with your cursor. It's a good idea in theory; in practice, however, many areas of AppleWorks are balloon-free.

- **AppleWorks Help.** Opens the AppleWorks 6 help system, which runs in the Mac OS's Web-browser-like Help Viewer application. Keyboard equivalent: ⌘-?. See page 20 for more on AppleWorks help.

Word Processing Menus

The commands in the word processing menu set are focused on helping you manipulate and move the text in your document.

Edit Menu

The Edit menu commands focus on copying, pasting, selecting, inserting, and editing text.

- **Undo.** When you choose Undo, the last action you took—deleting the paragraph, formatting a word, and so on—is undone. Your document is restored to exactly the condition it was in before you took that step. Once you've undone something, the Undo command changes to say Redo—in case you've changed your mind about changing your mind. Keyboard equivalent: ⌘-Z.

Note: The Undo command can't take back *every* kind of AppleWorks action. Fortunately, you'll generally be notified before AppleWorks executes a command for which there's no Undo—such as using the Find and Replace commands.

- **Cut.** Deletes the selected text (or object) from the document and puts it on the invisible Macintosh Clipboard, in readiness to paste elsewhere in the document (or in another document). Keyboard equivalent: ⌘-X.

- **Copy.** Copies the selected text (or object) to the Clipboard, ready to paste. Keyboard equivalent: ⌘-C.

- **Paste.** Deposits copied or pasted text or other objects into your document at the location indicated by the insertion point. Keyboard equivalent: ⌘-V.

- **Clear.** Deletes the selected text (or object) from the document *without* putting it on the Clipboard.

- **Select All.** Highlights everything in the document. You might use this command just before the Copy command, for example, when you want to paste everything you've just typed into an email message, or when you're about to change the typeface for the entire document. Keyboard equivalent: ⌘-A.

- **Object Info.** Opens a window that identifies the selected object, whether it's a picture, movie, or frame, and offers controls that govern its appearance. The wording of this command reflects the kind of object you've selected—it may say Corner Info, Frame Info, and so on. If only text is selected, or if nothing is selected, this command is dimmed and unavailable.

- **Insert Equation.** Fires up the Equation Editor, a mini-program installed by AppleWorks (see Figure A-4). After you've constructed your equation, close the window; the equation now appears in your document as an independent drawing object, which you can move, resize, and reformat like any other text block.

Figure A-4:
The Equation Editor, a stripped-down edition of the more powerful commercial product, MathType, lets the mathematically inclined go beyond simple arithmetic equations in AppleWorks documents. With Equation Editor, you can create elaborate, typographically correct equations by using the pop-up menu buttons at the top of the window.

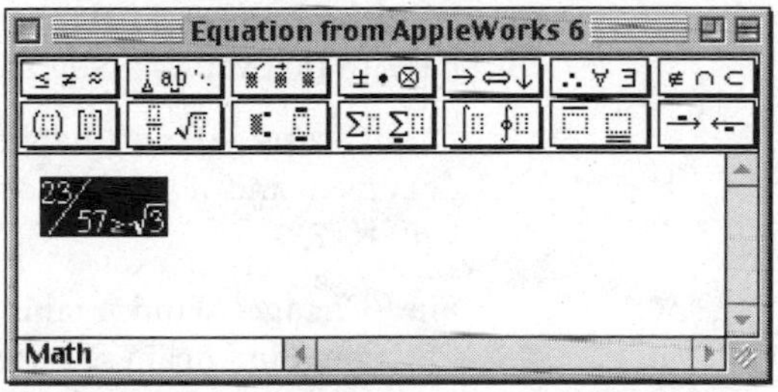

- **Insert Date, Insert Time.** Inserts the current date or time into your document, in either fixed or self-updating formats; see page 83 for details.

- **Insert Page #.** Opens the Insert Page Number window, which you can use to insert the current page number at the cursor. See page 84 for more on page numbers.

- **Sort Selected Paragraphs.** Opens the Sort Paragraphs window, which you can use to sort the selected paragraphs alphabetically according to the first characters in each one. Of course, you may not often need to sort your *prose* paragraphs alphabetically. But this command can be extremely useful if you've just typed up a list of any kind, one entry per line, and would like to see them listed alphabetically.

- **Writing Tools→Check Document Spelling.** Opens the Spelling window and begins a spelling check of the entire document (see page 50). Keyboard equivalent: ⌘-=.

- **Writing Tools→Check Selection Spelling.** Opens the Spelling window and begins checking only the text you've highlighted. Keyboard equivalent: ⌘-Shift-Y.

- **Writing Tools→Auto Hyphenate.** Turns on AppleWorks automatic hyphenation (see page 40).

- **Writing Tools→Thesaurus.** Opens AppleWorks' thesaurus and looks up the selected word, if one is selected. Keyboard equivalent: ⌘-Shift-Z.

- **Writing Tools→Word Count.** Opens a dialog box that shows you how many characters, words, lines, paragraphs, pages, and sections are in the document. If the Count Selection box is checked, then Word Count counts only the text you first highlighted.

- **Writing Tools→Select Dictionaries.** Lets you select the dictionaries used for spelling, the thesaurus, and hyphenation (see page 51).

- **Writing Tools→Edit User Dictionary.** Opens the User Dictionary and lets you edit its contents—useful if you've accidentally added a misspelled word to your user dictionary and you want to get rid of it.

- **Writing Tools→Edit Hyphenation Dictionary.** Opens the Hyphenation Dictionary, so that you can edit it (see page 40).

- **Find/Change→Find/Change.** This command lets you find specific text in your document and, if you like, change it to a different piece of text. Keyboard equivalent: ⌘-F.

- **Find/Change→Find Again.** Only available after you've used the Find/Change function, Find Again searches for the *next* appearance of whatever text you just found using the Find/Change command. Keyboard equivalent: ⌘-E.

- **Find/Change→Find Selection.** Finds the next occurrence of whatever text you've highlighted—a great shortcut. Instead of having to use the Find/Change dialog box, you can leap directly to the next appearance of a particular phrase. Keyboard equivalent: ⌘-Shift-E.

- **Preferences→General.** In common Macintosh fashion, the Preferences command, which technically has little to do with editing your documents, has found its home in the Edit menu. (See Chapter 11 for details on all three of the Preferences commands described here.)

The dialog box that appears when you choose Edit→Preferences→General controls five different areas of AppleWorks' behavior: General, Files, Text, Graphics, Spreadsheet. (See Chapter 11 for descriptions.) If a word processing document is open, then this window displays the Text panel; if no document is open, this window opens to the General panel.

- **Preferences→Button Bar.** Opens the Button bar preferences window, which lets you customize how the Button bar behaves and what buttons show up.

- **Preferences→HTML Import/Export.** Opens the Configure HTML window, in which you can tweak and configure how AppleWorks translates its own documents to the HTML Web-page language and how it translates HTML tags when *opening* an HTML document.

Format Menu

The Format menu governs text styles, headers, footers, and other formatting aspects of your text. Chapter 3 covers these commands in great detail.

- **Document.** Opens the Document dialog box, which controls margins, footnote placement, page numbering, and other aspects of your word processing document.

- **Section.** Opens the Section dialog box, which controls how *sections* look (including columns, headers, and footers).

- **Paragraph.** Opens the Paragraph dialog box, in which you can set indents, spacing, labels, and alignment for the highlighted paragraphs.

- **Show Styles.** Opens the Styles palette, where you can create style sheets that format selected text (or other AppleWorks data types) in complex ways with a single click.

- **Tabs.** Opens the Tab window, where you can set the tab stops for your document.

- **Rulers→Copy Ruler.** Copies the ruler settings in the paragraph where the cursor is currently located. Keyboard equivalent: ⌘-Shift-C.

- **Rulers→Apply Ruler.** Applies the ruler settings copied by selecting Copy Ruler to the selected paragraph, like a Paste command for ruler settings (see page 46). Keyboard equivalent: ⌘-Shift-V.

- **Rulers→Show/Hide Rulers.** Shows or hides the ruler itself. Keyboard equivalent: ⌘-Shift-U.

- **Rulers→Ruler Settings.** Opens the Ruler Settings dialog box, where you can change the ruler type, the units it uses (inches, centimeters, and so on), and the number of marks that you want to subdivide each unit.

Tip: The units you set up in the Ruler Settings dialog box also affect the spacing of the invisible grid lines—and the Autogrid—described in Chapter 6.

- **Scale By Percent.** Opens the Scale By Percent dialog box, where you can enlarge or reduce a selected object (such as a picture or a QuickTime movie). (This command doesn't affect text.)

- **Descent.** Opens the Descent dialog box for the selected graphic object, where you specify how high you want to shift it relative to text on the same line. For example, imagine that you have some text sitting next to a rectangle that's 200 pixels tall. When the rectangle's Descent setting is 0, the text sits on the baseline, even with the bottom edge of the rectangle. If the descent is 100, the text appears about halfway down. If the descent is set to 200, the bottom of the text appears at the image's top.

- **Insert Page Break.** Starts a new page at the cursor's current location. Text after the page break appears at the top of a new page (see page 73). Keyboard equivalent: Shift-Enter.

- **Insert Section Break.** Starts a new section (see page 73) at the cursor's location. Keyboard equivalent: Option-Enter.

- **Insert Column Break.** In documents that have multiple columns, this command forces the text to begin at the top of the next column (see page 73). Keyboard equivalent: Enter.

- **Insert Blank Footnote.** Puts the footnote number at the cursor's location (even if that's in the middle of a word) and then creates a blank footnote at the bottom of the page, as described on page 48.

- **Create Link→Internet.** Turns the highlighted text into a *hyperlink*, just like those found on a Web page. For instructions, see page 296.

- **Create Link→Anchor.** Creates an *anchor* from the selected text or object—a bookmark that makes it easy to navigate your document, as described in Chapter 12 (page 359).

- **Create Link→Document Link.** Turns the selected text or object into a document link that, when clicked, opens another AppleWorks document. Instructions on page 360.

- **Turn Active Links Off/On.** If you try to edit the text of one of the links you've created, you may wind up launching that corresponding Web page, AppleWorks document, or AppleWorks anchor. This command temporarily turns such links back into ordinary text so that you can edit them. If active links are already off, it turns them back on.

- **Show/Hide Links Window.** Shows the Links floating window if it's hidden; hides it if it's showing. The Links window lets you add, edit, or remove links within a document, and it shows all of the document's links. Keyboard equivalent: ⌘-Shift-M.

- **Insert Header, Insert Footer.** Inserts a *header* or *footer* at the top or bottom of all pages (in the document or in the section), as described on page 82.

Text Menu

You might expect that text-formatting commands would appear in the Format menu; instead, they appear in the four Text submenus (Font, Size, Style, and Text Color):

- **Font.** This submenu lists the fonts installed on your Mac. Like most of the commands described on this page, this one affects either the highlighted text or (if nothing's highlighted) your next typing.

- **Size.** Changes the font's size. The submenu lists nine common font sizes, plus these extra commands:

- **Size→Other.** Lets you specify whatever font size you please, even if it's something not listed in the Text→Size submenu, such as 22.3 points. Keyboard equivalent: ⌘-Shift-O.

- **Size→Smaller.** Decreases the font size of the currently selected text by one point. Keyboard equivalent: ⌘-Shift-<.

- **Size→Larger.** Increases the font size of the currently selected text by one point. Keyboard equivalent: ⌘-Shift-→.

- **Style→Plain Text.** Removes all styles from the selected text. Keyboard equivalent: ⌘-T.

- **Style→Bold.** Makes the selected text bold. Keyboard equivalent: ⌘-B.

- **Style→Italic.** Makes the selected text italic. Keyboard equivalent: ⌘-I.

- **Style→Underline.** Underlines the selected text. Keyboard equivalent: ⌘-U.

- **Style→Double Underline.** Puts two underlines under the selected text.

- **Style→Strike Thru.** Puts a line through the middle of the selected text—a common editing mark.

- **Style→Outline.** Creates hollow letters, with a white center and black outline.

- **Style→Shadow.** Puts a simulated drop shadow behind a hollow rendition of the selected characters.

- **Style→Condense.** Compresses the selected text horizontally by removing some space between letters—for tighter headlines, for example.

- **Style→Extend.** Expands the selected text horizontally by creating more space between letters.

- **Style→Superscript, Subscript.** Moves the selected text slightly upward or downward from the baseline.

- **Style→Superior, Inferior.** Makes the selected text smaller *and* moves it slightly upward or downward from the baseline, as you would do when writing chemical formulas such as H_2O.

- **Style→Uppercase.** Capitalizes every letter of the selected text.

- **Style→Lowercase.** Makes every letter of the selected text lowercase.

- **Text Color.** Use this palette of 256 shades to change the color of the letters in the highlighted text (or, if nothing is selected, of the text you're about to type).

Tip: The palette that appears in the Text Color submenu is determined by your current selection under the Text button in the Accents palette.

Outline Menu

The Outline menu lends structure to your word processing documents. For complete details on outlining and using this menu, see page 174. In the following discussion, the *selected outline topic* refers to the line that contains the blinking insertion point.

- **New Topic.** Creates a new outline topic at the same hierarchy level as the selected topic.

- **New Topic Left.** Creates a new outline topic—one that's farther to the left of, and therefore more important than, the selected topic. (Does nothing if the insertion point is already at the left margin.) Keyboard equivalent: ⌘-L.

- **New Topic Right.** Creates a new outline topic that's indented from, and therefore less important than, the selected topic. Keyboard equivalent: ⌘-R.

- **Move Left.** Moves the selected topic to the left, promoting it. *With Subtopics* moves all of the subtopics attached to the topic, too (keyboard equivalent: ⌘-Shift-L); *Without Subtopics* moves the topic but leaves its subtopics in place, therefore shifting the relative importance of your topics. (Oddly enough, this command has no keyboard equivalent.)

- **Move Right.** Moves the selected topic to the right, therefore demoting it. As with Move Left, you can choose to do so with or without the subtopics attached to the selected one.

- **Move Above.** Moves the selected topic and its subtopics upward in the outline at its same hierarchy level—that is, Topic II becomes Topic I.

- **Move Below.** Moves the selected topic and its subtopics downward in the outline at the same hierarchy level; subtopic A switches places with subtopic B, for example.

- **Collapse.** Hides all of the selected line's subtopics—everything at a lower hierarchy level. (Double-clicking the heading number does the same thing.)

  For example, if you're using the Harvard outline style (see page 75) and the insertion point is blinking in Topic III, the Collapse command hides all lettered subtopics (A, B, C, and so on), leaving only the I, II, and III headings visible. AppleWorks underlines the number of (or otherwise visually identifies) any topic that "contains" collapsed subtopics.

- **Collapse All.** Identical to Collapse—with one difficult-to-explain exception. The *immediate* effect of the Collapse and Collapse All commands is the same—all subtopics of the selected heading disappear. The only difference is what happens when you *then* use the Expand command, as described next.

- **Expand.** Reveals the subtopics of the selected heading. If it had been collapsed using the Collapse command, *all* subtopics (all levels) expand. But if you'd used the Collapse All command, only *one more level* of subheads appears—not all of them.

- **Expand All.** Reveals all subtopics, to all levels, of the selected heading, regardless of whether you'd previously used Collapse or Collapse All.

- **Expand To.** Opens the Expand To dialog box, which lets you specify how many levels of the outline you want expanded.

- **Raise Topic.** Promotes the selected topic (and its subtopics) by moving it to the left—beneath any of its own subtopics. (Compare with Move Left→With Subtopics, which promotes the topic *in place,* making what were equivalent topics its subtopics.)

- **Label Style.** Lets you select the style of symbol that appears before each topic, such as Roman numerals, diamonds, bullets, and so on. You can see these illustrated on page 75.

Table Menu

The Table menu lets you create tables in your documents and customize them, as described in Chapter 12.

- **Insert Table.** Opens the Insert Table window, which lets you select how many rows and columns you'd like for the new table you're about to create. Keyboard equivalent: ⌘-Y.

- **Convert to Table/Convert to Text.** If you highlight a "table" in your word processing document or frame whose columns have been created using tab stops, the Convert to Table command turns it instantly into an AppleWorks table, as described on page 352.

  If, on the other hand, you highlight an AppleWorks table and then choose Convert to Text, AppleWorks converts a table once again into plain text, where each row of your table becomes an independent paragraph, and tabs separate the items in each column. (Because other programs don't understand the AppleWorks table structure, converting text in this way is a good idea before you export your document, or even copy and paste it, to a different word processor.)

- **Select Current Cell.** Highlights the contents of the cell that contains the insertion point.

- **Insert Cells.** If a table *row* is selected, this command inserts a new row of cells above it. If a *column* is selected, this command inserts a new column to its left.

(Unavailable unless you've highlighted an entire row or column.) Keyboard equivalent: ⌘-Shift-I.

- **Delete Cells.** This command deletes the currently selected row(s) or column(s) of the table. Unavailable unless you've highlighted *entire* row(s) or column(s). Also unavailable when *all* the cells are selected, because AppleWorks doesn't know whether to delete rows or columns. Keyboard equivalent: ⌘-Shift-K.

Tip: If you wish to insert *multiple* rows (or columns), select the equivalent number of rows (or columns) in the *existing* table before choosing this command. AppleWorks grants you exactly the same number of *new* rows or columns.

- **Merge Cells.** Merges several selected cells into one table cell by removing the dividing borders and putting the contents of those cells into the newly created super cell. Keyboard equivalent: ⌘-M.

- **Distribute Columns Evenly, Distribute Rows Evenly.** Makes the selected columns or rows equal in width or height.

- **Subdivide Cells.** The opposite of Merge Cells—divides the selected cells further into the number of cells that you specify in the dialog box that appears. Keyboard equivalent: ⌘-J.

- **Vertical Alignment.** Controls how the text within cells is aligned vertically— whether it flows from the top, middle, or bottom of the cell.

- **Line Styles.** Lets you choose from among six different line types for the borders of the selected cells—double outline, dotted line, and so on.

- **Diagonal Line.** Opens the Diagonal Line dialog box, where you can choose from, and edit the look of, a variety of diagonal lines to fill the selected table cells (for the purposes of marking them empty, for example).

- **Auto Resize.** Permits the rows of your column to grow taller as you type more text into them. You can turn this feature on or off for an entire table at a time.

- **Use Grid.** Turns on (or off) the magnetic feature of the graphics grid. If it's on, when you drag one of the table divider lines, you'll feel it "snap to" these invisible guidelines, making it easier to align different rows and columns with each other. You can turn this feature on or off for an entire table at a time.

- **Line Segment Selection.** Under most circumstances, when you drag one of the lines that forms a table, you move the *entire* line, from end to end (or top to bottom) of the table. When this option is turned on for a table, however, you can drag the individual segments that border a cell, thus throwing that cell out of alignment with the rest of its row or column lines.

Spreadsheet Menus

See Chapter 5 for complete details on the Spreadsheet module. Here are its menus:

Edit Menu

Most of the commands in the Edit menu are the same in the Spreadsheet module as they are in the Word Processing module described earlier: Undo, Cut, Copy, Clear, Paste, Select All, Writing Tools, Preferences, and so on. Among them, however, are a few spreadsheet-specific commands like these:

- **Copy Format.** Copies a cell's format—but not its contents—so that you can apply that formatting to another cell. Keyboard equivalent: ⌘-Shift-C.

- **Apply Format.** Applies a cell's format—copied from another cell—to the currently selected cell or cells without changing the contents. Keyboard equivalent: ⌘-Shift-V.

- **Paste Special.** Opens the Paste Special window, where you're offered several special pasting options. For example, you can choose to paste only the contents of what you had cut or copied, but not the formulas behind them. As described in Chapter 5, you can also use the Paste Special command to *transpose* a range of cells (swap rows for columns).

- **Insert Function.** Inserts one of the AppleWorks financial, logical, statistical, or other functions into the selected cell. Use the pop-up menu at the top of the dialog box to view the functions in only one category (such as Date & Time or Trigonometric). See the Functions Appendix at *www.missingmanual.com*.

Format Menu

When you're working with the spreadsheet, many of the commands in this menu are the same as in the Word Processing module described in the previous section. A few important spreadsheet-only commands also appear here, however:

- **Numbers.** Lets you format the numbers in the selected cells, so that you don't have to type in, for example, the dollar sign, the decimal point, or the commas in large numbers—AppleWorks does all that for you. Using the "Show Negatives in Parentheses" checkbox, you can request that AppleWorks display parentheses around negative numbers, as is typical in financial statements. The Date and Time pop-up menus let you tell AppleWorks that the highlighted cells contain dates and times, not regular numbers—and lets you specify how you want them written out.

Tip: Double-click a cell to summon this dialog box to format a single cell. When formatting a range of cells, you can also Control-click the selected region and choose Number from the pop-up menu.

- **Borders.** Lets you specify which edges of the selected cells you'd like to display solid borders (which you can design using the Accents palette)—right, left, bottom, top, or fully outlined.

- **Show Styles.** As described in Chapter 5, spreadsheet cells can have style sheets, too—the window that appears when you choose this command gives you access to them.

- **Font, Size, Style, Text Color, Alignment.** When you're working with a spreadsheet, AppleWorks presumes that you'll be doing less text formatting. As a result, these commands and their submenus (which, when word processing, appear in the menu called Text) appear here in the Format menu.

- **Insert Cells.** Inserts new cells in the spreadsheet, pushing the existing cells either downward or to the right, depending on what you specify in the dialog box that appears. It's important to understand that the number of cells that AppleWorks inserts depends on the number of cells you highlight before using the command. If you highlight a block of three cells (even if they contain numbers), AppleWorks will insert an identical block of three empty cells. Keyboard equivalent: ⌘-Shift-I.

- **Delete Cells.** Deletes the selected cells. You can choose whether the cells are pulled up or to the right in the Delete Cells window that appears. Keyboard equivalent: ⌘-Shift-K.

- **Column Width.** Lets you set the widths of the columns of the selected cells. The default size is 72 pixels: each cell is one inch wide.

- **Autosize Columns.** Resizes the column to match the width of the data in the widest selected column. This is a great option if you're trying to conserve space on the spreadsheet, because it ensures that even the widest number in the column will fit in the cell—but that even that cell is no wider than necessary.

- **Row Height.** Lets you set the height of the rows that contain the selected cells. The default size is 14 points.

- **Autosize Rows.** This relative of Autosize Columns automatically makes rows taller—but no taller than necessary—to accommodate any extra-large font sizes you've established.

Tip: Several of the commands described here are also available in the contextual pop-up menu that appears when you Control-click the selection in your spreadsheet.

Calculate Menu

This menu appears only when you're working with a spreadsheet or spreadsheet frame.

- **Move.** A dialog box appears, in which you're supposed to type in cell coordinates. When you click OK, AppleWorks moves the selected cell or cells to that location in the spreadsheet. (This method of moving cells is generally more trouble than simply copying and pasting, or even simply dragging the highlighted selection elsewhere on the sheet—on the other hand, it may be useful if the destination cells are very far away on the spreadsheet. Note, too, that the Move command doesn't involve the Clipboard, so something you had previously cut or copied remains on the Clipboard even after this process.)

- **Fill Right.** Copies the contents (data or formula) of a cell into as many cells to the right of it as you've highlighted. Keyboard equivalent: ⌘-R.

- **Fill Down.** Copies the contents (data or formula) of a cell into as many cells below it as you've highlighted. Keyboard equivalent: ⌘-D.

- **Fill Special.** Fills the selected cells with a logical pattern, such as successive serial numbers, months of the year, days of the week, dates of the month, annual quarters, and so on—a terrific shortcut when you're setting up a spreadsheet. (See the tutorial on page 164.)

  When the Fill Special dialog box first appears, AppleWorks makes an attempt to *figure out* what the pattern should be based on data you already entered in the first couple of cells in the selection. For example, if the first two cells contain January and February, AppleWorks proposes filling in the subsequent highlighted cells with the names of subsequent months.

- **Sort.** Opens the Sort window, where you can sort the selected cells in ascending or descending order. Keyboard equivalent: ⌘-J.

- **Auto Sum, Auto Average.** Adds together, or calculates the arithmetic mean of, the cells in the selected range; puts the result in the rightmost or bottom cell (if it's empty).

- **Calculate Now.** Forces AppleWorks to recalculate all of the formulas in the spreadsheet. Keyboard equivalent: ⌘-Shift-=.

- **Auto-Calculate.** When this is on, AppleWorks keeps the results of all formulas current and "live," so that if you change a number in the spreadsheet, the formula that refers to it displays the new answer instantly. Turning this option off may make the spreadsheet faster on very slow Macs and very large spreadsheets.

Options Menu

This menu appears in the Spreadsheet, Drawing, Painting, and Presentation modules; but the commands in it differ in each case. Here's how it works in the Spreadsheet module:

- **Make Chart.** Opens up the Chart Options window, where you can choose from a dizzying array of charts to create from the cells you've selected, as described in Chapter 5. Keyboard equivalent: ⌘-M.

- **Lock Cells, Unlock cells.** Locks or unlocks the selected cells. When they're locked, you can't change their contents or formulas—a good way to prevent changing such information accidentally. Keyboard equivalent: ⌘-H.

- **Add Page Break, Remove Page Break.** Inserts or removes a *page break*. On the screen, the page break looks like a dotted line; when you print the document, the page break will force the spreadsheet to split onto a new page.

- **Remove All Breaks.** Removes all page breaks that you've inserted in the spreadsheet.

- **Lock Title Position.** Locks the cells above and to the left of the selected cell so that they print on every page and don't scroll along with the rest of the spreadsheet. Great for column and row headings—as you scroll way down in the list, the column headings remain fixed on the screen.

- **Set Print Range.** Lets you specify that you want to print only a portion of your spreadsheet. (If you highlight some cells before choosing this command, AppleWorks fills in the coordinates of the selected cells automatically, saving you some typing.) You can specify that you want the entire identified range printed, or only the cells within it that have information in them (so that you don't waste paper printing empty cells).

- **Default Font.** Lets you specify the spreadsheet's default font and type size.

- **Display.** Opens the Display window, in which you can change your spreadsheet's look—such as whether columns and rows have headings, whether formulas are displayed, or whether the cell grid is enabled.

- **Go To Cell.** Displays the Go To Cell dialog box, in which you can specify the coordinates of the spreadsheet cell to which you'd like to jump. Keyboard equivalent: ⌘-G.

Database Menus

The Database menu set appears whenever a database is active in AppleWorks.

Edit Menu

Once again, many commands in this menu are identical to those described in "Word Processing Menus," earlier in this chapter. Some have special functions, however:

- **Cut, Copy, Paste, Clear.** When you're editing text within a database field, these commands work exactly as they do when you're editing text.

  If, however, you click anywhere inside a record *except* on a field, you highlight the entire record. You can now use the Edit menu commands to cut, copy, paste, or clear the entire record. You can even paste the copied record into another program, such as a word processor or email message.

- **Select All.** When you're in Browse mode, this command highlights all of the contents of a selected field. If you're in Layout mode, it selects all of the objects in the layout. Keyboard equivalent: ⌘-A.

- **Copy Summaries.** Copies the contents of all of the visible summary fields to the Clipboard. (See Chapter 4 for details on summary fields.)

- **New Record.** Creates a new, empty database record in the currently active database. Keyboard equivalent, one that's well worth memorizing: ⌘-R.

- **Duplicate Record.** Creates a new record that contains exactly the same information as the one that had been selected. Very useful when you need to enter a lot of data where most of the information is the same from one record to another, such as several employees who have the same company address. Keyboard equivalent: ⌘-D.

- **Delete Record.** Deletes the selected record from the database. Keyboard equivalent: the Clear key.

Caution: The Delete Record presents no "Are you sure?" message before vaporizing your record. You can, fortunately, use the Edit→Undo Clear command to restore the obliterated record.

- **Find/Change.** These commands work exactly as they do in the Word Processing module. It's worth noting, however, that a Find in Browse mode works on data within records, but a Find in Layout mode works on the text and labels on the layout. If you want to be sure to change a particular phrase *everywhere* in the database, in other words, run two separate Find/Change procedures, once in each mode.

Format Menu

The Database module's Format menu is a subset of those described for the Spreadsheet module in the previous section. Several of the menus have special functions in the Database module, however:

- **Alignment.** This submenu is available only in Layout mode. It governs how the text within the selected cells is aligned, relative to the field's outline: flush left, centered, flush right, or fully justified.

- **Spacing.** These controls are also available only in Layout mode; they affect the spacing of the lines within each selected field: Single Space, 1-1/2 Space, or Double Space.

Layout Menu

This menu is central to the Database module. It lets you switch modes and create, edit, or manage custom layouts. See Chapter 4 for a much more detailed description of the various database modes.

- **Browse.** Puts the database in Browse mode, where you can create, edit, and delete database records. Keyboard equivalent: ⌘-Shift-B.

- **Find.** Puts the database into Find mode, which lets you search your records to round up only those that contain certain text. Keyboard equivalent: ⌘-Shift-F.

- **Layout.** Puts the database into Layout mode, the drawing-program-like window where you design your database, arrange fields, and so on. (In Layout mode, the Edit menu changes. Now it contains the same commands it does when you're using the Drawing module.) Keyboard equivalent: ⌘-Shift-L.

- **List.** Puts the database into List mode, which looks like a spreadsheet, where your fields and records are arranged in rows and columns. Keyboard equivalent: ⌘-Shift-I.

- **Define Fields.** Opens the Define Fields window, where you create, modify, and delete database fields. Keyboard equivalent: ⌘-Shift-D.

- **Insert Field.** Inserts a field (which you've previously defined) onto a database layout. The Insert Field dialog box appears, from which you can choose the field you want.

- **Insert Part.** Opens the Insert Part window, which you can use to insert headers, footers, or summary parts onto your layout.

- **Tab Order.** Lets you change the order in which the database's fields become active when you press the Tab key.

- **Show Multiple.** This one's well worth noticing, because it confounds many beginners. If this option is turned on, Browse mode shows all your records at once, in a long, scrolling list. When Show Multiple is turned off, you see only a single record at a time. The others aren't lost—they're just hidden.

- **New Layout.** Opens the New Layout window, from which you can create new layouts for your database. You can choose from five fundamental layout designs, such as Standard, Columnar, and so on.

- **New Label Layout.** Opens the Create Labels Assistant, which walks you through the process of making a layout that will print on standard self-adhesive mailing labels you've bought at an office-supply store. Chapter 4 contains a complete tutorial.

- **Edit Layouts.** Opens the Edit Layouts window, which lets you make certain changes to your layout—such as specifying how many columns of labels you want to appear on the page, and whether or not you want AppleWorks to delete blank space between fields when printing labels—or delete layouts altogether.

- **[Layout names].** The bottom of the Layout menu lists the layouts you've created. AppleWorks names the very first, generic, default layout *Layout 1;* if you've given your layouts custom names (such as Mailing Labels), they appear here instead. The current layout displays a checkmark.

Organize Menu

The Organize menu appears only when you're editing the database, and contains commands that help you sort, find, hide, or show records.

- **Show All Records.** If you've performed a Find operation, some of the database's records may now be hidden. This important command reveals them all. Keyboard equivalent: ⌘-Shift-A.

- **Hide Selected.** Hides the currently highlighted database records so that you can work with a smaller set of records. Keyboard equivalent: ⌘-(.

- **Hide Unselected.** Does the opposite of Hide Selected—hides the records you have *not* highlighted. Keyboard equivalent: ⌘-). (See page 145 for examples of how to use this command.)

- **Go To Record.** Displays the Go To Record window, in which you can specify the number of a record you want to see. (You can find out the number of the record by examining the little "record book" in the panel to the left of the main database window.) Keyboard equivalent: ⌘-G.

- **Sort Records.** Opens the Sort Records dialog box, which lets you sort the records in your database according to simple or complex criteria. The Sort Records command affects the entire database, not just the records that are currently visible. Keyboard equivalent: ⌘-J.

- **Match Records.** As described in Chapter 4, Match Records lets you search for certain records using formulas—to find, for example, everyone in your address book who owes you between $50 and $2000. Keyboard equivalent: ⌘-M.

Drawing Menus

These menus appear whenever you're working in the Drawing module, the Layout mode of the Database module, and so on.

Edit Menu

The Edit menu in the Drawing module is very similar to the Edit menu in other modules. Only two of its items are unique to the drawing mode:

- **Smooth.** Smoothes a shape that you've drawn with the Polygon, Bézier, or Freehand tools, making them look less hand-drawn and turning shapes with sharp corners into rounder, more amoeba-like shapes. Keyboard equivalent: ⌘-(.

- **Unsmooth.** Reverses the effect of the Smooth command. Keyboard equivalent: ⌘-).

Format Menu

Start with the Spreadsheet module's Format menu, described earlier in this chapter; subtract the commands that have to do only with spreadsheets; and the result is the Drawing module's Format menu. Here, too, the commands for formatting text (font, size, text color, and so on) appear in submenus—except when you're actually editing a text block, in which case the Text menu described on page 36 reappears.

Arrange Menu

The Arrange menu helps you manage the front-to-back, side-to-side, top-to-bottom, and rotational arrangement of the objects in your drawing, slide show, or database layout.

The first several commands all pertain to positioning elements of your drawing from front to back—that is, specifying which ones overlap, and how. For example:

- **Move Forward, Move Backward.** If you've drawn several overlapping objects, these commands let you shift the selected object up or down in the "stack," closer to you or farther from you. For example, if you drew a circle and then drew a rectangle on top of it, Move Forward would bring the circle into view, concealing part of the rectangle. Keyboard equivalent: ⌘-Shift-plus sign (+) or minus sign (-).

- **Move To Front, Move To Back.** Moves the selected object *all* the way to the front (or back), so that it appears in front of all other overlapping objects (or behind all of them).

- **Align To Grid.** Forces an object that you're dragging to snap to the intersection of the nearest two invisible gridlines. Of course, when the Autogrid is turned on (using the second command in the Options menu), objects *always* align in this way—Align To Grid can therefore be useful when the Autogrid feature is turned *off*. It can also be handy when you want realign objects you've just duplicated or resized (which don't necessarily align with the Autogrid, even when it's on). Keyboard equivalent: ⌘-Shift-L.

- **Align Objects.** Opens the Align Objects dialog box, which you can use to align several selected objects with each other—their top edges, right edges, and so on. Keyboard equivalent: ⌘-Shift-K.

- **Scale by Percent.** Makes a selected object larger or smaller by an amount that you specify.

- **Rotate 90°.** Turns the selected object 90 degrees counterclockwise.

- **Rotate.** Opens the Rotate window, in which you can specify the number of degrees by which you want to rotate the selected object.

- **Free Rotate.** Turns on Free Rotate mode, in which you can select objects in your drawing by clicking them, and rotate them by dragging their selection handles. (Don't forget to turn off Free Rotate off again—by choosing the same command the second time—when you're finished with this maneuver.) Keyboard equivalent: ⌘-Shift-R.

- **Flip Horizontally, Flip Vertically.** Flips the selected object or objects right-for-left (horizontally) or upside-down (vertically).

- **Reshape.** Adds special handles to certain kind of drawing objects, such as those you've drawn using the Freehand or Bézier tools, which you can drag to adjust the object's shape.

- **Group, Ungroup.** The Group command combines several selected objects into a single combined blob; Ungroup splits them apart again into the original component objects. (As noted in Chapter 6, you can also group grouped objects.) Keyboard equivalent: ⌘-G.

- **Lock, Unlock.** When you lock a drawing object, AppleWorks doesn't let you move, change, or delete it, as indicated by its gray (not black) selection handles. Unlock it when you want to manipulate it. Keyboard equivalent: ⌘-H.

Options Menu

The Options menu contains a miscellaneous assortment of drawing-related commands.

- **Show/Hide Graphics Grid.** Makes the background of blueprint-like dots visible or invisible. (This matrix of dots has no effect on your drawing, and doesn't print out.)

- **Turn Autogrid Off/On.** When the Autogrid function is turned on, then whenever you release a drawing object that you've just dragged or drawn, it jumps from your cursor to the nearest intersection of underlying grid lines. The idea is that the Autogrid makes it easy to align drawing objects as you draw them—you can imagine how much easier it makes, for example, drawing many little rectangles meant to represent different houses on the same street. When you're trying to create less regimented kinds of drawings, however, you may prefer to turn this feature off.

Tip: You determine the spacing of the Autogrid's gridlines by choosing Format→Rulers→Ruler Settings.

- **Edit Master Page.** There are two ways to create slide shows in AppleWorks, as described in detail in Chapter 8—by using the Presentation module, or using the older, more limited Drawing module. If you're using the Drawing module, you use this command to open the document's Master page, where you can add text, graphics, or any other items that you want to show up on every "slide." (You can also use this feature to add some element to every page of a drawing you *don't* intend to present—a watermark or "Confidential" stamp, for example.)

- **Object Size.** Opens the Object Size floating window, in which you control the selected object's position in the document, its size, and its rotation, and give it a name.

- **Frame Links.** Creates a *linked frame* that lets an article or spreadsheet "flow" from one frame to another on different parts of the page (or on different pages of the document), as described in Chapter 12.

- **Text Wrap.** Opens the Text Wrap window, where you can control how text wraps around the currently selected object or frame (see page 228, where you'll be reminded that the text frame must be *linked* before the Text Wrap feature works).

- **Edit Patterns, Edit Wallpaper, Edit Gradients.** Chapter 6 offers details on these tabs of the Accents palette. By using these commands, you can edit these accents (or design your own from scratch). The key to remember is that the changes you make to your Accents palette become part of *this document only.* When you open a new document, the Accents palette becomes its old, unmodified self.

Tip: To preserve changes you've made to the Accents palette, save the affected document as a template, as described on page 276.

Painting Menus

These menus appear when you open a painting document (or frame):

Edit Menu

The Edit menu in the Painting module is nearly identical to the one in the Word Processing module—but instead of cutting, copying, and pasting *text,* its Cut, Copy, and Paste commands apply to *regions of artwork* you've selected using the Lasso or Selection Rectangle tools.

The only command in the Painting Edit menu that isn't also available when word processing is the Duplicate command, which creates a floating copy of whatever artwork area you've selected. While the copy is still selected, you can drag it, delete it, or apply Transform-menu commands to it. (Keyboard equivalent: Option-drag the selection.)

Of course, you could also use the Copy and Paste commands to duplicate an area of the art—but then you lose whatever was on the Clipboard. In some circumstances, the Duplicate command is useful just because it preserves whatever you'd previously cut or copied to the Clipboard.

Format Menu

The Format menu commands are almost exactly the same as those in the Drawing module. Most of the text-formatting commands apply, of course, only to text you create with the Text tool—and are available only while you're still editing the original text box you've drawn. Once you click outside that box, the text becomes a frozen piece of the artwork; you can no longer change its formatting.

There's only one Format command unique to the Painting module: **Resolution & Depth.** While these may be important traits in a potential spouse, they're even more important in a painting document. They determine how many dots per inch this painting has, and how many colors are available to it. For a complete discussion of these technical parameters, and of the dialog box that appears when you choose this command, see page 246.

Transform Menu

The Transform menu contains some of the same commands as the Arrange menu in the Drawing module; the various rotation, resizing, and flipping commands work identically. When you're painting, however, it offers a few special commands for transforming a *selection* you've made (see page 240).

- **Slant, Stretch, Add Perspective, Resize.** These commands make small, black, square handles appear around your selection, When you drag these handles, you warp, shrink, twist, or enlarge the selection, as illustrated on page 240.

- **Fill.** Fills the selected area with the color, pattern, wallpaper, or gradient that's currently selected in the Accents palette.

- **Pick Up.** Lets a selection inherit the image directly beneath it, as illustrated on page 243.

- **Invert.** Inverts the colors of the selection: black for white, yellow for blue, and so on.

- **Blend.** Blurs together the colors in the selected region.

- **Tint.** Adds, to the selected area, a tint of whatever color is selected in the Accents palette.

- **Lighten, Darken.** Adds a white or black tint to the selected area, which makes it appear lighter or darker.

Options Menu

As described in "Drawing Menus" earlier in this chapter, some of this menu's commands affect the AppleWorks grid, which helps you align newly drawn or dragged pieces of the artwork, and let you design new wallpaper, patterns, and gradients. Some of the Options commands unique to the Painting module include:

- **Grid Size.** Opens the Painting Grid Size window, where you can adjust the distance between gridlines in the Autogrid.

- **Paint Mode.** Opens the Painting Mode dialog box, where you can choose between three paint types; opaque paint, transparent paint, or a tint (see page 245).

- **Edit Brush Shape.** Opens the brush shape dialog box, where you can edit existing "nib" shapes for the Paintbrush tool and create new ones. You can also create special-effect brushes (which blend and tint) in this dialog box.

- **Edit Spray Can.** Opens the Edit Spray Can window, where you can control how the Spray Can tool works—its dot size and flow rate.

Presentation Menus

The Presentation menu set is very similar to the Drawing menu set—which makes sense, because presentations are little more than specialized drawings.

Edit Menu, Format Menu, Arrange Menu

These menus are identical to the menus described in "Drawing Menus," earlier in this chapter.

Options Menu

Most of the Presentation module's Options-menu commands work exactly as they do in the Drawing module. It offers only one unique command:

- **Edit Background.** When you choose this command, you enter Edit Background mode, where you can specify background elements (such as a full-screen color block, a logo, the presentation's title, and so on) that will appear on every slide in your show. Any changes you make in this mode instantly appear on every slide.

When you're finished creating these consistent elements, choose Options→Edit Background again to exit this special mode.

Now, if you've read Chapter 8, and you're duly awed by the power and cleverness of the Master slide concept, you're entitled to wonder what the point of Edit Background mode is. After all, aren't *Master slides* designed for creating background colors and logos?

Yes. Still, the Edit Background mode can be useful in two situations: First, when your presentation is so simple that you don't feel like bothering with learning or exploiting the master-slide feature. Second, when your presentation is so *complex* that you need a *master* Master slide. The Background lurks behind *all* Master slides.

Installing and Upgrading AppleWorks

Installing AppleWorks on your computer is fairly straightforward; the Installer program on the AppleWorks CD-ROM does most of the work for you. (If AppleWorks came pre-installed on your Macintosh, you've got even *less* work to do.)

AppleWorks 6 for Macintosh requires a PowerPC-based Mac, running Mac OS 8.1 or later. The Mac needs 24 MB of memory with Mac OS 8.1, or 32MB if you have a later OS version; more, of course, is better. To use AppleWorks' Internet-based features, you also need an Internet connection.

CD Contents

The AppleWorks 6 CD-ROM contains everything you need to get started with AppleWorks. It also has some extra fonts, dictionaries, software updates, and so on. When you browse the AppleWorks CD's main window, you see the following items:

News and Web Site

At the top of the AppleWorks 6 CD window are two documents meant to give you news bulletins about AppleWorks: *AppleWorks Late-Breaking News* and *AppleWorks Web Site*. Late-Breaking News is a text document containing last-minute information about AppleWorks, including recently discovered problems with installation, hardware, upgrading, or third-party software. It's worth reading, especially if your copy of AppleWorks seems to need troubleshooting.

The AppleWorks Web Site document is a Web-page location document. Double-click it to launch your Web browser, which loads the AppleWorks Web site at *www.apple.com/appleworks*. There you'll find product information and—especially important if you're still using the original, not-completely-polished 6.0 release of

AppleWorks—any AppleWorks patches or updaters (to AppleWorks 6.0.3, for example) that Apple has made available.

Installers

The first window of the CD-ROM includes two installers: Install-US/Canada and Install-All Other Countries. Double-click the appropriate icon to begin the installation process.

Tip: As with any software installation, turn off your virus-protection software before you begin. Virus software, thinking that 100 evil viruses are invading it at once, interferes with many software installations.

AppleWorks Extras

The AppleWorks Extras folder contains seven folders full of fonts, dictionaries, and special offers. These are software modules that *don't* get installed by the Installer; if you want to install them, you must drag their icons manually from the CD to your hard drive. Here's a look at each.

- **AWUG.** This folder contains information about the AppleWorks Users Group, or AWUG—an outstanding resource for AppleWorks users (especially in education) in search of help, tips, tutorials, news, and a Web site full of add-on software. This folder contains a sample electronic edition of AppleWorks Journal, the user group's monthly newsletter.

- **ITC Fonts, School Fonts.** These folders offer additional TrueType typefaces, which you can use to spice up your AppleWorks (and other) documents. Some of them are extremely useful; some of them, furthermore, are required by the AppleWorks templates that you can download from the Internet. To install them, drag their "suitcase" files onto the System Folder icon.

- **Nova Documentation.** For those times when the thousands of AppleWorks Clippings aren't enough selection, this special offer saves you money on additional clip art from Nova Development.

- **Spanish Dictionaries.** This folder contains a Spanish hyphenation dictionary, spelling dictionary, and thesaurus. To make them available in AppleWorks, see page 51.

- **System Software Updates.** This folder contains three Macintosh system-software updates (Mac OS 8.1 Update, Mac OS 8.6 Update, and Font Manager Updater) for three English-language regions (North American, British, and International) of the Macintosh operating system. If you're using Mac OS 8.0, install the free Mac OS 8.1 update—a requirement if you want to use AppleWorks—and if you're using Mac OS 8.5, you can use the Mac OS 8.6 update for greater stability.

- **UK and US English Dictionaries.** This folder contains two additional dictionaries (UK English and US English) and two additional thesauruses (UK English and US English). Again, see page 51 for installation instructions.

AppleWorks 6 Documentation

As you probably discovered, AppleWorks doesn't come with a printed manual—if it did, you probably wouldn't be reading this book. Moreover, the AppleWorks 6 Documentation folder does not, in fact, contain documentation for AppleWorks. Instead, it contains several "getting-started"-type documents like these:

- **Electronic Documentation Info.** This text document offers instructions on reading the *other* documents in this folder (such as how to install the Acrobat Reader program necessary to open them).

- **AppleWorks Getting Started.** This 66-page Acrobat Reader document walks you through the very basics of AppleWorks. You can read it on the screen or print it out.

- **AppleWorks Install Manual.** This eight-page Acrobat Reader document covers the basics of installing AppleWorks on your computer.

- **Install Acrobat Reader FIRST.** This folder contains the installer for Adobe Acrobat Reader, the program you need to read the two documents just described. (If Acrobat Reader is already installed on your computer, you can ignore this folder.)

Installing AppleWorks

When you double-click the Installer program on the AppleWorks CD, you're shown the AppleWorks 6 Installer welcome screen; click Continue. Now you see the AppleWorks license agreement, which points out, among other things, that Apple is limited to $50 in liability for damages. If you plan to continue with the installation, click Accept. The main installation screen now appears.

At this point, you can choose where on your computer you want AppleWorks installed, specify which AppleWorks elements get installed, read a description of what's about to be installed, and so on. On the Macintosh, the upper-left corner offers a pop-up menu offering three options: Easy Install, Custom Install, and Uninstall. Each of these three choices is explained below.

Figure B-2:
The default setting for an Easy Install is good enough for most purposes. It installs most of the components that you'll need when using AppleWorks, and it puts them on the hard drive identified by the Install Location pop-up menu (lower left). At the end of the installation process, you'll find the AppleWorks 6 folder in this hard drive window; you're welcome to move the folder to a new location.

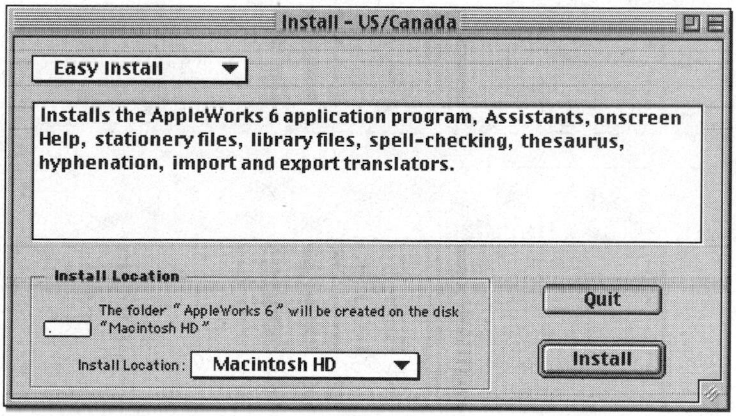

Install – US/Canada

Easy Install

Installs the AppleWorks 6 application program, Assistants, onscreen Help, stationery files, library files, spell-checking, thesaurus, hyphenation, import and export translators.

Install Location

The folder "AppleWorks 6" will be created on the disk "Macintosh HD"

Install Location: Macintosh HD

Quit

Install

Easy Install

The Easy Install puts AppleWorks and the files Apple thinks you'll need to accompany it onto your hard drive—nearly 1,000 files in all (including many pieces of clip art, fonts, and 700 help screens). You'll be asked to restart the computer to complete the installation.

Custom Install

The Custom Install lets you choose how much—or how little—of AppleWorks you want to install. Installations can range from just the AppleWorks 6 program (and a few small support files needed to run it) to a gigantic, many-megabyte collection of files, everything the installer is capable of putting on your hard drive, as identified by the checkboxes shown in Figure B-3.

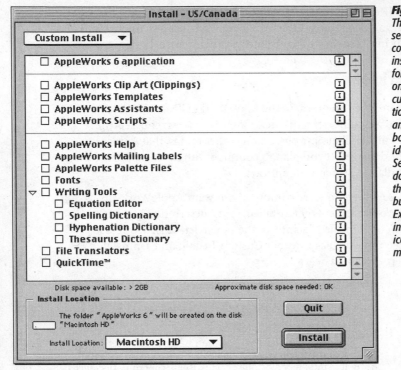

Figure B-3:
The Custom Install lets you select which of AppleWorks' components you want to install, which is great when, for example, you want to add only one component to your current AppleWorks installation. If you're not sure what an item is, click the I in the box to the right for a small identifying window. (Note: Selecting every item in this list doesn't install everything from the CD—some software bundles in the AppleWorks Extras folder don't get installed unless you drag their icons to your hard drive manually.)

Uninstall

Choosing the Uninstall option lets you remove AppleWorks (and many of its associated files) from your hard drive. If the AppleWorks 6 folder isn't in your main hard drive window, where the installer originally put it, then the uninstaller removes all components *except* the AppleWorks folder (and anything it may contain), the CarbonLib extension, and the AppleWorks bonus fonts. You'll have to delete the AppleWorks 6 folder yourself.

Upgrading to AppleWorks 6

If you own AppleWorks 5 or any earlier version of ClarisWorks, you can upgrade to AppleWorks 6 without interfering with your previous installations. The AppleWorks 6 Installer will place an AppleWorks 6 folder on your hard drive, without touching your older copies. Just follow the previous steps for the Easy Install or Custom Install.

After you've installed AppleWorks 6, however, you may want to import some of the macros, buttons, templates, dictionaries, and other items you created using the older version of the software. Here's the story:

- **Macros and custom buttons.** Unfortunately, macros and buttons created in earlier versions of AppleWorks or ClarisWorks aren't compatible with AppleWorks 6. You have no choice but to re-create them in the new version of the software.

- **Custom dictionaries:** While you can't *use* custom user dictionaries created in previous versions of AppleWorks or ClarisWorks, you don't have to re-type all of your custom dictionary terms. Instead, export your custom user dictionary as a text file (from your old version of AppleWorks or ClarisWorks), and then import those terms into a new AppleWorks 6 user dictionary. You'll find step-by-step instructions at the end of Chapter 2.

- **Custom templates:** After installing AppleWorks 6, drag any custom stationery that you made using previous versions of the program (or aliases of these files) into AppleWorks 6→Starting Points→Templates folder. The next time you launch AppleWorks, they'll show up in the Templates tab of the Starting Points window.

- **Libraries (now called Clippings).** You can import older versions of AppleWorks or ClarisWorks clip art libraries into AppleWorks 6. To do so, drag the *individual* libraries into the AppleWorks 6→Clippings folder. (The library files must not be in individual folders.)

Tip: Upgrading to AppleWorks 6 from an older version of the software offers a useful benefit: the MacLinkPlus file translators that were available in AppleWorks 5 remain in your System Folder, making these translations automatically available to AppleWorks 6. (See page 365 for details on MacLinkPlus and file conversion.)

AppleWorks Installation and Networks

You can use AppleWorks over a network in any of three ways: you can install AppleWorks *from* a network server; install it *onto* a server; and *run* it from a server.

AppleWorks Installer on a Server

If you put the AppleWorks Installer on a remote file server, citizens of your network can install AppleWorks from wherever they're seated. (Of course, you're legally obligated to buy enough AppleWorks licenses to cover all of the copies of you plan to install.)

To put the AppleWorks Installer on a server so that AppleWorks can be installed

---

across a network, create a new folder on the server. Copy all of the files from the AppleWorks CD into the new folder.

Then share this folder the way you would any folder. For example, on the Macintosh, highlight the folder, and then choose File→Get Info→Sharing. In the Get Info box that appears, make sure that the User/Group section has *read privileges* but not *write privileges,* so that your network members can install AppleWorks without making changes to the installer files. Close the window and save changes.

Installing AppleWorks on a Server

If you install AppleWorks onto a network server, several citizens of your network can launch and use that copy of AppleWorks simultaneously. To set up this arrangement on the Macintosh network, make sure that the most recent versions of the CarbonLib, QuickTime 4, and Internet Config extensions are all installed on the Macs that will be involved. (If these Macs are running Mac OS 8.1, also make sure that the Navigation Services extension is installed, too.)

Next, install AppleWorks onto the server from the server's CD-ROM drive, exactly as described earlier this chapter. Restart the server Mac; AppleWorks is now ready to be run remotely.

Running AppleWorks from a Server

If AppleWorks is installed on a server, users connected to that server can launch AppleWorks and use it remotely—all at the same time. This arrangement can be slow (AppleWorks puts out a lot of data through your network wires), however, and it imposes several limitations. For example, only one person at a time has access to the spell-check function or to any AppleWorks Assistants; file translators don't work at all; and the self-illustrating Font menu (in which the name of each typeface appears in the appropriate font) only works for the *first* person to open AppleWorks.

Tip: You can work around the one-person-at-a-time spell-checking and file-translating problems. To do so, create a folder called AppleWorks 6; inside, create a folder called AppleWorks Essentials. Put an alias of the server's copy of AppleWorks 6 itself in this folder, too.

Create this folder structure on every machine that will be using AppleWorks across the network. Copy the ASCII, EPSF, HTML, and TEXT translator files, plus the Dictionaries folder, from the AppleWorks 6→AppleWorks Essentials folder on the server into the corresponding AppleWorks Essentials folder on each of the other computers. You've successfully fooled AppleWorks into permitting the spell-checking and file-translation features to work on every networked Mac.

Index

Colophon

The authors regret to report that they did not write the text of this book in AppleWorks 6—not because it isn't up to the task, nor that the authors wouldn't have *loved* to, but because publishing industry staffers (and PageMaker) accept nothing but Microsoft Word.

From their various Pogue Press "branch offices" in California, Connecticut, and Massachusetts, the creative team generated the chapters as Word files, using a couple of Power Macs and an assortment of PowerBooks. The graphics were created in Apple-Works 6 and captured with Ambrosia Software's Snapz Pro 2 *(www.ambrosiasw.com)*; Adobe Photoshop *(www.adobe.com)* and Macromedia FreeHand *(www.macromedia.com)* were called in as required for touching them up.

The book was designed and laid out in Adobe PageMaker 6.5 on a Power Mac 8500 and Power Mac G3. The fonts used include Formata (as the sans-serif family) and Minion (as the serif body face). To provide the and ⌘ symbols, a custom font was created using Macromedia Fontographer. The index was created using EZ Index, a Mac-only shareware indexing program by John Holder, available at *www.northcoast. com/~jvholder*. The book was then generated as an Adobe Acrobat PDF file for proofreading, indexing, and final transmission to the printing plant.

More Titles from Pogue Press/O'Reilly

The Missing Manuals

Mac OS 9: The Missing Manual

By David Pogue
1st Edition March 2000
472 pages, ISBN 1-56592-857-1

The latest system software for the resurgent Macintosh platform is Mac OS 9, which includes over 50 new features. However, Apple ships Mac OS 9 without one of the most important features of all: a manual. O'Reilly/Pogue Press comes to the rescue with *Mac OS 9: the Missing Manual*. Award-winning author David Pogue brings his humor and expertise to Mac OS 9 for the first time in this lucid, impeccably written guide. Readers will appreciate the step-by-step guides to setting up small networks, the tutorials on Mac OS 9's new Multiple Users control panel, and the coverage of Mac OS 9's speech-recognition, color printing, digital video, and self-updating software features.

AppleWorks 6: The Missing Manual

Jim Elferdink & David Reynolds
1st First Edition May 2000
450 pages, ISBN 1-56592-858-X

AppleWorks, the integrated application that arrives in 4 million homes, schools, and offices a year, includes everything—except a printed manual. In *AppleWorks 6: The Missing Manual*, authors Jim Elferdink and David Reynolds guide the reader through both the basics and the hidden talents of the new AppleWorks, placing special emphasis on version 6's enhanced word processing, Internet, and presentation features. As a Missing Manual title, the book is friendly, authoritative, and complete, rich with clever workarounds, examples, and step-by-step tutorials.

iMovie: The Missing Manual

By David Pogue
1st Edition June 2000
400 pages, ISBN 1-56592-859-8

iMovie:The Missing Manual takes you through every step of iMovie video production, from choosing a digital camcorder to burning finished films onto CDs. The book also explains how to run iMovie on any recent Mac model (not just the iMac DV); uncovers the two secret clip-editing techniques that Apple's online help doesn't mention; and provides a powerful workaround for iMovie's weak soundtrack-editing feature.

Windows 2000 Pro: The Missing Manual

By Sharon Crawford
1st Edition July 2000 (est.)
450 pages (est.), ISBN 0-596-00010-3

In *Windows 2000 Pro: The Missing Manual*, bestselling Windows NT author Sharon Crawford provides the friendly, authoritative book that should have been in the box. It includes detailed guidance for installing, removing, and troubleshooting new software and hardware; exploring basic networking and Internet survival; and info on Windows 2000's local-management options—security, user profiles, backing up, and so on—all crowned by a beefy troubleshooting guidebook.

Windows Me: The Missing Manual

By Kathy Ivens
1st Edition July 2000 (est.)
450 pages (est.), ISBN 0-596-00009-X

In *Windows Me: The Missing Manual* bestselling author and magazine columnist Kathy Ivens begins with a tour of the Desktop, the enhanced Start menu, and instructions for customizing the Taskbar and toolbars. More advanced chapters explore each control panel and built-in application, walk readers through every conceivable kind of configuration, and how to set up a small network—an essential skill in today's home or small office. Special appendixes cover more technical ground: the varous DOS applications that govern the startup and shutdown process, instructions for installing and updating Windows, and so on.

POGUE PRESS™
O'REILLY®

TO ORDER: **800-998-9938** • **order@oreilly.com** • **http://www.oreilly.com/**
OUR PRODUCTS ARE AVAILABLE AT A BOOKSTORE OR SOFTWARE STORE NEAR YOU.
FOR INFORMATION: **800-998-9938** • **707-829-0515** • **info@oreilly.com**

International Distributors

UK, EUROPE, MIDDLE EAST AND AFRICA (EXCEPT FRANCE, GERMANY, AUSTRIA, SWITZERLAND, LUXEMBOURG, LIECHTENSTEIN, AND EASTERN EUROPE)

INQUIRIES
O'Reilly UK Limited
4 Castle Street
Farnham
Surrey, GU9 7HS
United Kingdom
Telephone: 44-1252-711776
Fax: 44-1252-734211
Email: information@oreilly.co.uk

ORDERS
Wiley Distribution Services Ltd.
1 Oldlands Way
Bognor Regis
West Sussex PO22 9SA
United Kingdom
Telephone: 44-1243-779777
Fax: 44-1243-820250
Email: cs-books@wiley.co.uk

FRANCE

INQUIRIES
Éditions O'Reilly
18 rue Séguier
75006 Paris, France
Tel: 33-1-40-51-52-30
Fax: 33-1-40-51-52-31
Email: france@editions-oreilly.fr

ORDERS
GEODIF
61, Bd Saint-Germain
75240 Paris Cedex 05, France
Tel: 33-1-44-41-46-16 (French books)
Tel: 33-1-44-41-11-87 (English books)
Fax: 33-1-44-41-11-44
Email: distribution@eyrolles.com

GERMANY, SWITZERLAND, AUSTRIA, EASTERN EUROPE, LUXEMBOURG, AND LIECHTENSTEIN

INQUIRIES & ORDERS
O'Reilly Verlag
Balthasarstr. 81
D-50670 Köln
Germany
Telephone: 49-221-973160-91
Fax: 49-221-973160-8
Email: anfragen@oreilly.de (inquiries)
Email: order@oreilly.de (orders)

CANADA (FRENCH LANGUAGE BOOKS)

Les Éditions Flammarion ltée
375, Avenue Laurier Ouest
Montréal (Québec) H2V 2K3
Tel: 00-1-514-277-8807
Fax: 00-1-514-278-2085
Email: info@flammarion.qc.ca

HONG KONG

City Discount Subscription Service, Ltd.
Unit D, 3rd Floor, Yan's Tower
27 Wong Chuk Hang Road
Aberdeen, Hong Kong
Tel: 852-2580-3539
Fax: 852-2580-6463
Email: citydis@ppn.com.hk

KOREA

Hanbit Media, Inc.
Chungmu Bldg. 201
Yonnam-dong 568-33
Mapo-gu
Seoul, Korea
Tel: 822-325-0397
Fax: 822-325-9697
Email: hant93@chollian.dacom.co.kr

PHILIPPINES

Global Publishing
G/F Benavides Garden
1186 Benavides Street
Manila, Philippines
Tel: 632-254-8949/637-252-2582
Fax: 632-734-5060/632-252-2733
Email: globalp@pacific.net.ph

TAIWAN

O'Reilly Taiwan
No. 3, Lane 131
Hang-Chow South Road
Section 1, Taipei, Taiwan
Tel: 886-2-23968990
Fax: 886-2-23968916
Email: taiwan@oreilly.com

CHINA

O'Reilly Beijing
Room 2410
160, FuXingMenNeiDaJie
XiCheng District
Beijing, China PR 100031
Tel: 86-10-66412305
Fax: 86-10-86631007
Email: beijing@oreilly.com

INDIA

Computer Bookshop (India) Pvt. Ltd.
190 Dr. D.N. Road, Fort
Bombay 400 001 India
Tel: 91-22-207-0989
Fax: 91-22-262-3551
Email: cbsbom@giasbm01.vsnl.net.in

JAPAN

O'Reilly Japan, Inc.
Yotsuya Y's Building
7 Banch 6, Honshio-cho
Shinjuku-ku
Tokyo 160-0003 Japan
Tel: 81-3-3356-5227
Fax: 81-3-3356-5261
Email: japan@oreilly.com

ALL OTHER ASIAN COUNTRIES

O'Reilly & Associates, Inc.
101 Morris Street
Sebastopol, CA 95472 USA
Tel: 707-829-0515
Fax: 707-829-0104
Email: order@oreilly.com

AUSTRALIA

Woodslane Pty., Ltd.
7/5 Vuko Place
Warriewood NSW 2102
Australia
Tel: 61-2-9970-5111
Fax: 61-2-9970-5002
Email: info@woodslane.com.au

NEW ZEALAND

Woodslane New Zealand, Ltd.
21 Cooks Street (P.O. Box 575)
Waganui, New Zealand
Tel: 64-6-347-6543
Fax: 64-6-345-4840
Email: info@woodslane.com.au

LATIN AMERICA

McGraw-Hill Interamericana
Editores, S.A. de C.V.
Cedro No. 512
Col. Atlampa
06450, Mexico, D.F.
Tel: 52-5-547-6777
Fax: 52-5-547-3336
Email: mcgraw-hill@infosel.net.mx

O'REILLY®

TO ORDER: **800-998-9938** • **order@oreilly.com** • **http://www.oreilly.com/**
OUR PRODUCTS ARE AVAILABLE AT A BOOKSTORE OR SOFTWARE STORE NEAR YOU.
FOR INFORMATION: **800-998-9938** • **707-829-0515** • **info@oreilly.com**

O'REILLY

O'Reilly & Associates, Inc.
101 Morris Street
Sebastopol, CA 95472-9902
1-800-998-9938

Visit us online at:
http://www.ora.com/
orders@ora.com

O'REILLY WOULD LIKE TO HEAR FROM YOU

Which book did this card come from?

_____

Where did you buy this book?
- ❏ Bookstore   ❏ Computer Store
- ❏ Direct from O'Reilly   ❏ Class/seminar
- ❏ Bundled with hardware/software
- ❏ Other _____

What operating system do you use?
- ❏ UNIX   ❏ Macintosh
- ❏ Windows NT   ❏ PC(Windows/DOS)
- ❏ Other _____

What is your job description?
- ❏ System Administrator   ❏ Programmer
- ❏ Network Administrator   ❏ Educator/Teacher
- ❏ Web Developer
- ❏ Other _____

❏ Please send me O'Reilly's catalog, containing a complete listing of O'Reilly books and software.

Name _____ Company/Organization _____

Address _____

City _____ State _____ Zip/Postal Code _____ Country _____

Telephone _____ Internet or other email address (specify network) _____

Nineteenth century wood engraving
of a bear from the O'Reilly &
Associates Nutshell Handbook®
Using & Managing UUCP.

POST CARD

NO POSTAGE
NECESSARY IF
MAILED IN THE
UNITED STATES

BUSINESS REPLY MAIL
FIRST CLASS MAIL   PERMIT NO. 80   SEBASTOPOL, CA

Postage will be paid by addressee

O'Reilly & Associates, Inc.
101 Morris Street
Sebastopol, CA 95472-9902